Nationalism and Eth

P.32-39 for Suharto framework
for role. –

Since 1998, which marked the end of the thirty-three-year New
Order regime under President Suharto, there has been a dramatic
increase in ethnic conflict and violence in Indonesia. In his
innovative and persuasive account, Jacques Bertrand argues that
conflicts in Maluku, Kalimantan, Aceh, Papua, and East Timor
were a result of the New Order's narrow and constraining reinterpretation of Indonesia's "national model." The author shows
how, at the end of the 1990s, this national model came under
intense pressure at the prospect of institutional transformation,
a reconfiguration of ethnic relations, and an increase in the
role of Islam in Indonesia's political institutions. It was within
the context of these challenges that the very definition of the
Indonesian nation and what it meant to be Indonesian came
under scrutiny. The book sheds light on the roots of religious
and ethnic conflict at a turning point in Indonesia's history.

Jacques Bertrand is Associate Professor of Political Science,
University of Toronto.

CAMBRIDGE ASIA–PACIFIC STUDIES

Cambridge Asia–Pacific Studies aims to provide a focus and forum for scholarly work on the Asia–Pacific region as a whole, and its component sub-regions, namely Northeast Asia, Southeast Asia and the Pacific Islands. The series is produced in association with the Research School of Pacific and Asian Studies at the Australian National University and the Australian Institute of International Affairs.

Editor: John Ravenhill

Editorial Board: James Cotton, Donald Denoon, Mark Elvin, Hal Hill, Ron May, Anthony Milner, Tessa Morris-Suzuki, Anthony Low

Published titles in the series are listed at the back of the book.

Nationalism and Ethnic Conflict in Indonesia

Jacques Bertrand
University of Toronto

CAMBRIDGE
UNIVERSITY PRESS

PUBLISHED BY THE PRESS SYNDICATE OF THE UNIVERSITY OF CAMBRIDGE
The Pitt Building, Trumpington Street, Cambridge, United Kingdom

CAMBRIDGE UNIVERSITY PRESS
The Edinburgh Building, Cambridge CB2 2RU, UK
40 West 20th Street, New York NY 10011–4211, USA
477 Williamstown Road, Port Melbourne, VIC 3207, Australia
Ruiz de Alarcón 13, 28014 Madrid, Spain
Dock House, The Waterfront, Cape Town 8001, South Africa

http://www.cambridge.org

First published 2004

Printed in China by Everbest Printing Co.

Typeface Plantin 10/12 pt.   *System* LATEX 2$_\varepsilon$ [TB]

A catalogue record for this book is available from the British Library

National Library of Australia Cataloguing in Publication data
Bertrand, Jacques, 1965–.
  Nationalism and ethnic conflict in Indonesia.
  Bibliography.
  Includes index.
  ISBN 0 521 81889 3.
  ISBN 0 521 52441 5 (pbk.).
  1. Religion and politics – Indonesia.   2. Indonesia – Politics and government – 1998–.
  3. Indonesia – Ethnic relations.   I. Title.
305.8009598

ISBN 0 521 81889 3 hardback
ISBN 0 521 52441 5 paperback

À Lisa et Liam

Contents

Figures and tables

Figures

Tables

Preface

During the New Order regime, most political scientists working on Indonesia focused primarily on the intricacies of "behind-the-scenes" politics in Jakarta. They analyzed the competition for power, resources, and representation around President Suharto, his generals, and a small clique of the regime's clients. They considered that the rest of the political elite jockeyed for influence and protection from this group, while few openly resisted. Jakarta was the uncontested center of rule, where decisions, directives, orders, and commands originated. Localities, regions, and provinces of this large archipelago were at the receiving end of a pyramidal hierarchy with Suharto at its apex. Few insights could be gained, therefore, from studying them.

While these political scientists were largely correct in their assessments of New Order Indonesia, they left out some important dimensions of politics. Virtually no centralized, authoritarian political system can boast of commanding full authority and control over its subjects. Pockets of resistance appear in the elite as well as the broader society. While analyses focusing on the political elite captured such resistance in Jakarta, they ignored the signs of resistance occurring in various areas of the archipelago. For sure, the *coup de grâce* of the regime in 1998 would come from cracks in the elite, but the full mobilization against Suharto, and the subsequent political instability, were revealing. The scale of riots, demonstrations, and ethnic and religious conflicts displayed an array of grievances that had been little detected in previous years. What were missed were the rising signs of "nibbling" at the regime's fundamental structure, much in the same way that society nibbled at the former communist systems of Eastern Europe and the Soviet Union until they collapsed. Such nibbling at the edges is rarely studied, partly because it can not only reveal deep fissures in a regime or in society but it can also lead to many false assessments. Studying non-events or small-scale acts can be a risky venture.

Nevertheless, it is precisely an interest in these understated, often hidden, acts of politics that began my journey with this book. As a graduate student, I had spent one year studying small acts of resistance and analyzing sources of compliance in villages of Java and Ambon. From this study, I had gained the insight that nibbling forms of politics could have tremendous cumulative power to limit the reach of the state. I returned to Indonesia for several months in 1996 to understand why the New Order regime appeared to have achieved ethnic and religious peace. The cases of East Timor, Irian Jaya, and Aceh were presented largely as anomalies within the archipelago. How had the New Order managed to eliminate virtually all of the conflicts that had raged during the 1950s? I proceeded with a skeptic's eye to seek out whether hidden grievances lay beneath this apparent peace. It became clear, during that research trip, that conflicts had not disappeared but had been transformed by the New Order state. Repressive measures had not eliminated discontent but caused it to be either expressed through different channels or silenced. More importantly, old grievances had evolved under the New Order's institutional structures and redefined conflicts in different ways.

Most significantly, I was struck by rising tensions between Christians and Muslims in Maluku, Flores, and other regions with significant numbers of Christians. It became clear that Suharto's courting of some Muslim groups was having important consequences for inter-religious relations. Combined with the destabilizing effects of the tight competition for the regime's patrimonial resources, these increasing tensions appeared to me as potentially destabilizing.

In other regions, I found that the relative peace of the New Order had been achieved by co-opting the regional elites, but not without cost. My conclusions were similar to those of Indonesian scholar Ichlasul Amal, who had convincingly shown how previously rebellious elites in South Sulawesi and West Sumatra now benefitted from the patronage of the New Order regime. Yet, many were also dissatisfied with its centralization and were beginning to openly demand more autonomy for Indonesia's regions. There was also a growing sense that the regime had reached its limits and had to change.

Soon after this particular research trip, my book project had to be completely transformed. Riots across Java and other parts of the archipelago began to reveal some of the tensions I had observed. These riots gave way to larger conflicts as the regime was hit by the Asian financial crisis in 1997 and then collapsed with Suharto's resignation in May 1998. From a study that had primarily focused on hidden tensions and on the nibbling at the edges of the regime, my project became an analysis of increasingly violent and open events involving ethnic and religious groups. As new conflicts unfolded and old ones intensified, my research trips in subsequent years targeted conflict areas while recognizing the insights gained from prior observation in generally peaceful areas of Indonesia.

It is within this changing political context that the comparativist in me developed the explanation contained in this book. I became increasingly convinced that we could not treat these conflicts as isolated events but rather as direct consequences of the New Order regime and its vision of the Indonesian nation. I did not espouse the view that Indonesia had longstanding conflicts between ethnic and religious groups that simply rose to the surface with the lifting of authoritarian rule. Nevertheless, the democratization that followed the end of the New Order regime had a direct impact on existing tensions and lifted some constraints on political action. These tensions had arisen as a response to the institutionalization of the requisites of unity and the policies designed to preserve the vision of national unity. This book explains, therefore, how different forms of what I call the "national model" were institutionalized, primarily under the New Order but also during previous historical periods in the twentieth century. The regime adopted a narrow conception of the Indonesian nation and institutionalized it in ways that contributed to the marginalization and exclusion of particular groups, to the failure to develop adequate means of inclusion for groups considering themselves as distinct nations (such as the East Timorese, Acehnese, and Papuans), and to the deepening of tensions between religious groups. Historical institutionalist theory helped me to explain conflicts in the late 1990s as a new critical juncture in the evolution of Indonesia's national model. These conflicts emerged from the prior means by which groups were included, or not, within this national model at various junctures of Indonesia's modern history.

Many people helped to make this book possible. Colleagues provided useful comments on parts of the manuscript or related papers. Some influenced my ideas in discussions at various venues where I presented my work, or forced me to revise my analysis significantly in light of their constructive criticism. Others helped me at various stages of developing the research project, from providing contacts throughout Indonesia to giving key advice in North America or Indonesia. Many thanks to Donald K. Emmerson, Michael Malley, Robert Hefner, Rita Smith Kipp, Sidney Jones, Donald Schwartz, Gwen Evans, Annette Clear, Rizal Sukma, Muhammad Hikam, John Sidel, Donald L. Horowitz, Alfred Stepan, Juan Linz, Richard Stubbs, Judith Nagata, Elizabeth Fuller-Collins, Lorraine Aragon, Mochtar Mas'oed, Leslie Butt, David Webster, and Richard Sandbrook. Thanks to many other colleagues for useful comments at various conferences. A special thanks to Bill Liddle, who has been a strong source of support and advice for many years, and who has provided invaluable comments on my work for more than a decade.

In Indonesia, I cannot begin to name the large number of people who helped me in the different stages of my research. I wish to thank all of them, despite naming only a few. Several would also wish to remain unnamed for their safety. Colleagues and friends at various universities across Indonesia were very helpful, especially at Syah Kuala University in Aceh, Universitas Cendrawasih in Papua, and Universitas Gadjah Mada in Yogyakarta. Many thanks to Hadi Soesastro, Clara Joewono, and other colleagues at the Centre for Strategic and International Studies for their help while in Jakarta. A special thanks to colleagues and friends at Universitas Pattimura in Ambon, who were tremendously helpful during various trips I made to Ambon and Maluku. Many of them were severely affected by the fighting and destruction that ravaged the region. I only hope that my work, in its very small way, can help to elucidate some aspects of the conflict and perhaps contribute to the reconciliation process. Many people from various non-governmental organizations across Indonesia provided me with assistance, contacts, and resources. Many thanks to all of them. I have great admiration for their struggle to make a difference in almost impossible circumstances. A very warm but sad thanks to Jafar Siddiq Hamzah, who accompanied me on my first trip to Aceh. His murder was one of many tragedies of the conflict in Indonesia. To all Indonesians affected by these crises and whose lives have been destroyed, I ask forgiveness if this book fails to convey an appropriate level of sensitivity. I have sought to understand the conflicts that affected them without having shared their experience.

At the University of Toronto, I would like to thank Rita O'Brien, Mary-Alice Bailey, and Van Bui for all their support with logistical issues relating to my research and writing. The chair of the political science department, Rob Vipond, allowed me the time and flexibility to finish the manuscript. Thanks also to Michael Donnelly, the director of the Asian Institute, for his support. I appreciate very much the work of the University of Toronto's cartography office, in particular Byron Moldofsky and especially Jane Davie, who drew the maps. I owe much appreciation to all of the very patient staff of the inter-library loan office of Robarts Library for processing quickly and efficiently the dozens of requests I made for materials that were sometimes very difficult to obtain. A special word of gratitude to my research assistants Michael Sheehan and Char Bhaneja for all their work.

Many organizations provided financial support and other resources for this research project. The Social Sciences and Humanities Research Council of Canada funded most of the project. Thank you also to David Dewitt, Carolina Hernandez, and their project on Development and Security in Southeast Asia, funded by the Canadian International Development Agency, for partially funding two trips to Indonesia. A Connaught grant from the University of Toronto, as well as other internal grants, provided some additional funding. Finally, the North-South

Institute, my previous employer, allowed me some time to travel to Indonesia during the early stages of the project. The Canadian Embassy in Indonesia provided some helpful assistance on a few trips. I would like to thank, in particular, Ambassador Gary Smith, Ginette Martin, and René Cremonese.

Chapter 7 was published in a slightly different form as "Legacies of the authoritarian past: Religious violence in Indonesia's Moluccan Islands," *Pacific Affairs*, vol. 75, no. 1, April 2002. I wish to thank the editors for allowing me to use the article for this chapter.

At Cambridge University Press, I would like to thank Phillipa McGuinness, Marigold Acland, Karen Hildebrandt, and Amanda Pinches for leading the manuscript to its final publication. Many thanks as well to Raylee Singh for superb copy-editing.

Finally, many friends and family provided the emotional support that made this book possible. Among those many friends, a special word of thanks to Marius Paraschivoiu and Chantal Benoit-Barné. I reserve the last words of gratitude for my wife, Lisa Isaac, and my son Liam. To Lisa, many thanks for the patience, support, and love that made this possible. To my son Liam, who was born when the manuscript was only partially completed, my thanks for his unique understanding of his father's commitment to the book. They have made it all meaningful.

INDONESIA

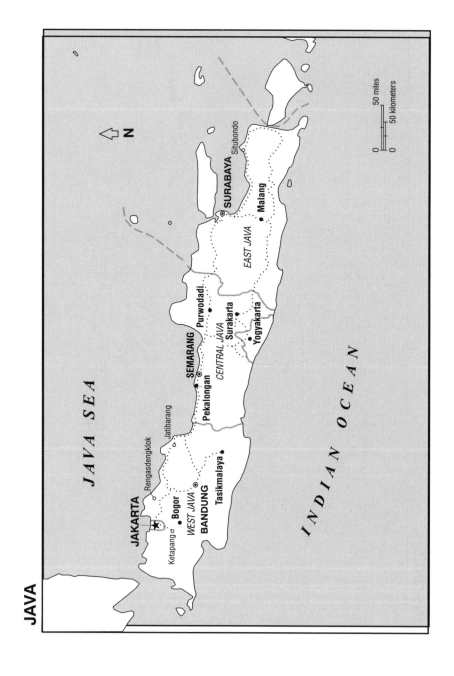

JAVA

JAVA SEA

JAKARTA
Ketapang
Rengasdengklok
Jatibarang
Bogor
WEST JAVA
BANDUNG
Tasikmalaya

Pekalongan
SEMARANG
CENTRAL JAVA
Purwodadi
Surakarta
Yogyakarta

SURABAYA
Situbondo
EAST JAVA
Malang

INDIAN OCEAN

N

50 miles
50 kilometers
0
0

KALIMANTAN (BORNEO)

SOUTH
CHINA
SEA

N

Sulu
Sea

BRUNEI
DARUSSALAM

MALAYSIA

SARAWAK

EAST KALIMANTAN

Singkawang • Sambas

KALIMANTAN
(BORNEO)

Ngabang
• Sanggau

◉ Pontianak

Samarinda ◉

WEST KALIMANTAN

CENTRAL KALIMANTAN

Ketapang •

Palangkaraya
◉

SOUTH
KALIMANTAN

• Sampit

Banjarmasin ◉

JAVA SEA

| 0 | | 100 miles |
| 0 | | 100 kilometers |

MALUKU

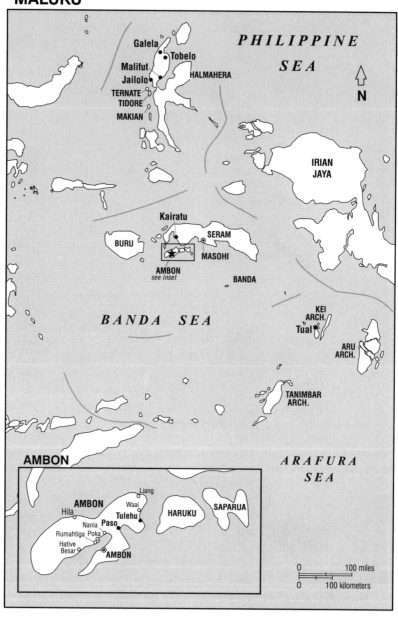

EAST TIMOR

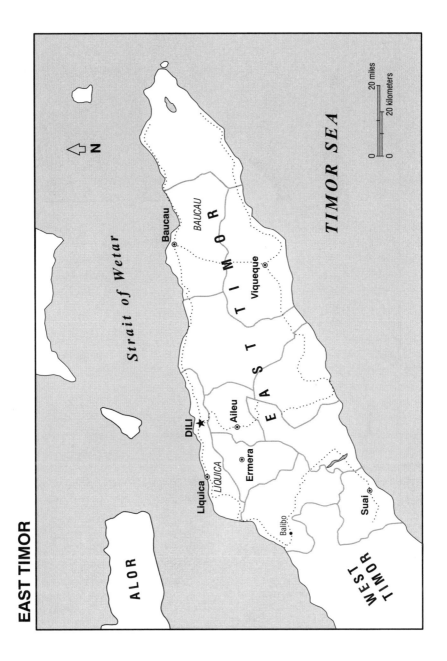

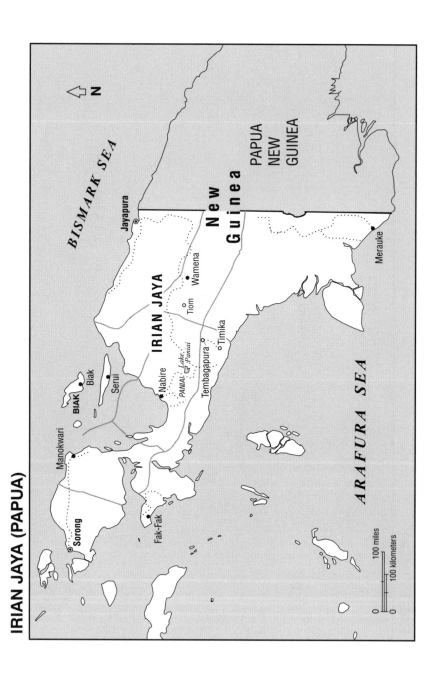

IRIAN JAYA (PAPUA)

N

BISMARK SEA

PAPUA
NEW
GUINEA

New Guinea

IRIAN JAYA

Jayapura

Merauke

Wamena

Tiom

Timika

Tembagapura

PANIAI Lake Paniai

Nabire

Serui

Biak

BIAK

Manokwari

Sorong

Fak-Fak

ARAFURA SEA

0   100 miles

0   100 kilometers

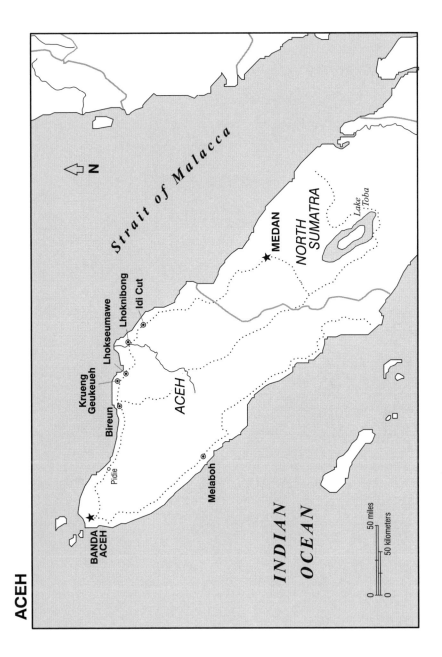

ACEH

N

Strait of Malacca

BANDA
ACEH

Pidie

Bireun

Krueng
Geukeueh

Lhokseumawe

Lhoknibong

Idi Cut

Melaboh

ACEH

MEDAN

NORTH
SUMATRA

Lake
Toba

INDIAN
OCEAN

50 miles

50 kilometers

0

0

1   Introduction

In the late 1990s, Indonesians experienced unprecedented levels of ethnic conflict.[1] During 1995 and 1996, riots in Situbondo, Tasikmalaya, and other parts of Java caused numerous deaths and the destruction of private property. They had ethnic and religious overtones that suggested serious tensions cutting across several dimensions of relations between Indonesia's ethnic groups. The wave of riots was perceived, in part, as a new phase in anti-Chinese sentiments that had regularly led to violence against the Chinese before and after Indonesia's independence. The targeting of places of worship, however, had others argue that relations between religious groups were deteriorating and reaching dangerous levels of tension. In either case, the riots were sufficiently different, numerous, and larger in scale from violent events since the 1960s to suggest a worrying trend.[2]

These worries were confirmed in the following years. Between 1997 and 2002, at least 10,000 people were killed in ethnic violence throughout the archipelago. In 1996–97 and 2001, two waves of violent clashes between Dayaks and Madurese in West and Central Kalimantan led to the deaths of at least 1,000 people and the displacement of hundreds of thousands of Madurese. In Maluku, at least 5,000 people were killed in a war between Christians and Muslims that began in January 1999 and escalated during the following three years. In East Timor, approximately 1,000 people were killed and 200,000 displaced in violence against the civilian population, following a referendum in August 1999. In Aceh, a renewal of conflict between the Free Aceh Movement and the Indonesian armed forces began in 1999 and intensified in the following years. At least 1,800 people were killed in 2000–01.[3] In Irian Jaya (Papua), the emergence of a civilian movement for independence during 1999 and 2000 led to several people dead in clashes with the Indonesian armed forces.

On 12 October 2002, a bomb exploded in the popular tourist resort of Kuta, in Bali. Almost 200 people were killed, mostly foreigners. Some of the perpetrators admitted that foreigners, especially Americans, had been targeted in retaliation for US policies that were perceived anti-Muslim.[4] Investigations blamed the Jemaah Islamiyah, an obscure, radical Islamic group that was unknown only a few months before the attack. Links to the Al-Qaeda terrorist network were also suspected. This terrorist attack was the largest in scale after those in New York and Washington on 11 September 2001. It was also the deadliest and most violent incident ever perpetrated in the name of Islam in Indonesia, where moderate Islam was always predominant.

What was happening to Indonesia? As it gained attention in the world press, observers abroad and within Indonesia wondered whether it would implode, break up, or disintegrate like the Soviet Union or Yugoslavia in the early 1990s. Violence on such a scale had not been seen since the massacres of 1965–66 that accompanied the change of leadership from Sukarno to Suharto.

Conflicts in East Timor, Aceh, and Irian Jaya had constituted exceptions to the relative stability of the previous thirty years. After the Indonesian government invaded East Timor in 1975, a guerilla war caused many deaths over the following decade. In Aceh, an armed secessionist movement arose in the mid-1970s and, once again, in 1989. In both cases, significant proportions of the civilian populations were also affected by the violent conflict. In Irian Jaya, a less organized secessionist movement nevertheless remained active and occasionally engaged in violent actions. Civilians were often caught between armed groups and the Indonesian armed forces, especially during the latter's military campaigns. In all three areas, violence was higher and the armed forces maintained a stronger presence than elsewhere in Indonesia.

Yet, the conflicts in East Timor, Aceh, and Irian Jaya did not destabilize the central government nor were they perceived as a threat to other regions. For more than thirty years, the New Order regime of President Suharto was stable and its institutions were solid. Although undemocratic, it was able to weave a considerable amount of support, or acceptance, among Indonesia's political elite in Jakarta as well as in various provinces. The conflicts in East Timor, Aceh, and Irian Jaya were perceived as important and clearly challenged Indonesia's national unity but did not constitute a threat to the New Order's political stability. For most Indonesians, these conflicts remained marginal and occurred in remote ⁿ⁺ the peripheries of the archipelago.

⸱⸱ ⸱ ᴄonflict in the late 1990s was considerably more dan-
⸱ spread and destabilize the whole country.
⸱rtones were most prone to contagion. The in-
f conflict in Aceh, and new conflicts in Maluku
ɔwed the weakness of the armed forces. In the
containing armed secessionist movements and
ɔriods without any open conflict. During most of

the 1990s, in fact, conflicts in all three secessionist regions had been considerably reduced and there was relatively little violence. The armed forces were incapable, however, of containing conflicts in Kalimantan, Maluku, East Timor, and Aceh after 1996. In some cases, the violence spread and continued, with little effective containment by the armed forces. In other cases, such as in East Timor and Maluku, the armed forces were accused of involvement in the local conflicts. At least two presidents, B. J. Habibie and Abdurrahman Wahid, lost their power in part because of the central government's inability to stop the violence.

The resurgence of ethnic violence coincided with the end of Suharto's rule but this political change cannot, in itself, explain the number and intensity of conflicts. A crisis of succession, growing awareness of corruption involving the New Order regime and Suharto's family, a financial crisis in 1997 that severely affected Indonesia's economy, and other factors contributed to the weeks of rioting that led to Suharto's resignation in May 1998. What began afterwards was either a resurrection of a weaker New Order regime, under the leadership of Habibie, or a difficult transition to democracy, depending on one's analytical perspective. In any case, some significant changes were undertaken during the months after Suharto's resignation, including the introduction of new electoral laws, autonomy laws for regions, as well as constitutional changes that strengthened the legislative assemblies relative to the very powerful executive under Suharto's rule. Although many of the conflicts appeared or became more intense after Suharto's downfall, there were signs of growing ethnic tensions prior to his departure. The riots of 1996–97 occurred well before any indication of the regime's financial woes and Suharto's resignation.

A historical institutionalist explanation

This book argues that ethnic violence in the late 1990s can be partly explained by analyzing Indonesia's national model and its institutionalization during the New Order of President Suharto. The late 1990s constituted a critical juncture in Indonesia's post-independence history, during which institutional transformation opened up channels to renegotiate the elements of the national model: the role of Islam in political institutions, the relative importance of the central and regional governments, the access and representation of ethnic groups in the state's institutions, as well as the definition and meaning of the Indonesian "nation." The institutional transformation of this period was one of three important junctures that have redefined this national model and modified the balance of constraints and opportunities for renegotiating relations between ethnic groups.

A broader theoretical context emphasizes the structures and meanings of different institutional settings. As Chapter 2 explains in greater detail, the causes of ethnic violence can be traced to the institutional context that defines and shapes ethnic identities, the official recognition of groups, their representation in state institutions, and their access to resources. Ethnic identities become politicized and the potential for mobilization is heightened when groups feel threatened by the structure and principles embedded in political institutions. Most obviously, when groups are excluded from representation or the ability to pursue their interests within given institutions, they may become increasingly alienated from the state.

At a fundamental level, institutions reflect a particular national model. Prior to the adoption of institutions, there are debates over the definition of the nation, or relations between nations, within a given state. The principles that come to define the nation or relations between nations – that is, the national model – establish inclusion/exclusion of its members and the terms of inclusion. Members might be included within a national model with conditions, for example, that imply the shedding of group identities or the acceptance of a particular hierarchy of ethnic relations. The content of these terms of inclusion can be quite varied and numerous from one context to another but usually includes a definition of the role of religion in the state (on secular or religious bases); the relative importance of group and individual rights, particularly in relation to ethnic group representation; the means of implementing and enforcing the principles of the national model (broad consensus or strong, central government directive); or the hierarchy or absence of recognition of ethnic groups and nations within the state. National models become embedded in a particular configuration of institutions that involve decisions over unitary or federal states, autonomy, and the means of representation of ethnic groups.

Ethnic violence tends to occur during periods of renegotiation of national models and state institutions. There is a tendency for waves of resurgence or intensification of violence that coincide with critical junctures of institutional reform. These junctures can occur in reaction to tensions built into past legacies of institutions and national models. They can also occur because of exogenous factors leading to institutional change. In both instances, these periods of reform become occasions to renegotiate national models or the way in which they are institutionalized. Periods of institutional instability offer possibilities for important changes but can also heighten the fears of groups that feel potentially threatened. Groups seek to position themselves either to protect past gains, favorable definitions of national models, or institutions that provide them with protection and representation. Other groups fear that they will be subjected to discrimination or exclusion. As a result, periods of stable political institutions and ethnic relations are followed by periods of institutional reform accompanied by more ethnic violence. At the end of the juncture, a national model is reconfirmed or a new one adopted, and a different structure of political institutions reflects newly achieved gains/losses for ethnic group inclusion or terms of inclusion.

This was the pattern in Indonesia. Clusters of ethnic violence tended to occur during periods of institutional reform and renegotiation of the national model, followed by periods of political stability with little or less intense ethnic conflict. As Chapter 3 explains, three critical junctures were particularly important: first, the period of formation of Indonesia's national model during which a concept of an Indonesian nation took form and was institutionalized in a unitary state in 1950; and second, the period of institutional reform that began around 1957, with the abandonment of liberal democratic institutions and their replacement by a strong, centralized system of authoritarian rule. During this juncture, which ended in 1968, President Sukarno and his successor Suharto reaffirmed the principles of the national model established in 1950 but institutionalized them in different ways. Resulting less from a broad agreement, the model became increasingly imposed by the state under Suharto's New Order rule, thereby developing unsustainable tensions from groups that were excluded or that rejected the terms of their inclusion. These tensions led to ethnic riots, with growing signs of institutional change as Suharto's rule reached its last years. The third juncture began with the resignation of Suharto in May 1998. This period of instability exacerbated tensions that had accumulated during the previous thirty years and led to violent outbreaks of several ethnic conflicts.

When democratization began in 1998, therefore, the eruption of ethnic violence was an outgrowth of path dependent choices about the national model and institutions defining ethnic relations. The financial and political crises that led to Suharto's downfall were not causes of the ethnic violence that subsequently occurred. They triggered a period of institutional reform, during which debates, demonstrations, and other forms of political action aimed not only at defining new democratic institutions but also at negotiating claims for ethnic representation and access to resources. Islamists wanted to reopen questions relating to the role of Islam in the polity, Dayaks refused to continue to be marginalized, East Timorese seized the moment to push for independence, and Acehnese vied to regain new terms of inclusion in Indonesia or independence.

The institutionalist analysis in this book explains two aspects of the eruption of violence. First, it presents an account of how institutions shaped and modified ethnic identities through different periods of Indonesia's history. Path dependent choices of institutions defining the relationship between ethnic groups and nations within a state constrain the possibilities that are offered at any period of institutional reform. Second, these choices are also constrained by concepts of nation and national models that are implicit or explicit in these institutions.

Violent ethnic conflict, therefore, is not always a product of conscious effort to redesign institutions or modify existing national models. An analysis of grievances, insecurities, choice of targets, and form of ethnic violence – the "fire-power" of ethnic mobilization – complements the clearer objectives spelled out by ethnic leaders during periods of mobilization. It reveals the relationship of this fire-power to the structure and meaning of institutions that shape ethnic relations and create conditions for violence.

The argument in this book consequently differs from other studies that have addressed various aspects of the ethnic violence of the late 1990s. We can classify these explanations in roughly three categories. The first emphasizes the role of elites (state, military, and their political opponents) in Jakarta, usually known as the "provocation" thesis. Under this analysis, instances of ethnic violence have been linked to Jakarta elites, with speculation about sources of funding and clientelist relations with criminal gangs in local areas. Conspiracy theories abound to explain the motives for inciting this kind of violence.[5] Although the evidence for provocation, or some role of outsiders, has surfaced in some cases, it has generally been weak, especially in the identification of elites responsible for master-minding conflicts. Certainly, no good evidence has surfaced linking in a credible way the elites in Jakarta with local actors in most of the cases where ethnic violence occurred.[6] Furthermore, provocation could only unleash such conflicts where tensions were high. While possibly igniting a conflict, it could not explain why so many people joined and why it became so intense.

A second line of explanation has focused, instead, on local elites and the competition for resources and power.[7] The violence is explained by the intense competition at the local level for state resources, access to positions in the civil service, or control of the top leadership positions in the province or district. Groups mobilized along religious lines in part because of existing social structures, in which religion has been a strong identifier of group differences, but the crucial factor lies in elite interests and their capacities to mobilize client groups. Conflict and violence became especially acute as a result of two decentralization laws that gave more power and resources to the districts. Violence increased in 1999, in Maluku, Kalimantan, and Poso, after these laws were implemented and as elections for leadership positions became more important. While elites certainly played a key role in mobilization, these

analyses are limited. They share a similar weakness with ar
on conspiracies and provocation. Elites cannot mobilize mas
dering each other, or pursue long-term conflicts, without s
discontent.

A third approach concentrates local grievances and their
to state policies. From this perspective, the uniqueness of context is
stressed.[8] The conflict in West Kalimantan, for example, resulted from
unique circumstances as well as reactions to state policies on access to
resources and Dayak exclusion from political and economic benefits.[9] In
Aceh, the conflict between the Free Aceh Movement and the Indonesian
state resulted from policies on natural resources and army practices in
the region. The Acehnese resented their exclusion from the benefits of
exploiting the province's natural resources, as well as their treatment at
the hands of the armed forces.[10]

While each case of violence has a unique blend of grievances explaining
the emergence of conflict, however, there are some factors that tend to
recur. The violence by the state's armed forces, for instance, has been
an important factor in these explanations. Repeated use of terror, intimidation, and killings of civilians by the armed forces in many conflict regions shaped grievances against the state and conditioned groups
to use violence in response. Beyond local sources of conflict, therefore,
broader factors have shaped the context for many of them to erupt into
violence.

While the emphasis on state violence under the New Order helps to
explain links between different cases of ethnic violence, it is not sufficient.
Why did the armed forces resort to such tactics? Why was the Indonesian
political elite supportive of or indifferent to the use of strong repression
by the armed forces? In large part, because the armed forces have always
been seen as an essential state instrument in maintaining and preserving
the integrity of the state and the unity of the nation. Even if the New
Order regime used violence beyond acceptable norms within Indonesian
society, there was at least a partial acceptance of the necessity of its use,
especially in regions facing secessionist movements. The institutionalist
approach in this book traces why a broad political elite extended some
legitimacy to the armed forces in its use of harsh repressive instruments.
Indonesia's political elite was locked into a compromise over the definition
of the Indonesian nation as institutionalized in a strong, unitary state.
Secessionist movements were seen as the worst threat to the unity of
the nation and the integrity of the state. These issues were particularly
sensitive, given Indonesia's past history of challenges to the concept of
nation and to the state.

Indonesia's past, the struggles over nation and ethnic representation,
defined the parameters of state action and group responses in the late
1990s. In order to understand the emergence of various forms of conflict

and, most importantly, their eruption or intensification after 1998, local grievances and contexts alone can explain little. Where explanations have focused on the New Order regime, they have been better able to account for the non-coincidental resurgence of violence in various areas of the archipelago. They have fallen short, however, of analyzing the New Order regime's institutions and the legacies of past historical periods when ethnic identities were formed and crystallized in particular ways. These responses to the institutional evolution of the Indonesian state, and the particular national model it came to represent, explain in large part why conflicts emerged in particular places and periods of time, while not in others.

The book presents a historical institutionalist analysis to explain many aspects of ethnic violence in Indonesia. Chapter 2 presents a theoretical framework that emphasizes the role of institutions, as they are renegotiated at various critical junctures. How a particular national model becomes institutionalized and renegotiated at these junctures defines the nature of ethnic relations, the inclusion/exclusion of ethnic groups, and the terms of inclusion. Chapter 3 provides an overview of changes to Indonesia's national model and its institutionalization at three critical junctures. Chapter 4 explains how this national model excluded some groups from an otherwise largely inclusive concept of the Indonesian nation. It discusses the issue of conflict against the ethnic Chinese as well as the conflict between Dayaks and Madurese in Kalimantan. The latter is explained as a result of the Dayaks' marginalization in the Indonesian nation because of their status as a "backward" group in Indonesian society. Chapters 5, 6, and 7 address conflicts between Muslims and Christians, particularly the violent conflict in Maluku. They situate the violence in Maluku in relation to the evolving role of Islam in Indonesia's national model and its effects both on inter-religious relations and among Muslims themselves.

Chapters 8 and 9 cover the resurgence of ethnonationalism in Aceh, East Timor, and Irian Jaya (Papua) after 1999. They explain the sources of conflicts in these three regions as they evolved from ethnic differentiations created by past conflicts. Their resolution institutionalized terms of inclusion that were unfavorable to all groups. In the cases of the East Timorese and Papuans, the problem was worse because the means of integration into Indonesia created deep resentment. Chapter 10 considers the regional autonomy laws introduced in 1999 and the special autonomy laws for Aceh and Papua. It discusses whether they constitute a new institutional departure for Indonesia's national model.

2   Critical junctures, nationalism, and ethnic violence

Ethnic conflict is shaped and mediated by the institutional context in which it occurs. Political institutions have a direct impact on the development of ethnic identity, its use in political mobilization, as well as the means available to negotiate group claims. They define citizens and non-citizens, majorities and minorities, and the allocation of political and economic resources. They define or deny group rights while also delimiting the means available to advance group interests.

Ethnic identities are malleable, multiple, and not always politicized. Identities defined in racial, religious, and cultural terms may be fixed over long periods of time but they can also change. Voluntary or forced conversion, conquest and redefinition of political boundaries, or colonial policies are all examples of events that can reshape them. Furthermore, any single individual possesses multiple, overlapping ethnic identities as a member of a religious, cultural, or regional group.[1] Which identity becomes a stronger source of group differentiation may vary from one set of circumstances to another.[2] Even more so, these identities do not necessarily become sources of competition for resources, access to the state, or conflict. While group differentiation may be prevalent, it may not have an impact on the structure of socio-political organizations or the character of political mobilization.

Political institutions are part of the context that shapes ethnic identity and mediates conflict. Differences in electoral systems might provide varied incentives to mobilize ethnic identity, sometimes even contributing to the formation of ethnic political parties. Federal structures can give control to ethnic groups over territory where they are majorities, whereas a unitary state might otherwise reduce them to permanent minorities with little political power. Formalized power-sharing agreements between ethnic groups can establish the foundation for coalition cabinets, veto rights, and quotas for positions in the civil service. To the extent that groups can channel their grievances, ensure their protection, and negotiate new powers and access to resources, conflict is less likely to be violent. When groups are denied such institutional channels, violence is more likely. Its intensity and scope might

9

vary, in turn, with the state's willingness and capacity to use repressive instruments.

Political institutions are also bounded, however, by fundamental principles that define the nation or the political community coincident with the state. Electoral systems, legislative structures, types of executives, and federalist or unitary systems embody a certain conception of the nation or relation between nations. Those that define their membership in terms of equal citizens sharing individual rights and fundamental political principles are unlikely to have political institutions that formally recognize ethnic groups. Conversely, nations that give primacy to ethnic identities are likely to develop political structures that reflect the dominance of particular ethnic groups or a negotiated allocation of power.

A historical institutionalist approach explains why violent conflict is often generated during periods of change. When institutions are weakened during transition periods, allocations of power and resources become open for competition. More fundamentally, ethnic groups can renegotiate the concept of the nation that underlies institutional structures, perpetuates an uneven distribution of power and resources, or specifies terms of inclusion that disadvantage them. These periods of institutional change constitute "critical junctures" during which the institutionalization of ethnic relations is modified along with a reaffirmation, contestation, or renegotiation of the principles upon which these relations are based.

Explaining ethnic violence

Explanations for ethnic violence have not sufficiently emphasized the link between nationalism, institutions, and relations between ethnic groups. Instead, they have focused on such factors as the nature of ethnic identity and its consequences, the role of elites, socio-economic disparities, group opportunities, or comparisons based on group legitimacy and group worth. Institutions have been studied in static comparisons of alternative arrangements for managing conflict and preventing its occurrence, but rarely in terms of the impact of change.[3] Yet, periods of institutional change are often associated with violent ethnic conflict. Changing institutional structures and their relationship to concepts of nationalism can contribute to the polarization of ethnic identities and the potential for violence.

Three broad approaches explain why ethnicity sometimes becomes a channel for political struggle and conflict. "Constructivist" approaches emphasize the social and historical context that shapes, transforms, and delineates ethnic boundaries, as well as the bases of conflict.[4] "Instrumentalist" approaches focus on the role of ethnic elites in mobilizing identities. Leaders and political entrepreneurs use the emotional appeal of ethnic identity to mobilize mass support in a competition for state power, resources, and private interests.[5] "Primordialist" approaches emphasize the inheritance of ethnic traits by birth and the immutability of group boundaries. In the purest version of this perspective, ethnic groups are seen as inherently prone to hostility by nature of their group differences.[6]

Most scholars reject the argument that conflict emerges from the mere sense of group identity. Aside from the existence of multiple identities around which ethnic groups may be formed in any given society, the relevant identities for political mobilization require a coalescence of group identity with political claims.[7] These claims arise out of group anxieties that are created by a changing political, economic, social, or cultural context. Political mobilization becomes a means of obtaining power as an end, to secure group entitlement and reduce group anxieties: "Power in these two latter senses – confirming status and averting threat – usually entails an effort to dominate the environment, to suppress differences, as well as to prevent domination and suppression by others . . . The fear of ethnic domination and suppression is a motivating force for the acquisition of power as an end. And power is also sought for confirmation of ethnic status".[8] When group anxieties become the basis for political mobilization, the struggle for power takes different forms depending on the available channels to express and advance the group's interests and claims.[9]

Group fears and grievances are therefore rooted in the context in which ethnic identities are constructed and mobilized. Members of an ethnic group may fear violence, for example, when tensions have been rising as a result of political discrimination. The fear and ensuing potential for violence are direct results of a political system in which one group dominates the instruments of state power and uses them to deny similar access or privileges to other ethnic groups. In another example, an ethnic group may demand redress for denial of education or services in its language. Such a grievance would result from discrimination against a minority's language. While context may not determine conflict, it may powerfully contribute to the delineation of ethnic boundaries and the definition of grievances.

Most often, group fears, tensions, or grievances are concealed, with the most common forms of political action remaining in the realm of the "hidden transcript".[10] In the public realm, ethnic groups can display cordial relations, support inter-ethnic cooperation and initiatives, and live peacefully with one another. This outward expression of harmonious relations may disguise, however, a hidden transcript of acrimony, grumbling, suspicion, and even hatred. Members of an ethnic group complain to each other about discrimination by other groups, threats to their livelihoods, or loss of relative status in the state. They develop stereotypes about members of other groups as being greedy, untrustworthy, aggressive, or arrogant. They view other groups' motives as being suspicious and are prone to conspiracy theories. Such disjuncture between the public and private realm can maintain a balance in ethnic relations for a long time, without leading to the open expression of grievances and tensions, or open conflict.

How or why the hidden transcript becomes public, or an event triggers a violent response, varies from one context to another. The passage from non-violent to violent action is complex, and can be attributed as much to "background" conditions as to immediate events that precede the violent outbreak. As Donald Horowitz argues, in his explanation of ethnic riots, "there is a trade-off between the precipitant and environmental conditions supporting the use of violence. What the underlying conditions may lack in conduciveness to disorder the precipitant may possess in provocativeness . . . This trade-off between the precipitant and the underlying conditions heightens the unpredictability of riots".[11] Which event or underlying conditions will be sufficient to trigger violence remains difficult to determine with any degree of analytical precision.

Elites play an important role, at times, in intensifying or orchestrating a precipitant event.[12] They may tap the potential for mobilization following a triggering event. Spontaneous rioting may be followed by a systematic, violent reaction that is coordinated by ethnic leaders using established networks for mobilization. Violence could also be triggered by a well-orchestrated act of provocation with the deliberate intention of raising fears and anger in a context where ethnic tensions are high. Any sustained violence is likely to involve both strong underlying conditions for violence as well as ethnic elites with an interest in initiating or perpetuating violent acts.

Changes in underlying conditions, however, constitute the "firepower" of ethnic violence. Rising tensions between ethnic groups can be related to a number of factors. If ethnic groups are subjected to economic discrimination or have a significant economic disadvantage relative to other groups, for example, they might resort to violence if their situation deteriorates. Similarly, if a group has enjoyed a relative advantage for some time but faces a sudden relative loss of its privileged position, it might also resort to violence to defend its status.[13] Tensions will rise also when an ethnic group is denied political rights, lacks representation in the state, has little control over policies that affect its interests, is severely repressed, or systematically excluded from citizenship rights. Violence is more likely to occur when these conditions first appear or when they worsen. Sources of tension might be related, as well, to cultural discrimination such as restrictions on religious practise, on the use of language in education or other official purposes, or on the application of cultural customs, from marriage tradition to dress codes.[14] Whether grievances are based on economic, political, or cultural conditions and comparisons, the likelihood of violence increases when significant changes lead to worsened conditions for disadvantaged groups or offer potential threats to the privileged status of dominant groups.

This categorization of underlying conditions, however, is underspecified. Many actions fall under the category of "discrimination" or "disadvantage" and, certainly, changes in these conditions can be quite varied. The analysis becomes particularly difficult when one accepts theoretical propositions that emphasize both a defensive reaction as well as an opportunistic moment. Many scholars have been divided on whether ethnic violence mainly stems from a strategic calculation of benefits and costs to the group (or its leadership) or from emotional responses to perceptions of threat. Rational choice scholars have been more likely to argue that cases of ethnic violence can be both a defensive or offensive response to changing opportunity structures, whereas other scholars have placed more emphasis on the psychological and passionate responses that modify groups' perceptions of events and cast them as threatening, insulting, degrading, or inhuman.[15]

When analyzing the changing social, political, and economic context, an institutionalist approach helps to narrow the field of possibilities. Political institutions define the parameters of this context by specifying the allocations of group rights and obligations, political representation, privileges or restrictions, access to resources, channels to express grievances, and repressive instruments of the state, among others. At a fundamental level, the structures of these institutions are defined by particular conceptions of the nation that characterize the common bond uniting individuals and groups within the state. The nation defines inclusion and exclusion, as well as the terms of inclusion that set out the relative power and representation of various groups.

The characteristics of a nation and political institutions restrict the range of possibilities, as well as the limits and effects of change that affect ethnic group relations. By analyzing institutions and how they change, one can better grasp why ethnic groups will sometimes choose violence over peaceful means of addressing grievances. Economic, social, cultural, or political grievances can underlie conflict and be important sources of change in ethnic relations but only in relation to the institutional environment that defines how grievances can be expressed, repressed, or negotiated. It is often at the level of the nation itself or its expression in particular forms of political institutions that the roots of conflict are located.

The types of violent conflict can be varied. Riots are one of the most common forms, in which groups react to an event that provokes violence when tensions are running high. A first incident can become a repeated series of riots in a chain of violent events that are increasingly independent from the original sources of tension between groups. Violence becomes the product of cycles of anger and revenge, of reinterpretation of group relations, and of a new discourse about violent events that sets the stage for future conflict.[16] Other forms of ethnic violence may involve smaller groups of people, such as terrorist acts or large-scale ethnic warfare. Ethnonationalist conflict is a specific type of ethnic warfare that pits an ethnic group against the state, is territorially concentrated, and seeks the establishment of a new nation-state through secession. The latter forms involve more systematic organization of violence, mobilization of resources, and role of ethnic elites in directing violent acts, but they share common underlying conditions of conflict with riots.

It is difficult, however, to explain why one form of conflict will erupt rather than another. In general, theories of ethnic conflict have been poor at differentiating between forms of conflict and better at developing theoretical propositions about the causes of all forms of ethnic conflict.[17] Just like the difficulties in identifying clear factors that trigger violent events, what form the violence takes requires much more theoretical analysis.

While recognizing this limitation, a historical institutionalist explanation can nevertheless provide an analysis of conditions that lead to violence even though they are limited and partial. The following two sections develop this approach in two ways. The first explains how nationalism constitutes an important source of construction of ethnic identity and, at times, of ethnic conflict. By understanding how "national models" are formed, how they shape ethnic relations, and how they change, one can better understand the conditions that lead to violence. The second section shows how these national models and related political institutions are most conducive to violence at critical junctures. When exogenous events or processes of change from past experiences cause political institutions to be transformed or national models to be renegotiated, established patterns in ethnic relations become very unstable and, often, more conflictual. Analysis of these critical junctures helps in understanding the factors of contextual change leading to ethnic violence.

Nationalism and ethnic conflict

The characteristics of a nation ultimately limit the shape and functions of state institutions and, therefore, of ethnic relations. Nations specify boundaries of inclusion and exclusion. They are organized around political, cultural, or ethnic principles of membership that may be broad or limited to a particular group. Since nations rarely coincide with state boundaries, such principles have effects on ethnic groups, either by providing a basis for ethnonationalist movements to emerge or, more subtly, by shaping the political relevance of non-nationalist ethnic mobilization.

In the Westphalian nation-state system, individuals are members of nations and they live in states. Although these two units are not always congruent, they are difficult to dissociate. Members of national groups seek to obtain control of states that coincide with their national boundaries. Similarly, state leaders attempt to define common national values to legitimize their jurisdiction over particular national groups.

Nationalism is the fundamental organizing principle that links nations to states. A "hard" view of nationalism views it as a principle or ideology that dictates a coincidence between the state and nations defined in ethnic terms.[18] Nationalism is viewed as a negative force, even a disease. By dichotomizing states as either imbued with nationalism or not, it denies the vast diversity of principles and characteristics that underlie the foundation of states and are imbedded in nations within states. A "soft" view of nationalism recognizes it as the principle that nations and states should coincide but argues that it can be positive or negative.[19] It is better suited to an understanding of nations as diverse and representative of a variety of common bonds.

State boundaries and institutions express values and identities shared by citizens living under their jurisdiction. Without a sense of common experience and a common set of political values, the boundaries of a state are meaningless. On what basis does one legitimize the affiliation of a citizen to a particular state? Even where several national groups coexist within a state, there must be some common identity. As Will Kymlicka notes: "multination states cannot survive unless the various national groups have an allegiance to the larger political community they cohabit".[20] At a minimum, a historical evolution beginning with the creation of the state provides a justification for maintaining boundaries and providing institutions to represent and govern the community of citizens within them.

Nations are defined as groups that share a sense of common belonging, common experience, and, oftentimes, common cultural traits.

Nations are "imagined communities" of citizens sharing common characteristics that differentiate them from other such communities.[21] They also seek sovereignty and resist subjugation to other nations. They seek to govern themselves and to obtain their own states as an institutional expression of their common bond, values, and history.

In the current nation-state system, two types of political movements seek the coincidence of state and nation. First, secessionist movements seek to create new states with boundaries that coincide with their nation's homeland. Second, state elites undertake "nation-building" efforts to create common bonds, foster common values, or craft a common culture that defines a new nation coincident with existing state boundaries. This form of state nationalism attempts to eliminate bonds to a prior national or ethnic group and to form new loyalties to the state based on membership of a new nation.[22]

Whether associated with a secessionist movement or created by a state elite, the nation defines principles of inclusion and exclusion. In each case, these principles entail a definition of the common bonds that define membership of the nation. These bonds can be traced to cultural characteristics, adherence to a particular religion, native languages, common histories, or political principles, such as the sharing of particular democratic ideals.

The principles characterizing a nation, or relationships between nations in multination states, are often sources of ethnic conflict. These principles constitute "national models" that specify membership inclusion as well as the terms by which such inclusion can occur. They usually refer to cultural as well as political characteristics. Sometimes, conflict can develop from group exclusion but, at other times, it is related to discrimination or unequal status as conditions of inclusion.

The vast diversity of ways in which nations combine cultural and political characteristics makes it particularly difficult, except in extreme cases, to associate particular categories of nations with ethnic conflict. One common classification divides different forms of nationalism as either "civic" or "ethnic." The former defines the nation's citizenship in the broadest inclusive terms, based primarily on birth or long-term residence in a territory. The latter limits citizenship to members of particular ethnic groups. Civic nationalism tends to be associated with open societies that emphasize individual rights and liberal values. According to Liah Greenfeld, it tends to be peaceful, while ethnic nationalism is considered to be aggressive. Violence occurs when the nation takes precedence over the individual, she argues, and when members who do not share common ethnic characteristics are excluded.[23]

The dichotomy between "civic" and "ethnic" nationalism, however, is misleading. It is premised on the idea that some states, such as the

United States, are devoid of any ethnic criteria of membership and are therefore open to members of any ethnic origin.[24] In these states, the nation is defined purely on the basis of rational principles of individual rights and democratic representation. Yet, while membership may be inclusive, there are conditions of adherence to the nation. Some degree of assimilation is expected to occur in order to conform to certain cultural norms. As Kymlicka argues: "What distinguishes "civic" and "ethnic" nations is not the absence of any cultural component to national identity, but rather the fact that anyone can integrate into the common culture, regardless of race or colour".[25] While cultural diversity may be respected, civic nations must still choose official languages among many more spoken in a given territory of the state, impose limits on religious or cultural customs that transgress accepted norms of civic behavior, and make choices in a common educational curriculum that place emphasis on the history and cultural customs of certain groups over others. Political identity is built around cultural memories, even if their most important components are based on political symbols and a discourse emphasizing political principles, as opposed to linguistic or ethnic bonds. Bernard Yack offers a good summary of such an argument by agreeing with the nineteenth-century French theorist on nationalism, Ernest Renan, that:

Two things make a nation: present-day consent and a rich cultural inheritance of shared memories and practices. Without consent our cultural legacy would be our destiny, rather than a set of background constraints on our activities. But without such a legacy there would be no consent at all, since there would be no reason for people to seek agreement with any group of individuals rather than another.[26]

A community requires a set of common characteristics that provide an emotional bond, make it unique, and differentiate it from other communities.

Even attempts to implement a civic nationalism along liberal principles may create serious problems of representation for particular groups. For instance, Deborah Yashar has shown in the case of aboriginal people in Latin America that a shift in "citizenship regime" had the unintended consequence of eliminating the means by which "Indians" negotiated power in the state. As a group, they had more power to negotiate on behalf of group interests under a corporatist, more authoritarian regime than after the implementation of democratic, neo-liberal regimes because their existence as a group was not recognized.[27] With the implementation of principles of individual rights without some level of group recognition, many other cultural groups find themselves excluded.

The dichotomy between civic and ethnic nationalism clouds some of the most important elements of debate that determine common characteristics for the nation, define inclusion and exclusion, and determine as well the terms of inclusion of various groups. Issues such as the representation of minorities, official languages, special status, and autonomy can occur in predominantly civic or ethnic nations. These debates involve negotiations about the particular mix of civic values, cultural expression, and ethnic representation embedded in national conceptions and institutions.

I suggest that these negotiations, compromises, and deliberations amount to the development of a national model that defines more than inclusion and exclusion along ethnic or civic criteria. They define the common cultural and political bonds of the nation, the conditions for recognition of particular groups and their representation, and on what terms they are included in the nation. Are they given special kinds of status, institutions, and rights over other groups? Are immigrants provided with equal rights to cultural support, use of language, or practise of religion? All of these characteristics correspond to an implicit or explicit articulation of a national model, from basic principles enshrined in constitutions to institutional forms or regular legislation. Conflict can arise from tensions revolving around any of these characteristics, not only broad principles that one can associate with civic or ethnic ones.

Two broad sets of issues can lead to conflict. First order principles, related to questions of membership inclusion and exclusion, resemble the distinction between civic and ethnic nationalism. The broadest criteria for inclusion tend to be the most stabilizing, while the most restrictive, most often associated with the worse kind of ethnic nationalism, tend to create violence against those who are excluded. Violence can also occur when groups are included as individuals but not recognized as groups. In this case, inclusion is broad and follows an individualist criterion along liberal principles, but there is no recognition of particular groups, their cultural difference, and interests arising from this difference. Repeated denial of recognition can lead to violence.

Second order principles defining a particular national model relate to the terms and means of inclusion. While membership criteria may be broad and some groups recognized, their inclusion might give preponderance to a hegemonic group's particular culture or preferences. In this case, official language, educational curriculum, national symbols, religious practise, or formal representation in political institutions give rise to debate and conflict. Negotiation might occur through peaceful means, if the polity is equipped with appropriate channels to voice grievances and create pressure on the dominant group. Groups might make claims and advance their interests through formal institutional means such as representation in the legislature, or more informal means such as open criticism through the media or peaceful political protest.

Knowing whether groups are included or excluded as citizens, therefore, is not sufficient for understanding how a particular national model may lead to conflict. The criterion of inclusion on restrictive ethnic bases or broader civic terms is only a first level of conflict. Once included, groups may seek more formal recognition, with accompanying changes to formal institutions to reflect their political representation, their cultural distinctiveness, or their particular needs. This "politics of recognition," as Charles Taylor has named it, becomes relevant even in the most democratic and liberal states, where the debate then shifts to the relative importance of collective and individual rights.[28] In less than fully democratic states, such issues are particularly prone to conflict. The less available are the means to negotiate peacefully, the more probable that violence will occur. At stake is the survival of the group:

[It is] a question of whether cultural survival will be acknowledged as a legitimate goal, whether collective ends will be allowed as legitimate considerations in judicial review, or for other purposes of major social policy. The demand there was that we let cultures defend themselves, within reasonable bounds. But the further demand we are looking at here is that we all *recognize* the equal value of different cultures; that we not only let them survive, but acknowledge their *worth*.[29]

If cultural survival can be threatened under a liberal democratic regime, it is more so when there are weak judicial and political institutions. Group survival is the most fundamental issue, followed by recognition of worth. Violent conflict is most likely when groups feel threatened and have few peaceful instruments available to guarantee their survival. Violence can also occur when groups are included and their recognition acknowledged, but on terms that maintain them perpetually in the status of "backward" group or "second-class" citizens.[30]

National models define and limit the legitimacy of the pursuit of group survival and equal worth. Groups appeal to fundamental principles underlying the state and its national model to justify claims to group survival and worth. Where historically a nation has defined itself as a homogenous cultural group or, in liberal terms, as a nation of equal individuals, the pursuit of group survival and worth may be severely constrained. In national models emphasizing multiculturalism, group survival may be guaranteed through provisions recognizing the legitimacy of cultural groups, but they may not be given equal status in the polity. These inequalities are likely to take a variety of forms, including the absence of representation in formal institutions that can threaten their survival, constitutional provisions that, de facto, give more power to certain groups over others, or legislation that limits the ability to protect a group's language, limits its use for official purposes, or curtails the group's perception of cultural advancement. A negotiation occurs between groups seeking further cultural and political guarantees, and dominant groups upholding the principles of the national model. National models limit the domain of legitimacy for pursuing claims to survival and worth, which can be resolved peacefully or violently.

Critical junctures, institutions, and "national models"

Ethnic violence often occurs during periods of institutional change. For the most part, "national models" and associated political institutions are stable. They define and shape relations between ethnic groups that are either peaceful or conflictual. A particular configuration of ethnic relations, political mobilization of ethnic identities, and tensions and grievances can be traced, historically, to their institutionalization at some point in the past. Only occasionally do critical junctures occur, when political institutions and the principles of national models are renegotiated. These junctures constitute historical moments of institutional change when the grievances of ethnic groups tend to surface. The analysis of these junctures can explain some important conditions associated with ethnic violence.

Formal political institutions reflect conceptions of the nation. Constitutions and special laws define the terms of citizenship, enshrine principles of representation, and give meaning to the structure and procedures of institutions. In the extreme ethnic case, citizenship is extended only to one particular ethnic group while it is denied or restricted for ethnic minorities, who are also given limited or no political rights and representation. Further along a continuum, some institutional arrangements explicitly recognize ethnic group identities and provide power-sharing arrangements, veto powers, and other special measures that give equal political weight to each major ethnic group in a polity.[31] Other institutional arrangements give special emphasis to individual rights and duties, and follow principles that prevent the institutionalization of ethnic identities. In such contexts, political representation is exclusively defined along territorial lines or proportional to population, with no special prerogatives for ethnic groups. In many cases, strategies are designed to enhance civic values and inclusiveness, while recognizing the complexities arising from ethnic diversity.

Past institutional choices and their justification in relation to a national model constrain the range of institutional forms that affect ethnic group relations. In a society in which the nation has been defined in ethnic terms, with institutions reflecting the dominance of one ethnic group, it is much more difficult to suddenly change course and adopt a national model defined along broad, inclusive terms. The reverse is also true. Where a broad, inclusive national model has been adopted in the past, ethnic group relations may be better protected from the attempts of one group to dominate another. Debates, negotiations, and conflict over power and resource allocation, as determined by political institutions, draw on the past national model as a tool of legitimation for status quo institutional solutions, modifications, or departures from established compromises. Where these changes also require a redefinition of the principles of the nation or national model, the stakes are seen as higher and therefore more difficult to surmount.[32]

Scholars have often proposed institutional solutions to reduce the propensity of ethnic conflict. Consociationalism is one of the main approaches that have been suggested. It is a variant of power-sharing approaches that are essentially targeted at elite accommodation. It is characterized by grand coalition governments that include representatives from all major ethnic groups; cultural autonomy for these groups; proportionality in political representation and civil service appointments; and minority veto over vital rights and autonomy.[33] Other approaches favor particular institutional incentives that foster a broad participation of society and elites in the political process. According to Horowitz, the actual techniques may vary according to different contexts, but five principles are likely to reduce conflict: dispersing the points of power; fostering intra-ethnic conflict; creating incentives for inter-ethnic cooperation; encouraging alignments based on interests other than ethnicity; and reducing disparities between groups. Among the structural reforms that use some of these principles, those that have been successful in several cases include federalism, regional autonomy, and electoral fine-tuning.[34] Overall, there is some variance between mixes of power-sharing, public participation, and state control.

These institutional solutions, however, are designed in a historical vacuum. Very few societies have the opportunity to engineer new constitutions and institutions that can better address group grievances. Debates over consociational arrangements, power-sharing, "ethnically blind" institutions, and cross-ethnic incentives are mainly relevant in exceptional circumstances.

Opportunities for significant changes arise only at critical junctures. Long periods under particular political regimes, stable institutional forms, and fixed national models are punctuated by points in time when

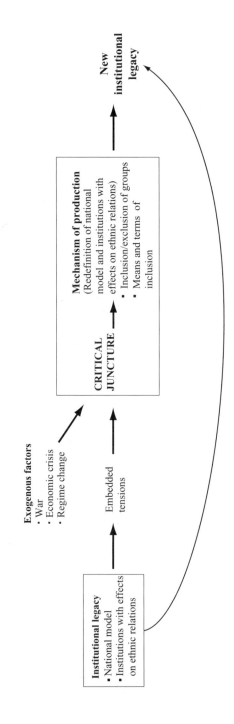

Figure 1 Critical junctures, national models, and ethnic relations

they collapse, unravel, or are strongly challenged.[35] These periods are critical junctures because they are characterized by transformation and change rather than the preceding stability and routine politics. They refer specifically to historical moments when either the principles of the national model or political institutions were changed in such a way that the nature and character of ethnic relations were altered (or expected to be altered). The analysis is restricted to an analysis of institutional change concerning the principles of the nation and those political institutions that regulate, represent, manage, control, or give voice to ethnic groups.[36]

An analysis of critical junctures can provide compelling explanations of the sources of ethnic violence. Figure 1 provides an illustration of the framework used in this book. Critical junctures are triggered by exogenous factors or emerge out of tensions created by previous institutionalized forms of ethnic relations. At these junctures, violence tends to occur as anxieties rise and ethnic groups become uncertain about past compromises and institutional settings. The violence and negotiations during these periods of uncertainty revolve around the first order principles (inclusion/exclusion) or second order principles (terms of inclusion) of a national model. A new pattern of ethnic relations is established during this juncture and gives way to a new period of institutionalized relations between groups and, usually, less violence. At a fundamental level, new institutions might reflect a new national model but, more often, these constitute new terms of inclusion that address previous grievances and tensions.

While critical junctures may end with more stable and peaceful outcomes, they increase the propensity for ethnic conflict when they are unfolding. The boundaries of ethnic compromise become blurred. Past achievements and gains, privileges, or injustices rise to the surface with debates over new institutional configurations. During these debates, national models may become open for renegotiation as well, thereby reopening fundamental issues about the nation and state themselves.

Group anxieties rise dramatically. The wider opportunity to renegotiate inclusion or exclusion, the terms of inclusion, and the allocation of power and resources is also accompanied by a rise in the uncertainty of outcome. Before a critical juncture occurs, tensions may be high because of perceived injustices, discrimination, or disadvantage but the range of possible courses of action and expected responses from other groups remains relatively clear. Violence may already be used but it operates within a relatively predictable context. It is often used as one of many simultaneous instruments to advance group interests. For instance, it is not unusual in countries with relatively stable institutional environments to find an armed branch of an ethnonationalist movement pursuing a guerilla war in favor of secession, while a political group also seeks the same objective through available formal political or diplomatic channels. Yet, at critical junctures, the predictability of the institutional environment is lost and the stakes rise dramatically. Dominant as well as minority groups are aware that a new, stabilized set of institutions may offer opportunities for unprecedented advancement for their groups or great loss of status and past gains.

Two types of negotiation or contestation are likely to occur. Groups might use violence or make claims on the basis of first order principles. These involve questions of inclusion and exclusion, recognition of new groups, or a new definition of the nation. Such principles are rarely negotiated and mainly occur at the time of the first declaration of the existence of a nation or the creation of a new state. Second order principles are more common as they relate to the terms of inclusion. Despite formal inclusion, groups might still require negotiations to erase differences of status, access, representation, or other discrepancies with other groups. These differences tend to express differentiated terms of inclusion or, in other words, the constitution of "second-class" citizens or minorities with restricted rights.

Critical junctures are important, in this context, because they are defining moments when new paths are set. As Paul Pierson notes: "some original ordering moment triggered particular patterns, and the activity is continuously reproduced even though the original event no longer occurs . . . The crucial object of study becomes the critical juncture or triggering events, which set development along a particular path".[37] Once a new legacy is established, new factors affect the causes and processes that lead to ethnic violence. A new institutional context defines the parameters of national identity, ethnic identity, and the processes leading to ethnic violence or its absence.

New paths are not necessarily sweeping or revolutionary changes from the past. At critical junctures, the field of choice is more widely open and can allow the kinds of institutional reforms offered by theorists espousing particular solutions to resolve ethnic conflict. Even then, the choices are constrained by past decisions on institutional forms and national models. It might be easier, at a moment of crisis, to agree on moving to a consociational arrangement from a majoritarian parliamentary system if the national model remains a broadly inclusive one. However, if such institutional choices involve a displacement of past ethnic hegemony by a particular group, these kinds of choices may provoke much more opposition from the dominant group and create higher potential for violence. Even when opportunities arise for drastic institutional reform, therefore, the field of possibilities remains constrained by past choices.

Critical junctures tend to be triggered by two sets of circumstances. First, they occur because of embedded tensions in past institutional compromises. At every juncture, certain groups gain and others lose in the negotiation over inclusion, power allocation, or access to state resources. At times, ethnic identities might be reconfigured because of the new institutional context. Where a new level of government is created, for example, minorities within the new jurisdiction may become more aware of their identities if they were previously part of a majority ethnic group under the larger territorial jurisdiction. Critical junctures widen the range of institutional choice at a particular time and allow groups to renegotiate their relative status, power, or representation. Groups also try to reconfigure institutions to reflect new compromises or outcomes of political struggle.

Exogenous factors constitute a second set of triggering factors. An economic crisis, a regime transition, a war, or other important event might offer the opportunity to renegotiate the institutions affecting relative group status. At more significant junctures, these changes may also entail debate and renegotiation of the most fundamental principles of the national model: choices between secular and religious state; equal recognition of all groups as opposed to a claim to group hegemony; or adoption of federalism and a formula for drawing a federal map along regional or ethnic lines, relative to a unitary state that emphasizes national unity and hegemony.

Most likely, however, exogenous factors are catalysts for processes already at work. Such factors themselves do not tend to alter ethnic relations, lead to ethnic violence, or trigger debates about the fundamental principles of a national model without tensions and cleavages already present. As the latter develop out of past institutionalization and conditions, a crisis or critical juncture occurs because of abrupt changes brought about by the exogenous factors.

Regime change, for example, is one such factor. This has been particularly prevalent during the third wave of democratization that began in 1974 and was associated with a higher incidence of ethnic violence.[38] Breakdowns of democracy, failures of democratic consolidation, and the concomitant rise of authoritarian regimes also constitute important junctures when ethnic group relations change. They can lead to the dominance of one group and severe threats to ethnic minorities. Conversely, they might reduce ethnic violence if repressive means are used to crush ethnic rebellions or ethnonationalist movements.

The period between the initial opening of an authoritarian regime and a fully consolidated democracy can be crucial for relations between ethnic groups. Questions are raised about citizenship, whose norms and practises the state is aligned with, and which groups are included and excluded.[39] In non-democratic political settings, inter-ethnic agreement is not necessary since acquiescence to the state's authority can be imposed.[40] Yet, when ethnic relations can be improved under authoritarian systems, the process of democratization can be facilitated.[41] If conflicts between the most powerful groups can be resolved immediately prior to a democratic opening, such as in South Africa, then it is possible to open up to less powerful groups through a pact-making process leading to transition. The achievement of relative equality between the English and Afrikaners in South Africa allowed for white unity and removed the underlying justification for racial segregation, thereby removing a major impediment to "national unity." White groups were then able to respond to black protests and riots by engaging in the pact-making process leading to democratic transition.[42] In other contexts, such as in Spain, Yugoslavia, and the Soviet Union, the sequencing of elections could be a determinant factor to ensure ethnic harmony. If all-union elections are held before regional elections, for example, ethnic conflict is less likely to arise during the transition period.[43]

Irrespective of whether such elite agreements can be made, democratic transitions trigger uncertainties over the future of the national model. Accepting the state, its boundaries, and a set of democratic institutions may be sufficient in some contexts, if groups are willing to accept politics as "the arena of uncertainty." Yet, more is often at stake. Without adopting an institutional framework that explicitly recognizes and congeals ethnic divisions, there may also be substantial demands for some forms of cultural recognition, equality of status, and extension of principles that will allow the pursuit of group interests: cultural preservation, use of language, education, or religious practise. These are conditions that go well beyond the agreement on new rules for electing leaders.

Regime change, therefore, can be an important exogenous factor that is accompanied by volatile relations between ethnic groups. While not necessarily conducive to violence, it is a period of important institutional change that opens up discussions and negotiations about resource allocations, representation, and status of ethnic groups. A crisis emerges out of tensions embedded in past institutional forms and compromises that are no longer sustainable or acceptable.[44]

By analyzing critical junctures in the historical evolution of national models and related ethnic relations, one can better understand the institutions that define and shape ethnic identities, tensions, and grievances. Although many factors might contribute to ethnic violence, they cannot be detached from particular institutional contexts. Institutions, in turn, reflect the past compromises, negotiations, imposition, or repression that have altered ethnic relations. Institutional forms in themselves cannot adequately explain sources of tensions and conflict. They only become meaningful in relation to their origins and to past critical junctures. Without an analysis of their expression of particular national models and the paths that have led to their present form, an emphasis on political institutions lacks explanatory power.

3   The national model and its
        institutional history

Indonesia's national model has been based on the concept of a single, Indonesian nation. Constructed out of diverse peoples spread across a vast archipelago, at its origins it was only a vision for establishing a new polity that would unify groups of different ethnicity, size, contact with the modern world, and experience with colonial rule. After independence, struggles within the political elite showed profound disagreements over its character and the best way to ensure its unity. They included issues such as the nation's secular or religious basis, and the degree of ethnic representation. Once a compromise was reached, subsequent institutional changes were highly constrained by the original concept.

Three critical junctures were particularly salient. The first corresponded to the decades during which the Indonesian nation was constructed. The rise of Indonesian nationalism competed with different political alternatives during decades of colonial decline, revolution, and war. At the end of the juncture in 1950, political leaders reached a compromise to institutionalize the Indonesian nation in the form of a unitary state and modern, liberal democratic political institutions. The second juncture began during the mid-1950s and ended only with the establishment of a military-dominated authoritarian regime, the New Order, which was consolidated around 1968. New political institutions were created to firmly entrench a vision of the Indonesian nation that focused on unity through the formation of homogenous political, social, developmental, and even some cultural characteristics for all of Indonesia's diverse ethnic groups. The legacy of this juncture lasted thirty years before the tensions and strains it created grew sufficiently strong to precipitate a crisis. With the sudden downfall of President Suharto in May 1998, a third critical juncture reopened many of the issues that had appeared to have been settled during the previous three decades. As institutional reform and democratization progressed, so did negotiations and struggles over questions of inclusion and its terms.

Several contentious issues characterized the debates about the principles of the national model and its institutionalization. First, questions of inclusion and exclusion varied from broad inclusive criteria to more restricted ones in which only *pribumi* (indigenous) Indonesians were considered to be full members. A related but subtler exclusion concerned criteria of modernity. Embedded in the concept of Indonesian nationhood was the idea of a "modern" people whose political, social, and economic life espoused the modern world. Some groups were considered "backward" and insufficiently modern to be full members of the nation because of their isolation and livelihood, which were considered pre-modern. As a result, although they were officially members of the Indonesian nation and citizens of the Indonesian Republic, they were marginalized and, therefore, not included on equal terms with other members.

Second, the role of Islam in the definition and character of the Indonesian nation was controversial. Some members of the political elite wanted to include adherence to Islam as a criterion of membership for inclusion or, at least, privilege within the Indonesian nation.[1] Others defended a national model that would be fully inclusive of people of all major religions.

Third, many of the struggles involved the representation of various ethnic groups, their access to power and resources, their cultural preservation, and their status as expressed in the political institutions of the Indonesian Republic. This set of issues led to many different conflicts and reforms of political institutions. The debates revolved around the means by which the Indonesian state should accommodate ethnic differences, given the unitary character of the state that was deemed most appropriate to represent the Indonesian nation at the time of independence. All of these issues were about the terms of inclusion in the nation.

At each critical juncture, incidences of ethnic violence occurred. Some of the violence involved religious groups that attempted to change the Indonesian nation and define it mainly as an Islamic nation. Other struggles involved groups seeking to reduce the dominance of the majority ethnic group, the Javanese, and to reduce the centralization of power in the central government that supported Javanese dominance. Some groups, such as the ethnic Chinese, were victims of rioting at various times as their marginalization from the Indonesian nation was perpetuated and even reinforced. Secessionist groups rejected the Indonesian nation and espoused, instead, a nation based on the majority ethnic group in their respective regions. At the end of each juncture, some issues were resolved while others surfaced. The violence that occurred, therefore, resulted in part from the institutional settlements that were made at the end of previous periods of change.

The rise of Indonesian nationalism

The 1920s to the 1940s constituted the formative period of the Indonesian nation. At no point during this time was any settlement reached over the meaning of the Indonesian nation and stable institutions to represent it. Many groups debated and even openly struggled over various alternative political agendas to define its character and political goals. Self-defined nationalists focused on independence and a nation based on the modern, European principles of self-determination, democracy, and modern political institutions. Islamists preferred an Indonesian nation that would build unity around Islam as the common characteristic of the diverse peoples of the archipelago. They favored the establishment of an Islamic state or, at the very least, a recognition of Islamic law for Muslims. Finally, a third stream emphasized social revolution and favored the adoption of a communist program. Although the communist stream could arguably be seen as an alternative to nationalism, the Indonesian communist movement nevertheless promoted revolution for people included within the boundaries of the Dutch East Indies. As such, it was nationalist in orientation as it adopted, in practise, the Russian example of revolution by country, especially promoted by Stalin in the 1920s.[2]

The organizations that gained prominence reflected these divisions. The first major nationalist organization, Sarekat Islam (SI), was formed in 1912.[3] Although it used Islam as a unifying characteristic that would cross ethnic boundaries, there was only a small group that actually espoused Islamic ideas of the nation. As early as 1917, modernist Islamic leaders of SI had to contend with increasingly strong local branches that followed Marxist ideas and were influenced by the structures of communist movements elsewhere.

The Communist Party of Indonesia (PKI) was born in 1920 out of these branches of SI and a formal split within SI occurred with the formation of the Red Sarekat Islam in 1921.[4] Although the PKI was decimated and its leaders exiled or imprisoned after a failed rebellion in 1926–27, communism remained a strong ideology within the nationalist movement.

Many Muslim nationalists who were disgruntled at the struggle with communists within SI joined a non-political organization, Muhammadiyah, which was founded in 1912. Muhammadiyah followed modernist Islamic ideas. It was involved primarily in education and the provision of social services but it also had political overtones with clear nationalist orientations.

The Nationalist Party of Indonesia (PNI) was formed in 1927 and rapidly became the strongest nationalist organization. Its objectives were the full independence of Indonesia and the establishment of democratic political institutions. Its leader, Sukarno, excelled at using an inclusive rhetoric that drew from Western, Islamic, and Hindu–Buddhist concepts. With a program based on the unity of all Indonesians and Sukarno's abilities to appeal to a broad constituency, PNI membership and strength grew rapidly, especially after establishing an alliance with Sarekat Islam.[5]

In the years leading to the end of the Second World War, the nationalist movement was stunted by Dutch resistance and, later, the Japanese occupation. No sooner had the PNI gained strength than Sukarno was imprisoned in 1930 and the party outlawed. Other nationalists became prominent, such as Sutan Sjahrir and Mohammad Hatta, who formed alternative organizations with the same objectives as the PNI. After they had gained much influence within nationalist circles, they were arrested and exiled in 1934. Sukarno, who had been released from prison in 1931, was also exiled in 1933 after he had begun to rebuild a strong political base. When the Japanese occupied the Indies in 1942, they established a repressive military regime that imposed three years of hardship on the Indonesian population. The country was drained of food and resources to feed the Japanese war effort.

The nationalist movement re-emerged in strength only at the end of the Second World War. Ironically, the later period of the Japanese occupation had a beneficial impact on it. Sukarno and Hatta had joined other nationalist leaders in cooperating with the Japanese. The latter had promised self-government in return for participating in the Putera, an advisory council set up by the Japanese to rally support for its war effort. Nationalist leaders used the Putera to advance their ideas and gain broad support for independence, as they were encouraged to approach and mobilize the Indonesian population. When the Japanese withdrew in 1945, they were well positioned to take a leading role in declaring Indonesia's independence and forming a government.[6]

To consolidate unity, Sukarno and Hatta understood the importance of rallying support from political leaders of all political orientations. Most importantly, they wanted to obtain support from Muslim groups, organizations outside of Java, as well as groups on the left as well as the right in their socio-economic orientation. They wanted to present a broad consensus before declaring independence and adopting an Indonesian constitution.

The most controversial issue at the time of the declaration of independence related to the "Jakarta Charter." In June 1945, Sukarno outlined his view on the philosophical foundation of an independent Indonesia. It was based on five principles – Pancasila – (1) nationalism, in the sense of unity in one nation; (2) internationalism or humanitarianism, implying peaceful relations with other nations; (3) representative government or consent; (4) social prosperity or social justice; and (5) belief in God.[7] This last principle, which became the first principle of Pancasila shortly thereafter, was not well received by Muslim leaders, who wanted a more explicit reference to Islam in the Indonesian constitution. When a committee reviewed the Pancasila for its inclusion in the preamble of the constitution in preparation for independence, it included the first principle as "belief in one God with the obligation for adherents of Islam to carry out Islamic law." This compromise to Muslim leaders was referred to as the Jakarta Charter. A day after the declaration of independence, when the constitution was ready to be promulgated, Sukarno and Hatta decided to drop the clause and retain only "belief in one God." They abandoned the Jakarta Charter to ensure the support of Christians, Hindus, and secular nationalists but, at the same time, they alienated a number of Muslim leaders.[8]

Once the Republic was formed in 1945, its leaders faced a new struggle with several regions that proposed a vision of Indonesia based on ethnic identity. At the end of the Second World War, the Dutch returned and attempted to re-establish their authority. Over the next four years, they waged war against the Republic. The armed struggle was interspersed with cease-fire agreements that specified various political arrangements and divided territories under Dutch or Republican control. None of the agreements ever had time to be implemented when the armed conflict resumed. For the most part, the Republic maintained its strength in parts of Java and Sumatra, while the Dutch controlled the other areas, including East Indonesia, Borneo, West New Guinea, and West Java.

The Dutch were largely influential in exploiting ethnic identities to destroy the nationalist creed proposed by Republican leaders. They promoted the establishment of independent states based on majority ethnic groups, such as the state of Pasundan, in West Java, where the Sundanese were a majority, the state of Madura with Madurese majority, and the autonomous territory of the Great Dayak for the Dayaks. Ironically, the only state that was ever functional, East Indonesia, was not associated with a dominant ethnic group. Because parts of Maluku had been key centers of the colony, the state of East Indonesia gave strong support to Dutch-established institutions. As the Dutch seized more territorial control between 1947 and 1949, they created, de facto, a federal system. In three different agreements with the Republic, the concept of a United States of Indonesia was accepted but never fully agreed until 1949, at which point the Republic had to contend with several states representing various ethnic groups.[9]

When the Dutch left in 1950 under international pressure, the federal system quickly crumbled and a unitary state was adopted. In 1949, the

United States of Indonesia had been established with ten constituent states, including the Republic. After the Dutch departed, most areas supported the dissolution of their individual states and adherence to the Republic, under a unitary state.

The most important opposition came from Ambon and South Maluku, which had been important centers of the colony. Many soldiers had been recruited among Christian Ambonese during colonial times. When the state of East Indonesia was dissolved, former officers of the Dutch colonial army declared an independent state of South Maluku. This resistance was nevertheless short-lived as the Indonesian National Army (TNI) was able to crush the rebellion within a few months.[10]

Two other groups resisted the nationalist vision of Indonesia. Muslims and communists generally supported independence and were nationalist in orientation, but they had different views on the final form of an Indonesian state. The Darul Islam movement, formed in West Java in 1948, sought an Islamic state. It was the most important and persistent resistance movement as its support expanded and included rebellious groups in Aceh and Sulawesi in the late 1950s.[11] The communists, who had been absent during the last decades of colonial rule, began to reorganize. Because the left was very divided, there were socialists and even communists who joined the first governments of the Republic. As the Republic began to negotiate concessions with the Dutch in 1946–47, a group of communist leaders revived the PKI. The party began to rebuild its strength by encouraging small left-wing parties and organizations to disband and join it. A small group that was particularly disenchanted with the Republic launched a rebellion from Madiun, in an attempt to trigger a large-scale, second phase of the revolution that would supersede nationalist aims and establish a socialist independent Indonesia. The rebellion failed to draw wider support, in part because of the weakness of the newly recreated PKI. As a result, it was easily crushed and the Communist Party faded away for another decade.[12]

By 1950, the Indonesian Republic had reached a measure of stability that marked the end of the first critical juncture. Despite the continuing campaign by the Darul Islam, the new independent Republic had control over most of the former Dutch East Indies (except West New Guinea). A constitution was adopted, political institutions were generally functional, and there were no immediate threats to the state. For the next few years, political leaders of various orientations agreed to follow the established political rules and to build national unity within the institutional context that had been agreed upon in 1950.

Several characteristics defined the national model that emerged from the struggles of the previous decades. A broad consensus among the political elite agreed on the basic principle of the unitary state and had rejected federalism because of the negative experience with the Dutch attempt to destroy the unity of the Indonesian nation. Regions were considered to be autonomous within the confines of a unitary state.[13] The provisional constitution was based on liberal democratic principles and included a strong parliament and a weak president. Although the principles of Pancasila were not enshrined in the 1950 Constitution, the secular nationalist orientation of the state that they implied was in place, at least temporarily. There was agreement that political parties were to be the main vehicle through which various orientations would be expressed, be they organized along social goals, religious identities, or other political objectives. In general, Indonesian nationalism was sufficiently strong that, to preserve national unity, political parties refrained from organizing along ethnic lines. Yet, religion was a significant source of political mobilization and was perceived by party leaders as compatible with a nationalist orientation.

Several ambiguities were built-in to this institutional structure. It was always meant to be a temporary solution, even though the democratic parliamentary system had broad support among the political elite. The constitution was provisional, as well as the allocation of seats in the parliament. Elections were to be organized in 1955 for a new parliament and a Constituent Assembly that would draft a new, final constitution for the Indonesian state. The temporary institutional structure reflected the objectives mostly of secular nationalists, while the interests of Muslim groups and communists had been side-lined. Given the provisional nature of the 1950 settlement and the postponement of discussions over crucial issues involving the fundamental characteristics of the Indonesian nation and state, these pressures almost inevitably would give way to change in only a few years.

The crisis of the late 1950s and the establishment of the New Order

The tensions and cleavages embedded in the provisional constitution and political institutions of the 1950s were primarily responsible for the advent of the second critical juncture. Tensions surrounding the issue of the basic foundation of the state involved different views on the terms of inclusion in the Indonesian nation. Proponents of Islam challenged the compromise of 1950, while nationalists continued to favor Pancasila. Meanwhile, the regions became increasingly dissatisfied with political centralization and what some perceived as Javanese dominance, when the 1950 compromise had espoused regional autonomy as a basic principle for the unitary state.

These tensions and cleavages triggered an institutional crisis, while a number of conflicts erupted. The Darul Islam gained support from disgruntled regions in Aceh, Sumatra, and Sulawesi, and was backed by the Islamist party Masyumi. Leaders of Masyumi, who were joined by rebellious military commanders, proclaimed an alternative government on Sumatra. The latter rebelled against government centralization and, especially, attempts to establish a new political system based on even more centralized power, a strong president, and a greater role for the central military command.

Other conflicts arose in the midst of this juncture. With growing uncertainties about the future of the Indonesian state, its form, and what kind of nation it would reflect, communists saw an opportunity to redefine the state along their political program, especially as they received increasing support from Sukarno and members of the central government. In this context, the ethnic Chinese also saw an opportunity to become fully included, especially given the PKI support for their equal status within the Republic. The Dayaks, in Kalimantan, took advantage of the instability created by regional rebellions, and the role of Banjarese Muslims in this rebellion, to seek a province with a Dayak majority, Central Kalimantan.

The cleavage involving Islamists and secularist Muslims was most important. The first elections under Indonesia's liberal democracy were held in 1955 to fill seats in the national legislature as well as the new Constituent Assembly. Instead of creating more stability, the elections revealed the deep tensions that had only temporarily subsided with the compromise of the 1950s. As the electoral campaign heated up, the main issue dividing political parties concerned the fundamental question of the basis of the state. Sukarno, the PNI, and other secularists, mainly of the left, supported Pancasila and broad inclusive criteria for defining the Indonesian nation. Masyumi was most vocal in advocating an Islamic state, while other Muslim parties, such as Nahdlatul Ulama (NU), based on the largest Muslim organization in Java, used Islam as a vehicle for obtaining votes. Meanwhile, the Darul Islam rebellion gained more supporters. Most notably, a rebellion in Aceh was launched as it became evident that the central government had rejected the idea of an Islamic state. Many Acehnese joined when it became clear that Masyumi was losing the political battle in Jakarta.

A regionalist rebellion also erupted. Even in Aceh, the Islamist goals overlapped with strong regional discontent over the centralization of government control in Jakarta and over Javanese dominance. Elsewhere, rebellions in Sumatra and Sulawesi were based on coalitions of military commanders and civilians that had separate grievances against the central government. In South Sulawesi, Kahar Muzakkar, a former guerilla leader in the revolution, rebelled against the central government because of the army's refusal to integrate his troops into the TNI. He joined the Darul Islam in 1952 and continued his resistance for several years.[14]

More serious rebellions occurred during 1956–57, when military regional councils were established or regional coups were launched in protest at centralizing policies. Rebel commanders, in alliance with regional politicians in Sumatra, West Java, and Sulawesi, denounced Jakarta's exchange rate policies that stifled economic exports from the regions. They also resented the armed forces commander's move to transfer regional commanders, as they had established smuggling operations and regional power bases that they were reluctant to abandon.[15]

On the civilian side, regional politicians were also disgruntled at the centralist approach. Tensions had been rising steadily as Jakarta transgressed the principles of autonomy agreed upon in 1950. Furthermore, failure to reform the civil service and reduce the role of the *pamong praja*, the former colonial civil servants, only intensified the frictions. By retaining the former system, the central government kept an active hand in regional administration.

These tensions also coincided with a resurgence of ethnic sentiments. In West Java and West Sumatra, Sundanese and Minangkabau ethnic organizations had primarily cultural orientations but, after 1956, they denounced "Javanese imperialism" and became increasingly politicized. For example, a coalition of local ethnic groups demanded autonomy for East Sumatra in response to growing resentment at the increasing migration and dominance of the Toba Bataks.[16]

In February 1958, a coalition of politicians from Jakarta and regional leaders proclaimed an alternative government, the Revolutionary Government of the Republic of Indonesia (PRRI). Prominent politicians from Masyumi, including its leader Mohammad Natsir, joined regional military commanders and civilian leaders who had been rebelling for months. Most of these non-Javanese politicians supported regionalist claims, especially after Sukarno began to favor the establishment of new, even more centralized political institutions.[17]

The central government mainly responded to these challenges with the use of force. It conceded to some regionalist demands by the creation of some new provinces, such as Aceh and Central Kalimantan. Otherwise, the central command of the armed forces was strengthened and the government opted for military solutions. It continued to contain the spread of the Darul Islam and crushed the PRRI rebellion. The PRRI was short-lived, being defeated in June 1958.

The central government also abandoned liberal democracy and established a new political regime. Sukarno developed a concept of "Guided Democracy" that would give more power to the president, the military, and "functional groups." He suspended the Constituent Assembly in 1959 and decreed a return to the Constitution of 1945 and Pancasila as the basis of the state. In 1960, the national parliament was dissolved and was replaced a few months later with an appointed parliament. Masyumi, which had been most vocal in supporting the idea of an Islamic state and which had been supportive of the PRRI rebellion, was banned in 1960. Other political parties were restricted in 1961 to ten parties.[18]

The two major tensions that had been embedded in the compromise of 1950 were resolved through force. The regions had accepted the unitary state under the condition of obtaining wide-ranging autonomy. When the central government reneged on this commitment, they became increasingly rebellious. Ethnic tensions were one expression of this resentment. The question of an Islamic state, discarded in 1945, had been left to debate and negotiation within the Constituent Assembly. The campaign for the 1955 elections and subsequent deliberations within the assembly had increased the divide between Islamists and nationalists. The demands for greater autonomy and for an Islamic state ended with the use of presidential decrees and military force. Sukarno and the armed forces chose strong-arm tactics to secure the unity of the nation, stability of the state, and resolution of fundamental questions about Indonesia's national model.

Yet, the establishment of Guided Democracy was not the end of this critical juncture. Sukarno had difficulty maintaining his independence from the army and sought to balance its power by nurturing closer relations with the PKI. From 1960 onwards, after several previous attempts to build itself into a strong political party, the PKI gained rapid ascendancy. Sukarno's support helped to provide it with more legitimacy and popularity but it also offered an alternative vision for Indonesia. Its promises of land reform and better income distribution were welcomed by a large proportion of the population during years when the economy was in rapid decline. Sukarno's balancing act between the military and the communists perpetuated the transitional nature of Guided Democracy.

The final confrontation between the armed forces and the PKI ended with the assassination of six high-ranking generals on 30 September 1965. Military units under the command of Major General Suharto responded swiftly to the coup attempt that had allegedly been instigated by the PKI. Within a few days, Suharto had seized control of the armed forces and given himself greater powers to restore order and security. The PKI was banned and most its members killed, jailed, or internally exiled in a purge that was initiated by the armed forces. In the following months, the violence extended beyond attacks against the party and hundreds of thousands of people were killed. While many of the victims were communists, many others were killed in settlements of local conflicts.[19]

With the banning of the PKI, the armed forces gained full control of the polity. By March 1966, effective presidential powers had been transferred to Suharto, who formally acceded to the presidency the following year. He then eliminated all remnants of left-wing supporters in the armed forces and gradually placed loyal officers in key positions. He bolstered the military's role in civilian tasks by expanding the "dual function" (*dwi fungsi*) concept that was developed by a former armed forces commander, Nasution. Under this concept, the armed forces played an active role not only in external defense but also in preserving the integrity of the state. They justified increased involvement in civilian administration on the basis of their crucial role during the revolution.[20]

Building on military strength, Suharto reaffirmed Indonesia's national model but greatly modified its institutionalization. His New Order regime was based on a united nation coinciding with a unitary state, guided by the Constitution of 1945 and Pancasila as its foundation. He extended the core institutions of Guided Democracy, centralized political control, and curtailed opposition. By 1968, most of the elements of the political system were in place.

The New Order's national model was institutionalized on the basis of five pillars. First, Pancasila legitimized the regime's vision of the nation. Suharto firmly indicated that the basis of the state was final and Pancasila was the only legitimate ideology. He maintained that the question of an Islamic state was settled and would not be reopened. Adherence to Pancasila became compulsory for all social and political organizations in the mid-1980s but, already in the 1970s, Suharto had ensured that it was learned and followed. Appropriate political behavior, ideas about the Indonesian nation, and judgments about threats to the nation or state were made according to the regime's own criteria and its own interpretation of Pancasila.

Second, the Constitution of 1945 guaranteed a strong president with wide-ranging executive power, while the ultimate governing body was the People's Consultative Assembly (MPR). Suharto ensured that, over the course of a few years, he controlled the majority in the national legislature (DPR) as well as the large number of appointed members of the MPR.

Third, the hierarchical and centralized government bureaucracy was expanded and unified. Under government legislation adopted in 1974 and in 1979, the central government introduced a homogenous government bureaucracy across all regions (province, districts, and sub-districts) and homogenous structures of village government. With these two pieces of legislation, it firmly institutionalized the political structure that was already well in place under the late Guided Democracy and early New Order regimes. The regime ensured that the institutional hierarchy was paralleled by leaders with strong loyalties to the center by appointing active or retired military personnel as provincial and district heads. Furthermore, the central government continued to intervene in regional administration by maintaining the *pamong praja* structure under a different label. Civil servants with direct accountability to central government departments were appointed at all levels of government, except the villages. Finally, the military placed command units at the provincial, district, and sub-district levels. Such bureaucratic and administrative structures eliminated institutional differences in various regions and were intended to reduce the diversity of the ethnic, cultural, or religious landscape in favor of the common characteristics of the Indonesian nation.

Fourth, political parties had limited freedom. In the first election of the New Order, in 1971, only ten political parties could participate. By 1974, they were forced to amalgamate under two weak parties, the Democratic Party of Indonesia (PDI) and the Development Unity Party (PPP). While the latter represented Islamic parties, any reference to Islam was removed from the party's name and, in the 1980s, from its symbols and statement of ideological orientation. Golkar, an organization representing functional groups, effectively operated as a large government party. It was also given political rights that were taken away from other parties, namely permission to organize political activities at the sub-district and local levels. Other parties could only be active at those levels during election campaigns.

Fifth, "development" became a key objective of the regime. According to the architects of the New Order, communism had gained prominence because of the impoverishment of Indonesians under Sukarno's administration. "Development" would ensure that the Indonesian nation, under the guidance of the state, would not only reach a higher level of welfare but also transform itself from its still-remnant "traditional" characteristics – including ethnic affiliations – to a fully modern nation. The vision of the New Order's nation included the creation of what it perceived as a "modern" people, with cultural characteristics that resembled those of nations in the Western industrialized world but with unique Indonesian features. The regime developed a rhetoric that defined for the Indonesian nation codes of behavior and characteristics that reflected these features.

During the first few years, the uncertainty over the structure of the New Order's political institutions allowed two sets of tensions to arise. Suharto founded a temporary alliance with Muslim groups to purge the country of communist supporters. These groups had seen an opportunity to gain greater power in the state and, perhaps, to promote Islamic issues. By 1968, it became clear that Suharto had no intention of allowing the banned political party Masyumi or other organizations to use Islam for political mobilization. He used repression to ensure that Muslim groups remained non-politicized. A second source of tensions rose to the surface with renewed violence against the ethnic Chinese. Under Guided Democracy, some Chinese groups had gained the favor of Sukarno and had seen an unprecedented ability to participate in the political system. During the unstable years of 1965–67, the Chinese were again targeted. Some were accused of supporting the Communist Party, while others were resented for their control of commercial sectors.

Overall, the New Order government had firmly established its political system by the late 1960s. With tight control and emphasis on internal order, there were few opportunities for dissent, whether against the regime or along ethnic or religious lines. It had rejected the liberal democratic institutions of the 1950s and had supported the return to a strong central government. The national model that followed the principles of Pancasila and the unitary state was extended and interpreted to conform to the regime's priorities of maintaining order and preventing political dissent.

The end of the New Order and the era of political reform

When Suharto resigned in May 1998, a new critical juncture began. Despite its long stability, the New Order regime carried important weaknesses. Although exogenous factors were most important in Suharto's downfall, ethnic tensions created pressures for institutional change. In the months following Suharto's resignation, several violent conflicts erupted. They showed the failures of the institutional forms of the New Order's national model.

In principle, the New Order preserved the basic tenets of the nationalist vision but its means of implementation were quite different from the past. It adhered to the Constitution of 1945 and Pancasila, as had Sukarno during Guided Democracy, but used even more intrusive and repressive measures to contain political opposition. Measures to weaken political parties and depoliticize Indonesians were generalized but even more repressive policies were used against Islamist groups. They were denied access to important political positions and their organizations were curtailed. Any debate on questions of Islam and politics was interpreted by the regime as subversive.

Modernity was embedded in the concept of an Indonesian nation but, under Suharto, "development" and "modern" were the regime's central creeds. The purpose of development was to create a "modern" Indonesian nation. Many groups in places such as Irian Jaya and Kaliman-tan were marginalized as "backward" and excluded, de facto, from the Indonesian nation because of their "traditional" lifestyles. Government policies, bureaucratic pressure, and military intimidation were designed to force change.

Strong political control, vested in the central government, was main-tained but reached new peaks under New Order rule. Since independence, the central government had been reluctant to abide by agreed principles of regional autonomy. Instead, various measures ensured sufficient ambiguity in legislation and institutional processes to retain strong central control while supporting, in principle, more autonomy and decentralization. The New Order multiplied its tentacles by using the bureaucracy, the military command structure, and Golkar. New legislation in 1974 was even less clear on autonomy so that it allowed for strong, central control. Suharto used these institutional and legislative instruments to keep regions under control and submissive to the directives of the center. Patronage lubricated this system by maintaining some level of loyalty among regional elites.

Although regional problems were mostly resolved through this sys-tem, new grievances gave rise to secessionist movements. Previously rebellious regions during the 1950s showed no signs of renewed polit-ical opposition during the New Order. One exception was Aceh, where tensions from the past overlapped with new grievances. The rise of the Free Aceh Movement in the 1970s involved a relatively small group of Acehnese who were mainly concerned with central government con-trol over the region and its resources. Its resurgence in the late 1980s was also limited and its grievances basically unchanged. The Indonesian military, however, responded with brutal and violent repression that contributed to Acehnese alienation from the national model. During the 1990s, the conflict was quelled by strong military presence and intimidation.

Two other regions, Irian Jaya and East Timor, became part of Indonesia in 1969 and 1975, respectively, so they did not share with other regions the same institutional legacies. In these cases, the process of inte-gration was a critical juncture that produced different perspectives of Indonesia's national model and political institutions. When the New Order applied the same institutional framework and integrative means as in other regions, secessionist movements emerged in response. The national model was insufficiently flexible to allow for diversity. For Timo-rese and Papuans, it was a threat to their communities. Furthermore, the

use of military violence and intimidation, coupled with stronger bureaucratic control than elsewhere, only exacerbated an already precarious
situation.

By the mid-1990s, the New Order's national model began to produce
more ethnic violence. Riots in East and West Java carried ethnic overtones. Churches were targeted, while the property of Chinese Indonesians
was destroyed. In East Timor, violence erupted after several years of relative calm. In West Kalimantan, dozens of people were killed in conflict
between Dayaks and Madurese.

It was not coincidental that ethnic conflict was on the rise at that particular time. The New Order regime had already lasted thirty years. Its
institutional legacy and relative stability had been maintained through
force, intimidation, and state strength. Some ethnic grievances had been
resolved but many had been side-lined, while groups were controlled and
manipulated by the regime's leaders. With Suharto ageing, there were
several open debates about succession and it was apparent that institutional change might be near. Such uncertainty provoked ethnic tensions
to rise in spite of existing instruments of control.

Immediately preceding Suharto's resignation, riots continued to occur
but were more clearly directed against the regime. Clamors for reform had
begun to be heard. Opposition also came from supporters of Megawati
Sukarnoputri and her banned PDI-P (Democratic Party of Indonesia
for the Struggle). In the end, the election returned another majority for
Golkar and political riots began to subside.

The Asian financial crisis disrupted the normal course of affairs. By
January 8, 1998, the rupiah had declined to Rp10,000 per US dollar,
crossing a psychological line that created panic, fear of shortages, and
disbelief among Indonesia's middle class. Cries for reform began to be
heard as attention turned toward the deep structural problems that worsened the impact of the financial crisis. The International Monetary Fund
(IMF) and international donors also focused on the large number of
subsidies, the corruption, and the inefficient business practises in the
Indonesian economy. Moreover, resentment and muted criticism of the
large conglomerates built up by Suharto's family and friends changed
to open expressions of anger as the crisis unveiled the practises that
had weakened the economy. As the crisis deepened, students organized
demonstrations calling for reforms.

Yet, Suharto stayed the course as he ran once again for president.
The crisis was at its worst as the MPR session met in March 1998 to
elect a new president and vice-president. With few surprises, the MPR
chose Suharto as president and B. J. Habibie as vice-president. Suharto
held on to power and even appointed friends and family to the cabinet,
departing from past practise. By giving important cabinet positions to

his daughter Siti Hardiyanti Rukmana and to Mohammad "Bob" Hasan, a close business associate, Suharto lost the legitimacy he had left.

The mobilization that occurred in the subsequent months targeted Suharto specifically. Students increased the frequency of their demonstrations asking for reforms and the president's resignation. A consensus was settling in that it was time for the long-time ruler to step down and for necessary reforms to be made to the economy and to the political system.

By May 1998, as security forces were unable to stem the political chaos, Suharto was forced to resign. Student demonstrators were shot down by state security at Trisakti University, on 12 May, killing six people. During subsequent days, thousands of rioters rampaged through Jakarta and several other major cities across Indonesia, protesting the Trisakti killings. After most of his cabinet resigned and former allies began to call for his resignation, he stepped down on 21 May.

With Suharto's removal, reforms to the political system became almost inevitable. President Habibie, perceived as a weak leader with a strong dependence on Suharto, was eager to strengthen his independence, his image abroad, and his power, so he rapidly distanced himself from his long-time patron and launched deep reforms of the political system. Within weeks, political parties were allowed to organize, controls over the media were removed, political prisoners began to be released, and preparations were made to hold free and fair elections for the parliament and the president.

While ethnic tensions built into the New Order's national model did not bring about institutional change, they broke out into violence as the critical juncture unfolded. The riots of the previous years gave way to larger scale, more intense conflict after May 1998. The ethnic Chinese were victims, once again, of rioting crowds during the May crisis. Within a few months, secessionist movements intensified their activities in Aceh, East Timor, and Irian Jaya. Violence rose rapidly, as well as the number of victims. Conflict between Christians and Muslims in Ambon became violent and spread to other regions of Maluku. New incidents of violence occurred between Dayaks and Madurese in Kalimantan. Many regions began to make more vocal demands for autonomy and decentralization.

Presidents after Suharto even had difficulties maintaining their power. B. J. Habibie launched the reforms and lost political power in October 1999, in part because of his inability to resolve the ethnic violence. His successor, Abdurrahman Wahid, was impeached in July 2001 because of an alleged scandal, but he had also been deeply criticized for his mismanagement of regional crises and ethnic violence. Megawati Sukarnoputri faced most of these crises when she acceded to the presidency and muddled through them for some time before some stability began to be restored.

The conflicts worsened during the period of democratization, even though political reforms were initiated. Democratic reforms promised new principles and new means of accommodating ethnic groups. Indonesians debated and negotiated different aspects of their national model, amidst unprecedented ethnic violence. Their national model was subjected to the most important contestation and reform since its main principles were adopted in the compromise of 1950. Violence could be expected when uncertainty was high and groups feared that the new institutional legacy might preserve an unacceptable status quo or create worse conditions.

The years following the end of the New Order regime represented one of three major critical junctures that led to increased ethnic violence in Indonesia. Tensions were embedded in the struggles over the definition and terms of inclusion of the Indonesian nation. The compromise of 1950 built in some tensions that became violent when the institutions of liberal democracy eroded and then collapsed under Sukarno's decision to move to Guided Democracy. The New Order reached a new stable political environment that relied heavily on coercion. While some tensions disappeared, new ones resulted from this institutional setting. By the mid-1990s, a new set of violent ethnic conflicts erupted out of tensions that were produced by the New Order's institutional legacy.

4   Exclusion, marginality, and the nation

To chapter ... key case study? :

Indonesia's national model created categories of excluded and marginalized groups. Although it was based on a civic concept, namely that citizenship should be granted to all people living in the former Dutch East Indies, its expression in legislation excluded or marginalized certain groups. A process of differentiation set them apart from the state's construction of "Indonesian-ness."

During the third critical juncture that accompanied the end of the New Order regime, some of these groups were participants in or victims of ethnic violence. The marginalized Dayaks fought Madurese migrants on the island of Kalimantan in 1996, 1999, and 2001. Chinese Indonesians were targeted during a wave of small-scale riots between 1996 and 1998. They were also victims during the bloody riots of May 1998 that formally ended the New Order regime of President Suharto. Marginalization and exclusion differentiated the Dayaks and the Chinese from other Indonesians. They provided a basis for discrimination that partly explains their involvement in ethnic violence during the period of institutional transition in the late 1990s.

The marginalized included a large number of groups that were considered "tribal" or "isolated" communities. Typically, they lived in hinterlands or mountain areas, thereby geographically distant from urban centers and from the reach of the state. They were treated as second-class citizens, as "primitive" or "backward" groups that lacked the "modern" characteristics of "Indonesian" citizens.

In a separate category, the "non-*pribumi*" were excluded from all other Indonesians because they were considered non-indigenous. Chinese Indonesians were the only group in this category. Formal denial of citizenship rights for recently migrated Chinese was gradually replaced by legislation and practises that differentiated and excluded all Indonesians of Chinese origin, even after citizenship was granted. Irrespective of their diverse origins, spoken language, number of generations since arriving in Indonesia, or mixing with non-Chinese, they became increasingly considered as a single category of "Chinese."

After the second critical juncture that began with the New Order regime, more narrow definitions of the Indonesian nation intensified processes of exclusion and marginalization. State penetration of less accessible areas, greater exploitation of natural resources, and greater obsession with political control contributed to unprecedented intervention in the livelihoods of small, marginal groups such as the Dayaks. The non-*pribumi*, in turn, were transformed into pariah status, dependent on the state for their security, repressed in their identities, and clearly demarcated from other groups through legislation and institutional exclusion. They became targets of violence because of a stereotyped characterization of the Chinese as a threat to the majority of Indonesians, especially because of their economic strength.

Violence became a channel for solving the aggressor group's perceived "problem," at a time when the fear of state repression declined and no institutional channels were available to address group grievances. The Dayaks transferred onto the Madurese their anger and frustration at their treatment under the New Order. The *pribumi* targeted the Chinese, as they stereotyped them and blamed them for socio-economic inequities. The eruption of violent conflict coincided with the institutional decay of the New Order and of its means of reproduction.

Institutional reform and uncertainty during the third critical juncture had different consequences for both groups. There was little change in the Dayaks' condition so that violence continued to be seen as a means of defending their identity and their interests in the context of unstable political institutions and an unpredictable future. For the Dayaks, violence against the Madurese made possible the seizure of power and control over lost territory.

Violence against the Chinese declined after May 1998, as new institutional measures were implemented to reintegrate them as equal citizens. The end of the New Order in itself removed some of the *pribumi* grievances against the Chinese. The lull in violence can be explained by the removal of the Chinese conglomerates as "symbolic culprits" for the socio-economic inequality of Indonesia. When Suharto resigned, large Chinese conglomerates had lost their patron and their grip on the economy. Perhaps more importantly, the leaders of almost all the various streams of Indonesian politics strongly condemned violent acts against the Chinese in May 1998. Finally, President Wahid contributed to rehabilitating them as equal citizens by removing some discriminatory regulations and legislation.

Ethnic violence resulted from the prior institutionalization of marginalized and excluded groups. The Dayaks were subjected to periods of inclusion followed by subsequent marginalization as past institutional changes first gave them a province and an institutional expression of their identity. Under the New Order, they subsequently lost their representation and became increasingly marginalized. The Chinese had been a divided group in which non-citizens were primarily excluded after independence. Yet, it was after citizenship was extended to most Chinese during the New Order years that the informal means of exclusion became strongest. The violence of the late 1990s emerged out of the prior institutional compromises over Indonesia's national model and its effects on Dayak and Chinese identities relative to other groups.

Marginality and conflict in Kalimantan

Large-scale conflict between the Dayaks and Madurese broke out in December 1996. It occurred in two waves.[1] On 29 December, a Madurese stabbed two Dayak youths in Ledo, near Singkawang (West Kalimantan), apparently as a revenge for a beating incident on 6 December. The original beating was allegedly provoked by the Madurese's harassment of a young Dayak girl. As news of the stabbing spread and rumors of the youths' death circulated, several hundred people began to attack Madurese quarters, even brandishing posters demanding the eviction of Madurese and the return of their land. Within the next few days, various attacks in Sanggau Ledo and neighboring areas led to the mass destruction of several Madurese hamlets. Some Madurese groups retaliated but many more sought refuge in various military posts. By 6 January 1997, the situation had returned to relative calm.

The second wave was more extensive and deadly. Tensions had remained high during the month of January and isolated incidents had continued to occur. Fueled by rumors and an attack on houses and a small mosque by a Dayak crowd, on 28 January a group of Madurese attacked a Catholic boarding school and stabbed two Dayak girls. In the Salamantan district, a group of Madurese burned down the houses of several Dayaks, most of whom were civil servants. These attacks set off a war between the Dayak and Madurese communities. Attacks and counter-attacks occurred almost daily for two weeks. In one attack, 131 people were killed when Dayaks stormed Salatiga and burned down all the Madurese houses. In some areas, the armed forces intervened to protect the Madurese and opened fire on groups of Dayak attackers. Most of the violence occurred in three districts, Sambas, Sanggau, and Pontianak, all located near the capital city of Pontianak, but Dayaks from many other districts had apparently converged on the area and participated in the attacks. Human Rights Watch estimated that

500 people died as a result of the violence, although no official figures were ever released. In addition, more than 20,000 Madurese were displaced.[2]

Three main arguments were offered to explain the conflict. A cultural explanation emphasized the particularly incompatible relationship between Dayaks, for whom the spilling of blood is seen as an attack on the whole community, and the Madurese, who are quick to resort to fighting with sharp weapons.[3] A variant argued that, in addition, the Madurese were particularly disrespectful of Dayak values and local customs.[4] It was most often cited to explain why the Dayaks targeted the Madurese but not other migrant groups such as the Javanese, Malays, or Chinese. This cultural explanation, however, resorted to stereotypical depictions of actions and behaviors of Dayaks and Madurese, without looking at the context that shaped these stereotypes and, especially, perpetuated them. While the development of a stereotype of Madurese as "prone to violence" and "easily angered" has a basis in reality, it developed out of repeated incidents that were exaggerated and distorted.

Another explanation focused on acts of provocation. It argued that the events in Kalimantan were linked to conflicts in Java, and resulted from a conspiracy designed to provoke political instability.[5] The putative motive was the general election of 1997 and the following People's Consultative Assembly (MPR) meeting of 1998 that, at the time, was seen as crucial for the succession to President Suharto. Proponents of the provocation thesis pointed to indicators such as violent acts that occurred after tensions had subsided and the spread of rumors that were unsubstantiated by evidence. They also pointed to a conflict in 1967, when the army incited Dayaks to attack ethnic Chinese in Kalimantan, whom it suspected of being communist sympathizers. Yet, as in other cases, only local arrests were made and alleged provocateurs were more often participants who had been caught by the police and the armed forces, instead of agents of a broader conspiratorial network. For a short time, Islamic scholars (*ulama*) from East Java were suspected of inflaming Madurese and contributing to the second wave but subsequently these allegations were dropped. Furthermore, while some elements of provocation were perhaps present, they did not explain why such acts were particularly volatile.[6]

A socio-economic explanation emphasized economic competition. Most observers agreed that inequalities were irrelevant.[7] Among migrants, the Chinese were relatively wealthier than others but most groups were as poor as the Dayaks. Among the Madurese, some individuals achieved considerable business success but, overall, they were poor. Most were involved in transportation (river ferries, pedicab drivers), or were coolies, drivers, laborers, or petty traders. Those in the countryside were mainly involved in wetland (*sawah*) rice farming.[8] Their main competition, especially in urban areas, was with the Malays or Bugis but not with the Dayaks, who comprised less than 2% of the urban population of Pontianak.[9] Yet, it could be argued that competition for local jobs and land was high in West Kalimantan, as a result of high rates of migration and transformation of the area. Under these conditions, the Dayaks competed with the Madurese and other migrants for scarce resources that were largely controlled by wealthy entrepreneurs from outside the region.[10]

This explanation, however, failed to capture adequately the institutional and political environment that created tensions and reinforced ethnic boundaries. Why would tensions resulting from business ventures in West Kalimantan produce conflict between ethnic groups with similar socio-economic conditions rather than alliances against wealthy outsiders? Why did such tensions become expressed along ethnic lines?

The marginalization of the Dayak by the New Order regime was a particularly important factor. Nancy Peluso and Emily Harwell make a compelling case that Dayak discontent grew during the New Order in response to the state's alteration of the rules of access to resources, the Dayaks' exclusion from political and economic benefits from development, and state violence. Violent identities among Dayak and Madurese communities were produced as a consequence of New Order policies.[11]

Yet, this marginalization can also be traced to the New Order's institutional structure, as reflected in its normative interpretation of the basis of citizenship, of the modernity of the Indonesian national identity, and of the characteristics of inclusion and exclusion. Out of the diversity of ethnic groups across the Indonesian archipelago, Sukarno had defined a vague and mainly rhetorical set of criteria for an Indonesian culture of unity. It clashed with attempts, among Acehnese and other groups supporting the Darul Islam rebellion, to add an Islamic component, as he was adamant about the need to include non-Muslims. Beyond this distinction, however, Sukarno held a discourse of inclusion and unity as a revolutionary process of nation-building. Many individuals shed various ethnic or religious identities to foster and promote an Indonesian identity. Many large groups that were relatively untouched by revolutionary change, retained their customs and ways of life without much interference by the state and without being excluded. Nation-building was presented as a process, and these groups would be eventually included as a result of a linear progression toward the achievement of a modern Indonesian nation.

The Dayaks developed an ethnic identity that was ambiguous in its relationship to the Indonesian nation. The construction of a "Dayak" identity itself only emerged in the last years of the Dutch colonial regime and became politically significant only during the 1950s. For the most part, this identity was developed in response to changes in local power relations, as the Dutch and, subsequently, the Republic redrew the boundaries of territorial control. In particular, the divisions between West Kalimantan and South Kalimantan (and later Central Kalimantan), as well as the corresponding political institutions that governed these territories, defined particular "Dayak" struggles and their relation to the Indonesian Republic. Furthermore, only few occasions allowed for the creation of a pan-Dayak ethnic consciousness that crossed these boundaries. The violence of 1996–97, 1999, and 2001 showed that such a consciousness did arise out of the New Order institutional context and its concomitant policies.

During most of the Dutch colonial period, the Dayaks were barely reached by administrative controls and boundaries. Constituting a large number of tribal groups with different languages or customs, they did not see themselves as a single cultural group. They were scattered in the hinterland of Kalimantan, while colonial rulers were more concerned about coastal areas. These areas were populated by a variety of groups that, eventually, were grouped in the "Malay" category. Mostly Muslim populations, they were politically organized in a number of sultanates that enjoyed relative autonomy. The Dutch used the sultans under a system of indirect rule. Until 1848, there was little penetration of the interior of Kalimantan, after which Christian missionization became more active. The term "Dayak" itself was used by Europeans to mean people of the "interior" and to distinguish them from the Muslim Malays.[12]

Dayak identity was appropriated by indigenous elites and used to unify the people of the interior in response to an Islamic form of Indonesian nationalism. In the early twentieth century, the Banjarese Malays of South Kalimantan mobilized in support of Sarekat Islam, the first major nationalist organization to counter Dutch rule. They also supported other nationalist organizations that displayed an Islamic orientation. The Dayaks of South Kalimantan (mostly Ngaju Dayak) had been included by the Dutch under the same administrative unit as the Banjarese. They perceived the Islamic mobilization of the Banjarese as a threat. In 1919, a small group of Dayaks formed the Sarekat Dayak that became the Pakat Dayak in 1926. This organization stressed Dayak custom and culture, and sought to develop a consciousness about the cultural commonalities unifying the various Dayak tribal groups. Not only did it resist Banjarese and Muslim influences, it also competed with Christian missions for the leadership of the Dayak.[13] It was in some sense similar to other nationalist organizations such as Jong Java and Jong Minahasa that were organized along ethnic lines to mobilize against the Dutch.

At the time of the Indonesian revolution, however, the Pakat Dayak took an anti-nationalist direction to oppose Banjarese nationalists. The Banjarese, who had fought a war against the Dutch for almost forty years, were strong supporters of the Indonesian revolution, which they saw as the "Second Holy War".[14] They fought for the cause of establishing an independent Indonesia as an Islamic state. The Pakat Dayak supported the Dutch against the Republic to avoid inclusion in a potentially Islamic Indonesia.

The Dutch exploited this division so as to gain support among the Dayaks. Under the Linggadjati agreement of 1946, the Dutch and the Republic agreed to a federal arrangement that included the creation of the Great Dayak (Dayak Besar) semi-autonomous administrative unit. This new territory was separated from the southern part of Kalimantan with Banjarese dominance. Pakat Dayak and Christian leaders of the Dayak Synod controlled the newly established Dayak Council, which continued to fight for a firmer commitment to constitutional autonomy. When a second agreement on a federation was reached between the Dutch and the Indonesian Republic in 1949, the Great Dayak gained the status of constituent state.[15]

For the first time, the Dayaks obtained representation in modern institutions. The creation of the Great Dayak region marked a new juncture as it gave an institutional form to the nascent rise of a Dayak identity alongside the Pakat Dayak. These institutions were a significant departure because they were not solely instruments of Dutch manipulation and they fed a new Dayak identity in formation.

A different institutional unit was established in Western Kalimantan, which also gave some representation to Dayaks. The Dutch formed a West Kalimantan Council for the representation of various groups allocated across a variety of self-governing lands and territories under direct rule. The Dayaks received representation as equal members alongside other designated ethnic groups, since they constituted a significant proportion of the population but not a majority. Representatives to the council included 15 delegates from self-governing lands (Malay), 7 Dayaks, 6 Indonesians (that is, non-Dayak or Malay), 8 Chinese, and 4 Netherlanders. West Kalimantan obtained its own constitution and was to be included within the state of Borneo. In 1947, it was designated as the Special Region of West Kalimantan.[16]

When the federation was replaced by a unitary state in 1950, the Dayaks lost the representation they had so recently gained. The Great Dayak state and Special Region of West Kalimantan were replaced by a single province of Kalimantan that encompassed the entire Indonesian portion of Borneo. Only a few Dayaks were given significant positions in the new administrative structures. Most notably, Tjilik Riwut, who had headed the Dayak guerilla units in favor of the Republic, was appointed head of one of the districts in spite of strong opposition from Banjarese Malays. Riwut had been the editor of the *Dayak Voice* and a member of the Pakat Dayak. Along with Riwut, many other Dayaks had supported the Republic, yet greater numbers had chosen to support the federal state of Great Dayak. As a result, the term "Dayak" became pejorative and associated with treachery to the cause of Indonesian nationalism. Aside from Riwut's position as regent, the Dayaks were not represented in the Provisional National Parliament in Jakarta and poorly represented in the Provisional Council for Kalimantan. The governors of Kalimantan between 1950 and 1957 were all Javanese.[17]

After losing administrative recognition or any significant representation in the new provincial institutions, the struggle to regain Dayak representation moved to the electoral realm. For the first parliamentary elections of September 1955, the Dayaks were one of few groups that formed a political party based on their ethnicity, the United Dayak Party (PPD).[18] They demarcated themselves from other ethnic groups whose members joined national parties. During the 1950s, Indonesian nationalist discourse across the spectrum of various tendencies denounced allegiances along ethnic lines, which had been associated with Dutch divisive strategies. The main political parties were organized along ideological "streams" (*aliran*) and not along ethnic lines. The formation of a Dayak party and its relatively strong regional support showed that many Dayaks did not share the broad appeal of an Indonesian nationalist orientation.

Nevertheless, the results of the election showed a mixed success for attempts to gain a new form of representation for the Dayaks (see Table 1). The PPD (United Dayak Party) obtained the second largest number of votes in the West Kalimantan electoral district (33.1%), after the Islamic party Masyumi (35.2%), whose main base of support was the Malays and migrants. In the South Kalimantan district, which included much of the former Great Dayak region (Central Kalimantan), the results were different. It was not surprising that, overall, there was resounding support for the two largest Muslim parties, Masyumi (31.8%) and Nahdlatul Ulama (48.1%), given the overwhelming dominance and concentration of the Banjarese Malay population in the southern portion of the district. More surprisingly, however, the area predominantly populated by Dayaks produced only 6.2% support for the PPD, and only marginal support for the Christian party Parkindo (4.9%), while Muslim parties still obtained the most votes (23.2% for Masyumi and 21.7% for Nahdlatul Ulama). According to Douglas Miles, these results can be explained by the large number of Dayak conversions to Islam in this particular area of Borneo and a corresponding shift of identity to "Malay."

Table 1 Results of the 1955 elections, Kalimantan (%)

Parties	West Kalimantan	South Kalimantan (incl. Central Kalimantan)	Central Kalimantan
Muslim			
Masyumi	35.2	31.8	23.2
Nahdlatul Ulama	8.6	48.1	21.7
PPTI	–	2.1	5.6
Dayak and Christian			
PPD	33.1	1.5	6.2
Parkindo	–	1.3	4.9
Katholik	0.6	0.1	0.1
National			
PNI	14.6	5.9	15.5
IPKI	1.7	2.4	9.8
PKI	1.9	2.2	4.3

Note: IPKI = League of Upholders of Indonesian Freedom; PKI = Communist Party; PNI = Nationalist Party; PPTI = Association for the Practise of Islamic Mysticism. *Sources:* based on Miles, *Cutlass and Crescent Moon*, pp. 116–18; Feith, *The Indonesian Elections of 1955*, p. 69.

When the opportunity arose, former Pakat Dayak and Dayak party leaders shifted strategies once again and demanded their own province. When regional rebellions began to erupt in different parts of Indonesia, the Banjarese Malays joined them in support of the creation of an Islamic state. In response, the Dayaks also rebelled and demanded an autonomous province of Central Kalimantan to eliminate Banjarese dominance. Faced with more serious rebellions, Sukarno appeased the rebels and signed a decree creating the province of Central Kalimantan in May 1957. Tjilik Riwut was named governor.

Elections once again represented a setback for Dayak leaders but Sukarno gave them his support. The leaders of the new province were surprised when elections for provincial and district councils in 1958 returned a fairly strong support for Muslim parties. Nevertheless, when Sukarno introduced Guided Democracy shortly thereafter, he abolished elected councils, banned the Muslim political party Masyumi, and gave stronger powers to governors. Muslim representatives in Central Kalimantan lost their positions. In subsequent years, the governor ensured that Dayaks controlled most positions in the province and districts.[19]

By the early 1960s, an elite-driven Dayak identity had been formed and institutionalized through political representation. Sukarno banned political parties formed along ethnic lines, and therefore the Dayak party was abolished but, nevertheless, the Dayaks had their own province. It was ironic that in "their" province, Dayak identity was most ambiguous, given the large number of Muslim Dayaks. In Western Kalimantan, where support for an ethnic Dayak party was strongest, the Dayaks represented about 40% of the population and obtained little political representation in the provincial institutions. Nevertheless, the positions in Central Kalimantan gained symbolic importance, in the same way that the former Great Dayak once had.

The previous existence of a Dayak political party and representation within the Republic's institutions became part of the collective memories associated with subsequent marginalization. Analyses of the violence of the late 1990s recount the Dayaks' repeated complaints that they had lost the representation they once had in the 1950s.[20] These memories were crucial in reproducing the collective identity of the Dayaks and their shared experience.

The New Order regime represented a new institutional departure that marginalized the Dayaks. Shortly after its inception, Dayaks lost almost all representation in government institutions, as well as access to the central government. They were categorized as "backward" in the New Order's ideological emphasis on development. Furthermore, migration became perceived as a threat, as it accompanied state-sponsored seizure and exploitation of the land and forests of Kalimantan.

The Dayaks lost the little political representation they had obtained in previous years. During the New Order period, none of the governors of West Kalimantan were Dayaks, while in Central Kalimantan none were Dayak after 1984. Only a few district heads in either province were Dayak. At the national level, no Dayaks obtained top positions in the cabinet, the military, or other major national institutions. They were even denied, therefore, access to the center, which was an important source of recognition, legitimacy, and patronage under the New Order.[21]

Furthermore, the Dayaks were relegated to a marginal status. They were classified as "isolated" or "primitive," along with the Papuans in Irian Jaya and a large number of smaller groups in various remote places of the archipelago.[22] As such, they were deemed to be "not yet modern" and, by implication, not yet fully Indonesian. Resettlement programs were designed to move them from remote places to villages that followed "Indonesian" standards. Village government was reconfigured along a national norm, even though the new structures displaced local forms of authority and social order.[23] The customary forms of swidden agriculture and forest-based livelihoods were denigrated as inefficient and environmentally harmful relative to the wet-rice field cultivation of Javanese and other migrants.

The resource-management policies of the New Order further contributed to this marginalization. Under Forest Law no. 5 (1967), the
Indonesian government distributed generous and long-term logging concessions over most of West and Central Kalimantan's territory. Because
these concessions were allocated to business partners of the regime, they
regularly disregarded legal requirements for the protection of forests and
forest dwellers. Customary uses of the forest by the Dayaks were ignored
and the law recognized no rights.[24] One study estimated that about
20–30% of the population of West Kalimantan in 1997 practiced swidden
agriculture on land considered state forest land and therefore exploitable
by logging companies.[25] In the Ketapang district of West Kalimantan,
close to the capital city of Pontianak and the area where the 1996–97
violence broke out, 94% of the available forest area had been distributed
as concessions by 1994.[26]

While Dayaks lost political representation and felt pressure on their
land, migration patterns intensified their sense of displacement. Migrants
always constituted a good proportion of West and Central Kalimantan's
population. The large groups, such as the Malays and Chinese, established good relations with the Dayaks. New migration began to intensify
in the 1960s, as part of the official transmigration program and of an
increase in spontaneous migration. As a result, West Kalimantan's population, for instance, grew by 2.33% between 1971 and 1981.[27]

The Madurese were never the most important migrant group in numerical terms, but they became the most visible in this new wave of
migration. Their proportion relative to others grew the fastest. In West
Kalimantan, they increased from only 0.6% of the population in 1971
to 2.5% in 1979. In Pontianak, they constituted 13.09% of the population, relative to only 1.42% of Dayaks. Most importantly, they were
highly visible because they organized themselves in separate communities. Sudagung estimated that, in 1980, almost 70% of Madurese lived in
such communities. Many opened up forested areas and were established
along new roads that made more areas of the interior accessible to logging
companies, plantations, and migrant settlements.[28]

This visibility increased Dayak resentment. The Madurese in West
and Central Kalimantan represented a group that had progressed under
New Order policies. They became targets of, what Donald Horowitz
has called, a "cumulation of direct and displaced aggression".[29] The
New Order regime was strong and its armed forces capable of retal-
iating, so the Dayaks were less likely to select direct government targets in response to frustration at their increasing marginalization. They
transferred their grievances instead to the Madurese. This displaced
aggression was combined with direct aggression resulting from past
incidents of violence involving members of the two groups. Dayaks

recorded and interpreted past violent incidents as evidence of Madurese violent characteristics and developed stereotypes of the Madurese as "aggressive".[30]

The New Order's political institutions, therefore, created categories of marginalized people that lost economic and political control over their region. The Dayaks constituted one of many groups that were relegated to a "backward" status. Yet, they developed a new "Dayak" identity, thereby giving them sufficient numbers and a sense of shared experience. This identity was never sufficiently strong to develop into an articulated group mobilization against the government, such as an ethnonationalist movement or open rebellion. Instead, they targeted the Madurese, who most vividly represented the changes brought about by the New Order regime.

They did so at a time when the New Order's institutions were weakening. The violence occurred in 1996–97 when Suharto's regime was nearing its end and a succession crisis was looming. Riots in other parts of the country had shown the vulnerability of the state's repressive apparatus and opened up the horizon for political change. In this context, violence was more likely to erupt as potential institutional change created new possibilities for redressing past grievances.

Changing political institutions also influenced subsequent violence between Dayaks and Madurese. After the end of the New Order, political uncertainty affected all areas of Indonesia. Institutional change after 1998 raised local uncertainties about a potential redress for the Dayaks and an end to three decades of economic and political marginalization. The violence not only resumed in 1999 but also spread to Central Kalimantan in 2001, where Dayaks felt they had lost most of their prior achievements in political representation.

Violence against the Madurese in 1999 was more complex to explain, as it also involved the Malay. It began in the district of Sambas with a minor incident on 19 January when, on the last day of the holy month of Ramadan, a crowd of 200 Madurese attacked a Malay hamlet in retaliation for the beating of a Madurese caught stealing in the hamlet. Four people were killed in the brawl, which nevertheless remained contained. On 21 February, a Malay bus driver was injured in a fight with a local Madurese after the latter had been assaulted for failing to pay for his ride. The next day, 300 Madurese went searching for the Malay bus driver. When they were attacked with gunfire by a group of Malays, the riot erupted and quickly spread. Attacks and counter-attacks involving both groups continued well into March. When a Dayak was killed in one incident, the violence spread to include Dayaks who joined the attacks on local Madurese. The attacks continued in successive waves for several weeks until April.[31] By 26 March, the West Kalimantan government had reported 186 deaths, massive property damage, and at least 26,000 Madurese refugees.[32]

The process of marginalization produced by New Order institutions can only indirectly explain this particular set of incidents. Some press reports claimed that other migrant groups, including the Bugis from South Sulawesi and the Chinese, might also have joined the Malays and Dayaks in attacking the Madurese. This evidence would concur with an explanation that the Madurese were scapegoats for other sources of frustration and, in particular, that they were selected as targets on the basis of their seclusion and close-knit community. The violence was located in the same region as that of 1996–97, in an area where the Madurese community was the fastest growing one. Since the New Order had created an environment of impunity for land grabbing by plantations and timber concessions, disputes often arose when Madurese farmers took possession of land previously owned by Chinese, Malays, or Dayaks. Finally, the boundaries between Malays and Dayaks were blurred in the area. When Dayaks converted to Islam, they often espoused an identity as Malay. A sense of "brotherhood" was created between the two ethnic communities and they even had stories of common origins in their mythological repertoires.[33]

A wave of rioting in Central Kalimantan provided further evidence of the effects of marginalization on the conflict between Dayaks and Madurese. The violence began in Sampit on 17–18 February 2001 after tensions had been rising since a brawl between Dayaks and Madurese in a karaoke bar in December 2000. Small attacks and counter-attacks occurred until the violence began to intensify after 18 February. It spread to include even the capital of Central Kalimantan, Palangkaraya, situated 220 km away from the site of the original incident. Thousands of Dayaks participated in attacks against Madurese.[34] By early March, 486 people had been killed, mostly Madurese. By mid-April, an estimated 108,000 Madurese had fled Central Kalimantan and, a few weeks later, virtually the entire Madurese community in the province had left.[35]

As in West Kalimantan, the Dayaks had been marginalized economically by the rapid spread of timber concessions and other business ventures that diminished the land area they used. For example, forest land declined from 84% of Central Kalimantan's land area in 1970 to about 56% in 1999. More than in West Kalimantan, the Dayaks of Central Kalimantan, especially elite members, felt the political marginalization that resulted from the New Order, as they had lost the strong political representation they enjoyed under previous institutional arrangements.[36]

Furthermore, Madurese migration had also been strong, alongside other spontaneous migrants and transmigrants. According to the International Crisis Group report on the violence in Central Kalimantan, transmigration to Central Kalimantan increased dramatically after 1980, with approximately 180,000 new transmigrant settlers per decade, compared to 13,000 between 1971 and 1980. Furthermore, spontaneous migration, especially of Madurese, continued to increase. Sampit, the town where the violence began, had a majority of Madurese.[37] The districts most affected by the violence all had higher proportions of Madurese than elsewhere in the province.

The violence in Central Kalimantan, therefore, was linked to the violence of 1996–97 in West Kalimantan. Although some observers partly stressed local factors,[38] the location of conflict in areas with high concentrations of Madurese, and the frequent mentioning of resentment created by economic and political marginalization, especially forest degradation and loss of representation, were all consistent with an explanation that emphasizes the aggressive frustration among the Dayaks resulting from the New Order's institutional environment. The Dayaks of Central and West Kalimantan shared the same experiences under the New Order. The violent events of 1996–97 only intensified the tensions also present in Central Kalimantan.

Institutional change increased the potential for violence. In addition to the uncertainty surrounding the fall of Suharto, rapidly changing institutions opened up not only opportunities but also fears of further mobilization. When the Habibie government began to implement a law on regional autonomy in 1999, competition rose for the positions of district head and provincial governor. Under the new law, vast resources were decentralized to the districts and, therefore, became a source of intense competition. Dayak political elites, who had been frustrated at their loss of representation and control over resources, had a strong interest in winning many of these posts. They were also in a good position, given the numerical advantages of the Dayak in Central Kalimantan. Van Klinken emphasized the role of this elite competition among the Dayak elite, especially members of the Dayak and Central Kalimantan Representative Association (LMMDD-KT). Yet, these elites were only able to make political gains by tapping into the cumulated frustrations of the marginalized Dayaks. With a new critical juncture in the institutional configuration of Indonesia's political and administrative institutions, Dayak elites saw an opportunity to reassert the control they once had in the province.

The last years of the New Order regime and the subsequent democratic transition created an institutional environment that was conducive to violence. The marginalized Dayaks saw opportunities to act on their grievances while potentially improving their status relative to migrant groups, in particular the Madurese. Although the source of their grievances was the New Order state, they transferred their aggression onto the Madurese. The conflicts of 1996–97, 1999, and 2001 could all be interpreted in relation to this changing institutional environment.

Exclusion: Chinese Indonesians as non-*pribumi*

Violence against the Chinese Indonesians has its roots in the recurring institutionalization of exclusion. From the Dutch colonial system to different periods of post-independence Indonesia, various laws, regulations, and representative institutions aimed at differentiating the Chinese from other groups. They were singled out as outsiders, non-Indonesians, non-*asli*, non-*pribumi*.[39] This institutionalized exclusion made them visible targets when violent outbursts occurred. Grievances based on socio-economic differences were funneled through this process of group differentiation and conflict. Periods of violence occurred mostly during critical junctures and political transitions.

Socio-economic differences between the Chinese and non-Chinese Indonesians have been blamed as a primary source of grievance.[40] A minority of Chinese accumulated wealth and power, often accompanied by the impoverishment of peasants or the displacement of traders from other ethnic groups. Part of this wealth was gained by policies that protected certain Chinese business activities, especially under the New Order system of patronage.

While such grievances created frustrations and even anger, they cannot in themselves explain ethnic violence. Anger and resentment were generalized to all Chinese, irrespective of their socio-economic status. As Charles Coppel has noted, explanations based on socio-economic grievances are limited when one closely analyzes the violence against the Chinese. Many incidents were triggered by non-economic factors and even involved poor Chinese as the main targets of rioters.[41] Some of the motivations were mixed, such as the violence unleashed in 1965, which was triggered by a military purge of communist sympathizers. The categorization and exclusion of the Chinese perpetuated suspicions among non-Chinese Indonesians that their loyalties lay outside of Indonesia and that their business activities were exploitative.

The construction of the Indonesian nation left the Chinese in an ambiguous category. After independence, their citizenship became a focal point of struggles between Chinese political leaders and the Indonesian government. The Dutch as well as early Indonesian nationalists had differentiated them. While they later became more integrated and were given citizenship, their integration was incomplete. Various informal and formal categories to identify the Chinese, restrictions on their political or economic activities, and other forms of discrimination were institutionalized.

Dutch colonial policies first made the distinction between the Chinese and the "Natives".[42] As "Foreign Orientals," the Chinese were given more privileges and rights than the "Natives" but fewer than the Europeans. In the earlier period, the Dutch East Indies company gave Chinese merchants leases over entire administrative areas, including whole villages, for selling imports and, later, to extract agricultural produce for export or to mobilize labor. The colonial government granted them monopolies, including the collection of road tolls, bazaar fees, salt, and later opium.[43] Under the Culture System and Ethical Policies, many of these privileges were removed but the Chinese continued to be differentiated. A pass and zoning system required them to reside in restricted areas and to seek special permission to travel outside of these areas. Chinese men were required to wear Chinese long-dresses and were prohibited from cutting their pigtails.[44]

As a result of this differentiation, nationalist movements also followed group patterns. Chinese nationalists formed various groups and organizations to promote Chinese cultural characteristics and group interests. The Chinese Association (THHK), formed in 1900, emphasized the revival of Chinese culture, especially Confucianism and the Chinese language. Other organizations included a Chinese Chamber of Commerce (1906) and several Chinese newspapers, such as the *Sin Po*. After 1911, Chinese associated with the Sin Po group and the THHK increasingly advocated the adoption of Chinese citizenship and support for the Republic of China.[45]

The birth of Indonesian nationalism was closely linked to a differentiation from the Chinese and produced violence in some instances. The first major Indonesian nationalist organization, Sarekat Islam (1912), was initially a response from "Native" merchants to Chinese competition. One of its main activities was the organization of boycotts against Chinese entrepreneurs.[46] Riots broke out across Java between 1912 and 1914, as the Sarekat Islam expanded. The Chinese were increasingly eager to reach a new, equal status to Europeans, whereas the "Natives" saw the growing organizational strength of the Chinese as potentially usurping the power of Javanese rulers and further threatening their merchants.[47]

Yet, the Chinese community itself was divided. The mixed descendants of early Chinese migrants, born in the Indies, formed the *peranakan* Chinese community that was dominant. They had often shed many of their Chinese cultural characteristics and tended to speak local languages or a Chinese-Malay dialect. New migration from China in the late nineteenth and early twentieth centuries formed a *totok* (or *singkeh*) Chinese community that retained cultural practises, including the Chinese language, and rarely married "Natives".[48] The *peranakan* and *totok* communities formed political organizations with different objectives. In the 1930s, most *peranakan* supported the Chung Hwa Hui

(CHH), which advocated support for the Dutch and equal status to Europeans in the Indies. A smaller group joined the Indonesian Chinese Party (PTI), which promoted assimilation with indigenous Indonesians and full citizenship for the *peranakan* Chinese in an eventual independent Indonesia. The Sin Po group declined significantly and became mainly a representative group for the *totok*.[49]

In the decade preceding independence, the idea of including the *peranakan* Chinese in the Indonesian nation progressed. A majority supported a nation that was restricted to "indigenous" Indonesians. The Nationalist Party of Indonesia, for example, restricted membership to Indonesian *asli* (indigenous). A few secular nationalists, however, advocated a non-racial concept of nation. One of these was Amir Sjarifuddin, who would become one of the first prime ministers of Indonesia. His political party, Gerindo, opened membership to the *peranakan* Chinese in the late 1930s.[50]

After independence was declared in 1945, there was a moment when the divisions between the Chinese and indigenous Indonesians might have been significantly reduced. All Indonesian political parties changed their membership policies to accept full inclusion of the *peranakan*. At the same time, a small number of *peranakan* joined national political parties. The Socialist Party of Sutan Sjahrir, for instance, drew a good amount of support from pro-Republican Indonesian Chinese. Furthermore, Chinese representatives were included in governmental institutions such as the temporary legislative body (KNIP) and its working committee, as well as some cabinets in the late 1940s.[51]

The issue of citizenship, however, continued to divide Chinese and Indonesians. Indonesia's first citizenship law used the principle of *jus soli*, by which citizenship would be extended to all people born in Indonesia. Those who wished to reject citizenship were required to do so within twelve months. This law was not well received among indigenous Indonesians with anti-Sinicist orientations. More surprisingly, a large number of Chinese also disliked it because they feared that, on becoming Indonesian citizens, they might no longer be protected by China if they were victims of anti-Chinese violence and discrimination.[52]

The end of the first critical juncture and the adoption of democratic institutions did not end the differentiation of the Chinese. The 1946 citizenship law, the inclusion of Chinese in the Republic's political institutions, and the liberal democratic environment after 1950 were not sufficient. A major problem remained the differential status of the *totok* and *peranakan* Chinese. The success of the Maoist revolution in 1949 contributed to a growing suspicion among some Indonesians that many Chinese, especially those born in China, were supporters of the new communist government. In August 1951, the Sukiman government raided organizations that were deemed supportive of the People's Republic of China (PRC) and other communist-oriented organizations. Since the deadline for rejecting Indonesian citizenship had been extended to December 1951, it was no surprise that almost 300,000 consequently rejected it. Many *totok* considered the raid as evidence that the Indonesian government could not be trusted.[53]

When a new citizenship law was proposed in 1953, *peranakan* Chinese politicians increased their activism. The proposed law included more difficult access to citizenship, namely a minimum residency requirement of three generations, proof of one's parents' birth in Indonesia, as well as proof of at least ten years of residence in Indonesia. Many Chinese saw these measures as very restrictive, given the mass destruction of documents during the Japanese occupation.[54] In response, a group of Chinese politicians created in 1954 the Consultative Body for Indonesian Citizenship (Baperki).

Baperki was presented as a mass organization that promoted citizenship based on equal rights and democratic principles. It rapidly became popular among the Chinese. Although it was not officially a political party, it played a similar role when it decided to field candidates for the legislative elections of 1955. It supported constitutional guarantees and the elimination of racialism. It stood for the "integration" of the Chinese, meaning a recognition of their right to exist as a group and to be included as one of the many ethnic groups constituting the diversity of the Indonesian nation. By doing so, it rejected the "assimilationist" orientation of other *peranakan* Chinese who advocated inter-marriage with non-Chinese, the adoption of Indonesian names, and the full abandonment of Chinese cultural practises.[55] While many Chinese decided to support other political parties in the 1955 elections, Baperki nevertheless obtained 63–74% of *peranakan* votes in Java, where the greatest number lived.[56]

The efforts by Baperki and other organizations to settle the question of Chinese exclusion failed during the liberal democratic period. While some initiatives were taken to integrate the Chinese, past suspicions, a weak state, and events in China revived suspicions toward *totok* Chinese and, by extension, *peranakan* Chinese. Baperki offered a political channel to voice concerns and it succeeded in mobilizing a large number of Chinese. By doing so, however, it drew attention to itself as a "Chinese" organization, which became a severe handicap by the mid-1960s.

Under Guided Democracy, Baperki and Chinese Indonesians reached an accommodation with the Indonesian government. After parliament and the Constituent Assembly had been suspended, there were more narrow channels for influencing political decisions. Positions in cabinet and access to President Sukarno became highly prized, as well as alignments with the military and the Communist Party (PKI), two strong pillars of power in the early 1960s. The Chinese Indonesians in Baperki associated themselves with the PKI, which was gaining favor with Sukarno. They were also represented in the cabinet.

The short period of accommodation between 1963 and 1965 had three main aspects. First, the question of citizenship was temporarily resolved. A new law was adopted in 1958 with many more restrictions than the 1946 law, but it was acceptable to Baperki. It required that foreigners meet certain residency requirements for gaining citizenship but did not alter the citizenship status of Chinese who had already become Indonesian citizens. In addition, with the implementation of a dual nationality treaty that was signed in 1955 but implemented in 1963, some ambiguities about citizenship were removed: all Chinese in Indonesia were either citizens of Indonesia or aliens. They could no longer be citizens of both Indonesia and China. Second, businesses owned by Chinese Indonesians were allowed to operate and expand as a source of national development. Third, anti-Chinese violence was kept in check. When riots erupted in West Java in 1963, the government suppressed them before they spread.[57]

Yet, this accommodation occurred against a background of further restrictions against non-Indonesian Chinese. The government banned Indonesian citizens from attending alien schools, which meant that Indonesian Chinese could no longer attend Chinese language schools. A head tax was imposed on aliens in 1957. Finally, in 1959 the government imposed a ban on retail trade by foreigners in rural areas. Indonesian Chinese had to prove their citizenship to avoid these restrictions. As a result of these measures, thousands of Chinese left Indonesia.[58]

To seek protection and advance the interests of Chinese Indonesians, Baperki became sufficiently close to the PKI that it divided the Chinese community. As Sukarno and the government had taken a turn to the left, an association with the PKI was favorable. "Assimilationists" who favored the dissolution of the Chinese as a distinct group, however, sided with the military against the communist-oriented Baperki and formed a rival organization, the Institute for the Promoters of National Unity (LPKB). In the competition between the two organizations, Baperki remained most popular, with its membership reaching 280,000 in 1965, compared to 40,000 in 1955.[59]

Baperki and the Chinese were caught in the struggle between the military and the PKI that ended with a new institutional legacy. After the coup attempt of 30 September 1965, the military and other organizations moved against the PKI and its supporters. Baperki was banned and its leaders imprisoned. The large-scale killings across Java and other parts of Indonesia during 1966 were largely attacks against communists. Of the estimated 500,000 people who were killed, around 2,000 were

Chinese. Most of the anti-Chinese violence was targeted at Chinese-owned property but did not only affect wealthy Chinese.[60]

Sporadic actions against the Chinese continued to occur throughout 1966 and 1967 in various locations in Indonesia. In addition, some military commanders took radical action. In Aceh, for example, 10,000 alien Chinese were expelled from the province. In West Kalimantan, 5,000 alien Chinese were moved from the Sarawak border to Pontianak, with the intention of expelling them. A few months later, the military provoked the Dayaks to attack the Chinese, with the intention of uprooting communist sympathizers and former guerillas who had been involved in the confrontation against Malaysia. An estimated 50,000 Chinese fled the interior of West Kalimantan and sought refuge in coastal areas.[61]

The scale of the violence revealed the weaknesses built into the prior rules and institutions defining the terms of inclusion for the Chinese. Their socio-economic distinction created under Dutch rule remained in a different form. The Chinese continued to be suspected of unfair business practises toward non-Chinese Indonesians. Furthermore, the association of Baperki with communism created greater suspicions among non-communists of a specifically Chinese threat to the Indonesian nation. Although "alien" Chinese were particularly targeted, all Chinese were affected. They were viewed as one group. The ambiguities relating to the citizenship status of many of them during the 1950s contributed to heightened suspicions and blurred distinctions between "aliens" and citizens. Both the liberal democratic environment and the more authoritarian context of Guided Democracy perpetuated the differentiation and exclusion of the Chinese.

Violence in the mid-1960s resulted more from the context of institutional change, therefore, than from socio-economic grievances. As Jamie Mackie has noted, explanations based on socio-economic rivalry are insufficient: "The extreme instability of the entire political situation in Indonesia during the next two years [after 1965] should perhaps be regarded as the most important element common to the various outbursts of anti-Chinese hostility in that period." Mackie then provides a list of explanatory factors, divided among predispositions for violence, restraining factors, and precipitating ones. Five out of eight predispositions related to the way the Chinese were constructed as "separate" from others during the colonial period and the rise of nationalism, thereby intensifying other factors such as the xenophobic aspects of nationalism (both in its Indonesian and Chinese forms).[62] These factors relating to the "separateness" of the Chinese were direct consequences of the institutionalization of exclusion that was perpetuated after independence.

As a result, the period of institutional change in the mid-1960s was seen as an opportunity to reshape and redefine the institutional status of the Chinese. When the New Order regime began to consolidate itself, a new set of institutions redefined the relationship of the Chinese to the Indonesian nation and clarified the terms of inclusion. Yet, once again, contradictions in the policies and regulations exacerbated tensions and reinforced elements of exclusion over time.

The new regime clarified the rules and regulations regarding citizenship. The remaining non-citizen Chinese were stateless, since an association with the PRC would have branded them as communist. Instead of a policy of mass expulsion or mass naturalization, which were both politically unacceptable to the regime, the Suharto government simplified the naturalization procedures and allowed all non-citizens to apply for Indonesian citizenship. In July and August 1967, Suharto personally approved the naturalization of thirty-eight Chinese. He also confirmed in his Independence Day speech on 17 August that the Chinese Indonesians should not be discriminated against and racism should be eliminated.[63] A Presidential Instruction (no. 2, 1980) streamlined the procedures for naturalization and made it more acceptable.

The government also committed itself to the protection of the lives, property, and businesses of the "alien" Chinese. In its official formulation of policy of June 1967, no mention was made of the 1959 ban on retail trade in rural areas that remained in place. Instead, it encouraged the mobilization of domestic foreign capital (that is, of the "alien" Chinese) for the purposes of national development. It also proposed to phase out foreign capital in certain sectors over the following decade, thereby leaving ample opportunity for non-citizens to apply for naturalization before the phase-out.[64]

The regime sided with the assimilationist perspective of the LPKB, instead of the integrationist approach that Baperki had propounded. Chinese Indonesians who had joined the anti-communist movement and who were close to the regime viewed assimilation as the best option. The New Order regime consequently adopted policies to eliminate the distinctions marking Chinese Indonesians from other Indonesian citizens. It banned alien schools and urged all Chinese (citizens and non-citizens) to attend Indonesian national schools. It strongly encouraged the adoption of Indonesian names. It also issued a decree banning Chinese religious observances or cultural forms in public areas.[65] Chinese-language publications were restricted and only one Chinese-language newspaper was allowed.

In the late 1970s and early 1980s, the government pursued even more coercive methods. It reaffirmed and reinforced the 1967 decree that religious observances with cultural affinities to China should be restricted to private homes. After the closing of alien schools, the government allowed new private schools to be formed after 1968, where Chinese was the language of instruction. After several years, however, it began to worry about their increasing numbers and abolished them all in 1974.[66]

The assimilationist approach was accompanied by formal and informal discriminatory measures that increased the differentiation of the Chinese rather than fostering their integration. In 1976, the Bank of Indonesia issued a publication specifying different conditions for extending credit to *pribumi* and non-*pribumi*.[67] To obtain certain permits or official documents, Chinese Indonesians were required to show proof of citizenship, while non-Chinese Indonesians were not. In 1979, all Chinese were required to reregister. Special codes were added to their identity cards, clearly identifying them as Chinese.[68] Chinese Indonesians were virtually barred from the civil service and the military, especially top positions. Only a few got involved in political parties but none ever acceded to cabinet positions even if they had attained influential positions within the government party, Golkar. In sum, as Frans Winarta, a prominent Chinese Indonesian lawyer and political activist, concluded: "There is not much difference between the Dutch policy of divide and rule and the existing policies. Differentiation of the *pribumi* and the Chinese only breeds divisiveness".[69]

The differentiation was intensified by the New Order's nurturing of a small minority of very wealthy Chinese businessmen. During the 1950s and 1960s, this group profited from close business relationships with top military officers such as Suharto. The restrictions on the Chinese, the New Order's emphasis on mobilizing domestic foreign capital for development, and existing patron–client relations with a few Chinese businessmen created a class of very wealthy owners of vast business conglomerates. These conglomerates grew under the protective wing of and favorable contracts from the New Order government.[70] In the 1980s and 1990s, this network of large conglomerates was extended to a number of *pribumi* businessmen and Suharto's family members but the Chinese retained the greatest economic strength. A widespread public perception held that Chinese Indonesians dominated 70% of Indonesia's economy, despite the absence of clear evidence.[71]

In the early to mid-1990s, however, old grievances about socio-economic inequalities resurfaced. The close relationship between conglomerates and the regime came under public scrutiny. Resentment grew not only against the large conglomerates but also, by extension, against all Chinese Indonesians, especially small retailers in towns across the country. These anti-Chinese sentiments were a consequence of new and old policies that reinforced the position of the Chinese in the economy while perpetuating their political and social exclusion.

They surfaced as Indonesia was entering a new critical juncture. There were many public discussions about the high possibility of Suharto's departure from politics. The uncertainties ranged from speculation about the potential policies of possible successors to expectations of institutional change. In a post-Suharto world, the future of Chinese conglomerates close to the regime would be questioned. As in other times of political uncertainty and institutional change, the *pribumi* made greater demands for the reduction of socio-economic inequalities with the Chinese. There were more open and more frequent expressions of grievances against the power of the conglomerates and their association with the New Order regime.[72]

Violence erupted during this period. Riots across Java targeted Chinese property. Some of these were intrinsically related to religious tensions (see Chapter 6). It is analytically difficult to disassociate the causes of these violent eruptions since the Chinese were mostly Christians. Nevertheless, in riots in Medan, Rengasdengklok, Pekalongan, Situbondo, and Tasikmalaya, Chinese shops and homes were burned to the ground. Rioters consciously distinguished the Chinese from others and targeted their property. They displayed resentment against the socio-economic status of the Chinese and, in particular, because they were non-*pribumi*.

The Asian financial crisis heightened these grievances. Hundreds of people were laid off by Chinese-owned businesses and many blamed the conglomerates for the severity of the crisis. Hundreds of Chinese-owned shops were looted in various parts of Indonesia, partly in fear at rising prices for basic necessities and partly because rumors abounded of a conspiracy by the Chinese behind the rise in prices. In early 1998, members of the armed forces and Suharto himself even accused some Chinese businessmen of triggering the crisis. This turn against the close business associates of the regime was felt even more strongly when one prominent Chinese businessman, Sofyan Wanandi, was questioned in the press for alleged links to bombings in Jakarta. The Centre for Strategic and International Studies, a think-tank led by prominent Chinese Indonesians formerly close to the regime, was also the target of demonstrations, with apparent support from some members within the regime. These manifestations of anti-Chinese sentiment as the crisis progressed led many Chinese Indonesians to secure their capital abroad and make preparations to leave the country.[73]

When riots broke out in Jakarta and across several cities in mid-May 1998, Chinese Indonesians were again targeted. Hundreds were killed. Dozens of Chinese women were raped.[74] The violence was more extensive and involved many more targets than the Chinese, but these particular incidents were the most brutal. In addition, there was mass destruction of Chinese property.

More than other instances of violence, the targeting of Chinese in May 1998 was orchestrated by provocateurs. A report by a special investigating team revealed that these actions were largely provoked and undertaken by members of Indonesia's armed forces, including Suharto's son-in-law Prabowo Subianto. Of all the instances of ethnic violence in Indonesia, the May 1998 riots showed the most convincing evidence of provocation.[75]

Nevertheless, this provocation rested upon anti-Chinese feelings that were running particularly high. The outbreak of violence showed the accumulated frustrations and failures of New Order policies that were institutionalized throughout the 1960s and 1970s. The assimilationist orientation of these policies had not led to a blurring of distinctions between Chinese and Indonesians. Instead, they created a single "Chinese" group in the eyes of indigenous Indonesians. While the assimilationist policies and restrictions strongly diluted the difference between *totok* and *peranakan* Chinese, they maintained through formal and informal discriminatory practises the distinction between the Chinese non-*pribumi* and the *pribumi* Indonesians. As the regime created stronger and more evident socio-economic inequalities by nurturing Chinese conglomerates, the resentment against the regime was transformed into violence against the Chinese.

The period of reform and democratization after Suharto's downfall was marked by a significant decline in violence against the Chinese Indonesians and their property. After the numerous incidents of violence culminating in the events of May 1998, this sudden decline was noteworthy. It was doubly significant because political instability was still present and ethnic violence continued to occur in many parts of the archipelago.

This decline can be explained partly by a sudden, normative change regarding Chinese Indonesians. The killings of May 1998, and especially the brutality of the rapes, horrified the Indonesian political elite, especially once it became clear that the armed forces were involved. Islamic politicians who had been most vocal about the corrupt relations between Suharto and Chinese conglomerates were equally dismayed. After May 1998, the tone suddenly changed to one of sympathy. Public statements from politicians of all streams reaffirmed the inclusive values of the Indonesian nation and the place of the Chinese Indonesians as citizens and equal members.[76] The criticism aimed at the Chinese conglomerates and at socio-economic inequalities was replaced by praise for the role of Chinese capital in Indonesia's development.

The collapse of the New Order's authoritarian regime supported these normative changes. Capital flight and the large number of Chinese leaving the country were catalysts for a reversal of policies and attitudes toward the Chinese. More fundamentally, with the end of the regime, most large conglomerates had suddenly lost their patron. Many Indonesians expected the imminent dismantlement of this network of patronage. When some of the wealthy Chinese businessmen who had cooperated with the regime were investigated for corruption, these measures contributed further to the easing of tensions. The prosecution and subsequent imprisonment of Bob Hasan, one of Suharto's most famous cronies of Chinese descent, particularly pleased many Indonesians. Without eliminating socio-economic grievances, therefore, the end of the New Order regime removed suddenly one of the most significant symbols of resentment against the Chinese.

Institutional reforms, leadership change, and the violent results of the New Order's policies presented an opening to renew rules, laws, and customary practises. The impetus came from two directions. For the first time since the 1950s, Chinese Indonesians saw an opportunity to engage in political action, with the formation of new political organizations and new channels to voice their grievances. Furthermore, some non-Chinese politicians, who had been shocked by the failures of past policies and the nature of the May violence, were able to push some reforms without feeding the anti-Chinese sentiments that remained among some of their supporters.

Chinese Indonesians openly requested an end to discriminatory practises and became involved in political activities. Most directly, new political parties and political organizations were formed to represent Chinese Indonesians and their interests. The Chinese Indonesian Reform Party (Parti) was formed in early June 1998 with the objective of promoting racial harmony and protecting the interests of the Chinese. The Indonesian Unity in Diversity Party (PBI) used the country's motto in its name to promote equal rights and an eradication of racial, religious, and ethnic distinctions. Two other parties, the Indonesian Assimilation Party (Parpindo) and the Indonesian Citizen-Nation Party (Partai Warga Bangsa Indonesia), were short-lived. The quick disappearance of Parpindo was evidence of the disillusion among Chinese Indonesians with the assimilationist policies of the New Order. Many other groups and associations were formed to promote an end to discrimination, such as the National Solidarity Organization (Solidaritas Nusa Bangsa) formed after the May 1998 riots, and the Indonesian Anti-Discrimination Movement (Gandi) launched in November 1998 at the home of the prominent Muslim leader and future president, Abdurrahman Wahid.[77]

Most Chinese Indonesians, however, appeared to prefer national organizations to ethnic ones. Several were included and became influential members in the largest political parties, including the Democratic Party of Indonesia for the Struggle (PDI-P) of Megawati Sukarnoputri, the

National Mandate Party (PAN) of Amien Rais, and the National Awakening Party (PKB) of Abdurrahman Wahid. In the elections of June 1999, most Chinese Indonesians voted for these parties. Of the parties formed to represent them, only the PBI participated in the elections. It won one seat in parliament but received strong support only in West Kalimantan.[78]

Under all three presidents after the fall of Suharto, measures were taken to eliminate discrimination against the ethnic Chinese. Suharto's immediate successor, B. J. Habibie, who had obtained much support among Muslims critical of Chinese conglomerates, issued Presidential Instruction no. 26 in September 1998 to eliminate all forms of discrimination in the government, including the use of *pribumi* and non-*pribumi*. In January 2000, President Abdurrahman Wahid revoked Presidential Instruction no. 41, 1967, which had restricted the public celebration of Chinese religious practises and traditions. As a result, the Chinese New Year and other cultural events could be celebrated in public spaces. Under President Megawati Sukarnoputri, the Chinese New Year was declared a national holiday. More importantly, the MPR adopted a constitutional amendment in November 2001 that removed the requirement that the president be "indigenous" and replaced it with a condition of citizenship. This constitutional provision had long been an irritant for the Chinese community.[79]

Democratization did not end the exclusion of the Chinese but some formal and informal measures changed the course of past practises. Assimilation was abandoned as an official policy. Statements and some institutional changes were made to eliminate discrimination and continued distinctions between the Chinese and other Indonesians. These measures and the constitutional amendment of November 2001 provided political support for the full inclusion of Chinese Indonesians. They were combined with renewed calls for the importance of Chinese Indonesian capital in Indonesia's national development. With the investigation and prosecution of cases of corruption under the New Order, there was some sense that the privileges of the small class of Chinese conglomerates had ended. Where criticism was aimed at the government, it was because of its weakness in curbing corruption in general, and not specifically emphasizing Chinese businessmen.

Violence against Chinese Indonesians was almost absent after May 1998, in large part due to the change in institutional direction of post-Suharto Indonesia. As other Indonesians, the Chinese could pursue political activities, publish newspapers in Chinese, and establish a large number of organizations for cultural and social activities. Business activities could also resume normally. Many rules and legislation with discrimination against the Chinese remained in place but the normative environment spelled the beginning of institutional change. At that particular critical juncture, there was an opportunity to eliminate the exclusion of the Chinese and reduce future violence. Chinese political activity diminished a few months after the May events, but many activists continued to press for Chinese involvement in all political forums to maintain the momentum for change.

5   Islam and nation: The Muslim–Christian dimension

During the New Order period, religious identity emerged as the most important form of ethnic identification. The Suharto government increased the use of state instruments to repress Islamic demands and contain religious conflict. Yet, these policies ironically contributed to a reinforcement of religious identities. Over the three decades of Suharto's rule, identities as Muslim or Christian intensified, leading to greater demands for protection and recognition of their respective communities.

The question of an Islamic state had been one of the most important challenges to the nationalist vision of Indonesia. Rejection of the Jakarta Charter at the time of independence had not been well received by Muslim groups that had supported the Republic. The first critical juncture had ended with an ambiguous role for Islam in the polity: the question was left open-ended and subject to renegotiation during discussions for a final constitution. The Darul Islam movement followed the path of armed rebellion to promote an Islamic state. Other political organizations, such as the Islamic party Masyumi, chose to adhere to established political processes to further an Islamic agenda. Islamic parties failed to obtain strong support in the 1955 elections but subsequently wielded considerable power in the Constituent Assembly that was formed to negotiate the new constitution. They prevented the assembly from reaching a compromise that excluded Islam as a state ideology and negotiations were stalled as a result.

When regional rebellions arose in the late 1950s, several of them joined the Darul Islam. In February 1958, politicians from Masyumi joined rebel military groups in Sumatra and Sulawesi to declare an alternative revolutionary government (PRRI) that used Islam as its basic ideology.[1] That rebellion was easily put down by the Indonesian armed forces.

The Islamic state question was resolved by force. Sukarno moved decisively against Islamists by banning Masyumi, suspending the Constituent Assembly, and replacing the liberal democratic political system with an authoritarian regime, Guided Democracy. Later, the New Order regime followed a similar course by attempting to repress political Islam and eliminate demands for an Islamic state while promoting the alternative ideology of Pancasila. It sought to control Islamic organizations and create a strong, moderate Islamic clergy devoted to the private practise of Islam and to the nationalist orientation of the state. Using coercive instruments and positive inducements, it adopted policies on the assumption that the state could manipulate religious identities and reduce religiously oriented demands.

In the last few years of the regime, conflict intensified along religious lines. At first, tensions were revealed through growing worries about the New Order's apparent shift to Islam, through the creation of the Indonesian Association of Muslim Intellectuals (ICMI) and the removal of Christians from high-ranking positions in the armed forces and the cabinet. Subsequently, these tensions erupted into sporadic riots throughout Java and other areas. Finally, Muslim–Christian relations deteriorated further and led to open and violent conflict, especially in Maluku.

Violence between Christians and Muslims revealed a failure of the New Order to de-politicize religious identity and replace it with strong attachment to its definition of the Indonesian nation. Unity required that religious groups uphold the values of Pancasila, the core of the nationalist ideology. "Belief in one God" was its most consequential principle that differentiated Indonesia from a secular state but which avoided an explicit promotion of Islam. Other policies were designed to repress demands for an Islamic state, eliminate Islam as a basis of political organization, co-opt Islamic leaders, and shape a generation of scholars that would promote the New Order's vision of a modern Indonesian society. Violence between religious groups showed that the New Order was not able to reach its objectives.

The following two chapters demonstrate why religious relations became conflictual. In the years following its accession to power, the New Order government laid the basis of anti-communist policies and measures to curb the power of Islamic organizations. It then further tightened its control over these organizations by eliminating their ability to participate in politics, forcing their loyalty to Pancasila, and co-opting leaders to promote its objectives. These years also saw the consolidation of the alliance between nationalist Muslims and Christians. Tensions in this alliance appeared toward the end of Suharto's rule. In the 1990s, when Suharto turned to Islam to bolster his support, this change of direction also revealed the depth of the unintended consequences of his policies. An increase in religiosity had reaffirmed religious identities, especially among Muslims who sought in Islam a new basis to challenge the regime. The tensions broke out into sporadic rioting and violent conflict in the late 1990s, at the beginning of the third critical juncture.

The New Order's management of religion

From its inception, the New Order used coercive methods to foster religiosity. In its campaign to suppress the supporters of the Indonesian Communist Party (PKI), it stipulated adherence to a world religion. Indonesians without a clearly identified religion were suspected of espousing communist ideology. As a result, every Indonesian citizen was required to carry personal identification cards indicating their religion, while previous supporters of the PKI were also identified as such.

Thousands of people who were ex-supporters or who had abandoned religious practise fled to one of the officially recognized religions: Catholicism, Protestant Christianity, Hinduism, Buddhism, or Islam.[2] There was a spectacular revival of all religions in the rush to avoid being identified as an atheist and, by implication, a communist. Christian conversions were highest, with estimates reaching in the thousands or even hundreds of thousands.[3] Many adherents to religions not officially recognized by the government chose conversion as a refuge from potential accusations, discrimination, and imprisonment. Small communities following animist beliefs converted to officially recognized religions.[4] Many Chinese in Java and the Outer Islands converted to Christianity as Confucianism was excluded from the state's list of world religions and many were suspected of being communists.[5]

Many Muslims also converted to Christianity. Thousands of *abangan* Javanese,[6] who were nominally Muslim but whose beliefs included elements of Hinduism and Javanese mysticism, were either ex-communists or feared such identification. Some chose Christianity instead of turning to a stricter practise of Islam because they found Christian religions to be less constraining. Many others deplored the apparent fanaticism of Muslims who participated in the massacres of communists. They preferred Christianity, whose adherents had not participated in the purge and which appeared to be more tolerant.[7]

These policies had the effect of strengthening religion as a political category. Not only did Indonesians convert to avoid being labeled as communist, they also increased their regular practise of religion for the same reasons. Religiosity became an expression of anti-communism.

The accession to power of the New Order was accompanied by a brief revival of Islamic politics. The nationalist and *abangan* military rulers had counted on the support of Muslim groups in their struggle against the PKI. In many areas of Indonesia, *santri* Muslims from Nahdlatul Ulama and Muhammadiyah – the country's two largest Muslim organizations – had participated in the communist purge.[8] In Java, a *fatwa*[9] of the Muhammadiyah had declared the extermination of communists a religious duty. As B. J. Boland has argued: "Whatever the proper explanation may be of the events of September 30th, 1965 and thereafter, to the Muslim way of thinking it was a 'holy war' against atheistic communism, the archenemy of religion." After Sukarno's suppression of Masyumi in 1960, Muslim politicians and Islamic organizations hoped that their support for the New Order would allow more freedom to reorganize and revive Masyumi.[10] They thought that the New Order would begin a new, positive relationship between Islam and the state.

Yet, the consistency and unity of Islamic demands should not be overstated. In addition to divisions between *abangan* and *santri*, Muslims were also divided along traditionalist and modernist lines. The former followed a long-established Islamic practise that revolved around education in rural Islamic schools. A large proportion of these Muslims were based in East Java and were represented by the Nahdlatul Ulama (NU). Modernist Muslims adhered to a relatively newer current within Islam that was influenced by the Middle East. This group was represented by the largely urban-based Muhammadiyah.

Despite the diversity of Islamic orientations, the New Order applied restrictive policies in fear of an Islamic revival. The NU and traditionalists were seen as more moderate than modernists, who were more supportive of an Islamic state. Nevertheless, the regime minimized these differences and curtailed all political organizations with a basis in Islam.[11]

Through manipulation, co-optation, and repression, the New Order virtually disabled Islamic organizations. It maintained the ban on Masyumi and prevented its former leaders from leading a reinvented version of the party, Parmusi (Muslim Party of Indonesia), created in 1968.[12] By 1973, the government required all political parties to amalgamate under the Development Unity Party (PPP) or the Democratic Party of Indonesia (PDI). Parmusi, NU, and other Islamic parties were merged under the PPP, which was prevented from adopting a name referring to Islam. Its creation further weakened Islamic politics by forcing organizations with different objectives under the same umbrella.

Even the powerful NU was not spared. It had survived the New Order's first crackdown and emerged as a serious challenger to the government in the 1971 elections. It maintained the 18% share of the vote it had gained in the 1955 elections, despite widespread intimidation and fraud.[13] "No other politically organized group was in a position to form a coherent opposition . . . the traditionalist NU had largely escaped the attention of the authorities before the 1971 election campaign, in good part because of its past record of anti-communism and political pliability".[14] The government weakened the NU, however, by eliminating its long-lasting control of the Ministry of Religion. Instead of naming an

NU leader as minister, in 1972 Suharto appointed Professor Mukti Ali, a modernist Muslim. Furthermore, NU's integration into the PPP seriously diminished its ability to repeat the 1971 electoral challenge.

Modernists were also curtailed. They were already paralyzed by their inability to launch a new political platform through Parmusi and, since modernist organizations were mainly urban based and clearly identifiable, the government could control them more easily than the traditionalists who were organized around informal networks.[15] Measures were also taken to train a new generation of scholars that would be more supportive of the New Order's orientation. For example, the government began to encourage the training of modernist Muslims at McGill University in Canada to provide a counter-balance to modernists seeking higher education in the Middle East, which it viewed as fomenting potentially radical ideas.

Bureaucratic means were used to channel and control Islamic demands. The Ministry of Religion played an increasingly central role in managing religious affairs, from educational issues to coordination of the annual pilgrimage to Mecca. New institutions were created to attract Muslim scholars supportive of the state. In 1975, consultative councils were organized at all levels of government and headed by a National Council of Ulama (MUI). State Institutes for Islam (IAIN) were also established to offer modern qualifications to religious teachers.[16] With these new institutions, the government formed new *santri* Muslims with greater commitment to the state and its developmentalist project. Many were expected to join Golkar, the government's political vehicle, to complete the political submission of Islam to the state's objectives.

Pancasila provided the ideological justification for containing Islamic politics and controlling religion. It became the ideological counter-weight to Islam. Its first principle, "Belief in one God," but not the Muslim God Allah, had a strong symbolic force to unify the nation, as it transcended religious and ethnic boundaries.[17] Through public speeches, declarations, and preambles to a host of state initiatives in all sectors of society, the New Order state regularly reaffirmed its commitment to Pancasila as a necessary basis to preserving unity.

Instead of encouraging and nurturing support for Pancasila through positive inducements and debate, however, the government used repressive means. It imposed the teaching of Pancasila on the school curriculum and obliged all civil servants to follow courses on Pancasila. In a gesture that was perceived as a clear affront to Muslims, in 1984 it decreed that Pancasila would be the sole ideological basis for all social organizations (including political parties). The already weak PPP was forced to relinquish Islam as its basic ideology and to remove the *Ka'bah*, symbol of the Muslim shrine in Mecca, from its banner. Critics were angry at the possibility that the civil religion of Pancasila might replace Islam as a source of morality and guidance in social and political affairs.[18]

Muslims reached a low point in their relations with the state when tensions over repressive policies turned to violence. On 12 September 1984, soldiers opened fire on a Muslim crowd at Tanjung Priok, Jakarta's port area. Large assemblies had been led by Muslim leaders who denounced the regime's anti-Muslim stance. In one incident, two security officers were assaulted after they entered a prayer house without respecting the required decorum. Several people were arrested in the following brawl, including the leader of the prayer house. When an angry crowd marched on the army post where the men were detained and demanded their release, soldiers opened fire. Estimates of the number of people killed range from eighteen to hundreds. The incident subsequently intensified the resentment by Muslims who felt that the regime excluded and repressed them.[19]

The Tanjung Priok affair was dismissed by New Order officials as an attempt by a small group of fanatics and criminals to create havoc in Jakarta. In the following months, several bombs exploded in various areas across Java. Again, the regime accused Islamists of seeking to create instability through fanatical acts. The marginalization of these events by the New Order government showed its confidence that Islamic politics had been curtailed and eliminated from the mainstream.

Through a gradual process of bureaucratization, repression, and ideology, therefore, the New Order government sought to gain increasing control over Islam. As Ruth McVey concluded: "Indonesia's military rulers have not been kind to the spokesmen for Islam, however much they called on the religion's forces during their seizure of power in 1965–66." The regime limited political expression and even attacked the fundamental institutions of Islam in Indonesia.[20] It removed an Islamic agenda from politics, but the ensuing political stability depended on a tightly knit set of state instruments to contain Islamic groups rather than on a conviction of the virtues of policies.

The policies were primarily aimed at containing Islamic forces but they also affected Christians. Anti-communist policies led to greater religiosity among them and a surge in conversions. The curtailment of political parties forced the Catholic and Protestant parties to merge with the Nationalist Party of Indonesia and form the Democratic Party of Indonesia (PDI) in 1975. The churches also had to adopt Pancasila as the basis of their organization. Since the churches were less politicized and less potentially threatening than Islamic organizations, the government did not attempt to create alternative vehicles for co-opting Christians but their leaders were urged to join Golkar.

State policies, overall, contributed to a strengthening of religious identities and to the rise of tensions between Muslims and Christians. The New Order responded with measures designed to prevent conflict. Yet, it became increasingly clear that these same policies reinforced religious divisions and heightened the stakes in obtaining access to state resources to promote or protect one's particular religious group. Every step to promote Islam or Christian religions was being interpreted by the other group as a threat.

As early as 1967, outbreaks of violence occurred. In October, riots erupted in Makassar after reports that a Christian teacher had insulted Islam during group discussions in his home. Underlying this violent response, Muslims were most angry that Christians had constructed a large church in front of the central mosque, especially since few Christians lived in that area. Furthermore, they resented the growing number of conversions to Christianity and of Christian public activities.[21]

Proselytization had become a general source of friction. In the aftermath of the anti-communist campaign, there had already been massive conversions to Christianity as the churches gained new converts among ex-communist supporters, fearful Javanese *abangan*, and formerly Confucian Chinese. Christians proselytized through their school system, distributed religious information, and were conspicuously building new churches. The problem was exacerbated by the stronger missionary activities of "new" sects and faiths, reinforced by foreign missionaries.[22]

Muslims perceived Christian proselytization as a threat to Islam. They also resented the building of places of worship in areas with large numbers of Muslims. In 1967, a conflict erupted over the construction of a small Methodist church in Melaboh, West Aceh. In early 1969, a Protestant church was destroyed in one of Jakarta's new suburbs by crowds angered by the presence of the building in a predominantly Muslim area. Similar incidents subsequently occurred in Jatibarang (West Java) and Purwodadi (Central Java).[23]

Reflecting these growing tensions, the government organized interreligious consultations in November 1967. The minister of religion, who chaired the meeting, called for tolerance and respect between the two communities. Muslims were especially critical of Christian attitudes and activities. Ahmad Dahlan, then the leader of Muhammadiyah, fiercely accused both Protestant and Catholic missions of aiming to wipe out Islam in Indonesia. The government asked both Christians and Muslims to renounce proselytization targeted at other universal religions. While Muslims accepted this government limitation, the Protestant and Catholic churches refused to support a statement that would limit their missionary activities. The matter was left unresolved.[24]

During the following decades, the government intensified its control of religion. After failing to obtain self-restraint through dialogue, it adopted several decrees to circumscribe religious activities that could potentially lead to inter-religious conflicts. A joint instruction from the ministers of religion and of internal affairs in September 1969 required that a permit be obtained from the governor of a province for the construction of any new religious building. It further specified that places of worship could not be built in a community of another faith and that no private houses could be used as substitutes. In 1978, the minister of religion issued two decrees that further restricted religious propagation. Decree no. 70 imposed the proposal arising from the 1967 inter-religious dialogue. The propagation of religion could not be directed toward people who already adhered to one of the officially recognized religions, whether through gifts or other disbursements, reading materials, or house visits. Decree no. 77 restricted proselytizing by foreign missionaries in Indonesia.[25]

Reactions varied. Muslims were generally content with the new decrees as they responded to their main concerns. Christians were most angered by the new restrictions. As a minority, they would find it difficult to build new places of worship in communities with large numbers of Muslims and relatively fewer Christians.[26] Furthermore, restrictions on foreign missionaries mainly affected Christians, who received much support from abroad. Paul Webb notes that, whereas Christians had chosen not to protest against the communist purges because of their minority situation and the fear of Muslim reactions, "they were less silent in 1978 when the Minister of Religion brought down restrictions on proselytizing," which significantly curtailed one of their main activities.[27] The decrees contributed to a lessening of tensions between the two religious communities but Christians felt disadvantaged.

In addition to restrictive measures, the government sought to manage tensions through dialogue between religious leaders. In 1980, it institutionalized the process begun with the 1967 consultations by creating an inter-religious council (*Wadah musyawarah antar umat beragama*), under the auspices of the Ministry of Religion. In 1981, the body dealt with its first public case. A debate had arisen over Islamic participation in Christmas celebrations, after the MUI had issued a prohibition. The minister of religion demanded that the prohibition be revoked because it threatened religious harmony. The issue drew much attention when the chairman of the MUI resigned in protest against the minister's demands. The council played a crucial role in resolving the ensuing tensions between the religious communities. In subsequent decades, it met several times to defuse or resolve conflicts. Inter-religious meetings were also organized in localities where agreements were reached on issues such as the building of places of worship, propagation of religion, mixed marriages, and rules for the conduct of funerals.[28]

In parallel to this strategy, Suharto restricted public discussion of religious and ethnic issues. He limited the reporting of events of a religious or ethnic character. Although governmental authorities varied the intensity of this censorship over time, editors were always aware of the government's power to withdraw publishing licenses at any time, if desired. It was commonplace for newspapers, and radio and television stations, to receive phone calls from the Ministry of Information to remind them to be "responsible" in the reporting of events involving religious or ethnic conflicts. SARA became the acronym that referred to ethnic, religious, racial, and tribal issues that should not be publicly discussed. The strength of this censorship, and related elite management to diffuse conflict, gave the impression to the broader public that Indonesia lived by its ideal of religious harmony.

The New Order government managed religious issues primarily by using restrictive instruments and by engaging religious elites. It was never able to co-opt the leadership of the main religious organizations, such as Nahdlatul Ulama or Muhammadiyah, or the leaders of Protestant and Catholic churches. These organizations maintained their independence. Yet, the regime often tried to attract some leaders by offering paid government positions, either through their adherence to the MUI, for example, or through Golkar. It also set limits to the autonomy of religious organizations through bureaucratic and repressive measures. It provided some controlled platforms for dialogue, discussion, and the expression of grievances. Religious organizations were reminded of the need to adhere to the principles of Pancasila to safeguard national unity and were periodically warned about the consequences of actions deemed to threaten it.

Representation in the New Order's institutions

Once constrained by New Order policies, religious groups sought new channels to protect their interests. With the tightening of the authoritarian grip, political expression through political parties and legislative representation was less relevant. Instead, various groups paid greater attention to representation in the cabinet and the armed forces.

Religious groups played an ambiguous role in the cabinet and in the top positions of the armed forces. To a large extent, Suharto chose individuals for their skills or loyalty. Army leaders were most often selected on the basis of their achievements in military campaigns and past relationships to Suharto. Yet, cabinet ministers or leaders of ABRI (Armed Forces of the Republic of Indonesia) were occasionally approached by members of their ethnic or religious groups because of their access to the president and the ruling circles. Even though they could barely be seen as representing the interests of their regions or ethno-religious groups, their presence in cabinet or in the top levels of ABRI was valued by their respective groups, if only because of possible clientelistic access to the center and possible protection.

For several years, Christians were disproportionately represented in these institutions. Suharto strongly distrusted Islamic groups. Before the 1977 elections, he reportedly summoned Frans Seda and Kasimo, two former leaders of the Catholic party, and stated upon their arrival at the meeting: "Our common enemy is Islam!"[29] Suharto was an *abangan* Javanese, nominally Muslim but highly influenced by mystical and Hinduist Javanese beliefs. Most of the top core of the armed forces were also *abangan* and generally suspicious of Islamic groups. The Christians within and outside of the military shared the suspicions of the *abangan* Javanese officers.

A small group of *abangan* officers, with close associations to a few Christians, was most influential in creating the New Order's political structures and policies. Ali Murtopo, Yoga Sugama, and Sudjono Humardhani were three key advisors in the core group that had closest access to Suharto. They were closer and more influential than any ministers in the cabinet. Murtopo headed a special operations group (Opsus), while Sugama was the head of Bakin, the state intelligence agency. Murtopo and Humardhani created a think-tank in 1971, the Centre for Strategic and International Studies, which provided much of the intellectual backbone for their policies. The CSIS was constituted mainly of Roman Catholic Chinese intellectuals. They were instrumental in devising some of the New Order's core political strategies to increase its dominance over Indonesian society, such as Murtopo's "floating mass" concept, which led to the de-politicization of political parties, and the strengthening of Golkar as the government's electoral machine.[30]

Christian military officers also played key roles. The most influential was Sudomo, who was the army chief of staff and then commander of the Kopkamtib (Operations Command for the Restoration of Security and Order). He remained a close advisor and cabinet member until the late 1990s.[31] Benny Murdani, a Javanese Catholic intelligence officer and assistant to Murtopo, later became one of the most powerful armed forces commanders that Indonesia ever had. This was due in part to his past experience and his personal links to all of the organizations constituting the New Order's powerful intelligence and internal security apparatus. Other Christian generals also rose to top positions in the armed forces, such as the first head of Kopkamtib under Suharto and then later deputy commander of the army, Maraden Panggabean. He later became defense minister.

Successive cabinets saw several key positions held by Christians. Johannes Sumarlin and Radius Prawiro, for example, were key technocrats who were responsible for managing Indonesia's economy. Former top commanding officers in the armed forces who joined the cabinet included Panggabean, Murdani, and Sudomo.

The decade of the 1970s was marked by the establishment and strengthening of the New Order's instruments of political control, tainted by Christian–*abangan* dominance. Muslim groups were increasingly marginalized and paralyzed. By the 1977 elections, they had become severely weakened as all Muslim parties were forced under the banner of the PPP. Dissatisfied with the weakening of political parties through forced amalgamation, Murtopo also used covert operations to discredit Muslim parties. Faced with the possibility that Golkar would gain less than 50% of the vote in the 1977 elections, he allegedly thought it was necessary to create an "issue." *Agents provocateurs* created disturbances, suggesting a threat to the state from a fanatical Islamic group called the "Komando Jihad." As a result, the Kopkamtib could arrest potentially disturbing Islamic leaders and remind Islamic groups of the armed forces' position.[32] Muslim political activity was severely curtailed therefore by the state's security apparatus.

In the 1980s, Christian–*abangan* dominance was sustained. Murdani was named armed forces commander in 1983 and proceeded to build a power base that was unprecedented among former commanders. Many of his closest allies were *abangan* Javanese and Christian officers. In the cabinet, the technocrats were provided with even more power, as dwindling oil revenues in the 1980s led to a new economic strategy based on deregulation, liberalization, and diversification of export production. Among these technocrats, Christians continued to enjoy a favorable position, with the reappointments of Prawiro and Sumarlin. Many other cabinet positions were held by former military officers of the *abangan*–Christian group.

The first twenty-five years of the New Order regime showed a remarkable ability to use Pancasila and the instruments of state political control to advance a quasi-secular vision of the Indonesian nation. The New Order had affirmed its commitment to development and order, instead of a more open polity with the free expression of different political ideas. After crushing the communist threat, challenges to the New Order's authority were depicted as threats to national unity and to the national ideology of Pancasila. For Suharto and his collaborators, Islam represented the largest threat, while there were few signs of any ability of the PKI to re-emerge. SARA issues had to be censored and contained so as to preserve unity and stability. Because this careful attempt to equate Indonesian nationalism with the New Order's interpretations of Pancasila and goals of national unity produced a remarkable degree of political stability, it became assumed that all major groups in Indonesia had accepted this state of affairs.

The Islamization of the New Order

The strength of the political system disguised a profound disgruntlement among Muslim groups. There were occasional signs that they were waiting for an opportunity to re-emerge but the New Order machinery appeared sufficiently stable to minimize the importance of this discontent.

This apparent stability in relations between Islamic groups and the state was to change in the early 1990s, with important effects on relations between Christians and Muslims. After two decades of denying Islamic interests a political space to advance their demands, Suharto began to integrate Islamic organizations into the New Order's institutions. He gradually side-lined the *abangan* Javanese and Christians who had long formed the core of the regime's power base, thereby allowing a renewed sense of confidence among Muslims. This change indicated an abrupt modification in the favorable position of religious minorities. Since Christians had relied on political access to Suharto, they had no guarantees that the winds of change would not lead to repression and a loss of the means to protect the interests of their community.

The New Order's policy shift became apparent through a number of actions in the late 1980s and early 1990s. The government allowed students to wear the *jilbab* (Islamic head-dress) in public schools and assisted in the creation of an Islamic bank. With close family members and associates, Suharto performed the holy pilgrimage to Mecca in 1991. By the 1992 election and the nomination of the 1993 cabinet, the "greening"[33] of the New Order had taken place.

Most importantly, Suharto supported the creation of the Indonesian Association of Muslim Intellectuals (ICMI) that marked a departure from the New Order's previous policy of denying to Muslims potential political platforms. Portrayed as an initiative by students in East Java to arrange a conference of Muslim intellectuals, ICMI was in fact the outgrowth of several years of activism by these intellectuals seeking to organize themselves collectively. Previous attempts had failed to obtain the required permission from the government.

By some accounts, ICMI appeared to be a ploy by the Suharto government to co-opt Muslim groups. Indeed, many of its founding members and subsequent adherents were government officials. The choice of a protégé of Suharto, B. J. Habibie, as ICMI's head not only provided a clear stamp of presidential approval but also opened ICMI to accusations of manipulation and co-optation by New Order leaders. Habibie had very few credentials as a Muslim leader and had never before been associated with an Islamic organization. He was better known for his nationalist economic ideas and emphasis on developing indigenous technology. His positions as minister of research and technology, head of the state's Agency for the Assessment and Application of Technology (BPPT), and head of the state aircraft manufacturer IPTN made him a controversial figure in the international financial community and the armed forces because of his strong ideas about economic management, but not because of any involvement in Islamic politics.

This interpretation emphasized the military's growing challenge to Suharto's rule. Murdani, the president's former protégé, was critical of the business activities of Suharto's children and had even reportedly stated that Suharto should consider stepping aside. Suharto responded by promptly removing Murdani from his position as armed forces commander and by proceeding to a gradual removal of Murdani's allies from influential positions in ABRI. This process took several years, as many high-ranking generals were close to Murdani and their sudden removal might have been too disruptive.

It is within this context that Suharto gave his approval to the creation of ICMI. Some observers argued that he sought to use Islamic groups as a counter-balance to the power of the military.[34] This was especially significant since Murdani and his mentor, Ali Murtopo, had built a powerful network of *abangan* Javanese and Catholics within and outside of ABRI. The anti-Muslim policies of the New Order regime had been designed and implemented by this group. Suharto's shift to Islam, therefore, meant not only the removal of the Catholic Murdani but also the displacement of many *abangan* generals, as well as the Catholic and *abangan* civilians that had been associated with the Murtopo–Murdani group, such as the intellectuals from the CSIS.

Others contended that Suharto sought instead to co-opt Islamic groups for electoral purposes. William Liddle, for instance, argued that Suharto still had firm control over the military and did not need to balance its power.[35] In fact, his ability to remove Murdani and his allies showed that Suharto's position had not weakened. Instead, the creation of ICMI and the shift to Islam were means by which he could garner more support for the upcoming election in 1992. Following past practise, he simply gained control over potential rivals to Golkar by attracting them to the government's side. Habibie's leadership of ICMI and the large number of cabinet members who joined certainly reinforced the view that Suharto had a strong hand in the organization.

An alternative explanation for the rise of ICMI focused instead on the gradual Islamization of Indonesian society during the 1970s and 1980s.[36] The strong emphasis on mass education during the Suharto period was accompanied by mandatory religious education, which mainly benefitted the spread of Islam. Islamic institutions expanded in the social and cultural realm and their appeal increased because they provided guidance in understanding the rapidly changing environment. Urban areas and universities became the centers of this religious revival, as shown by the controversial movement in educational institutions that pressured the government to allow women to wear the *jilbab* on campus. One campus movement gained particular importance. The Salman mosque movement began at the Bandung Institute of Technology under the leadership of the well-respected Islamic leader Imaduddin Abdulrachim and rapidly spread to campuses throughout the country. Its activities included a wealth of seminars on religion and development, educational and economic programs, and even the sponsorship of pop bands sympathetic to the Islamic revival. Islamic cultural festivals were organized across the country. There was an explosion of publications that discussed the relevance of Islam to the social, economic, and political changes characterizing Indonesian modernization.[37]

The Islamization of society was accompanied by a change in the political strategies of Islamic leaders. The 1970s saw the rise of a generation of new leaders, many of whom were young, modernist, and educated abroad. Several of them had been student supporters of the New Order in the mid-1960s and had joined the technocratic elite of the government. Prominent among them were Nurcholish Madjid, Dawam Rahardjo, and Djohan Effendi. These modernist leaders were disillusioned with the policies of the 1950s and the ineffectiveness of a confrontational approach in response to the increasing curtailment of Islam. Instead, they advocated a reform of the New Order and the advancement of Islamic interests from within its institutions.[38]

The "*pemikiran baru*" (new thinking) movement, as it came to be called, also moved the locus of Islamic activity from the political to the social realm. By doing so, freedom of discussion and action was increased. New foundations and organizations were created. Leaders such as Amien Rais from Muhammadiyah and Abdurrahman Wahid from Nahdlatul Ulama called for reflection on how Islam could be more participative in the development and modernization of the nation. Much emphasis was placed on forming a generation of Muslims who would be strong in technocratic expertise and modern skills, so they could fully participate in development and in the state.[39]

Even the leaders of Indonesia's largest organization, Nahdlatul Ulama, abandoned the confrontational approach and espoused accommodation. The NU had remained part of the PPP after its amalgamation, while many modernist Muslims of the former Masyumi, or supporters of Muhammadiyah, either remained outside of politics or joined the PPP. Competition between the NU and various factions within the PPP significantly weakened the party. The PPP had pursued a confrontational strategy against the government in the 1978 MPR, when it walked out of the assembly because of a proposal to treat *aliran kepercayaan* (spiritual beliefs) equally with the five officially recognized religions. Shortly thereafter, the government manipulated the selection of a new leader for the PPP to ensure that one of its supporters, Djaelani Naro, would be chosen. Once elected, Naro proceeded to side-line the NU, which was deemed most responsible for the confrontational stance of the PPP. The gradual marginalization of the NU, and especially the sudden drop in its candidates for the PPP in the 1982 elections, greatly angered many NU members. Combined with the growing strength of the "new thinking" group favoring accommodation, this dissatisfaction led to the NU's withdrawal from the PPP and from formal political activity, under the initiative of Abdurrahman Wahid. The latter was subsequently chosen as NU leader in the 1984 Congress.[40]

In subsequent years, the accommodationist strategy included support for Golkar. The NU was the first organization to accept Pancasila as its sole ideology, while stating clearly that Pancasila did not replace religion. In the 1987 elections, many NU members supported Golkar instead of the PPP. After Wahid made some links to Golkar officials during the election campaign, the results showed a drastic decline in support for the PPP in NU dominated areas. The PPP obtained only 11.82% of votes (down from 15.96% in the 1982 elections), while Golkar reached a record 72.99% (from 64.34% in 1982).[41] With the NU gaining closer links to high officials of the New Order, as well as the tacit support for Golkar in the 1987 elections, the government eased its suspicions of the organization. Outside of the NU, other Muslim leaders, including Madjid, also supported Golkar. Along with Wahid and Madjid, many former PPP supporters found themselves representing Golkar in the 1988 MPR session.

By the late 1980s, the fruits of this strategy were apparent. In addition to the rapprochement of the NU and Madjid with the government, there was a growing number of well-trained Muslim intellectuals, technocrats, and professionals that were increasingly present in public institutions and playing stronger leadership roles, such as Amien Rais, Adi Sasono, and Sri Bintang Pamungkas. Also, many less prominent Muslims had joined the ranks of the state administration and even the mid- to upper-ranks of the armed forces.

In this context, the creation of ICMI and other pro-Islamic measures in the early 1990s did not represent such a drastic shift. The government was not anti-Muslim, despite its nurturing of *abangan* Muslims and Christians. It was already supporting Islam through a variety of programs and initiatives to promote religiosity in the private realm as a means of preventing a resurgence of communism. The Ministry of Religion was particularly active in supporting "cultural" activities of Islam and helping to strengthen Islamic practise, especially its intensification of Islamic education through the state's Islamic institutes (IAIN). Most strikingly, the New Order sponsored a construction boom of mosques and other Islamic prayer buildings throughout the three decades of its rule, although this intensified after 1990. One of Suharto's foundations supported the building of new mosques and even the work of Muslim proselytizers in remote areas of Indonesia.[42] From 1988–89 to 1992–93 only, the number of mosques grew from 548,959 to 587,435, while the government sponsored up to 1,000 Muslim proselytizers to transmigration areas, many of which were predominantly Christian.[43] During the New Order period, therefore, the government supported the "cultural" activities of Islam, while curtailing political activity.

ICMI was a result of the growing Islamization of society and the greater accommodation of Islamic leaders. Even though Suharto may have sought to co-opt these leaders through ICMI, he was facing changes in society that forced him in this direction. A continued marginalization of Islamic groups, and relative favoritism of Christians and *abangan*, would have required increasing amounts of societal repression, as the pressures for more political involvement among Muslims had been on the rise. The better-educated Muslim class was growing in numbers and had to be absorbed into the bureaucracy and private sectors. Arguments that the *abangan* and Christians maintained their relative advantage because of better education and more interest in government positions may have been acceptable to Muslims in the early decades after independence, but was difficult to sustain after twenty years of economic development under the New Order regime. Furthermore, the government's own emphasis on religious education and culture to counter communist tendencies contributed to the deepening of religious identities. When Muslim organizations began to adopt more accommodationist strategies and became less threatening to the New Order's rule, there were few arguments left to resist a greater inclusion of Muslims in the regime's institutions and policies favoring the Muslim majority. ICMI offered an institutional means of formalizing the channels between new Muslim intellectuals and the New Order state.

Muslim leaders thereafter enjoyed a strong position within the New Order's institutions. As a result of Suharto's rift with Murdani, the latter's allies in the top levels of the armed forces were replaced with officers known to be *santri* Muslims and closer to Muslim groups, such as Feisal Tanjung and Hartono who would become, respectively, armed forces commander and army commander. Tanjung, Hartono, and also Prabowo Subianto, Suharto's son-in-law, were key officers who played a strong role in the side-lining of Murdani's allies and their replacement with generals more sympathetic to Islamic groups.[44]

During the run-up to the 1992 elections and subsequent MPR meeting, the increasing power of Muslim groups, especially ICMI, became more apparent. The accommodationist strategy of the *pemikiran baru* group had already resulted in the inclusion of prominent Muslim leaders in Golkar. In 1988, for example, Wahid and Madjid had been named as Golkar representatives on the MPR working committee, and many prominent Muslims such as Slamet Effendy, from the NU youth organization, and Usman Hasan, a former activist of the Association of Muslim Students (HMI), gained important positions within Golkar. The CSIS group, associated with Murdani, had seen its role completely eliminated by 1988.[45] In the selection of candidates for the 1992 elections to the DPR and for the MPR meeting of 1993, Suharto rejected eleven candidates for Golkar, all of whom were close to Christians or associated with the CSIS group. Instead, there was a strong representation by all Muslim groups and the nomination of many members with prominent positions in ICMI.

The nomination of new cabinet members in 1993 also favored ICMI members. Suharto surprised the international financial community by removing even the Christian technocrats who had implemented successful economic reforms in previous years. He replaced them with a new generation of Muslim technocrats who were unknown to Indonesia's international creditors. Key cabinet ministers were now Muslims with mostly ICMI connections, such as Habibie, the head of ICMI and still minister of research and technology, Ibrahim Hasan, Akbar Tanjung, Aswar Anas, Ginandjar Kartasasmita, Abdul Latief, and Tarmizi Taher. A few of these ministers, however, were closer to Habibie, since they had held important positions in BPPT. These included Minister of Transportation Maynato Dhanutirto, Minister of Education and Culture Wardiman Djojonegoro, and Minister of Commerce Billy Satrio Joedono. It was not clear whether the new cabinet was mainly a victory for ICMI or whether it had principally bolstered Habibie's power base.[46] Nevertheless, it enshrined the change in the balance of representation in favor of Muslim groups.

The 1993 MPR and the nomination of the new cabinet launched a series of changes throughout the rest of the archipelago. They signaled the attainment of a new status for Muslims in the New Order government and for ICMI in particular. Bureaucrats joined ICMI in large numbers, so that by 1995 its members were the most influential faction within the New Order bureaucracy. Its publications, the daily *Republika* and news magazine *Ummat*, increased their circulation rapidly. ICMI also created the Centre for Information and Development Studies (CIDES), which gained prominence and influence. CIDES was a Muslim research institute designed to counter-balance and emulate the former role of the Catholic-dominated CSIS.[47] Even the Indonesian Islamic Preaching Council (DDII), one of the most conservative Islamic organizations and formerly most critical of the Suharto regime, played an important role in ICMI and began to establish better relations with the government: "Responding to the president's overtures, the DDII and its affiliates slowly reconciled with the regime. The DDII's transformation from a principled if conservative Islamist critic to regime supporter was essentially complete by 1996".[48] The inclusion of Islamic groups in the New Order was rapid and almost a revolutionary change from the first two decades of its rule.

The last decade of Suharto's rule was accompanied by increasingly numerous religious conflicts. Many of these originated in tensions arising from the creation of ICMI and the regime's nurturing of Islam. How far would Islamic organizations seek to change Indonesia if allowed to control the political agenda? For Christians who were displaced from their former position at the core of the regime, this question became a source of worry. The change in the New Order's orientation created an environment in which all political options were reopened. This could signal to Muslims with radical political agendas that they could potentially reach their objectives. It also indicated to Christians that their community could be threatened. The possibility of these extremes and the loss of former means of managing inter-religious relations through New Order repressive instruments laid the basis for the conflicts that erupted in subsequent years.

6   The escalation of religious conflict

The Islamization of the late New Order increased tensions between Christians and Muslims. The trend toward a greater role for Muslims in government, the creation of ICMI, and the simultaneous marginalization of Christians signaled that past practises were gone and a new basis of power was being created. How far would these changes go? For most Muslim groups, Suharto's change of heart was an opportunity to reverse past exclusion. Some still sought to advance an Islamic political agenda. Christians deplored their sudden displacement from core institutions that spelled an end to their protected status. Would their interests be preserved in the future? Would they be subjected to discriminatory practises and repression? The political relevance of religion and its importance for representation in the New Order's institutions solidified group identities and reinforced each group's perception that gains for one meant losses for the other.

Growing uncertainty about the future of the New Order regime added to these factors. Suharto had been re-elected by the People's Consultative Assembly (MPR) for another term but it was widely believed it would be his last. Succession was a central concern because no one knew whether it would lead only to Suharto's replacement or to the dismantlement of New Order institutions. Christians worried that the post-Suharto era might lead to an Islamic state or to majority rule that would exclude them. Muslim groups, especially ICMI, began to distance themselves from Suharto. They espoused a discourse of reform, democratization, and an end to the corruption of the past, but they also called for an elimination of policies benefitting minority groups instead of the Muslim majority. This position raised fears that minorities, especially Christians, would have little say after Suharto's departure.

This uncertainty over succession and institutional change marked the beginning of a critical juncture. It contributed to the heightening of tensions. In this context, groups were preparing for a weakening of the state or an imminent institutional change. As a result, fear of the future, anxieties over relative group status, and a sense of rising opportunities for change increased the potential for violence.

Several additional factors coalesced to create conditions which were ripe for the eruption of riots and, subsequently, larger-scale violence in Ambon and Maluku.[1] Tensions over socio-economic inequalities can explain the destruction of stalls, kiosks, banks, or malls in several of the riots. Grievances against the regime best account for the targeting of government offices. Migratory patterns fueled some of the resentment of local inhabitants against "outsiders" gaining control of local markets.

Where migration disrupted the local balance of numbers between Christians and Muslims, tensions rose. Policies of economic development were accompanied by intentional and unintentional migration throughout the archipelago. Economic inequalities between migrants and local indigenous peoples often fueled conflict, but they appeared to be worse where combined with differences in religious identity.

Throughout the archipelago, Christians and Muslims had lived side-by-side for decades without conflict. Their proportions in most communities had remained fairly static or changed only progressively. Communities prided themselves on maintaining good relations and even helping each other to build places of worship. This was particularly true where a single ethnic group, such as the Ambonese, had members differentiated along religious lines. Among some ethnic groups, such harmonious relations were even institutionalized. In Maluku, "*pela*" is a pact linking Christian and Muslim villages in a spirit of brotherhood designed to prevent inter-religious conflict. While conflicts in many areas arose over the building of churches or mosques, these were isolated events. Except for the period of mass conversion after 1965, there were few disruptions in the balance between Christian and Muslim numbers and few conflicts.

Migration disrupted the balance of representation. Inter-island movement increased dramatically in the 1970s and 1980s. Government-sponsored transmigration from densely populated areas to sparsely populated ones was one source of this changing balance. More importantly, economic development created more employment and business opportunities in several areas that were once less accessible. The means of inter-island transportation also expanded. As a result, many places that had once been relatively isolated and scarcely populated saw significant increases in migrant populations. Given the very large majority of Muslims in Indonesia, these migrants were often Muslim. Problems tended to occur in areas of Eastern Indonesia where some islands had majorities of Christians and relatively small local populations.

There was considerable debate surrounding the effects of the transmigration program. Some scholars imputed to Suharto a deliberate attempt to use transmigration as a tool for national integration through the dilution and assimilation of religious groups.[2] Foreign organizations were most critical of transmigration in Irian Jaya, for example, because they argued that the program aimed at Javanizing the Papuans. Yet, there are some important reasons to be skeptical of such objectives. According to George Aditjondro, it was Christian areas of East Nusa Tenggara that had been identified since 1986 as source areas for migrants to Irian Jaya. Similarly, Muslims from Eastern Indonesia were being sent to mainly Muslim Western Indonesia instead of Irian Jaya.[3] This evidence showed trends contradictory to Javanization or Islamization. Aside from accusations emanating from human rights organizations, the literature on transmigration contains little evidence of political objectives in the program.[4]

Spontaneous and voluntary migration had a much greater impact on ethnic and religious relations.[5] Generally, most studies concur that there were relatively few movements of population other than transmigration until the 1980s, after which there was a dramatic increase in migratory trends. By 1985–90, more than five million people were recorded as in-migrants across the country.

Total numbers of in-migrants were not as significant as the differences in the religious identities of migrant and local populations. Table 2 shows the extent of in-migration, expressed as total number of migrants and percentage relative to local population. In most areas, there was a significant increase in the total number of migrants across the three recorded periods, from 1975–80 to 1985–90. Those areas with the largest numbers of in-migrants expressed as percentages of the local population (West Java, East Kalimantan, Southeast Sulawesi, Central Kalimantan, Bengkulu, Jambi, Riau, Yogyakarta) were not the provinces where ethnic or religious conflicts broke out in the 1990s. Provinces where conflict was already present and which would see the greatest amount of violence, such as East Timor, Irian Jaya, Maluku, and West Kalimantan, had higher than average in-migrants relative to population but not significantly higher than areas with similar averages. Furthermore, West Kalimantan, where violence exploded in the late 1990s between migrant Madurese and local Dayaks, had a low percentage of in-migrants (1.4%) between 1985 and 1990. There was therefore little correlation between the quantity of migration and the later rise of conflict.[6]

In-migration created tensions in areas where migrants had different religious identities and where the balance of religious groups changed. In Irian Jaya, the proportion of Muslims changed rapidly in one decade, from 12% in 1981 to 20% in 1990. In Maluku, where Christians were slightly more numerous than Muslims, in-migration brought the proportion of Muslims to 56.8% by 1990, according to official government statistics.[7]

Table 2 Recent in-migration by province of residence, 1975–90

Province*	1975–80		1980–85		1985–90	
	N	%	N	%	N	%
Aceh	51,205	2.2	37,692	0.8	194,699	1.6
North Sumatra	95,586	1.2	59,600	2.6	107,882	1.0
West Sumatra	93,117	3.1	75,757	4.0	129,049	3.2
Riau	98,652	5.2	91,881	11.8	245,465	7.5
Jambi	107,273	8.8	52,647	–	136,397	6.8
South Sumatra	221,165	5.6	105,064	1.9	212,196	3.4
Bengkulu	66,902	10.2	33,386	–	82,831	7.0
Lampung	507,803	13.0	126,677	2.0	212,298	3.5
Jakarta	766,363	13.6	684,001	14.0	833,029	10.1
West Java	551,960	3.2	560,460	3.5	1,350,596	3.8
Central Java	183,761	0.8	171,473	9.5	384,753	1.3
Yogyakarta	98,856	3.8	112,331	2.7	161,740	5.6
East Java	203,175	0.8	165,731	–	328,607	1.0
Bali	37,254	1.7	23,565	1.9	65,997	2.4
West Nusa Tenggara	26,221	1.0	26,762	–	37,401	1.1
East Nusa Tenggara	25,976	1.0	20,050	19.4	27,107	0.8
East Timor	–	–	13,093	–	26,255	3.5
West Kalimantan	39,380	1.8	19,331	–	43,809	1.4
Central Kalimantan	46,699	6.1	33,328	–	78,791	5.6
South Kalimantan	61,704	3.4	55,752	–	98,330	3.8
East Kalimantan	112,620	10.6	83,976	0.8	194,531	10.4
North Sulawesi	45,498	2.4	14,783	–	34,736	1.4
Central Sulawesi	83,595	7.5	28,067	–	70,034	4.1
South Sulawesi	65,208	1.1	48,453	18.9	119,455	1.7
Southeast Sulawesi	51,014	6.4	69,547	3.9	71,143	5.3
Maluku	46,904	3.8	23,860	2.6	68,701	3.7
Irian Jaya	33,420	3.4	52,771	–	73,776	4.5
Total	**3,721,314**	**2.8**	**2,790,038**	**2.0**	**5,389,608**	**2.9**

*Percentages calculated using the total population of each province.
Source: Ida Bagoes Mantra, "Pola dan Arah Migrasi Penduduk Antarpropinsi di Indonesia Tahun 1990," Populasi 3, no. 2, 1992, p. 55.

Sources of tension between migrants and the local population were often due to economic interests. However numerous they were, migrants across Indonesia were often more competitive than the local population in small trade and the small business sector. They were often perceived as displacing local trading networks. In Irian Jaya, for example, this was the case with migrants from South and Southeast Sulawesi who were targeted more than the Javanese.[8]

Yet, these conflicts were not only motivated by economic factors:

Recent conflicts between migrants and the local populations in the provinces of eastern Indonesia strongly indicate that ethnicity and religion have intermingled with economic and political factors. The indigenous population in eastern Indonesia which can be classified as "Christian-Melanesian" generally has a lower human resource endowment and have "clashed" with "Moslem-Malay" migrants who have relatively higher human resource capacities.[9]

The differentiation along religious and ethnic identities was important in the expression of conflict. While economic motivations may have underlain some tensions, they tended to be stronger if combined with differences in religion.

The destruction of places of worship, as well as the religious polarization between group victims and perpetrators of the violence, however, cannot be explained by socio-economic inequalities or migration. The Muslim–Christian dimension of many of these conflicts confirms that institutional factors enhanced religious identity. It became the vehicle for the violent expression of various grievances filtered through the political context of tense religious relations.

When riots unfolded throughout the late 1990s, it became increasingly evident that they were related to each other. In every instance, local factors produced tense relations between Christians and Muslims. Yet, the explanation for violence could not be reduced to these local factors. After thirty years of relative peace between the two groups, the wave of religious riots that rocked Indonesia in the late 1990s was not a coincidence. With the dramatic increase in the number of instances of violence and their scale, factors relating these events to each were more important in explaining the changing political context that laid the basis for the conflict. In all of the following cases of riots and violence between Christians and Muslims, there was clear evidence of the prior heightening of tensions as a result of the Islamization of the New Order's institutions and its effect on religious relations.

The riots

The first major set of riots occurred in East Timor, pitting the Catholic East Timorese against Muslim merchants from South Sulawesi (Bugis). In November 1994, a massive uprising in Dili, East Timor's capital, followed the stabbing of a Timorese man by a Bugis trader. The riot led to the burning of several Bugis houses in the neighborhood. On 1 January

1995, a Timorese was stabbed by a drunken Bugis youth in a street incident in the town of Baucau. During the riots that followed, ninety-five shops and kiosks mostly owned by Bugis traders were burned down and five people were killed.[10] In the same town, another violent outburst came after unconfirmed reports that two Timorese youths had been killed by an angry Javanese woman trader. Rioters burned twenty shops and several people were injured.[11]

The most dramatic incident occurred between 7 and 12 September 1995. Riots broke out in Dili and other towns after reports that a man at the Maliana prison had made statements that were insulting to Catholics. After the governor ignored local complaints about the case, a demonstration was organized in protest but it soon turned into a riot. During the following days, youths burned kiosks and markets controlled by Bugis in Maliana, Viqueque, Dili, Liquica, Maubisse, and Suai. Two mosques were also destroyed. As a result of these riots, thousands of Bugis, Javanese, and Sumatran traders, civil servants, and other residents fled the territory in fear of further violence.[12]

In some respects, the tension might have been higher in East Timor than elsewhere, given the high levels of state repression endured by the Timorese since the Indonesian state forcibly annexed the territory in 1975. After the Dili massacre of 1991, the Timorese were subjected to more intense efforts by the government to erase separatist tendencies and accelerate integration. Reports of abuse by the Indonesian armed forces increased and the Timorese lived in a climate of continuous fear.

Yet, these incidents suggest a separate conflict. They occurred at a time when similar events began to occur in other locations across Indonesia. Their uniqueness was surpassed by the commonalities linking these riots to other instances of Muslim–Christian violence.

Muslim migration to the area could be perceived as an attempt to assimilate the Timorese and turn them into a minority in their land. The government's transmigration program was often seen in this light. More importantly, large numbers from South Sulawesi and other Muslim regions migrated to East Timor. Aditjondro estimated that these migrants represented ten times the number of officially sponsored migrants.[13] While important to a degree, migration could not explain the timing and nature of these particular events.

Economic disparities between migrants and Timorese were also part of the explanation. Bugis migrants had gained control over local trade in East Timor, while other Muslim migrants often came as civil servants. Young Timorese were often denied these positions and faced few job opportunities. As early as 1989, tensions had already become apparent. A Gadjah Mada University study on East Timor noted that "within indigenous East Timorese circles a feeling of hatred has arisen towards the Makassarese and Bugis [from Sulawesi]. They are seen as a new group of extortionists who stand in the way of their economic advancement".[14] Furthermore, in the aftermath of the demonstrations in Dili that led to the Santa Cruz massacre, Bishop Belo had argued that these demonstrations had been partly a result of the lack of job opportunities for educated Timorese: "All the teachers are from outside, all the civil servants are from outside. Go into any government office and all the employees are from outside. For the simplest jobs in road building, they bring in people from outside. And these workers bring their children and their brothers and sisters".[15] Timorese youths were frustrated at the economic progress of migrants and the sense of discrimination in obtaining jobs. This was certainly a dimension of the conflict.

There are reasons to doubt, however, that the riots were only an outgrowth of economic disparities. They occurred in the mid-1990s, but these tensions had existed for several years without leading to open conflict. Furthermore, prior to the 1990s, these types of disparities between migrants and local communities were common across the archipelago, yet they produced violence in only a few instances. More importantly, the Timorese had never been in control of local trade. Under the Portuguese, the Chinese were dominant and were gradually replaced by the Bugis.[16]

The timing of these riots and their nature suggest that they reflected rising tensions between Muslims and Christians in general, while they took on particular significance in the context of East Timor's unique political situation. Riots in Flores during the same year were quite similar to those in East Timor. The island of Flores is predominantly Catholic. A small minority of Florinese Muslims and Muslim migrants from Sulawesi were living peacefully with their Christian neighbors. As in East Timor, many new spontaneous migrants arrived in the late 1980s and early 1990s, especially from West Sumatra and from Java. Violent clashes involved mainly this latter group of migrants and the local Florinese.

The riots were linked to a number of incidents of host desecration in Flores and other Catholic areas of East Nusa Tenggara (NTT). During the 1980s and 1990s, there were reportedly over 45 cases of host desecration across the province, with a peak of 25 cases between 1990 and 1995. Typically, a recent migrant of unknown religious affiliation would attend a mass at a local Catholic church. At communion, he would either spit out, trample or otherwise desecrate the host, thereby insulting and angering the community. The desecrator was usually Protestant or Muslim, and a recent migrant from Sumatra, Java, or other part of NTT. Desecrators were often beaten or killed by a crowd, or arrested and prosecuted.[17]

In a few cases, serious rioting erupted. The offices of the Ende court were burned down by an angry crowd on 25 April 1994 after a judge sentenced a man to only one year in prison for having desecrated the host in Ende on 26 December 1993. Two days of rioting followed another sentence of a desecrator in Maumere on 28–29 April 1995. A judge sentenced Didi Warsito to three and a half years in prison for host desecration at a local Catholic church on 25 December 1994. The crowd was angered that the accused was not given a longer sentence. After stoning the courthouse, rioters attacked the local police station and shops owned by Javanese and Sumatran (Padang) migrants. Some youths controlled the town for two days as they blocked the access roads with trees to delay the arrival of troops. In Larantuka, a man was beaten to death after desecrating the host during mass at the cathedral on 11 June 1995. Rioters then destroyed at least nineteen kiosks owned by Muslim migrants.[18] These cases far surpassed the violence of prior incidents related to host desecrations, as rioting crowds were much larger and the array of associated destruction much wider.

The anger unleashed on Muslim migrants' property is most significant, especially the differentiation made between recent and old Muslim migrants and between Christian and Muslim migrants. There had been much frustration at the opportunities for these migrants to establish businesses in Flores when the local population did not have sufficient capital to do so. A transformation of the local economy had occurred quite rapidly with the arrival of these new migrants and they were specifically targeted in the riots, while local Makassarese or Florinese Muslims were spared.[19] The Makassarese had emigrated to Flores long before, when links between Sulawesi and NTT were driven by the trade in copra. While these links had been severed under the New Order, many Makassarese remained in Flores.[20] The Chinese, who also own kiosks and shops, were also spared. According to some interpretations, rioters did not target the Chinese because they were Christian.[21]

Furthermore, recent migrants and civil servants were frequently accused of transgressing local traditions. They often irritated the Florinese by marrying local women, who were subsequently obliged to convert to Islam. They also allegedly contravened local customs related to bridal wealth.[22]

Resentment against recent migrants was compounded by the accelerating inflow of Javanese or Balinese civil servants, as unemployment among the youths was widespread. With a greater penetration of the state during the 1970s and 1980s, many Javanese, Balinese, and other non-Florinese were sent to fill positions in Flores' expanding local bureaucracy. Because many of these positions were created in branches of national departments, they were often staffed by outsiders: "Before, if a position was vacant . . . one could suggest people [from here] to fill it. Now, even if we suggest, the centre finally determines and usually chooses someone who is from the centre [Jakarta or Java]".[23] The exclusion of local Florinese from these positions was worsened by the local perception of systematic discrimination. For example, they had difficulty accessing training programs for the civil service or the armed forces. Local interpretations blamed the strong tradition of "tribalism" (*sukuism*) in Indonesia, by which most groups favor their own ethnic group when they control positions in government institutions. The Florinese had a relatively weak network to tap and therefore lost out to outsiders from Java and Bali.[24]

Changes in local market control, unemployment, and discriminatory practises suggest a socio-economic explanation of the riots. Frustrations had been building up with the rapid increase in new migration. Clientelistic practises for access to state positions worked to the disadvantage of the local Florinese. Violence spread partly because of these factors.

This line of explanation, however, cannot explain certain aspects of the riots. Why, for instance, were only Muslims targeted while the Chinese were spared? For a long time, the Chinese had been a primary source of resentment across the archipelago for their control of local trade. Furthermore, why had the intensity of resentment occurred at that particular period of time and in Flores specifically? The explosion of violence at the same time as a similar event in East Timor, also involving Christians against Muslims, was not coincidental. Religious differentiation was important, especially in the mid-1990s.

The eroding legitimacy of the Suharto government as well as growing tensions between Muslims and Christians seem to have fueled much of the resentment. Reflecting on the causes of violence, the Catholic Church noted local suspicions of the police and security forces that were seen as over-stepping the law, government manipulation and failure to meet its promises, and corruption alongside socio-economic problems of unemployment and local impoverishment.[25] The attack on the court and the local police station in the Maumere riots, as well as the burning of a judge's house in the Ende incident, were signs of local frustrations against the system of order imposed from Jakarta. During the riots, the crowds also shouted political slogans and voiced their dissatisfaction against political authorities.[26]

The perceived attack on religion triggered a violent response by local people. They resented the relatively light sentence given to someone who had insulted their religion. It was less a question of religious doctrine, however, than of injustice imposed by the government in the only realm that was seen as free and relatively untouchable by government authorities: religion.

There was no fanaticism involved [in the riots]. It's not the host itself as body of Christ which made them angry, it was the fact that they were hurt in their self-respect [*harga diri*]. People here suffer socio-economically, they are poor and have no freedom left. They live in an atmosphere of governmental propaganda and pressure [*paksaan*], and their only area of self-respect left is their religion.[27]

By the early 1990s, religion was strengthening partly as a response to political repression.

For a long time, Flores was able to shield itself from the state's control. Under Dutch colonialism, the strength of the Catholic Church was enormous. Catholic missionaries expanded the Church's activities in the social realm, including health and education.[28] The Old Order government allowed the Church to retain its predominance, as President Sukarno had spent a long sojourn in Ende (Flores) and had good relations with the Catholic Church.[29]

Under Suharto, the relationship remained very good in spite of increasing competition in social programs and education. As it penetrated all regions of Indonesia, the state took control over education, health, and other areas formerly managed by the Church.[30] Nevertheless, the Church still represented the main source of influence on the island and this dominance was acknowledged by the government. Before appointing *bupati* [district heads] in Flores, for example, it always sought the approval of the Bishop of Ende.[31] Good relations in Flores reflected those at the national level where Catholics played a large role as advisors and key actors in the New Order state until the late 1980s.

In the 1990s, however, Florinese Catholics perceived a change: "Suharto is now different than before. There are no Catholics in influential positions in the center . . . [and] there has been an erosion of the relationship between Catholics and Islam".[32] As a result, the relationship between the government and the Church on Flores also suffered: "[In the early 1990s] almost all the *bupati's* staff were Muslim, so it was difficult to serve the interests of Catholics." The *bupati* authorized, for example, the construction of a mosque in Maumere in an area surrounded by Catholics, triggering demonstrations by students and seminarians. His actions transgressed rules on the construction of places of worship that were designed to maintain stable religious relations. The influential St Paulus seminary was pressured to transfer authority over its education activities from the Department of Education to the Department of Religion. Given that the latter department had always been led by a Muslim and was then controlled by ICMI, it raised suspicions among Catholics in Flores that ICMI was trying to diminish the influence of the Catholic Church. The police and the military also had tense relations with the local church, in part because their commanders were Javanese Muslims.[33]

Some religious leaders in Flores were concerned about the consequences of diminishing Catholic representation at the center. As a result of trends toward Islamization and policies hurting the interests of Christians, Frans Seda, a former minister in both the Sukarno and Suharto cabinets, reportedly reminded Suharto of Sukarno's pledge, at the time of the creation of the Republic, that the new state would be based on government and not on religion.[34] Although some of these facts may not be quite accurate, they reflected a local discourse expressing a growing distress at the directions of the Indonesian polity.

While riots in East Timor and in Flores were seen as marginal incidents in remote parts of Indonesia, similar outbreaks in Java drew more attention. The riots in Situbondo and Tasikmalaya carried religious overtones. They triggered a national debate on questions of ethnic and religious relations, as the violence was no longer considered marginal.

The first incident that caught national attention occurred in Surabaya, East Java. On 9 June 1996 hundreds of rioters descended onto the streets and burned down churches while services were being held. Ten churches were damaged, including those of the Batak Protestant, Pentecostal, and Bethel churches. This unprecedented event created sufficient worry among Protestant Christians that they launched a public and official protest against the rising incidence of attacks on their churches. Such attacks had escalated in the preceding years but had not until then occurred on such a large scale.

A few months later, riots in Situbondo increased tensions between Christians and Muslims even further. On 10 October 1996, riots began after a judge sentenced a Muslim man, Saleh, to five years in prison for "insulting and disgracing Islam." Saleh had reportedly insulted Allah as well as a respected local Ulama, KH As'ad Syamsul Arifin. After his arrest, the court proceedings attracted a large crowd. By the day of sentencing, the court was already well guarded by the local military command because of the sensitivity of the case. The crowd was angered by the apparently light sentence pronounced against Saleh, even though the judge had applied the maximum penalty. Rioters first attacked the courthouse and attempted to seize Saleh. According to unconfirmed reports, someone in the crowd shouted that he was hiding in a nearby church. After setting fire to the church, rioters marched through the streets and damaged several buildings. Five people were killed, and twenty churches were burned down in Situbondo and surrounding areas. Restaurants, shops, a few Christian schools, a movie theatre, and a billiard room were also damaged or destroyed.[35]

The Tasikmalaya riot was similarly unrelated to its triggering incident. In early December 1996, a *santri* (Muslim student), Rizal, was caught stealing at a local *pesantren* (Muslim boarding school) in Tasikmalaya, West Java. He was punished by two older students and brought to Ustadz Mahmud, one of the teachers at the school. The next day, Rizal's father, a local policeman, was invited to the school to discuss the theft. On the subsequent day, however, the two older students were summoned to the police station for questioning. When they did so, accompanied by Ustadz Mahmud and another teacher, Ustadz Ate, the latter was allowed to leave while the other three were interrogated. Rizal's father beat them and a fight broke out. Ustadz Mahmud was hospitalized. On 24 December, the police came to apologize but student groups and other organizations informed the police that a demonstration of 300–400 *santris* would take place that Friday outside the main mosque.[36]

On 26 December, the day of the riot, about 3,000 *santris* gathered in front of the mosque. A youth stood up and asked that the police apologize for its treatment of the teacher and students. The crowd became agitated and a small group began to riot. Rocks were thrown at the police station and the crowd began to spread through the streets of Tasikmalaya, targeting shops, churches, and other buildings. The riots resulted in four deaths. Eighty-nine stores were damaged or burned, as well as twelve churches, twenty-one offices, the police station, four factories, eight car dealers, seven houses, six bank offices, and three hotels.[37]

The targets in both riots indicated a number of different grievances. Churches were attacked even though Christians were unrelated to the triggering events. But shops, movie theatres, and bank offices were also damaged, which suggested that the crowds might have been targeting the ethnic Chinese more than the Christians. Anti-Christian and anti-Chinese motives were very difficult to separate because the Chinese were overwhelmingly Christian and many Christians in Java were ethnic Chinese. Nevertheless, the attacks also destroyed churches of non-Chinese Christian communities, such as the Batak. Furthermore, in both cases, rioters reacted violently against the system of order (courts, police). They reacted to perceptions of injustice and police misconduct. Rioters showed a strong frustration with these two institutions and, by extension, the government.

In West Java's Rengasdenklok, a rioting crowd damaged three churches but the main targets were shops and houses owned by ethnic Chinese. The violence was perceived as retaliation against an incident in which a Chinese woman had lashed out at Muslim youths calling to prayer with drums before dawn, during the holy month of Ramadan.

Although the violence was directed most clearly at the ethnic Chinese, religious undertones were nevertheless present. The conflict was initially triggered by the intolerance of a Christian Chinese for Muslim ritual practises. But as rocks were thrown by Christian children at the local *musholla* (Muslim prayer house), Muslims were offended. Furthermore, during the violence, those *pribumi* Indonesians wishing to defend their property against rioters placed signs on their buildings reading "This is Muslim property" or "Muslim shop," thereby using a religious rather than an ethnic identifier. In reaction to the riot, the local secretary of the Indonesian Council of Ulama (MUI) noted that people in Rengasdenklok were annoyed at the use of private houses as places of worship for non-Muslims: "We are not anti other religions, but houses whose functions are changed like this can be a time bomb." The local *bupati* concurred by also noting he had personally stopped the building of a church on a 400-m property because local residents objected to its construction and the government had not issued a permit.[38] The difficulty of obtaining such permits and of holding religious services in private homes was often raised by Christians throughout the archipelago as a source of increasing tension in the 1990s.

Between 1994 and 1996, the number of cases of violence between Christians and Muslims increased dramatically. From Flores to Tasikmalaya, triggering incidents differed but outcomes were similar. Riots targeted the churches, stalls, and shops of Muslim migrants or Christian Chinese, and government offices. What first appeared to be sporadic violence became a pattern. The conflict partly reflected economic grievances and resentment against the government but also a deteriorating relationship between religious communities with an increasingly uncertain future. Religious identity was the channel through which expressions of violence were made.

Suharto's fall and the intensification of religious conflict

The critical juncture that began with Suharto's sudden resignation in May 1998 was accompanied by an intensification of religious conflict. The tensions that had developed over the thirty years of New Order rule, and that evolved from its institutional management of religious relations, unraveled at the end of the regime and worsened after May 1998. Riots in Kupang and Ketapang revived worries of increasing religious conflict, but the violence in Maluku led to the unavoidable realization that there was a serious problem with religious relations in Indonesia. Only in the intense and lengthy conflict in Maluku were Indonesians forced to face the difficult questions pertaining to relations between Christians and Muslims that had been minimized under the Suharto regime.

Suharto's successor, B. J. Habibie, tapped into Muslim support to build his constituency. In the past, Habibie's political support had been weak and his appointment as vice-president had been greeted with much disgruntlement. He had long been disliked by members of the armed forces, which had prevented him from becoming vice-president in previous cabinets. His nomination as head of ICMI had been seen partly as an attempt to build the political constituency that he lacked.[39] ICMI and reformist Muslims were at the forefront of the reform movement that led to Suharto's resignation. The leader of Muhammadiyah, Amien Rais, emerged as a symbol of reform among student demonstrators in the days preceding the resignation. Rais and ICMI allies had been the strongest critics of the corruption in the regime and of the leader himself. As head of ICMI, Habibie could capitalize on its support and he did so as he donned the mantle of reform.

Some Muslim student groups also rallied in support of Habibie. Shortly after May 1998, Forkot (City Forum), which had been the main coalition of students behind the anti-Suharto riots, began to organize demonstrations in favor of deeper and more accelerated reforms, the removal of the armed forces from the parliament, and Habibie's resignation. They saw his rise to the presidency as a continuation of the New Order regime. Another Muslim youth group, Furkon (Islamic Forum for the Upholding of Justice and the Constitution), emerged in response to anti-Habibie protests. Recruiting from several Muslim organizations and students, Furkon began to stage demonstrations in support of Habibie's reform agenda. As the executive head of ICMI, Achmad Tirtosudiro, explained: "If they [Forkot and other groups] want to break up constitutional efforts, they must be confronted".[40] The alliance of ICMI, Furkon, and other reformist Muslim groups was aligning itself with Habibie against secular, nationalist organizations.

In November 1998, the Special Session of the People's Consultative Assembly (SI–MPR) further pitted Islamists against nationalists. The assembly had been called by Habibie to adopt political reforms leading to democratic elections. Forkot, supported by a number of leftist organizations and the reformist Barisan Nasional coalition, continued to oppose the legitimacy of the Habibie government. Furkon members were recruited as private volunteers to support the armed forces in ensuring that security was maintained during the special session. Violence broke out and only increased the sense of tension surrounding divisions between Muslims and nationalists, with the corollary impact on relations with non-Muslims.[41]

It is against this background that violent conflict exploded once again. Only a week after the SI–MPR, religious riots erupted in Ketapang (Jakarta). They began with a trivial incident on 22 November, involving a quarrel over parking at an entertainment center, controlled by a Christian Ambonese gang. A fight broke out between a local Muslim and an Ambonese parking attendant. The next day, the gang marched through the streets, threatening and harassing local inhabitants. Several were beaten and property was damaged. Angry Muslim mobs responded by destroying Christian property, including twenty-one churches. Thirteen people were killed and several wounded.[42]

The Ketapang incident was most significant because of its subsequent repercussions. On 30 November in Kupang, the capital of the province of Nusa Tenggara Timur, where most inhabitants are Christian, rioters targeted Muslims who were mainly migrants from other areas of Indonesia. The incident began with a gathering of local Christians to mourn the deaths and destruction in Ketapang. It was followed by a rally across the city that turned into a riot. Ten mosques were destroyed as well as a dormitory at a local Muslim university. The mob also targeted stores, stalls, and homes owned by Muslim migrants from Java and South Sulawesi. As a result of the Kupang violence, hundreds of people fled to their province of origin, South Sulawesi. The day of their arrival in the capital, Ujung Pandang, rioters set fire to a local Catholic church. Mobs also damaged two local churches in West Java.[43] Conflicts in one area reverberated in other regions.

Sulawesi was the site of more inter-religious violence at the end of December 1998. In the town of Poso, Central Sulawesi, rioters damaged more than one hundred businesses. Reports denied any inter-religious dimension to the incident that involved youth groups but created strong clashes between Christians and Muslims. Similar tensions were reported in the town of Palu, but the violence was contained.[44] A resurgence of violence in these towns in April and May 2000 confirmed that these earlier incidents were relevant to the growing insecurity between the religious communities. That they occurred shortly after the events in Kupang and Ketapang adds to the evidence in favor of interpreting these clashes at least partly in relation to the deteriorating state of inter-religious relations.[45]

These conflicts appeared in continuity with previous riots. The compendium of violent incidents involving religious groups had accelerated since the initial outbreaks in 1995. The parallels between these events and those of the Suharto period showed a commonality in the sources of tension, rooted in religious relations.

Compromise among Muslims and the presidency
of Abdurrahman Wahid

The rise to power of Abdurrahman Wahid occurred at the height of tensions between Christians and Muslims, and was symptomatic of Muslim divisions over the future of the country. Political mobilization was high, as Indonesians were preparing to vote in the first free legislative elections since 1955 and the first-ever presidential election. Between the election of the new parliament in June 1999 and that of the president in October, there was a period of instability that was marked by renewed calls for a greater role for Islam in the polity. Wahid emerged as a compromise candidate that reinforced the tolerant and open nature of mainstream Islam in Indonesia. More than anyone else, he was seen as the bridge-maker, a respected Muslim leader and scholar who had promoted democratic values and inter-religious understanding.

Religion was a major component of the legislative elections and the subsequent presidential contest. Political parties had mushroomed after Home Affairs Minister Syarwan Hamid announced on 8 June 1998 that they could be freely established. Many observers became worried about signs that parties would be created on the basis of religion, as Islam could now be used as a basis for party organization after having been suppressed since 1974. One of the most respected Muslim leaders, Nurcholish Madjid, recalled: "We have had traumatic experiences with religion-based political parties," referring to the political divisions in the 1950s around the question of the Islamic state, promoted by Masyumi.[46] The most prominent Islamic parties that emerged were the National Awakening Party (PKB), led by Wahid, the Development Unity Party (PPP), which had been the banner party under Suharto for former Islamic parties, and the Crescent Star Party (PBB). Amien Rais' National Mandate Party (PAN) was not presented as an Islamic party but could not shed its image as a strong representative of Islamic interests, given Rais' previous leadership of Indonesia's second largest Islamic organization, Muhammadiyah.[47] The PKB was the political wing of the largest Muslim organization, Nahdlatul Ulama, while the PBB attracted Muslims who had supported Masyumi in the 1950s and who were associated with more radical Islamic groups such as the Indonesian Committee for World Islamic Solidarity (Kisdi) and the Indonesian Islamic Preaching Council (DDII). Even Golkar had an ambiguous position. It was seen as both an organization that formerly served as the state's main vehicle for Suharto's version of secular nationalism, and one that encompassed ICMI members supportive of Habibie as a representative of Islam.

The campaign revived some of the ideological divisions of the 1950s. Walking in her father's footsteps, Megawati Sukarnoputri and the Democratic Party of Indonesia for the Struggle (PDI-P) represented the nationalist ideal of the founders of the Republic. The party drew a large following from non-Muslims, secularists, Muslims of nationalist orientation, and the poor Indonesian masses that longed for a return to the Sukarnoist era. The main opponents of the PDI-P came from Islamic parties that promoted, instead, a greater place for the majority of Muslims in the polity. None espoused, however, the idea of an Islamic state. Finally, Golkar faced a crisis of identity. It retained most of its powerful elite but had no clear orientation. The large number of politicians from ICMI that Golkar had attracted in the late Suharto years were divided in their outlook. One faction strongly supported Habibie as the representative of Islam, against the secular nationalists and non-Muslims. Another faction upheld the values of nationalism and unity under Pancasila that had been pursued under the New Order. The programs and policies of the various political parties remained ambiguous while personalities and the division between Islam and non-Islam were prominent.

Among Muslim parties, unity was difficult to attain. Muslim politicians who had opposed the New Order regime were less likely to want an alliance with Habibie and the ICMI faction in Golkar. Amien Rais and PAN were most representative of this group. The PKB, under Wahid, also found it difficult to ally itself either with Golkar or with PAN. There had long been a difference of views and orientation between the rural-based NU, behind the PKB, and the urban, modernist Muhammadiyah supporting PAN. Furthermore, personality clashes between Wahid and Rais prevented a rapprochement. The PPP had always been an uncomfortable coalition of Muslims forced to amalgamate under one banner and reduce the Muslim orientation of the party. It was perceived as more likely to support the ICMI faction in Golkar. The smaller parties had a variety of orientations. For the PBB, an alliance with Golkar and Habibie was feasible since its members represented the radical group within ICMI and it had some problems with the more moderate orientations being espoused by Wahid and eventually Rais. Perceived as close to non-Muslims, Wahid was not a likely ally. Rais found that in order to gain inroads among moderate Muslims, PAN had to present itself as a party open to all groups.

During the electoral campaign, many debates emerged about relations between Muslims and non-Muslims, as well as the role of Islam in politics. For example, retired Maj. Gen. Theo Syafei reportedly accused Islamic organizations of desiring the establishment of an Islamic state. The charge was made in a church in Surabaya in September 1998 but only reported in the press in January 1999 when a tape of the speech was discovered. The speech articulated the fears among the Christian community that Islamic organizations, especially Kisdi or the PBB, had a hidden agenda. Syafei was denounced by many Islamic leaders who re-asserted that the question of an Islamic state had been resolved and they had no intention of reviving it.[48] Nevertheless, these issues added to the climate of instability and uncertainty.

The June 1999 election appeared to confirm that Indonesians more strongly supported a nationalist vision than an Islamic one. Megawati's PDI-P won the largest number of seats (153) and 30.6% of the vote, followed by Golkar (120 seats, 24% of votes), PPP (58 seats, 11.6% of votes), and PKB (51 seats, 10.2% of votes). The PBB gained only 13 seats (2.6% of votes), while smaller Islamic parties received a very small per-centage of the total vote. Clearly, Muslims were divided in their support for various parties. The greater success of the PPP could be attributed as much to voting for a known entity than to actual support for an Islamic party. The PKB support was relatively weak and defied expectations, given its large basis in Nahdlatul Ulama and the popularity of Wahid. PAN received only 34 seats (6.8% of votes), which meant that it did not gain the expected support from Muhammadiyah members. Golkar's suc-cess could be interpreted as voting for a known entity, support for a large patronage machine, for the status quo, or Muslim support for Habibie as an ICMI representative. This vote by no means indicated a strong role of Islamic issues in the election. Instead, Megawati's resounding success showed the strength of past nationalist ideas and compromises, as well as her personal popularity.

After their defeat in the legislative elections, Muslim parties and Golkar mobilized to prevent the election of Megawati as president. During the months preceding the presidential election by delegates of the MPR, only two candidates appeared to have sufficient support in the assembly to win: Megawati and Habibie. As they represented the parties with the largest number of seats in the MPR (PDI-P and Golkar, respectively), the competition revolved around gaining support from the smaller parties, as well as the seats held by the armed forces and the delegates from the provinces.

The campaign against Megawati began early. A large Islamic Congress was organized in November 1998 to discuss a variety of issues relat-ing to Islam in the era of political reform. The most significant issue to emerge was the understanding among a large number of delegates that the next president should be a Muslim and should not be a woman. Megawati was directly targeted and these statements stirred much con-troversy. Many Muslim politicians feared the election of Megawati and her supporters in the PDI-P, as the party represented the nationalist vision of Sukarno and included many non-Muslims. The controversy paralleled a statement made by one of Habibie's ministers, Ahmad Muflih Saefuddin, who dubbed Megawati a Hindu and boasted of his ability to counter her candidacy on the basis of his Islamic religion. Although he was forced to resign, his statements reflected the prejudices of many Muslims against her.[49]

The Islamic card became crucial in preventing Megawati's election. Despite the small percentage of their total number of seats, Islamic parties began to circulate the idea of an alliance. The idea of a Central Axis force was first floated in July 1999 by Hamzah Haz, the leader of the PPP, and Achmad Tirtosudiro, the head of ICMI, during discussions in Bandung that also focused on the possibilities of forming a single Islamic party. While the latter idea encountered numerous obstacles, the Central Axis movement gained momentum in the following months. It comprised the PPP, PAN, PBB, and Partai Keadilan, while Wahid's PKB only gave its support much later. As political brokering for the presidency accelerated near September, Rais seized the opportunity to propose Wahid, his rival but a widely respected Muslim leader, as the presidential candidate of the Central Axis.[50] Originally perceived as a ludicrous and far-fetched idea from parties that had been frustrated by their poor showing in the legislative elections, the Central Axis became a crucial power in the final days leading up to the October election.

Support for Wahid as president crystallized in the last few hours before the MPR vote. In the preceding days, support for Habibie had begun to wane. He was perceived as a representative of Muslim interests among a faction of Golkar members, as well as some members of the Central Axis parties, especially those close to ICMI.[51] But resentment against the Habibie government was rising. His administration was criticized for allowing East Timor to leave Indonesia, and members of his cabinet were being accused of corruption linked to loans by the Bali Bank. As it became evident that student protesters and Megawati's supporters would unleash mass demonstrations in the event that Habibie were elected, Golkar split into two camps. Many Golkar members began to espouse the idea of Wahid as president. Habibie withdrew from the race the day before the vote, as his report to the MPR had been rejected by a majority of members. Support for Megawati remained steady and was bolstered by the support of Wahid's PKB. But there were growing indications that Wahid could emerge as a serious candidate, and members of his party increasingly joined forces with the Central Axis. On Habibie's withdrawal, support for Wahid firmed and the Central Axis was able to gain a majority of votes and defeat Megawati. The last-minute deals had been made under the banner of an anti-Megawati coalition.[52]

The presidential contest mainly showed the opportunism of politicians who were positioning themselves for power, but the issue of Islam was also important. It was obvious that Islam had not been a sufficiently strong source of appeal for Central Axis parties to gain a large number of seats in the MPR. They were also very divided, since the PKB tended to support the nationalist orientation of Megawati, PAN projected itself as a non-religious party with a nationalist orientation, and many Muslims thought that their interests would be best served by supporting Habibie, and Golkar. Only a small minority supported parties that presented themselves exclusively as representatives of Muslim interests. Nevertheless, Rais' maneuver and his support for Wahid, a Muslim scholar, showed the strong desire to oppose Megawati's election and create an opportunity to show a strong Islamic front.

In subsequent years, the politicization of Islam continued. During the August 2000 annual session of the MPR, thousands of people demonstrated in front of the MPR building to demand amendment of the constitution and inclusion of the Jakarta Charter. They touched upon one of the most crucial compromises in Indonesian politics: the compromise at the time of independence of Pancasila and nationalism, over Islam, as a basis for the state. The revival of such an issue under democratic government showed that the question of Islam and its place in Indonesia remained unresolved. The Jakarta Charter was discussed by an MPR committee appointed to propose constitutional amendments after Megawati came to power in 2001, but it was rejected and the nationalist compromise upheld. The demands were made by marginal Islamic organizations but they were significant in showing that Islamic mobilization was persistent in Indonesia.

Sources of religious conflict

Religious conflict is mainly the violent expression of grievances that use religion as a basis of group identity. The Indonesian riots were responses to socio-economic inequalities, economic displacement by migrants, declining political legitimacy, and perceived threats to group identity. In some cases, the riots involved more direct grievances over rights to religious practise. The use of religious identity requires explanation beyond the various immediate causes of violence. The previous analysis points to the incessant sensitivity of religion in Indonesian politics.

Religion has always stirred high emotions in Indonesia. As former finance minister Radius Prawiro commented about the riots: "Ethnicity can be an instrument. If someone wants to create a social spasm, he can find an issue for that group and stir its emotional feelings. Religion is most easily used this way. It is most sensitive".[53] In the Indonesian context, one's religious identity is often more important that one's ethnic identity as Javanese, Ambonese, Madurese, or other.

Yet, because of its sensitivity and New Order restrictions, the discourse on the riots focused on issues other than the politicization of religion. The tendency was strong to blame unknown provocateurs or socio-economic inequalities. It was a remnant of the New Order when ethnic or religious conflict could not be openly discussed.

Few observers, if any, would argue that there was any intrinsic hatred between the communities or any dogmatic differences that would produce violent outcomes. "None of the conflicts are purely religious. Conflicts are not caused by religious doctrine," argued Cardinal Julius Darmaatmadja.[54] Instead, religion is used as the channel through which dissatisfaction is expressed.

To many Indonesian observers, socio-economic inequalities created frustrations that expressed themselves violently. A study of the Tasikmalaya riot concluded that economic inequality was the primary cause.[55] The National Human Rights Commission (Komnas HAM) came to similar conclusions about most of the riots during this period. According to Munawir Sjadzali and Miriam Budiarjo, "religious problems in the riots were not an immediate cause; economic disparity was." Furthermore, "a big problem is that we have many university graduates who are unemployed; hundreds and thousands of them are unemployed . . . this is a very dangerous situation".[56] Commenting in the national press shortly after the Tasikmalaya riot, Secretary General Baharudin Lopa concurred that social inequality is the ultimate trigger of riots, not religion.[57] NGO activists expressed similar views: "Social inequality creates the potential for these kinds of riots, combined with civil rights that are not respected and reinforced through legal means".[58] Reflecting on several of the riots, lawyer and long-time human rights activist Mulya Lubis stated: "There is a problem with the management of disparities in economic levels. Religion is used as an instrument".[59]

Socio-economic inequality was the most widely cited factor to explain the riots. The discourse favoring such a basis of conflict was strong. It coincided with an emerging critique of the Suharto government's lack of distribution of economic resources, and a growing awareness of the corruption surrounding the regime and especially of the wealth accumulated by the first family and its business associates. The riots of 1996–97 triggered a public debate in the press that fed this critique of the regime and suggested that violence was one of its consequences.

The second most-often cited reason for the riots was provocation. Instead of pointing to structural deficiencies in the system, some government officials, academics, and social and political leaders looked for evidence that the riots were willfully instigated to serve the interests of some small political grouping. Nahdlatul Ulama, and its leader Abdurrahman Wahid, were most vehemently outspoken about the role of provocateurs. The NU White Paper on the causes of the Situbondo riot concluded that it was engineered by people seeking to discredit NU and Wahid, and even ultimately to dislodge Wahid from the leadership of the organization.[60] Many government officials accused unknown provocateurs, although some pointed to the familiar target of communist activists. Minister of Religion Tarmizi Taher spoke of groups wanting to make use of Islam to raise the emotions of the masses and especially the possibility of active members of the PKI taking advantage of the situation.[61] The governor of East Java, Basofi Soedirman, asserted that the riots had been planned for a long time and drew parallels with PKI actions because of the burning of bibles, *qur'ans*, and *mushollas*.[62] Almost every riot produced evidence pointing to suspects that could have started the riots or aggravated the anger of the masses.

Although provocation might have occurred, no evidence was uncovered of any broader conspiracy. Certainly, the thesis that the PKI had been involved only showed the extent to which the New Order government had become powerless to find culprits to justify its style of rule, especially as the PKI had long been eliminated and communist movements had almost disappeared on a global scale in the aftermath of the demise of the former Soviet Union and Eastern Europe.

Beyond communist agitators, it was also difficult to identify other possible provocateurs, nor did such accusations indicate the source of the riots. According to Marzuki Darusman, the deputy head of Komnas HAM, the government accused provocateurs as a means of pacifying the situation so that the issues involved would not spread to other areas. He saw it as a calming instrument rather than a problem-solver. Mulyana Kusuma of the Legal Aid Institute added that provocateurs were accused by the government because it feared that, otherwise, its own institutions would be blamed for the instability and its authority would be eroded.[63] Although provocateurs might have been involved in the riots, there had to be other reasons why crowds were susceptible to violence. As Munawir Sjadzali, chair of Komnas HAM, noted: "If leaves are dry, it doesn't matter how many matches one throws in, they will burn".[64] Provocation might explain how the riots began or increased in intensity but it does not explain the conditions that made them possible.

Many analyses of the riots implied that the government had some responsibility. Religious relations deteriorated, according to Laksamana

Sukardi, one of the top officials of the PDI-P, because of a "complete absence of institutionalization. The system depends too much on individuals and on personalities. In such a system, the use of religion to reach one's ends can be quite strong and powerful".[65] Lukman Soetrisno, a sociologist and director of the Center for Research on Rural and Regional Development at Gadjah Mada University (Yogyakarta) argued that the core problems leading to the riots included the "domination of the state over its subjects, leaving the latter helpless before its power, and people's lack of trust in the bureaucracy, due to the latter's insensitivity and poor service".[66] Cardinal Darmaatmadja partly blamed the "decline in morality in almost all areas of livelihood . . . [resulting from] insufficient attention to law enforcement, human rights and human values not sufficiently respected, and a sense of justice not maintained".[67] Sociologist Hotman Siahaan argued that political communication between people and political institutions was shattered so people could not channel their aspirations. Instead, there was always a monologue, never a dialogue with the people: "People are treated as if they don't understand anything. They are considered stupid [bodoh]".[68] These critical attacks targeted the Suharto regime itself as being the ultimate culprit for creating conditions leading to the riots.

Even those who had been more supportive of the Suharto regime were having serious doubts about the future direction of the regime. Juwono Sudarsono, vice-governor of the National Defense Institute, argued that the riots were partly explained by "inertia":

The system depends so much on one man who has been in power for more than thirty years . . . [There is] inertia of the same man on television, every day, the tributes to him and his family, and the corruption everywhere. He maintained this system through patronage . . . The children of Suharto are in Golkar and quite bold in injecting patronage . . . [But] the further one gets from the traumatic events of the 1960s, the harder it is to maintain the system. Money alone will not be sufficient to maintain Golkar anymore. The balance of patronage is no longer sufficient . . . Twenty years ago, the population gave the government the benefit of the doubt. People were traumatized by the events of 1966, and didn't like party politics. Now things have changed. People are more "politically enfranchised," even though probably "economically disenfranchised." It is a crucial stage in this transition of development.[69]

Remarkably, these analyses were made before the Asian financial crisis began to affect Indonesia and well before Suharto resigned. They show the extent to which a political crisis was brewing underneath a veneer of strength and continuity. The riots were the first symptoms that the regime had produced conditions leading to violence and, eventually, to its own demise.

Political manipulation of religious groups created suspicions and divisions between communities. The riots occurred in this context of heightened tensions between Muslims and Christians. These tensions coincided with growing frustrations at the ineffectiveness of the New Order regime to address socio-economic inequalities and, more importantly, with a growing realization that the government had been responsible for increasing these inequalities. A crisis of legitimacy was growing and it became apparent among the elite and the masses that Suharto's reign might be coming to an end. The riots expressed many of these tensions but they took on a religious dimension as a result of the imbalance that had been created between communities. Religion had become one of the major forms of identity in the late New Order period, in part because of the regime's own anti-communist rhetoric, political repression, and the allowing of religion as the only means of public expression for Indonesians.

7   Conflict in Maluku

In January 1999, sudden and surprising violence broke out between Christians and Muslims in Indonesia's province of Maluku.[1] Previously seen as a stable region in the archipelago, it quickly became the site of devastating inter-religious strife. Thousands of people were killed in a spiral of violence over the following years. Little known in the rest of Indonesia and mainly neglected under the Suharto regime, Maluku became a core preoccupation of the Habibie, Wahid, and Megawati governments.

The conflict was a consequence of New Order policies that disrupted the balance of forces between the two communities. One of the few regions where both religious groups were almost equal in number, Maluku was the site of a silent, fragile competition for power between Christians and Muslims. Patrimonial networks reinforced group identities, as powerful and lucrative positions in the civil service became major sources of resources and protection for each religious community.[2] Under the New Order, access to such networks represented one of the few channels through which groups could advance their interests.

The Islamization of the Suharto regime in the 1990s disrupted the fragile balance in Maluku. Muslims gained a new sense of confidence to challenge the longstanding Christian dominance. Christians concomitantly felt threatened. With a growing fear that the government was becoming Islamized, they were worried about losing the positions of power that ensured the security of their community.

At the third critical juncture, when Habibie began to democratize the New Order's institutions, there was a period of high uncertainty concerning the future of the polity. No one knew the extent to which the patrimonial features of the New Order system would be dismantled or whether the Pancasila ideology, which had maintained a quasi-secular orientation for the state, would continue to define the principles of the Indonesian nation. As a result, Muslims and Christians in Maluku feared losing their relative positions and access to resources. Muslims could be concerned that Christians might reassert their regional dominance,

114

while Christians feared an erosion of their status in a state more strongly inclined to favor its large Muslim majority.

Factors that would otherwise not have been sources of tension fed group fears because of this particular context. Spontaneous migration from Sulawesi and policies designed to encourage migration had been occurring for decades. They had created few frictions between Muslim migrants and local Christians but this situation changed with fears of Islamization. As Muslims became the largest group in Maluku, the disruption in the numerical balance of the communities in the region was seen as a threat for Christians. Well before the violence of 1999, therefore, religious identities in Maluku were highly politicized and the communities were poised for conflict.

Ambon and Maluku in the Indonesian Republic

The ambiguity of the role of Islam in the Indonesian nation and patrimonial relations sustaining the New Order regime reinforced divisions between Christians and Muslims. The regime's policies and manipulative use of religion for political support had negative consequences, particularly since Dutch colonial policies had already created a divide among the religious communities.

Ambonese Christians were favored during the colonial period, while Muslims were marginalized. The city of Amboina (Ambon) became one of the most important towns in the Dutch East Indies: it was the administrative center and major port of the Moluccas islands. The Dutch required the use of local people to staff positions in its colonial administration and to serve in the colonial army. Many Ambonese converted to Christianity as a result of missionization and opportunities for work open only to Christians. They occupied staff positions in the administrative center of Ambon but, more importantly, they were the principal group in the Dutch colonial army. Meanwhile, Muslim Ambonese were marginalized and isolated. They pursued their livelihoods in villages across the region, with little involvement in Dutch colonial institutions.[3]

When the Indonesian Republic declared its independence in 1945, many Ambonese Christians resisted, as they feared inclusion in a new country with a Muslim majority. After the Second World War, the new Republic fought for four years the returning Dutch. When they finally left in 1949, the Republic adopted a unitary state and dissolved the federation that had been created by the Dutch. Ambon and Maluku had been part of the state of East Indonesia, one of the only functioning states during the four years of Dutch–Indonesian conflict. Bolstered by some support among the Christian Ambonese community, disgruntled officers of the former Dutch colonial army declared the independence of the South Moluccan Republic (RMS). The Republic rejected the new state and sent the Indonesian National Army (TNI) to quell the resistance. Within a few months, the South Moluccan Republic was defeated.[4]

As a result of the RMS incident, the position of the Ambonese in the Republic remained ambiguous. Many Christian Ambonese had joined the Republic in the struggle against the Dutch. Some of these nationalists played important roles as cabinet members and prominent leaders of the Protestant Party of Indonesia under the regime of President Sukarno. Yet, the RMS incident marked the region as rebellious. After being the center of the Dutch East Indies, Ambon and Maluku were subsequently marginalized. The once thriving trade among islands in Eastern Indonesia was significantly reduced and even purposely curtailed. Shipping routes were diverted to Surabaya (Java), which became the hub for eastern trade instead of major eastern ports such as Makassar (Sulawesi). Government policies favored the more populous areas of Java and Sumatra. Rice production became a high priority and funds were therefore channeled to rice-producing regions in Western Indonesia, while Maluku stagnated.[5]

The shadow of the RMS was used in the Suharto era to raise threats against the Ambonese. Opposition and criticism were met with accusations that the Christians were still supporting the movement. More often than in other provinces, the positions of governor and regent (*bupati*) were filled by military officers and non-locals. Governor Akib Latuconsina, appointed in 1992, was the first civilian governor and Moluccan under the New Order. The region remained relatively calm and passive, as critics of the government were accused of supporting the RMS.[6]

Nevertheless, Christian Ambonese benefitted from the Pancasila state. Christians in general were well represented in the New Order regime and its patrimonial system extended to the region. Because of their strong role in the colonial civil service and the dominance of missionary schools, Christians in Maluku were well positioned to play a stronger role than Muslims. They maintained their educational advance and an overwhelming representation in the regional bureaucracy. Furthermore, the Ambonese prized civil service employment, which had been highly regarded under the Dutch, so they sought these positions over any other occupation. Below the regional command that was firmly held by military outsiders, Christian Ambonese maintained a strong presence regionally and promoted the interests of their community.

With the integration into Indonesia, however, a greater role for Muslims would inevitably occur. The introduction of a secular system of education allowed Muslims to catch up and expect positions previously dominated by Christians:

After independence, Maluku was integrated into a state with a very large majority of Muslims, and Christians are not yet able to accept this. They still think of themselves back in the Dutch colony. It makes sense that since Christians controlled most positions after independence, of course many of them would be displaced and replaced by Muslims, even more so since they have obtained higher education and were better able to compete with Christians.[7]

Christians resented the growing presence of Muslims in areas they previously controlled, but they did not dare voice their protest.

Religious identity played a strong role in the competition for positions in Maluku. This competition occurred beneath an outwardly balanced and cordial relationship. Blood relations were created between Christian and Muslim villages in recognition of their common origins. This traditional institution, "*pela-gandong*," was designed to ensure peace between the different religious groups.[8] Furthermore, Muslims and Christians were often distant relatives in many Ambonese families, so they wished to maintain harmonious relations.

In reality, these institutions did not prevent Muslims from competing for positions or Christians from trying to retain their own. Within the regional and municipal bureaucracies, Christians resented the growing presence of Muslims in areas they previously controlled, while Muslims saw their advancement as a just redress since they had been previously marginalized. A particularly interesting example was the University of Pattimura. Mostly led by Christians, the university was nevertheless divided along religious lines. The powerful education faculty (FKIP), one of the largest in the university, was almost exclusively staffed with Christians well into the 1990s, while other departments included more Muslims.

Local historical factors therefore set the stage for tensions to grow along religious lines. The Ambonese Christian role under the Dutch had created a political divide between Christians and Muslims, even among Ambonese with common origins, and it remained salient under the independent Republic. The looming RMS issue gave the New Order state the means to repress opposition and maintain a strong military presence, while allowing elites to benefit from patronage networks. Policies designed to contain potential uprisings and the marginalization of the region under the New Order regime allowed religious networks to be a source of access to government positions and to protect one's respective communal interests.

Islamization and the struggle for government positions

Tensions began to rise more steadily when Muslims became favored under Suharto's change of policy in the 1990s. With the creation of ICMI, Muslims throughout Indonesia saw growing opportunities for advancement while Christians at all levels of government were replaced. According to Nicolas Radjawane: "The tendency for Islamization has always been present in Indonesia but only with ICMI has it become open public policy to promote Islam at the expense of other religions".[9] In Maluku more than elsewhere, these policies had the effect of heightening tensions. Moluccan Christians became defensive, as they were worried about the Islamization trend and a loss of their dominance. Moluccan Muslims, on the other hand, found a political opportunity to break this dominance and establish a more equitable balance in government positions.

The governor of Maluku, Akib Latuconsina, faced many difficulties in his attempt to redress past imbalances in the allocation of positions and resources. Appointed in 1992, Latuconsina, a Muslim, was the first Moluccan governor since the beginning of the New Order. Shortly after his nomination, he accelerated the appointment of Muslims to the higher echelons of the bureaucracy, thereby displacing Christians from former strongholds. These nominations further politicized religious identities.[10]

Between 1992 and 1996, the governor managed to place Muslims in all of the most important positions within the regional bureaucracy. All of the regents (*bupati*) were Muslim in 1996, even in Central and Southeast Maluku where Christians are a majority. Regional heads of national departments, previously almost all Christian, were replaced with Muslims, even positions long held by Christians, such as head of the education and health departments. By the mid-1990s, Christians were left with very little control over top positions.[11]

Furthermore, most new teachers hired by the government were Muslims, even though the majority of graduates from local education faculties were Christian. Christians had long dominated education and 90% of teachers were Christian. The FKIP at Pattimura University (Unpatti) produced most new teachers and almost all were Christian. The new head of the education department, a Muslim from Southeast Sulawesi, had decided to hire mainly Muslims and the FKIP saw its share of new teachers decline to 10%. Many new teachers originated from outside of Maluku since there were insufficient numbers of Muslims being trained in the region.[12] Christians increasingly resented these kinds of policies, even though they were designed to create a fairer balance between Christians and Muslims.

Struggles for two key positions were especially crucial in the mid-1990s. The positions of mayor of Ambon and rector of Unpatti were seen as Christian strongholds and the Christian community strongly resisted attempts to fill these positions with Muslim candidates. A military officer, Yohanes Sudiono, a Javanese Catholic close to the Protestant community, held the position of mayor. During his tenure, he had promised that Christian Ambonese positions would be guaranteed. He had even hired Christians, who then represented about 90% of employees in the city district office. Governor Latuconsina, who sought more Muslim representation in the city government, was unhappy with Sudiono's approach. When the time for renewal was up, the Democratic Party of Indonesia (PDI) representatives in the local assembly (DPRD-II) proposed that Sudiono be returned to his position. Latuconsina, however, favored Diponegoro, another military officer but a Muslim. The PDI and Christian Ambonese rejected the candidate and mounted a strong resistance to the governor's choice.[13] In the end, the governor chose not to further alienate the Christian community and selected a Christian candidate, Chris Tanasale.

Governor Latuconsina provoked another strong protest from Christians in his attempt to appoint a Muslim as rector of Unpatti. As a former head of the economics faculty, Latuconsina had apparently had tense relations with Nanere, the Unpatti rector. The latter was accused of favoring Christians in the sponsorship of staff being supported to pursue graduate studies abroad at the masters and doctoral levels. The governor asked Nanere to step down from his position, citing an age limit as the official cause. His proposed replacement was the local head of ICMI, a candidate supported by the governor but not on the list proposed by Unpatti's senate. The deadlock lasted eight months. During this time, 230 Unpatti professors threatened to resign and student demonstrations were organized on several occasions. In the end, Secretary of State Moerdiono resolved the issue, and a Christian, Mus Huliselan, was finally appointed. Muslims had been rectors in the past but religion had not been as politicized. In the national context of the time, this kind of event stirred high emotions among Ambonese Christians and Muslims.[14]

The allocation of government positions assumed a heightened symbolic value that, interpreted within a context of growing religious tensions, could be particularly conflictual. As pointed out by many Ambonese, it was normal to expect a gradual increase in the number of positions for Muslims to redress the imbalance that had favored Christians since Dutch colonial times. Furthermore, Muslims in powerful posts had appointed Christians to high-level positions and Christians had appointed Muslims: "[even the former governor], a Catholic, gave Muslims important positions in government . . . Since [Muslims] represented more

than 50% of the population, it was important to start giving them important positions".[15] But as the context changed, and Christians became
displaced on a national basis, the effects in Maluku were multiplied.
Every position lost became a threat to the position of Christians in the
region and heightened the fear that Islamization was occurring across
Indonesia: "If you look at Java, it was not impossible that a Christian
be appointed as *camat* (sub-district head) or *bupati* (district head). In
the past there was no problem but now it is impossible. In the army there
are still some Christians, although less. And Ministers, from 6 or 7, there
are now 1 or 2".[16]

In this kind of political context, the rapid inclusion of Muslims at the
top of the bureaucracy created concern. Even those, such as Sammy
Titaley, the head of the Protestant Church of Maluku (GPM), who supported the governor's attempt to create a balance between Muslims and
Christians, and who thought that the threat to Christians was overstated,
still expressed some worry:

I reminded the governor that Christians also need to be taken care of. It is right
to promote the interests of Muslims to create an equilibrium but I tell him:
"Don't forget you're not the governor of Islam but the governor of Maluku, of
all Moluccans." One recent example is the regional head of the Department of
Education and Culture. Now, he is a Muslim and caretaker until a new person
is found. There is a Christian who is quite good and most capable of being in
this position. If the governor takes a Muslim from Java and promotes him as a
candidate and does not promote the Christian, then he is not respecting Pancasila
and he has ulterior motives in mind, because this is a clear example of where an
Ambonese Christian is competent and able to assume the responsibility. This
would be a clear sign that he is not respecting the need for equilibrium between
Christians and Muslims.[17]

This line of argument was one of the most moderate among Christian
Ambonese leaders. Many others expressed views that more directly accused the governor of pursuing the interests of Muslims in general and
of ICMI in particular.

Even some Muslim leaders acknowledged the growing impact of ICMI
and the national context on regional politics. Abdullah Soulissa, one of the
most respected Muslim leaders in Maluku, argued that it was difficult to
contain the flow of Islam in a country with 85% Muslims. He thought that
it should be easy to create a balance in Maluku, since the two communities
were almost equal in numbers. Yet, he acknowledged that he understood
Christian fears about government positions in Maluku and, furthermore,
about the increasing amount of Islamic programming on television that,
he thought, was excessive and should be more sensitive to ensuring good
Muslim–Christian relations.[18]

Therefore, the allocation of government positions was being interpreted within the context of the perceived Islamization of Indonesia.
The result was an intensification of the political value to both religious
communities of gaining positions in top levels of the bureaucracy.

The impact of migration

Tensions were compounded by rapid migration that changed the balance
between Christians and Muslims. Migrants from Sulawesi and Java significantly increased Muslims' advantage relative to Christians in the region.
Furthermore, some of the Muslims who migrated to Maluku, such as the
Bugis or Butonese, gained greater control of local trade and established
successful small businesses.

The transmigration program attracted many Muslims to Maluku and
triggered accusations against the government. Through official sponsor-
ing of migrants from overpopulated areas, the government sought to alleviate pressures on scarce land. The program targeted Java in particular,
and Maluku was chosen as a recipient area because of its vast land and
relatively small population. Given that Java and the rest of Indonesia
is overwhelmingly Muslim, it could be expected that the great majority
of transmigrants would be Muslims as well. "Before, the majority was
Christian [in Maluku] but with transmigration, Muslims are a majority
in the province . . . [Given the population problems], it makes sense to
have transmigration, which is necessarily going to be mainly Muslim since
90% of the population is Muslim. Locations with population problems
are mainly Muslim so of course Muslims are the ones who go to Buru
and Seram," the main transmigration areas in Maluku.[19]

Yet, some Ambonese were suspicious of the government's intentions.
They feared that there was a deliberate attempt to prevent Christians
from migrating to Ambon. Mgr Andreas Sol concurred with this view:
"Almost all of the transmigrants are Muslim. If they write down that they
are Catholic or Protestant, they don't have permission to transmigrate.
Sometimes, they write down 'Muslim' and, once they get here, they see
the minister/priest and say that they declared themselves as Muslims just
to transmigrate".[20] This example suggests that, at the very least, rumors
abounded linking Muslim transmigration to the government's turn to
Islam:

Transmigration is mainly Muslim and, as a result, there are more and more
Muslims in Ambon and more mosques being built. There is a limit to this. Eastern
Indonesia won't accept this . . . In East Timor, many Bugis were encouraged

to establish commercial ventures and all their shops were burnt down. They had to leave. This is a sign that the Timorese won't accept this. It's the same in Irian . . . This is a sign that Eastern Indonesia is not willing to accept Islamization on that scale.[21]

Ambonese Christians were therefore viewing the increase in the number of Muslims as a deliberate government policy. But the evidence for specific discrimination against Christian transmigration is not very strong. Given the large number of Muslims in Java, such a policy might not in fact have affected the overall numbers, anyway.

Instead, most migration to Maluku was spontaneous. While the influx of Javanese resulted from the transmigration program and affected mainly Buru, Seram, and parts of Halmahera, most migrants came from Sulawesi. The Bugis and Butonese had long migrated to Maluku in search of economic opportunities. Along with economic development in Indonesia, many were attracted to Ambon and other Moluccan areas to establish commercial enterprises.

The increasing presence of Butonese and Bugis had an impact on the economy: "Moluccans have difficulty competing with people from outside. So all the middle economy (commerce) is controlled by Butonese and people from other regions. The big problem is that the Ambonese and the Moluccans don't have the capacity to compete in the area of commercial enterprise. They are only interested in salaried jobs, especially civil servants".[22] As the government opened up more areas by building roads and infrastructure in transmigration and other areas, the Bugis and Butonese moved in and took control of commerce. So, as a result, the Ambonese and Moluccans saw Muslim outsiders, who increased their wealth relative to the Ambonese, dominate these areas of the economy.[23]

Meanwhile, economic opportunities were diminishing for Christian Ambonese. The civil service offered few options in urban areas, and traditional agriculture was on the decline. Villagers in many parts of Central Maluku relied on the production of spices as their main livelihood. As the price of cloves and other spices plummeted in the 1990s, they found themselves deprived of an important source of revenue. The fisheries industry also encountered difficulties as large-scale over-fishing in the region contributed to an important decline in fish stocks.[24]

Economic differences between the Butonese/Bugis and Christian Ambonese raised tensions along religious lines. Christians noted the effect not only on the distribution of wealth but also, more importantly, on the proportional numbers of Christians and Muslims in Maluku and the resulting tensions. While the ethnic Chinese were also heavily involved in the commercial economy, they were rarely mentioned by Ambonese

Christians as a problem. The fact that they were Christian may well have contributed to the relatively lesser sense of threat from their strength in the middle economy. Furthermore, tensions in Ambon city were mainly between Christian Ambonese and Muslim migrants. Frequent fights had occurred between youths in the predominantly Christian area of Mardika and the neighboring one of Batu Merah with its high concentration of Butonese and Bugis migrants.[25]

Migration to Maluku became a source of tension when relations between Christians and Muslims deteriorated. While there was no a priori reason why migration should contribute to conflict, in the context of the growing polarization of the two groups in the region it became one of many factors that would lead to violence.

The eruption of violence

The outbreak of violence and its intensity were a direct outgrowth of the tensions brewing between religious groups. It began with a small incident that degenerated into a large-scale riot and ethnic war. Initially contained to Christian Ambonese and Muslim migrants, the conflict rapidly included Muslim Ambonese against Christian Ambonese as well, thereby showing underlying tensions. The riots spread to other areas of Central Maluku and then to South and North Maluku, and involved large sections of the population in a continuous stream of rioting.

The explanation for this violence is complex. There is no doubt that unique factors caused initial riots to degenerate into prolonged ethnic warfare. Among these, one can point to the potential role of provocateurs and the involvement of security forces. The use of unknown provocateurs and the bias of security forces are not uncommon in Indonesia's history. Violence can be explained in part by the habitual use of extrajudicial forces, such as gangs and thugs, by the authoritarian state and its continued use after the demise of Suharto.[26] Yet these factors, in turn, occurred in a changing institutional context. Rapid democratic transition followed thirty years of authoritarian rule. This transition created much uncertainty about the future of Islam in the polity and changed the patrimonial structures that had sustained authoritarian institutions.[27] In addition, policies to decentralize power to the regions intensified the religious dimension of local competition, as was evident in the spread of conflict to North Maluku.

The following description of the conflict's evolution shows that the changing institutional context tipped already tense relations between Christians and Muslims into violent conflict. Provocation and the involvement of security forces had such repercussions because of the already high regional tensions, which were explained as an outgrowth of fears of Islamization, attempts to redress past injustices toward Moluccan Muslims, the unintended effects of migration patterns, and competition for resources and government positions. Rapid democratic transition tilted these tensions into conflict by raising the potential costs associated with the new Indonesia that would result from this institutional change.

The first large-scale riot erupted in January 1999. It began on 19 January, Idul Fitri, the last day of the holy Muslim month of Ramadan. A minor incident involving a local minibus driver and local youths turned into three days of bloody rioting. Accounts of the incident vary according to different sources, with some blaming the Christian driver of the minibus of wounding his Muslim attacker with a knife, while others recount that the driver was attacked and had to flee. Nevertheless, supporters of both the Christian driver and the Muslim youth began to spread word of the incident and emotions ran high in their respective communities, the Muslim quarter of Batu Merah and the neighboring Christian quarters of Amantelu and Mardika. Again, there are contradictory accounts of which group attacked dwellings in the others' quarter and began the subsequent rioting. Groups began rampaging through the area. The destruction subsequently spread to other areas of Ambon city. When news began to spread that churches and mosques had been burned down, the violence escalated further.

The conflict continued during the subsequent three days.[28] It spread to the communities of Batu Gantung, Waringin, Benteng Karang, Passo, Nania, Wailete, Kamiri, Hative Besar, and others. Violence was also reported in the village of Hila, several dozen kilometers away from Ambon city. It appeared that news of the violence in the city had spread rapidly and caused other communities to mobilize. In most cases, Christians tended to target Muslim migrants, the Butonese and Bugis. They burned down many of the markets and shops dominated by these groups, whereas they spared the Chinese, who were mainly Christian. As for the Muslims, they attacked houses and districts where Christians were majorities and several of these areas were burned to the ground.[29]

The incident resulted in several deaths and widespread destruction across Ambon city. At least forty-eight people were killed, and several churches and mosques were burned. Buildings, cars, and motorbikes were also destroyed.[30] Several hundred people sought refuge in churches, mosques, and government offices.

The original incident and subsequent brawl between local residents was not unprecedented. Local Ambonese recall regular outbreaks of violence between the Christian residents of Mardika and the mainly Muslim Batu Merah.[31] Usually, they were fights between youth gangs from both quarters and remained contained. When a soldier tried to attend a village dance party held by Christians in Hative Besar on 12 December 1998, a fight broke out between Christian youths and soldiers, with subsequent rioting leading to the destruction of a few houses. Again, such incidents were not uncommon since Muslims, both local migrants and personnel from other areas in Indonesia, often disapproved of Christian parties that involved ballroom dancing and drinking. This incident was resolved through traditional appeals to religious and inter-cultural tolerance.[32]

The greatest surprise was the spread of the violence to other parts of Ambon and the rapid increase in its scale. This development was a departure from past occurrences. While Muslim–Christian relations had been tense in the past, they were contained through dialogue between Muslim and Christian leaders while the military and police ensured that order was promptly restored.

This time, the violence erupted when tensions were at a high level and rapid democratic change was under way. Moluccans were aware of the instability following the transition to the government of President Habibie. They were also aware of the inter-religious violence in Ketapang and Kupang only a few months before. Compounded by the regional sources of tension between Christians and Muslims, the Ambon incident triggered conflict because conditions were ripe for violence.

After a very short respite in Ambon city, the conflict began to spread to neighbouring islands in Central Maluku. On 3 February 1999, Christians armed with sharp weapons attacked Muslims whom they had initially invited for a peace initiative in Kairatu, on Seram island. The following day, Muslim Ambonese and Butonese burned Christian houses in the Waitasu hamlet. On another island close to Ambon, Saparua, Christians burned down a Muslim dormitory, leading to a mobilization of Christian and Muslim communities that fell short of open violence when local leaders successfully calmed their followers. On 14 February, at least twenty-three people were killed in a fight between Muslim villagers of Pelauw and Christians from the neighboring hamlet of Kariu, which was almost completely burned to the ground. Many of the deaths were apparently a result of gunshot wounds inflicted by police and army units attempting to stop the rioting. The violence involved local Muslims, with some support from Butonese migrants and Muslims from neighboring islands who rushed to Haruku upon hearing about the beginning of hostilities. Accusations were made by both Christians and Muslims that security forces had assisted the other camp. These were the first reports that security forces appeared to be taking sides, rather than restoring order, and were willing to use live ammunition against local residents.[33]

Continuing violence around Ambon island soon fed renewed rioting in Ambon city. The city had remained very tense after the January trauma.

Isolated incidents continued to occur and small indications of possible renewal of conflict made crowds panic. The Haruku incidents spread fear among residents in Ambon city who stayed at home and closed their shops. Small groups attacked a few houses, including that of the head of the Al-Fatah mosque foundation, Abdullah Soulissa. On 23 February, several people were killed, mainly Butonese, and houses were destroyed by rioting mobs. Armed conflict in the villages of Waai (Christian), Tulehu (Muslim), and Liang (Muslim) became an "all out war".[34]

By early March, Ambon city was a "war zone." Violent clashes on 1 March set Christians from Ahuru hamlet against people from the Muslim Rinjani hamlet, with contradictory reports about the instigators of the violence. Again, police opened fire on the rioting crowd. At least thirteen people were killed and nine others wounded. The incident angered Muslims even beyond Maluku because of rumors that the initial attack had taken place in a mosque. Although these reports were highly contested, they had the effect of increasing Muslim outrage. Similarly, an attack close to Ambon's Silo church on 6 March enraged Christians. Barricades were set up by local residents to protect their respective Muslim and Christian districts, as well as local checkpoints.[35] The conflict was settling in and escalating.

Much of the initial reaction to the violence focused on finding the provocateurs of the January incident. The media, military and police personnel, as well as many politicians, especially the leader of Nahdlatul Ulama, Abdurrahman Wahid, pointed to evidence of provocation in the series of violent conflicts between religious groups in Ketapang, Kupang, and then Ambon. Public accusations were made against Yorrys Raweyai, a leader of Pancasila Youth, an organization that had been known to use illegal and often violent methods to support the interests of Suharto's New Order. Although not in Ambon himself, Yorrys was suspected of fueling the violence there, in coordination with a disgruntled former mayor of Ambon city, Dicky Wattimena. Some pointed to the events in Ketapang, which had involved a gang of Ambonese criminals, who were subsequently rumored to have gone to Ambon shortly after the conflict in Jakarta in December 1998.[36] The press dissected the details of the events to prove the theory of provocation. Army and police personnel also engaged in the speculation while never publishing any names of suspects. It was common among the security forces to blame provocation since it provided a means of containing the conflict and avoiding the confrontation of more serious underlying issues. Yet, despite months of speculation about provocation and demands for the instigators of the Ambon violence to be prosecuted, only local rioters were arrested and charged, while no strong evidence emerged to condemn any of the suspected provocateurs.

When it became apparent that the conflict was spreading and intensifying, the public focus shifted to concern about its management. By March, Christians and Muslims were accusing the local security forces of taking sides in the attacks. Much evidence was presented to suggest that police and army personnel were responsible for many of the deaths that occurred. Troops from the elite army strategic reserve, Kostrad, were sent to Ambon after the January incident to support the local army command. Many of the soldiers, however, were Bugis and Makassarese, which only raised the suspicions of local Christians. Moreover, Christians were worried about the partiality of troops, given that the head of the Ujung Pandang regional command was a Muslim Ambonese. Under pressure from these accusations and from failure to control the violence, the armed forces commander, General Wiranto, ordered the removal of the Maluku regional police head. Wiranto admitted that some security personnel had participated in the conflicts and taken sides.[37] A marine corps from Java was sent to Ambon as reinforcement and as a force that could be perceived as more neutral in the conflict.

These responses came amidst rising emotions across the country about the conflict in Maluku. Groups demonstrated in many major cities, including Jakarta, Semarang, Surakarta, and Pekanbaru. They demanded that the government take immediate action to stem the violence in Maluku and protested against the massacre of their Muslim brethren. Most of the demonstrators were Muslim student groups and youth organizations. In Jakarta, the Indonesian Committee of Muslim Students (Kammi) organized a large demonstration at the Al-Azhar mosque. Many demonstrators called for a *"jihad"* (holy war) to protect Muslims in Ambon and organizations registered volunteers to be sent to Ambon for the war. Organizations such as Furkon (an Islamic youth organization), the youth wing of the Islamic Crescent Star Party (PBB), Kisdi (Indonesian Committee for World Islamic Solidarity), and the FPI (Front for the Defense of Islam) all called for volunteers to defend Islam in Maluku.[38] While none were sent at the time, they illustrated the high sensitivity of the religious conflict.

In the following months, the conflict began to spread to other areas of Maluku. In April, violent clashes set Catholics against Muslims in Kei, Southeast Maluku, located far away from Ambon. Initially triggered by an incident involving the exchange of insults between two youths on 27 March, a subsequent fight between religious groups degenerated into fighting and destruction of property for the next six days. The violence spread to more than thirty villages and to the local capital city of Tual. Eighty people were killed, more than sixty were wounded, and hundreds of houses were destroyed. Explained by the local police as an outgrowth of a local conflict, the violence in fact mirrored the clashes in Ambon, with Muslims adopting the label "White group" against the Christians identified as the "Red group," as they had done in Ambon.[39]

With the conflict spreading beyond Ambon and Islamic groups mobilizing across the country, the government sought solutions. In March, it sent a delegation from the military, composed of prominent military officers of Ambonese origin who had spent much of their life in the region. This delegation met with various groups in Ambon to try reconciling the differences. These efforts were met with more bombs and violent outbreaks, in part because of the local population's growing resentment of the armed forces' role in the killings of the previous months.[40] Having earlier removed the head of the regional police, the government then created a new military command for Maluku (Kodam XVI Pattimura), with a Moluccan, Brigadier-General Max Tamaela, in charge. This measure was taken to downgrade the role of troops from Sulawesi, many of whom were Bugis, and restore confidence in the armed forces. There was also the hope that it would enhance the control of the armed forces in the region. Ironically, on the day the new command was inaugurated, renewed conflict exploded between groups from Batu Merah and Mardika. They had been brought together for the annual celebration of the regional Moluccan hero, Pattimura, but the event turned into another wave of violence and destruction instead of an occasion for peaceful reconciliation.[41]

The last months of the Habibie presidency were marred by a continued recurrence of incidents throughout the region. In July, violence broke out in the village of Sirosiri on Saparua island and in the town of Saparua after Muslims discovered that a Christian from a neighboring village was intentionally damaging the village's clove trees. As tension rose again in the region, Christians and Muslims fought each other in Poka and Rumah Tiga on the outskirts of Ambon and the violence eventually spread to the city itself. For many days in July and August, both sides unleashed almost unprecedented destruction and fury. The whole city was engulfed in violence, hundreds of shops and houses were destroyed, and fighting broke out in villages all over Ambon island. The armed forces opened fire once again on Muslims in front of the Al-Fatah mosque. By the end of the month, Ambon city and surrounding hamlets were severely damaged and an increasing number of people were living as refugees in the Al-Fatah mosque and Silo church, as well as other places of worship around the city.[42] It was the most severe violence since the January outbreak, with a higher number of casualties.

Ambon was left in a state of disarray after this second wave of large-scale conflict. Thousands more people began to leave the city and the area. Refugees who had returned in March with expectations of a more peaceful future left with no intention to return. Violent incidents continued to erupt on a regular basis and normal activities could not be restored. Provincial and district departments were relocated to other regions of Maluku, as employees could not safely reach their offices. Local markets and schools were segregated along religious lines and opened in territory secured by each community. Permanent outposts and borders were set up between Christian and Muslim quarters.[43]

The armed forces continued to demonstrate its inability to control the violence and to prevent its members from taking sides. Various reports implicated different units present in Ambon. The mobile brigades (Brimob) of the regional police were accused of favoring Christians during clashes in September, while the Kostrad forces were accused of supporting the Muslim side. There were even reports of clashes between members of these forces, although such incidents were not clearly confirmed. Nevertheless, there was enough evidence to force Brig. Gen. Tamaela to admit to some irregularities. Pressures began to rise for Tamaela's removal from his command.[44]

The crisis in Ambon began to take on a dynamic of its own but reflected the deep distrust that had grown between Christians and Muslims. Local competition for resources and positions, the polarization of religious identity, fears over future opportunities, and threats to each community provided fertile ground for conflict. Rapid democratic transition increased the uncertainty of outcomes over these struggles that had already created high tensions between Christians and Muslims well before Suharto's resignation.

The Wahid presidency and the spread of violence

The conflict escalated within the first month of President Wahid's accession to power. Previously confined mainly to Central and Southeast Maluku, it spread to North Maluku with some of the worst violence to date. In November 1999, twenty people were killed when conflict erupted in the cities of Ternate and Tidore. In late December and early January, the violence reached unprecedented levels in North Halmahera, a predominantly Christian area of North Maluku. Conflict began in Tobelo on 26 December and several hundred people were killed in subsequent days in Tobelo, Galela, and Jailolo. According to the official military account, 907 people were killed between 26 December and 7 January, while less conservative estimates reached more than 2,000.[45]

According to the sociologist Thamrin Amal Tomagola, a Moluccan and a specialist of the region, local issues were at the heart of the violence. The violence actually began in August 1999, shortly after a government decree was issued to create a new district, Malifut, located at the border between North and Central Halmahera. Malifut included a majority of Muslim villages inhabited by Makianese, who had been resettled in 1975 when their place of origin was threatened by volcanic eruption. Other local villages populated by Christians rejected the creation of this district and initiated the violence. They viewed the new district as a loss of territorial control for Christians and an attempt to prevent the spread of Christianity to Central Halmahera.

Tomagola also blamed competition between the sultans of Ternate and Tidore for some of the violence. The Sultan of Ternate, drawing his support in part from Christians in North Halmahera, had long been a rival of the Sultan of Tidore whose basis of support was greater among the Muslims in Central and South Halmahera. When the Habibie government decided to create a new province in North Maluku, the Sultan of Ternate vied for the position of governor, while an ally of the Sultan of Tidore, Bahar Landily, a career bureaucrat, was also in the running. Tomagola viewed the ensuing violence as a result of competition for the governorship, as well as the destabilizing factor in Malifut. Finally, the violence was also caused by the Australian exploitation of a local gold mine, the proceeds of which were the subject of highly contested claims by Christians and Muslims allied with the two sultans.[46]

In the same analysis, however, Tomagola recognized the importance of "contextual" factors in explaining the conflict in North Maluku. He noted that the area of the new district of Malifut had been contested for a long time. The territorial competition between Christians and Muslims in Halmahera stretched back to the initial settlements and conversions by the Dutch in North Halmahera. This competition was particularly significant in the 1990s when Christians were worried about the political gains of modernist Muslims after the creation of ICMI and the 1993 elections, in which they obtained a significant share of seats in the parliament and cabinet.[47]

It is not coincidental that the violence erupted after months of conflict between Christians and Muslims in other parts of the region. These events could only raise the tensions and stakes for both religious communities in the North and therefore make local issues appear much more significant. News and contacts with the rest of Maluku intensified the sense of threat felt by Christians in Ambon and other local areas long before the violence first erupted. The former rector of Pattimura University, Nanere, was at the center of one of the growing controversies between religious communities in Ambon during the mid-1990s. His involvement would have an impact on Christian communities in North Halmahera, since he was born and raised in that region. Thus local issues, while important, provided the trigger and the filter through which tensions at the national and regional level were expressed.

The subsequent reverberations show how conflicts were not only local but also fueled tensions among Muslims and Christians across the region and elsewhere. In Ambon, the violence resumed at roughly the same time. On Christmas day, a new wave of rioting was triggered by a minor incident. One of the city's major churches, Silo church, was burned down. The attack on this important Christian site intensified the violence. News of an "attack on Christians" spread to other regions of Central and Southeast Maluku and set off similar rioting. In Tanimbar, Southeast Maluku, Christians attacked several mosques in retaliation. Violence erupted on the island of Buru, which had been spared thus far.[48] Such outbursts were now closely linked to events in other parts of the Moluccan archipelago. Furthermore, their eruption during Christmas and Ramadan provoked particularly intense emotions.

Reports of these events enraged Muslims and Christians throughout Indonesia as it also became evident that the security forces had failed to remain neutral. The forces were taking sides along religious lines and senior military officers admitted that troops were firing on rioting crowds, thereby increasing the number of casualties. The head of the armed forces command, Admiral A. S. Widodo, publicly acknowledged this but justified it by arguing that soldiers had intervened to protect their families. Despite past complaints about the role of security forces, it became widely reported that the Brimob, who were 75% Christian, were siding with Christians while the overwhelmingly Muslim Kostrad was siding with Muslims.[49]

Groups began to mobilize as a result of the increased violence. Two hundred thousand people demonstrated in Jakarta to denounce the government's inaction in Maluku. The demonstrators were mainly supporters of Islamic parties and organizations. Prominent leaders included Amien Rais, the leader of PAN and head of the MPR, as well as Ahmad Sumargono, a prominent Islamic leader associated with the staunchly pro-Islam organizations Kisdi and DDII (Indonesian Islamic Preaching Council). In other parts of Indonesia, especially Yogyakarta and Makassar, more recently formed Islamic organizations such as the FPI and Forkap-Malut (People's Communication Forum for the Province of North Maluku) began recruiting volunteers for a *jihad* to Maluku. Several hundred had already been recruited by mid-January. A *jihad* force formed in Ternate had already been sent to North Halmahera to defend Muslims, as more deaths were recorded in Tobelo and Galela.[50]

By April and May 2000, *jihad* volunteers began to leave for Maluku. A group calling itself the Ahlus Sunnah Wal Jama'ah *jihad* fighters staged demonstrations in front of the presidential palace and the parliament.

They called for a holy war in Maluku. Three thousand of them had been training in Bogor, near Jakarta, and were ready to depart. Although they disarmed themselves under government orders and ceased their training sessions, many left for Ambon at the end of April. The armed forces allowed them to enter Maluku, as long as they came strictly for humanitarian purposes, which they claimed to be their primary mission. Yet, by mid-May, there were almost 4,000 reported in Ambon and their presence was blamed for a resumption of the conflict.[51]

Violence intensified in Maluku with the presence of this group of "Laskar Jihad." At the end of June 2000, the Wahid government declared a state of emergency but conflict continued as more Laskar Jihad forces penetrated the region. In the following months, they took over Christian villages, forcing Christians to flee or to convert to Islam. It took a few months before the Indonesian security forces could build up sufficient resistance to the presence of the Laskar Jihad for the violence to diminish.[52]

In the meantime, religious conflict broke out in other parts of the archipelago. On the island of Lombok (East Nusa Tenggara), Muslims attacked churches in the local capital of Mataram. The riot began after a meeting of Muslims was held to show their support for Muslims in Maluku. Despite being asked to calmly disperse, at least 2,000 people began to burn down churches. The rioting lasted two days. This event was significant in that the two major religious groups in Lombok are Muslims and Hindus. Christians represent only a tiny minority, many of whom are ethnic Chinese. The event was a direct result of heightened emotions among Muslims at the perceived massacre of their Muslim brethren in Maluku, with no apparent local source of tension. Smaller incidents occurred in Padang (North Sumatra), where a church was burned down, and in Makassar, where people began stopping vehicles and demanding identity cards, which show religious identity. They targeted Christians and beat them.[53]

More sustained violence erupted in the town of Poso, in Central Sulawesi. In mid-April, a fight between drunken teenagers degenerated into a large-scale riot the next day. Churches, schools, and hundreds of houses were burned down. After a pause of a few weeks, the conflict resumed for several weeks in mid-May and early June. At least 120 people were killed and many houses destroyed. Some observers explained the violence as the result of competition for the position of district head (*bupati*) that began in December 1998. Christians wanted the position but failed to secure it. They accused Muslims of corruption and rigging the selection process. These tensions led to clashes and were believed to have created a cycle of revenge that resulted in the ensuing violence.[54]

It is unlikely that a contest for district head alone could stir such high emotions. More importantly, the competition involved groups identifying themselves as Muslims and Christians and interpreting their respective defeat as a loss for their respective religious communities. The explosion of violence in Poso is consistent with the analysis in other regions, which suggests that, where Christians and Muslims were in competition with each other for political positions, tensions were highly exacerbated by the deteriorating relations between the religious communities nation-wide. With the widely reported mobilization of Muslims for *jihad* in Maluku, the intensity of the conflict in the region, and the long series of events that have pitted Christians against Muslims, the Poso and Lombok events can be understood at least partly as a "snowballing" effect from the conflict in Maluku. It was especially significant that these events occurred during a renewed phase of violence in Maluku and the concomitant radicalization of certain Islamic groups seeking to defend Muslims there.

During most of 2001 and 2002, the fighting in Maluku was considerably reduced. As the security forces applied more pressure on the Laskar Jihad and as the involvement of police and military troops in the conflict was reduced, the number of incidents and casualties declined. North Maluku returned to a peaceful state while conditions in Maluku greatly improved, despite continuing tensions and a perpetuation of divisions between Christian and Muslim zones.[55]

An uneasy peace pact was reached in 2002 but tensions remained high. The Malino peace pact was signed in February 2002. In subsequent months, violence continued sporadically as bombs exploded and fighting resumed in some locations. Nevertheless, a more stable government under Megawati Sukarnoputri and more effective security forces complemented the peace pact and ensured that conflict remained limited. By 2003, stability appeared to be returning to the archipelago. The Laskar Jihad had disbanded in October 2002 around the time of the Bali bombing that radically shifted the Indonesian government's attention to fighting terrorist organizations.[56]

The conflict between Christians and Muslims in Maluku was unprecedented. When rioting broke out in January 1999, no one suspected that it would spread from Ambon's Mardika plaza to numerous other locations in Maluku. It occurred during a time of increasing violence across the archipelago but few would have expected a large-scale conflict in the region. Furthermore, it was the first time in Indonesia that Christians and Muslims were pitted against each other in such ethnic warfare.

Institutional factors provided the context for potential violence but do not explain its intensity and scale. Combined with local factors such as the historical divide between Christians and Muslims, the almost equal numbers of both communities, and the effects of migration, they made Maluku particularly prone to conflict. Provocation may well have been a factor in triggering violence, where it was ready to occur, but certainly cannot explain why it had such devastating consequences. An analysis of reasons for the first riots degenerating into ethnic warfare would require an examination of the cycle of revenge, further provocation, and participation by security forces.

8   Late integration into the nation: East Timor and Irian Jaya (Papua)

Ethnonationalism has been a significant manifestation of ethnic conflict in New Order Indonesia. In conflicts in East Timor, Irian Jaya, and Aceh, groups identified as "East Timorese," "Papuan," and "Acehnese" conceived of themselves as distinct nations on the basis of ethnic differences. The process by which these groups were integrated into the Indonesian state, and subsequent policies designed to maintain those boundaries, contributed to their alienation from an otherwise inclusive Indonesian nation.

The development of ethnonationalist resistance in East Timor and Irian Jaya differs in some respects from that in Aceh. East Timor and Irian Jaya were integrated into Indonesia well after the revolution of 1945, and no significant Indonesian nationalist sentiment developed among East Timorese and Papuans prior to that time. The Acehnese joined the Indonesian nationalist movement and fought with other ethnic groups against the Dutch. Whereas groups of East Timorese and Papuans resisted from the moment of their integration, in Aceh such resistance emerged much later. Consequently, for many East Timorese and Papuans, ethnonationalism reflected a rejection of the fact and process of integration into the Republic, whereas in Aceh it represented a reaction to the treatment of Acehnese under the Indonesian state.

The process of late integration marks a traumatic critical juncture in the histories of East Timor and Irian Jaya. It defined the terms of inclusion and fixed in the imaginations of the East Timorese and Papuans a meaning to inclusion within the Indonesian nation that was different from other groups in the archipelago. For East Timorese and Papuans, being part of the Indonesian nation meant a loss of their own identity and freedom, instead of the liberating, modernist conception with which other groups identified.

The democratization of the late 1990s led to increased ethnonationalist demands rather than greater loyalty to the state, because of the absence of any historical moment that legitimized the adoption of an Indonesian national identity. Shortly after the fall of President Suharto and his replacement by B. J. Habibie, East Timorese nationalists increased

135

their mobilization and international lobbying, so that only fifteen months later they were receiving support from a large majority of the East Timorese population in a referendum that led to their independence. Papuan nationalists also increased their levels of mobilization as they formed a civilian movement demanding a referendum on independence.

East Timor: The integration that never was

When East Timor was integrated in 1975, it had few prior links to the rest of the archipelago. As a former Portuguese colony, it lacked a shared colonial experience with other regions. Initially an elite struggle to fill the vacuum left by the Portuguese, a nationalist movement intensified and spread with the invasion by Indonesia. The Indonesian national model was superimposed on a society for whom Indonesian symbols, political structure, culture, and even language were alien. Subsequent efforts to assimilate and integrate the Timorese through patronage, selective development, education, in-migration, and brute force failed. Rather than creating new bonds to the nation and state, the Timorese fed their own national consciousness and solidified their unity in resisting the Indonesians. Once offered an opportunity, they overwhelmingly chose independence.

East Timor was a relatively neglected region of the Portuguese colonial empire. As a result, little change occurred. The colonial system preserved some of the local socio-political structures, including the *liurai*, the traditional village heads. The territory was divided among various cultural groups that spoke different languages and dialects. Only 10% of the population spoke Portuguese in 1975, while many more spoke Tetum, the local lingua franca.[1]

The emergence of a nationalist elite in the 1960s resembled patterns in many other parts of the developing world. Nationalist leaders were influenced by the ideas and actions of the broader decolonization movement in Africa, Latin America, and Asia. When a coup in Lisbon signaled an end to colonial rule in 1974, several organizations sprang up. The Democratic Union of Timorese (UDT), the Social Democratic Association of Timor (ASDT), and the Popular Democratic Association of Timorese (Apodeti) shared the common goal of an independent or autonomous East Timor. They also promoted freedom of expression and opposed racial discrimination, colonialism, and corruption.

These organizations differed in terms of social base and ultimate goals. The UDT, with a more conservative base of administration officials and Catholic smallholders, advocated a federation with Portugal during a transition period toward full independence. The ASDT was more vocal in its rejection of Portuguese rule, and sought a more rapid transition to independence. Apodeti was formed around the principle of integration into the nation but wanted autonomous status. The latter appeared to draw little popular support from the population and was suspected of being promoted by Indonesian agents.[2]

The UDT was initially the most popular group but was quickly overrun by the ASDT, renamed the Revolutionary Front of Independent East Timor (Fretilin) in September 1974. Influenced by the ideas of Paulo Freire and by the experience of the nationalist movement Frelimo in Mozambique, Fretilin launched literacy campaigns and provided agricultural technical assistance in rural areas.[3] To foster a trans-ethnic national consciousness, it began to use the term "Maubere," previously used by the Portuguese as a derogatory term to designate the "backward natives".[4] Fretilin's popularity rose rapidly with the appeal of its program and emphasis on the common people.

The Indonesians intervened early to undercut the nationalist upsurge and prevent an independent East Timor. Under operation "Komodo," they began radio transmissions at the end of 1974 to undermine specifically Fretilin and its coalition with the UDT. When that failed, General Ali Murtopo, a close advisor to Suharto, met with UDT leader Lopez da Cruz to convey the message that Indonesia would not tolerate a communist government but might support independence if an anti-communist party led the country. The UDT severed its coalition with Fretilin in May 1975 and staged a coup on 10 August 1975. The UDT's new government lasted only a couple of weeks before Falintil, Fretilin's military wing, gained control of East Timor's main towns during the last days of August and seized Dili on 1 September. UDT troops fled across the border into Indonesian Timor, while their leaders were allowed to cross only after signing an appeal to Suharto for East Timor's integration into Indonesia, even though UDT leaders and supporters in Dili did not support such integration.[5]

Fretilin's brief administration enjoyed widespread support. According to several Australian parliamentarians who visited the territory, support for Fretilin was high during its brief hold on power. James Dunn, former Australian consul to Dili and a long-time observer of the territory, concurred: "Whatever the shortcomings of the Fretilin administration, it clearly enjoyed widespread support from the population, including many hitherto UDT supporters".[6] Fretilin's goals and programs captured the grievances of the East Timorese and provided a response in a way that the UDT, and certainly Apodeti, were unable to achieve.

Fretilin declared independence while the Indonesians began a military invasion. Caught between the invasion and the need for more foreign support, Fretilin precipitously declared independence on 28 November, as the Portuguese and other East Timorese parties refused to negotiate a settlement. The Indonesians launched a large-scale invasion of Dili on 7 December after obtaining a declaration from the UDT and Apodeti that accepted full integration. Fretilin leaders and their supporters fled to the mountains.

After establishing its control over Dili, the Indonesian military waged a campaign against Fretilin-held territory. While the Indonesians had planned a quick, decisive victory they became embroiled in a much longer and deeper military operation, as Fretilin's resistance grew incredibly resilient. By the end of December, Indonesian troops numbered around 15,000–20,000. They terrorized the population with indiscriminate shootings, looting, and maltreatment as they faced an enemy that was difficult to locate and had broad support among villagers. According to the Indonesian-appointed deputy-governor of East Timor, Lopez da Cruz, 60,000 people had been killed by February 1976. He even admitted "excesses" against Fretilin suspects.[7] In the subsequent couple of years, 40,000 soldiers occupied East Timor and waged campaigns of "encirclement and annihilation." Following intense bombing, troops would advance and burn villages and fields, forcing the local inhabitants into more confined areas until they were completely surrounded. The subsequent "annihilation" would consist of population displacement, executions, imprisonment, and relocation into camps. USAID estimated that close to 300,000 people were relocated in 150 such camps, which were presented as resettlements for development but where the emphasis was clearly on security. Many were surrounded by barbed wire and the conditions were miserable.[8]

Despite large losses and casualties, Falintil survived the numerous attempts by the Indonesian military to eliminate it. By the end of 1978, for instance, one of its main leaders, Nicolau Lobato, was captured and killed. Falintil split into several small groups scattered across the territory. Although several of them surrendered or were decimated, some survived and reconstructed the resistance.

Meanwhile, the Indonesian military continued to wage campaigns for the final elimination of Falintil/Fretilin. In 1981 and 1984, thousands of troops were sent again to East Timor. Indonesian soldiers used a "fence of legs" strategy, in which local inhabitants formed a human chain ahead of soldiers to sweep large areas suspected of hiding Falintil soldiers.[9] Along with these periodic campaigns, the Indonesian military used intimidation, torture, arrests, beatings, and other violent means on a regular basis. Over more than a decade, therefore, the East Timorese were subjected to a war of attrition perpetrated by the Indonesian armed forces.

In parallel to their military action, the Indonesians also ran a civil administration. Once integrated, East Timor was given equal status to other provinces, with an identical governmental structure. The provincial governor was responsible to the minister of the interior and the president. The province was also subdivided into districts (*kabupaten*), sub-districts (*kecamatan*), and villages (*desa*). The traditional heads, the *liurai*, were given positions as village heads (*kepala desa*), with a different set of expectations and responsibilities as defined in the 1979 village law (Undang-undang no. 5, 1979) which was applicable to all villages in Indonesia. This model followed the structure of Javanese villages and had little resonance in East Timor.

During the 1980s, the Indonesian government attempted to show that its policy of integration had succeeded. The Fretilin/Falintil resistance was less significant and development projects were being implemented. Funds were allocated particularly to the building of paved roads, schools, and health clinics. While in many other provinces the governors were often former military officers and not indigenous to the province, in East Timor the appointed governors were all East Timorese and civilians.

Yet, this apparent normalcy only slightly disguised the reality that the East Timorese were effectively governed by the Indonesian military with little concern for the welfare of the population. Roads were built for security reasons, to allow better transportation of troops to all areas of East Timor. Resettlements presented as new social experiments for development were effectively camps located close to roads, where people could be kept under better surveillance. The local population was also forced to provide free labor for the construction of roads and often for personal services to soldiers. While the governor was East Timorese, the regional secretary (*sekwilda*) was a military officer from outside of the region and had more real power. The arbitrary use of violence was common and included various forms of torture and sexual assault.

The East Timorese were not treated equally to those of other provinces, as the military played a stronger role and was more violent than elsewhere. They did not have representatives in the higher echelons of the military, civil service, or cabinet, and therefore had no influence with central authorities. The territory was effectively closed until the late 1980s when the East Timorese gained the right to travel freely to other areas of Indonesia. Visits by foreigners remained nevertheless under tight scrutiny and control.[10]

The economy was dominated by the military. As a reward for the integration campaign, the military was provided with commercial monopolies through PT Denok, a company owned by top military officials, including General Benny Murdani. In particular, the company obtained a monopoly over the commercial trade in coffee. Local producers were forced to sell their coffee at low prices to village cooperatives that subsequently sold to PT Denok. The military also expanded plantation areas for coffee and cloves, even doubling their production between 1977 and 1983.[11]

Schools were built and education was expanded but the curriculum was exclusively Indonesian. As for all Indonesian children, classes were conducted in the Indonesian language, whereas Catholic schools had previously used Portuguese or Tetum. Many courses at the primary level emphasized Pancasila, Indonesia's national history, its heroes, symbols, and common culture promoted by the government (especially elements of Javanese culture). Uniformity was encouraged through learning national songs and wearing national school uniforms, as well as using the same textbooks across the country. Hundreds of teachers were brought in from other regions, especially Java and Sulawesi.[12]

Many migrants came to settle in East Timor and controlled most government positions and small businesses. The transmigration program was often seen by foreign observers as a ploy by the Indonesian government to assimilate the East Timorese. Yet, only a few hundred families migrated to East Timor under the auspices of this program. More importantly, civil servants were hired from outside the region to fill the numerous positions as administrators, technicians, and instructors. Thousands of spontaneous migrants from Sulawesi, Sumatra, and West Timor settled in the territory and increasingly dominated the small business sector. The main towns of Dili and Baucau, in fact, became populated by majorities of non-Timorese.[13]

The increased migration was combined with a policy of population control. Under its family planning program, the government applied the same policies as in the rest of Indonesia, where children were limited to two per couple. Contraceptives were actively promoted by thousands of field agents who often used intimidation to force the adoption of contraceptive use. In 1985, the Bishop of Dili, Mgr Carlos Felipe Ximenes Belo, opposed the program, not because of the Vatican's views on contraception but because there were 20% more family planning agents relative to the population than in other regions of Indonesia. There was also evidence that some agents were misleading the Timorese by promoting injectable contraceptives as vaccines against tetanus. The fact that injectables were used in much higher proportions than anywhere else in Indonesia indeed raised suspicions.[14]

The Indonesian government used a variety of means to foster integration. The strong use of repression by military forces overshadowed other attempts to create new loyalties to the state through development funds and education. Sponsored by the provincial government and the Bank of Indonesia, a study by Gadjah Mada University scholars concluded on observing the years of military occupation and abuse: "This feeling of trauma is reflected in different types of behaviour. For the government administrators and officials it manifests itself in rigid and authoritarian actions and policies, while it has made the East Timorese uncooperative, apathetic and constantly suspicious . . . Protracted 'war conditions' in the province must be ended quickly".[15] Instead of being assimilated and more integrated, those East Timorese who were not fighting for Falintil withdrew into a state of passive resistance.

Active resistance to the Indonesians continued and added diplomatic initiatives. Despite severe defeats, Falintil/Fretilin was rebuilt in the 1980s under the leadership of Xanana Gusmao. The movement took a more diplomatic turn as well, with increased lobbying by NGOs and foreign governments. Youth and student underground movements were formed and periodically staged anti-Indonesian demonstrations. For example, when the Pope visited East Timor in 1989, students successfully raised nationalist banners in front of the Dili cathedral.[16]

The Catholic Church also came to play a more active role in the resistance. Initially conservative and supportive of the Portuguese colonial government, it kept its distance from the Indonesian government. At first, it was suspicious of Fretilin because of the latter's flirtation with Marxist ideas, but by the 1980s the Church was increasingly critical of the Indonesian government and supportive of Fretilin's resistance under a veneer of neutrality.[17] Carlos Belo, the Bishop of Dili whom the Indonesians had favored over more openly critical candidates, made a very critical statement only two years after being named to his position: "Having experienced with the people all the events which, since 1975, have deeply affected the social and political life of this same people, the Church bears anxious witness to facts that are slowly leading to the ethnic, cultural and religious extinction of the people of East Timor".[18] As the only location where people could legitimately express their grievances, the Church became a strong force in East Timor.

The decade of the 1990s marked the end of East Timor's isolation and closed status. By the late 1980s, Fretilin had become a more neutral organization. It had joined other organizations in the unified National Council for the Maubere Resistance (CNRM), founded in 1989 with Gusmao as president. The CNRM used more intense lobbying and diplomatic approaches, especially through its main representative abroad, José Ramos-Horta. In East Timor itself, the CNRM advocated peaceful resistance. As a result of a reduction in military activity, the Indonesian government relaxed its tight controls in 1988, allowing the local people to travel more freely inside and outside of East Timor. The use of torture and arbitrary military violence were also reduced, while the Indonesians attempted to polish their image abroad on human rights issues. Instead of a guerilla war, the conflict increasingly pitted young peaceful protesters in urban centers against soldiers.[19]

East Timor gained renewed attention from governments around the world when the Indonesian armed forces opened fire on a peaceful demonstration in Dili on 12 November 1991. During a procession to the Santa Cruz cemetery following a memorial mass for the death of Sebastio (Gomes) Rangel, a young Timorese killed in a skirmish between Indonesian soldiers and young nationalist activists, some demonstrators shouted pro-independence slogans and showed support for Fretilin. Despite the peaceful nature of the demonstration, the Indonesian soldiers opened fire and killed at least fifty people.[20] A foreign journalist captured the shooting on camera and smuggled out the footage. The worldwide broadcast of the incident ended the Indonesian information clamp on East Timor. The government was severely criticized for the incident and more generally for human rights abuses in the territory.

During the subsequent decade, the limelight on East Timor never dissipated. Indonesia was pressured to find a negotiated solution to the problem, as domestic constituents among its major international partners, including the United States and Australia, maintained a greater scrutiny over their governments' stance on human rights abuses in East Timor. When the Nobel Peace Prize was awarded in 1996 to Ramos-Horta and Carlos Belo, the resistance movement gained even further international recognition and legitimation.

The status quo altered quite rapidly when political conditions suddenly changed, with the fall of Suharto and the beginning of a period of democratization. President Habibie was unable to maintain his predecessor's tight control over the military, whose image was severely weakened by the events that had led to Suharto's downfall.

East Timor's future became a central issue for Habibie's new government. Demonstrations in East Timor and in Jakarta demanded a resolution of the conflict.[21] East Timorese representatives stepped up their diplomatic efforts internationally now that authoritarian rule appeared to be diminishing. Faced with difficulties in consolidating his power, Habibie came to rely on the military's ability and willingness to quell dissent as it arose across the country. The military was over-stretched and the government continued to suffer from the effects of the 1997–98 economic crisis.[22] East Timor was a thorn in Indonesia's relationship with foreign donors, and the benefits of retaining the province appeared few.

In a surprise move to create allies abroad and to solidify his leadership at home, Habibie offered a special autonomy package for East Timor. At first, he announced in June 1998 that Indonesia was prepared to offer wide-ranging autonomy, thereby setting a new basis for the stalled negotiations between Indonesia and Portugal on the latter's former colony.

Faced with mass protests demanding a referendum, a resurgence of violence by armed groups in the province, and little enthusiasm for the proposal from the East Timorese leadership, Habibie proposed on 27 January 1999 that if the offer of wide-ranging autonomy was rejected, East Timor would be given its independence.[23] Considerable uncertainty surrounded the means by which this decision would be made. Finally, an agreement was reached to hold a referendum on the autonomy proposal. Indonesia and Portugal spelled out the terms of the referendum on 5 May: it would be monitored by the United Nations; Indonesia would be responsible for security during the referendum; and the results would be ratified by Indonesia's supreme legislative body, the People's Consultative Assembly (MPR).

The months leading up to the 5 May agreement, and subsequently to the referendum scheduled for August 1999, showed the fragility of the new government. While Habibie favored a diplomatic solution, the armed forces were infiltrating East Timor and arming para-military groups to create a civil war aimed at disrupting the referendum and ensuring that the territory remained in the Republic. Habibie's attempts to portray Indonesia as a new democracy and to consolidate his leadership were being undermined by Operasi Sapu Jagad (Operation Global Clean-Sweep) that undertook a covert campaign threatening pro-independence Timorese and preparing for violent outbreak if autonomy was rejected in the August referendum. Violence escalated between November 1998 and August 1999, with pro-autonomy militias undertaking increasing numbers of attacks against pro-independence groups. A small United Nations mission, UNTAET, was dispatched to East Timor to support the organization of the referendum but did not have a mandate to prevent the mounting violence.[24]

The referendum was held on 30 August 1999 in relative peace but the announcement of results unleashed an unprecedented wave of violence against the civilian population. The vote was freely held and pro-integration militias refrained from intimidating the population at the polls, although they had been issuing warnings and death threats for months before then. Out of 451,792 registered voters and with 97% of these voters having cast their ballots, 78.5% rejected Indonesia's wide-ranging autonomy proposal (against 21% in support). This result was widely considered to show strong support for independence.[25] Only hours after the results were announced, pro-autonomy militias descended on villages, burning, looting, and displacing the local population. Within a few days, 200,000 refugees had fled to the mountains and to the neighboring province of West Timor, while the militias engaged in vast destruction. Supported by elements of Indonesia's armed forces, and apparently with the tacit approval of the high levels of military command, the militias undertook to either maintain Timor through violence or, at least, to punish the Timorese for favoring independence.[26]

The vote had wounded the armed forces, which was unable to keep the territory within Indonesia because of intense international pressure to accelerate the transition to independence after the results of the referendum. Hundreds of people were killed and thousands became refugees as a result of the systematic destruction of the capital, Dili, and hundreds of villages. Although the United Nations sent a peacekeeping force with a mandate to stop the violence, the damage had already been done by the time it arrived and the militias had retreated into West Timor.

Under UN occupation, the transition to independence occurred swiftly. The territory was under de facto UN rule during the months leading up to the MPR session in October 1999, even though Indonesia continued to assume official responsibility for security. Police forces and some troops from the armed forces patrolled side-by-side with UN troops. The Habibie government was under fire from the rest of Indonesia for losing East Timor, and the armed forces were widely criticized for actively arming the militias and were humiliated by their inability to integrate the territory into the Republic. The MPR approved the transfer of authority to a temporary UN body that would oversee the gradual transfer of power to an independent East Timorese government. Gusmao, the Fretilin leader, was released from prison and returned triumphantly to East Timor. The newly elected president, Abdurrahman Wahid, gave his support to East Timor's independence and offered Indonesia's fullest cooperation.[27]

Irian Jaya (Papua)

Irian Jaya shares a history similar to that of East Timor.[28] The main difference is its former inclusion in the Dutch East Indies that, in theory, meant it shared a similar historical experience with other regions of the archipelago. In fact, the colonial experience in West New Guinea was quite different from elsewhere and, as a result, the Papuans had very little contact with people from other regions. Certainly, when young nationalists from Java, Sumatra, Ambon, and other areas shared ideals to create an independent Indonesia, Papuans were shielded from this movement. They did not join the revolution and did not become part of the new Indonesian state in 1949. Instead, they remained under Dutch colonial rule until an international agreement sealed their fate. In 1963, without broad consultation, they were integrated into the Indonesian

Republic. Then, in 1969, they were subjected to an "Act of Free Choice," which saw unanimous support by the chosen representatives for the integration.

Although the consultation was accepted by the United Nations, the process was not democratic and was widely criticized by Papuans and many foreigners. It strengthened and expanded a Papuan nationalism that had emerged in the previous decades. For almost thirty years, many Papuans resisted the Indonesians by joining the Free Papua Movement, while the Indonesian administration intensified its control over the territory. With democratic transition, the nationalist movement mobilized and clearly showed that a majority of Papuans desired independence.

For most of the official period of Dutch colonialism, West New Guinea remained isolated from other areas of the archipelago. Prior to the arrival of the Dutch, a few coastal villages had contacts with some Moluccan islands. The Dutch made an official claim over West New Guinea in 1848 but only indirectly by including it within the territorial control of the Sultan of Tidore. The Dutch only allocated a first, small budget for its administration in 1898, and established an actual presence in the territory only in the 1920s and 1930s. In 1938, there were still only 15 European administrators for the whole colony and 200 European residents. With no known economic resources, West New Guinea was considered a buffer zone to protect the Moluccan islands, which were at the centre of the Dutch colonial venture.[29]

West New Guinea became the subject of an international dispute at the end of the 1940s. During the four years of fighting and various agreements between the Dutch and the Indonesian Republic after 1945, it was excluded. The Dutch considered it a separate colony, to be dealt with separately. When they finally agreed to leave Indonesia in 1949, they retained control over West New Guinea.[30] This issue continued to divide Indonesia and the former colonial power.

The Indonesians and Dutch had divergent interests over West New Guinea. The Dutch wanted to retain some colonial prestige after losing most of the Dutch East Indies. There were few other interests since there were no economic or strategic benefits at the time. Some groups wanted a new homeland for Eurasians and the creation of a "tropical" Holland but, on the whole, this project was short-lived.[31] For the Indonesians, the question of "Irian" became a symbol of their nationalist struggle. As President Sukarno stated in his Independence Day anniversary address of 1950: "The Irian question is a question of colonialism or non-colonialism, a question of colonialism or independence. Part of our country is still colonized by the Dutch . . . In our present Constitution it is expressly laid down that the territory of our State comprises the entire former Netherlands Indies, that is from Sabang to Merauke".[32] This nationalist credo defended a territorial homeland that included West New Guinea.

Both the Dutch and the Indonesians ignored the Papuans' stance on their future. Papuans were left out of every conference where their future was negotiated, except the first meeting in Malino. According to Robert Bone, both the Dutch and the Indonesians discarded the option of a democratic process involving consultation with the Papuans, since more than 50% had never been in contact with the outside world and were considered to be still in a Stone Age culture. The Papuans were also considered too diverse and always at war with each other.[33]

Yet, the Dutch shifted their strategy after 1949 and began to invest heavily in Papuan economic and political development. As Arend Lijphart observed, this development was impressive and led to remarkable achievements, especially in education and health. Large government subsidies were invested in a variety of programs.[34] The Dutch relied on the Protestant and Catholic churches for health and education, while also training the Papuans in business and administration. For those who benefitted from this development, Dutch colonialism was welcomed: "With this kind of pattern, Papuans did not feel colonized. It strengthened the Papuans' desire to become their own nation".[35]

The Dutch educated and shaped a Papuan elite, with the ultimate goal of self-determination. Negotiations became increasingly tense with the Indonesians throughout the 1950s. Failure to obtain support in the United Nations prompted Sukarno to nationalize Dutch corporations, expel Dutch citizens, and suggest Indonesia's readiness for war over West New Guinea. In response, the Dutch gave an impetus to Papuan nationalism by creating a West New Guinea Council in 1961 composed of twenty-eight members, most of whom were Papuans. Queen Juliana herself declared that the objective was self-determination.[36]

Stimulated by these Dutch policies, this elite increasingly thought of a Papuan nation. Clearly, the nationalist movement included only a small proportion of Papuans. In 1960, there were only 1,000 Papuan teachers and 9,000 occupying government positions. Along with those involved in the private sector, only about 50,000 Papuans had left their traditional lifestyles. Most Papuans who would play any significant leadership role in the future had all attended the same public administration school created in 1944.[37] Yet, this group was thinking of itself as a nation: "The Dutch used the church (especially boarding schools) and various tribal groups, from Merauke, Fak-Fak, and elsewhere. We met there and formed bonds. That generation saw itself as becoming a free nation. Inter-ethnic conflict existed, but we started to think in terms of one nation".[38] With the rise of this national consciousness, in October 1961 a group of Papuan leaders signed a nationalist manifesto and adopted a flag and a national anthem, and designated West Papua as their homeland.[39]

In some ways, the Dutch can be accused of creating an elite serving its own interests, as most of the Papuans were excluded. There is little doubt that nationalist thought had not reached most of them, who were still unaware even of the presence of the Dutch and for whom the notion of a united Papuan people did not exist. Yet, as in most other places, a nationalist consciousness usually began with a small elite and then spread as an idea through mobilization and socialization. As Benedict Anderson has aptly argued, nations are "imagined communities" and Papuans were no different. As a result of colonial policies, elites from various Papuan groups were brought together, and developed the shared experience and common bond that has characterized many nascent nationalist movements.[40] The absence of such a shared history, common experience, or interaction with elites from other areas of the Dutch East Indies explains why the Papuans did not adhere to the Indonesian nationalist movement from the 1920s and 1930s.

The basis of nationalism in a common culture may overstate the distinctions between the Papuans and the Indonesians. During negotiations over West New Guinea, the Dutch made the argument that the Papuans, as Melanesians, were racially distinct from the Malays of the rest of the archipelago. The Indonesians, on the other hand, argued that links with the rest of the archipelago had always existed and West Irian had been an integral part of past empires that encompassed the whole archipelago. Furthermore, they argued, Indonesia was composed of many different ethnic groups speaking dozens of languages and therefore could accommodate racial differences. Consistent with its logic of national unity, in 1956 Indonesia even named a Moluccan as first governor of the province of West Irian, based in Tidore, Maluku.[41]

These debates show the absence of objective cultural bases underlying any particular form of nationalism. There are many reasons why either Indonesian or Papuan nationalism might have prevailed. Once created, a nationalist movement can either capture the imagination of a wider group or become irrelevant and die. According to Gabriel Defert, most observers around 1962 agreed that a majority of urban Papuans preferred independence to the option of joining Indonesia.[42] This is not surprising, given that no alternative, Indonesian national movement had taken root.

Papuan nationalism might also have arisen out of a proto-nationalist movement based on millenarian imagery. The Koreri millenarian movement that surfaced on and around Biak became more political with the rise of a leader called Angganitha Manufaur, one of its *konoor*.[43]

Previously based on the promise of a better and richer eternal world, the movement also incorporated Judeo-Christian symbols and beliefs. In the 1930s, Angganitha transformed the movement into a more political one, involving the ability to take its own destiny in its hands, especially by resisting the colonial presence. A flag was adopted, with the use, for the first time, of the Morning Star as its most important symbol. After Angganitha, the movement was more explicitly designed to foster unity among all tribes in West New Guinea, with the objective of resisting foreign intrusion. As it lost more of its religious character, it began to fade away. Nevertheless, it laid the basis for future such movements, the rise of common objectives and unity among various tribes, the beginnings of ideas of self-determination (or forging one's destiny by resisting outsiders), and some of the symbols that were later adopted by the nationalist movement.[44]

Once a Papuan nationalism had begun to emerge, it would persist despite the attempts of Indonesians to fully integrate West New Guinea. The Indonesians proceeded first from a logic of territorial integration, prior to finding the means to assimilate the Papuans to the common national characteristics of Indonesia. In the name of an Indonesian nation and state, the Papuans were subjected to an intensive military, political, and social program of integration.

The formal means of integration provided a crucial moment for Papuan nationalism, as the process was deemed illegitimate. The Dutch ceded West New Guinea to Indonesia in the New York agreement, which transferred the territory to a temporary UN administration (UNTEA) on 1 October 1962 and to Indonesia on 1 May 1963. The agreement stipulated that a plebiscite be held before 1969 to consult Papuans on their preference for integration into Indonesia or self-determination.

The Act of Free Choice in 1969 was highly contested. After 1963, the Indonesian military had banned political parties and activities. Soldiers plundered the territory, stealing and selling outside of the province the technical equipment and other valuables left behind by the Dutch, including air conditioners from the Hollandia hospital. Military activity increased during the years leading up to the Act of Free Choice. After months of military intimidation and repression prior to the consultation, delegates cast a unanimous vote in favor of integration. During the process, the UN observers were restricted in their movements and their ability to properly monitor the consultation, a revolt in Paniai was crushed by Indonesian troops, Papuans were arrested in all areas where opposition to Indonesia was suspected, and the UN authorities received many petitions demanding a West Papuan independent state. Nevertheless, the results of the consultation were accepted by the United Nations, and West Irian became officially part of Indonesia.[45]

For Papuan nationalists, this event marked the beginnings of their re-solve for independence. Even some who later served in the upper echelons of the civil service saw the Act of Free Choice as an illegitimate pro-cess: "Papuans were forced [to accept the results] . . . forced! [Because at that time, the regime was] very authoritarian. In addition, Papuans were considered primitive and so unlikely to be able to cast a vote in the Act of Free Choice with a one man, one vote system. But all of this is false!"[46] The Act was seen as a faulty process in which delegates had been either hand-picked by the Indonesians or intimidated to support integration.[47]

Resistance to Indonesia mainly took the form of a guerilla movement. Many Papuans fled to the jungle or across the border into Papua New Guinea, forming small groups of armed resistance that became known as the Free Papua Movement (OPM). Its members were armed with scarcely more than bows and arrows, or the occasional rifle from the First World War. The movement's first action had been in 1965, a short hit-and-run attack. Among the Arfak people, where the movement first appeared, it had sparked a rebellion that was brutally repressed by Indonesian forces. By some estimates 2,000 people had been killed. As the military increased its repression against the OPM leading up to the Act of Free Choice, the movement spread to several areas of Irian and many small uprisings were organized. Although it was a weak movement, divided, poorly organized, and poorly armed, it became a symbol of resis-tance to Indonesian rule.[48] The group continued to organize in various regions in the following years.

After 1969, the Indonesians used a multi-faceted approach to integra-tion. Military force was the main instrument used to quell the resistance and intimidate the population against joining any opposition group. There were some indications that the ultimate objective might be to inculcate a sense of belonging to Indonesia as well, although programs and policies in this direction were minimal. Instead, the Indonesian government seemed to encourage assimilation by making Irian its primary target area for transmigrants. Spontaneous migration also increased rapidly after 1969. Whether or not the government actually intended to use it to assimi-late the Papuans, in-migration was certainly consistent with its political objectives.

From the 1960s, military campaigns were regularly waged. In 1977, when more than 15,000 Dani and related clans rose up in opposi-tion to the Indonesians, military forces dropped napalm on villages across the region. Military airplanes strafed a whole area where an incident occurred in a village 40 km away in Timika, near the American-owned Freeport-McMoran mining company. In retaliation, a group of Papuans sabotaged a Freeport pipeline, which was met with an even more brutal response by the military.[49] Military campaigns throughout the 1980s were on a smaller scale and were most often concentrated around the provincial capital, renamed Jayapura, and along the Papua–New Guinea border, where the OPM sought refuge after its hit-and-run raids.[50] Nevertheless, their consequences were quite important. An Amnesty International report estimated that at least 11,000 people fled across the border into Papua New Guinea between 1984 and 1986 in response to military retaliations following a failed anti-Indonesian uprising in February 1984.[51]

As reports of human rights abuses increased, the military diminished the scale of its responses but violence against civilians, torture, disappearances, and shootings continued. In 1995 for the first time, a local report denounced military abuses relating to more intense activity between the OPM and ABRI (the armed forces) between June and December 1994. Following several incidents near Timika, eleven people were shot dead in the village of Hoea. Also, twenty people in Tembagapura were arrested, beaten, and tortured during demonstrations in December 1994.[52] Several people were killed when troops opened fire on rioters near Timika in March 1996. Only a week later, five people were killed and more than one hundred arrested in a riot in Abepura, near Jayapura. Several among them were beaten and tortured.[53] In the following year, a military operation throughout the Timika area caused at least eleven deaths and two disappearances. Dozens of houses and several churches were burned down by military forces and, as of March 1998, more than thirty people had died of starvation related to the operation.[54]

The OPM was never able to mount a serious challenge to Indonesian rule. It did not change significantly from the loose organization of the late 1960s. In the early 1980s, there were at least four different groups, armed with only rudimentary weapons. They appeared to have fewer rivalries among them, as younger leaders replaced their predecessors who were even known to enter into fighting with each other. They also began to make diplomatic links to groups such as the World Council of Indigenous Peoples and Australian aboriginal groups.[55] Yet, they remained fairly separate, sharing only the ultimate objective of an independent West Papua. Otherwise, the tactics of resistance varied from groups involved in hit-and-run attacks to others using kidnappings to raise attention.[56] The OPM was merely a symbolic resistance.

Aside from the emphasis on crushing separatist rebels, the Indonesian government ruled the province in a way that was reminiscent of colonialism. The economy was developed primarily to the benefit of foreign investors and their partners in Jakarta. Education and social programs were aimed more at integrating Papuans with the rest of

Indonesia than adapting them to the specific context and character-istics of the Papuans. Cultural expression was viewed with suspicion, as it was usually interpreted as a manifestation of Papuan nationalism. Instead, cultural symbols of Java and the rest of Indonesia were imposed. These measures were combined with a laissez-faire approach to large in-migration that threatened the Papuans' economic well-being and even their demographic advantage.

Papuans received few benefits from the economic development of their province. Irian Jaya became a resource-rich province after the discovery of copper and gold. PT Freeport, the Indonesian business owned by Freeport-McMoran, was inaugurated in 1973 and produced large profits for its investors and the Indonesian government. It was estimated for the first three-quarters of 1980 that Freeport's gross sales were over US$122 million and the Indonesian government received $22 million in taxes. Yet, Papuans benefitted little from all these profits as few of them were hired at the mine and, if they were, obtained only low-skilled jobs.[57] Even Ginandjar Kartasasmita, the head of the National Development Agency (Bappenas), recognized in 1996 that the riots in Timika occurred, in part, because Papuans in the area felt few benefits from Freeport's min-ing activities.[58] As for the government's total development budget, vir-tually none of the funds were aimed at development of the Papuans. Of a budget of $34 million (compared to estimates of $600 million in revenue from exports from the province), most of the funds in 1990 were allocated to administrative costs (67%), roads (10%), and trans-migration (8%). The few agricultural development programs were all aimed at transmigrant communities, while Papuans were recipients of na-tional Indonesian programs and slogans with little impact on their daily lives.[59]

Education centered on an Indonesian curriculum. It had a strong emphasis on the learning of the Indonesian language but local lan-guages were not taught. Pupils learned Indonesian history with only a small reference to Irian, from an Indonesian perspective. They learned the slogans and songs of Indonesian nationalism, and would sing the Indonesian national anthem beneath the Indonesian flag. They were taught also the principles of Indonesia's national ideology, Pancasila. Courses placed much emphasis on local conditions in Java. Although this curriculum was no different from that in other parts of Indonesia, it ap-peared particularly irrelevant to the conditions, culture, and history of the Papuans.

Furthermore, Papuans rarely went beyond elementary school. High schools were scarce and entry levels to university were set by national exams in which Papuans did poorly. It was even difficult for them to gain access to Cendrawasih University, the main university in Irian Jaya.[60]

Migration threatened the Papuans' livelihood and their demographic majority. Most of the migration after 1969 was spontaneous but the Indonesian government certainly made no attempts to diminish the flow. In fact, its transmigration program contributed to this in-migration. In 1977, Irian Jaya was named a priority destination. Exact figures are not available but estimates for the number of transmigrants between 1979 and 1989 vary from 70,000 to 150,000 (compared to an estimated population of 1.2 million Papuans). The central government had actually fixed a target of 1.7 million, which would have rendered the Papuans a minority in their own province.

Spontaneous migrants came in much greater numbers and constituted the greatest threat to Papuans. Exact figures are not available but it is estimated that, out of a population of 2.6 million in 2000, 1.6 million were Papuan and 1 million were spontaneous migrants and transmigrants. Most of the influx came to the major towns of the province, with Jayapura growing from 50,000–80,000 in the 1970s to 200,000–300,000 in 2000. Timika and Sorong also saw their population quadruple. The migrant population increased rapidly while the Papuan population remained very stable, without much change since the 1950s, mainly because of poor health and high infant mortality.[61] In addition, migrants quickly gained access to resources, land, and jobs. The government encouraged rice cultivation, which expanded from 900 tons in 1974 to 52,000 tons in 1990, mainly in transmigration areas. No subsidies were allocated for the production of sago, the local staple. Furthermore, fishermen from South and Southeast Sulawesi could better compete, given the use of modern technologies.[62] Bugis, Madurese, and Torajan migrants controlled small businesses and were joined by many Javanese who abandoned transmigration sites. Migrants overwhelmingly occupied private sector and government jobs. This trend was reinforced by corrupt practises by which migrants controlling access to new positions hired friends and families over local Papuans. As a result, Papuans found themselves relegated to their traditional means of livelihood, isolated from the cities and decreasing in numbers.

Papuans were also denied the freedom to express their culture and were fed, instead, the symbols of Indonesian culture. Their own province was named "Irian," even after local Papuans saw it as an Indonesian fabrication.[63] It was renamed "Irian Jaya" (Victorious Irian) in 1973 and the provincial capital, "Jayapura" (Victory City), using Sanskrit words associated with Javanese culture. Shortly after 1969, the Indonesians undertook a campaign ("campaign Koteka") in the Papuan highlands to persuade people to abandon their penis-sheaths (*koteka*) and wear "modern" clothes instead.[64] Papuan songs or cultural expressions were deemed to be nationalist. The government sought instead to bring the

Papuans within the common realm of Indonesian culture. As Foreign Minister Mochtar Kusumaatmaja once stated on Australian television:

Culture is a changing thing, and I think it's a mistake to want to preserve a certain culture and freeze it at a certain time . . . What we are doing in Irian Jaya is to introduce the Irianese, which are admittedly of a different cultural level, into the mainstream of Indonesian life and I don't think there is anything wrong with that . . . They will be part of the Indonesian nation.[65]

The Papuans' culture was seen as an obstacle to their ability to become modern citizens of Indonesia.

For most of the post-1963 period, therefore, Papuan nationalism was curtailed while the Indonesian government fostered greater integration and assimilation. If Papuan nationalism survived, it was probably at least partly a result of the means chosen by the Indonesians to integrate the Papuans. With the heavy emphasis on military repression and territorial control, Papuans had few incentives to develop strong loyalties to the Indonesian nation.

Aside from the OPM resistance, there were few occasions when civilians openly expressed nationalist aspirations. In 1980, a group of six women attempted to raise a flag in front of the governor's office. They were arrested, raped, and imprisoned.[66] Arnold Ap, the curator of the ethnology museum at Cendrawasih University, recorded and preserved Papuan culture. Indonesian Special Forces (Kopassandha) shot him dead in 1983 because his cultural work and public appeals were seen as dangerously nationalist. In 1984, more than 100 Papuans from the local Brimob police forces (SWAT team) defected and protested after an ABRI corporal was shot when attempting to raise the Papuan flag over the ABRI regional headquarters. In 1988, Thomas Wanggai, a civil servant and former candidate for governor, was arrested after a flag-raising ceremony and declaration of independence of the "West Melanesian" state, at a large meeting in Jayapura. Wanggai, who had not been a popular leader among Papuans, became a symbol of Papuan resistance. When he died in 1996, riots broke out in Abepura, near Jayapura, when his body was returned for burial.[67] These events showed the resilience of the nationalist movement that seemed to gain broader appeal with every instance of repression.

With the Indonesian democratic transition in 1998, the popular appeal of the nationalist movement became clear. Democratization could have begun a period in which ethnonationalist appeals would be diminished, as institutions became better vehicles for the representation of interests. Yet, in the case of Irian Jaya, Indonesian democratization led to a resurgence of Papuan nationalism.

As President Habibie began to relax political controls, groups of Papuans mobilized in favor of independence. In July 1998, demonstrations were organized in major cities throughout Irian Jaya to demand demilitarization, a revision of the process leading to the Act of Free Choice, and a referendum on independence. Thousands of people demonstrated, singing the Papuan anthem and raising the Morning Star flag, symbol of Papuan nationalism.[68]

Despite more liberalization, the Indonesian armed forces repressed activities deemed to be separatist. Their commander, Wiranto, was clear on the government's perspective: "Wherever in Indonesia a flag other than the red-and-white flag [of the Republic of Indonesia] is displayed during a demonstration, this is a separatist act that shatters national unity and integrity".[69] In one incident, a student was killed in Abepura after the armed forces opened fire on the campus of Cendrawasih University. In Biak, the security forces fired rubber bullets at demonstrators who resisted calls to lower the Morning Star flag after it was raised on 2 July.[70] Attempts to make demands through peaceful demonstrations were limited by their link to demands for independence.

Yet, despite early responses involving the armed forces, the Habibie government and the Indonesian parliament were willing to investigate Papuan grievances and propose some solution. A fact-finding team from the national parliament (DPR) was sent to Irian Jaya at the end of July. According to Abdul Gafur, the leader of the team, Papuans were not primarily separatist but were dissatisfied with their experience within Indonesia. He conveyed their desire to see the name of the province changed to Papua and recommended that the planned autonomy provided to all provinces was the best course of action.[71] In October, Habibie lifted the status of Military Operations Region (DOM) after almost thirty years, which signaled a possible reduction in the military approach to the conflict. He also agreed to pursue a dialogue with the Forum for the Reconciliation of Irian Jaya Society (Foreri), which had been formed in June and included a wide range of representatives from local churches, universities, *adat* groups, women's groups, and students. Foreri denounced the process of integration into Indonesia and proposed three options: full independence, wide-ranging autonomy within Indonesia's unitary state, or federalism. Ultimately, it wanted a referendum for Papuans to choose their future and a process whereby autonomy would be implemented via the Indonesian legislative process (MPR and/or DPR).[72]

The discussions with Foreri culminated on 26 February 1999 in an unprecedented meeting of 100 Papuan representatives with President Habibie. Tom Beanal, the team leader, stood up and read a joint declaration that denounced the history of Irian's integration into Indonesia and formally demanded independence. Negotiators for the meeting had obtained guarantees that the group could speak freely without fear of prosecution, including on the issue of independence.[73] Yet, Habibie was shocked by the declaration. He listened carefully to their demands but reasserted that independence was impossible.[74] The plans for a national dialogue effectively ended that day.

The Indonesian government returned to a repressive approach. Across Irian Jaya, hundreds of volunteers had erected communication posts (*posko*) that supported the independence option. Discussions were organized with Team 100 members to inform the public of the meeting with Habibie. By April, however, the regional police head ordered a ban on these posts and discussions. Many Team 100 members were arrested or banned from traveling abroad.[75]

Instead of a dialogue, the government unilaterally decided to divide Irian Jaya into three provinces. This measure was supposedly intended to increase not only the amount of resources that could be retained but also the capacity of local governments to gain access to various parts of the area. The law dividing the province was passed by the DPR, and formalized on 25 September by a presidential decree creating positions for two new governors. Papuans protested and accused the government of attempting to divide them to prevent further separatist tendencies. The proposal was short-lived. When Abdurrahman Wahid was inaugurated as president on 1 November, he cancelled the planned division in response to the widespread protests.[76]

Wahid's presidency began with a more open approach. On 12 November, Theys Eluay, an *adat* leader and prominent nationalist, called for a province-wide hoisting of the Morning Star flag on 1 December 1999 to celebrate the declaration of West Papuan independence in 1961. This declaration was made at a large gathering for his birthday that even included the local police chief and military commander. The government already appeared to tolerate flag raisings as Morning Star flags had been displayed in Timika since 10 November without any intervention from security forces.[77] In the end, the flag-raising ceremonies were allowed, as long as the Indonesian flag was also on display. On 1 December, Morning Star flags were raised in eleven towns and massive gatherings occurred everywhere to celebrate West Papuan independence. Tens of thousands of people participated in these events and, by some local NGO accounts, perhaps up to 800,000 people.[78] The flag raisings raised high emotions as many Papuans imagined independence to be near. In the days preceding the flag raising, one frequently heard statements such as: "We will raise the flag on December 1st and then it will be over; we'll be independent".[79] Wahid then visited the province on 31 December. He discussed Papuan grievances with community representatives and nationalist leaders and, in a symbolic gesture, decided to rename the province Papua, although he reiterated the government's position that independence was not an option.[80]

The next year was characterized by a struggle between Papuan nationalists and a fragile democratic government. Some of the Papuan nationalist elite saw an opportunity from the democratic opening to organize the nationalist movement and mobilize Papuans for independence. Given his democratic approach, Wahid sought to appease nationalist fervor, while setting limits to dialogue and compromise. Yet, he was attacked by parliamentarians who focused on the hesitations and contradictions in his actions and decisions, and denounced him for threatening national unity. Furthermore, this debate occurred as East Timor gained its independence and the former president, Habibie, was widely criticized for allowing the referendum that led to its loss. Still wounded by the Timorese issue, much of the Indonesian political elite wanted to take fewer risks toward Irian Jaya.

Papuan nationalists formalized their movement by organizing two congresses. The first (Mubes) was arranged only a few weeks after Wahid's visit to the region, from 23 to 26 February 2000. Every district in Irian Jaya was asked to send ten representatives from a variety of groups, including youth, women, religious, and *adat* leaders. For the Papuan People's Congress from 29 May to 4 June 2000, another ten representatives per district were added.[81] According to the organizers of both congresses, however, it was difficult to restrict access to the meetings as they represented the first democratic opportunity for Papuans to express themselves openly. It was especially difficult because many Papuans wanted to ensure they would not be manipulated: "Both the Mubes and Congress were flooded with people. Thousands came to ensure that the organizing committee and the PDP would not be like the Pepera [the Act of Free Choice]".[82]

At the Mubes, three main issues were discussed: the need to re-examine the history of Papua's integration into Indonesia; the definition of a political strategy and coordinated approach for the Papuan movement; and the consolidation of the movement.[83] In its resolutions, the Mubes stated its strong opposition to the Act of Free Choice and the process of integration. It criticized the Papuan people's experience with Indonesia, including human rights abuses, impoverishment, and cultural genocide. It reiterated demands for independence.[84] The Mubes finished its deliberations by naming a Presidium of the Papuan Assembly (PDP).

The Papuan People's Congress (Kongress Papua) consolidated the nationalist movement. After several days discussing the same issues as the Mubes, it condemned the failures of the international community to acknowledge past historical injustices, demanded its involvement in recognizing the Papuan right to self-determination, and reaffirmed calls for independence.[85] The structure and function of the PDP were reaffirmed and Congress members were named as representatives of the Papuan Assembly (Dewan Papua).[86]

The Congress appeared to seal the nationalist elite's objectives and strategy. The elite was previously divided along ethnic and personal lines. Some leaders had espoused a more cautious approach and disapproved of Theys Eluay's calls for flag raisings on 1 December 1999, an act that the Indonesian government would inevitably consider provocative. Suspicions of Theys Eluay ran high because he was one of the representatives of the Act of Free Choice and was subsequently involved in the government party, Golkar. During his rise to prominence in 1998–99, he was also associated with Yorrys Raweyai, formerly close to the Suharto family. As a result, many thought they might be trying to manipulate the Irian issue to the advantage of elites close to Suharto. Other Papuan nationalists, such as Tom Beanal, had a long record of opposing the Indonesian government and supporting independence. Furthermore, ethnic groups from the Central Highlands were suspicious of the political activities of coastal groups, as they blamed the latter for having allowed the integration to occur while the Central Highland groups were still unaware of these events. Consequently, while the Mubes was still viewed with some suspicion, the Congress was widely recognized as democratic and legitimate among all groups, and Theys' leadership was acknowledged even if he had appointed himself Papuan leader and PDP head.[87]

The OPM's role diminished after the Congress. It had continued its usual tactics, such as hit-and-run attacks and kidnappings, but the PDP wanted a peaceful approach. As Theys Eluay stated: "The OPM already agrees with us. And we have already requested that they cease their hostilities".[88] In fact, some OPM factions were given representation within the PDP.[89] As a result, it lost much of the symbolic support and the PDP became the main vehicle for Papuan nationalism.

The government's response to the Mubes and the Congress was inconsistent. Wahid continued to espouse an open approach, while military and police forces in Irian Jaya used a more repressive one. Wahid had seen flag raisings as cultural expressions and not necessarily separatist acts. He had provided one billion rupiah to finance the Congress. He also arranged a meeting on 4 July 2000 with Theys Eluay.[90] He was severely criticized for these decisions, however, by MPR representatives. The August meeting of the MPR refused to endorse Wahid's proposal to change Irian Jaya's name to Papua and noted his ineffectiveness in addressing the issue of separatism. Meanwhile, the military and police forces in Irian Jaya continued to counter demonstrations and flag raisings. Several people were killed or injured in Nabire (July 2000),

Merauke (February 2000), and Sorong (August 2000) following clashes around flag-raising incidents.[91] For several months, therefore, the Papuan nationalist movement received different signals from Indonesian authorities.

The ambiguity ended after September 2000 when there was a definite shift to curtail the nationalist movement. Emerging scandals began to fully paralyze Wahid, whose power was already being challenged by political opponents. In Irian Jaya, as local authorities regained their ability to use repressive measures, they banned flag raisings. Serious clashes occurred in Wamena on 6 October, in which 37 people were killed, 89 injured, and dozens arrested. More than 13,000 people were reported to have left the area as a result of the violence. Ceremonies commemorating the declaration of independence were held across Papua on 1 December. Although flag raisings were tolerated on that day, several incidents occurred. Many people were killed in Merauke, Fak Fak, and Tiom as security forces tried to force people to take down the flags after the allowed time. Theys Eluay and several members of the PDP were arrested and jailed for two months in connection with a prosecution for separatist activities linked to the 1 December 1999 flag raisings, the Mubes, and the Congress.[92] The local police received orders to eliminate all separatist activities, repress the activities of the Papuan political elite, and gather intelligence information on local NGOs, foreigners, and political elites supporting separatism. It would also adopt a "preventive function" to "eliminate people involved in the separatist movement, followed by efforts to foster among the population a positive opinion so that it increasingly sides with the government of the Republic of Indonesia".[93] The Papuan movement was paralyzed by a return of repressive measures.

In parallel to the crackdown in the aftermath of the Congress, the Indonesian government offered its own proposal for special autonomy. It had already passed (in 1999) two laws that decentralized political and fiscal power to all regional-level governments (kabupaten). The MPR session of 1999, however, had gone further in adopting a motion instructing the government to develop a policy of special autonomy for Irian Jaya and Aceh. In its annual session in August 2000, it reiterated the urgency of implementing special autonomy.[94] In the following months, the governor of Irian Jaya, J. P. Solossa, put together a team to develop a draft on special autonomy. Presented to the DPR in April 2001, it included clauses protecting and reinforcing Papuan values and culture, substantially devolved power to the province, and proposed that 80% of revenue be retained by the provincial government.[95] The draft was revised and a special autonomy law was passed by the DPR in October 2001.

Special autonomy was not well received in Irian Jaya. During the drafting process, the governor's team had faced numerous protests. It had been unable to hold many special meetings to discuss the draft contents and, in the end, the process had been completed without much of the broad consultation that had been intended.[96] The new law received a very lukewarm response in the province. Many groups continued to view any form of autonomy with suspicion. The PDP, which was initially agreeable to special autonomy, later opposed it and reiterated its goal of full independence.[97]

After she became president in July 2001, Megawati Sukarnoputri reaffirmed the government's uncompromising position on the nationalist movement. In her address to the nation for the 17 August Independence Day celebrations, she apologized for the Indonesian government's treatment of Papuans and stated her commitment to rectifying past injustices, but clearly affirmed her strong opposition to Papuan independence. She continued to support military operations designed to curtail the nationalist movement, while supporting the adoption of the law on special autonomy.

Democratization created a dilemma for the Indonesian government. From Habibie to Megawati, efforts to increasingly democratize the polity had its limits: no president was willing to risk a referendum in Papua that might have the same results as in East Timor. Yet, whether created by the Dutch or maintained by a small political elite, Papuan nationalism was a reality that would not disappear. The nationalist movement tapped into the strong dissatisfaction among Papuans over their harsh treatment and marginalization since being integrated into the Republic. While the Indonesian government offered a substantial compromise with special autonomy, it would be difficult to make Papuans see the opportunities it offered. For the Papuans, there were fears that special autonomy could lead to the same results as the Act of Free Choice. Mistrust of the Indonesian government fueled the continued opposition to autonomy. In the meantime, further military and police operations against the OPM, the prosecution of PDP leaders, widely seen as representative of the Papuans, as well as the murder of Theys Eluay in November 2001, allegedly by Kopassus (special elite forces), could be seen as strong measures of force to show the government's unwillingness to compromise on state boundaries. Nevertheless, it certainly contributed to the continued climate of fear and repression that had characterized almost forty years of Indonesian rule.

Ethnonationalist violence in East Timor and Irian Jaya had its roots in the means and terms of inclusion in the Indonesian national model. In both cases, the territories were integrated by force and the people were never consulted democratically. The local populations were victims of military campaigns aimed at eradicating small groups of armed rebels. While the number of casualties was much greater in East Timor, the effects were similar in Irian Jaya. In both cases, weak identities as Timorese and Papuan were strengthened against a perception of occupation by the Indonesian government and military.

Democratization was insufficient to establish new terms of inclusion. At least in East Timor, it provided the opportunity to secede. In Papua, it offered the possibility for a civilian movement to emerge and promote secession. The government of Megawati Sukarnoputri chose to repress the movement while promoting special autonomy. There were few indications that, a year after special autonomy was implemented, secessionist objectives had diminished. Without a democratic process, the government resorted to measures designed to foster special autonomy and hope for the creation of loyalty and an Indonesian identity among Papuans. The path established at the time of integration remained almost unnavigable.

9   Aceh's ethnonationalist conflict

As in Irian Jaya and East Timor under the New Order, the conflict in Aceh took the form of an ethnonationalist struggle against the Indonesian state. When the New Order regime collapsed, the struggle broadened into a civilian movement requesting popular consultation on the future status of Aceh. In parallel to the rise of this civilian movement, the Free Aceh Movement (GAM) intensified its guerilla activities. The type of conflict and the effects of democratization on Acehnese ethnonationalism, therefore, were similar to those in Irian Jaya and East Timor.

Yet, the conflict in Aceh also had striking differences. Whereas East Timor and Irian Jaya shared a history of forced integration into the Indonesian nation, Aceh was always part of the Republic. When nationalist youth organizations organized across the archipelago to fight against the Dutch, the Acehnese joined them. Aceh was one of the regions that contributed financial support to the Indonesian revolution. Even the Darul Islam movement, the first major rebellion of the Acehnese against the Indonesian Republic, did not seek to secede but, instead, to transform the Republic. Regionalist claims and demands for independence came later and did not constitute, as in the case of East Timor and Irian Jaya, a reaction against the means of integration into the Indonesian nation.

The evolution from full participation in the Republic to strong support for secession requires explanation. At each historical juncture, when relations between Aceh and the central government were renegotiated and new institutional forms introduced, the terms of inclusion became increasingly unacceptable to a significantly high percentage of Acehnese. Once a distinct Acehnese identity was created, every subsequent institutional compromise was interpreted from the perspective of gains and losses to Aceh. With each step by the Indonesian government to implement and secure its vision of national unity, the Acehnese perceived an encroachment on Aceh. Even after obtaining special status or autonomy, the Acehnese often remained powerless to counter the Indonesian government's directives, security imperatives, or economic interests.

Analyzed from this perspective, successive rebellions in Aceh can be understood as consequences of the institutional context governing

161

identity, power, and economic distribution. The Darul Islam rebellion contested the Indonesian state that discarded the Islamic option in favor of a nationalist, secularist concept. The subsequent autonomy and provincial status of Aceh were sufficient to sway part of the elite back to the fold until the next juncture when, under Guided Democracy and the New Order regime, a more centralist, repressive institutional form of the nationalist unitary model was adopted. Some elite members became disillusioned when national imperatives and the central government's objectives superseded any claims on the basis of regional autonomy. Under the New Order regime, the state's mechanisms of response to regional rebellion were primarily based on military action, political control from the center, and limited institutional autonomy. These mechanisms were legitimated on the basis of Indonesia's established unitary state and requirements to maintain national unity. They were largely responsible for broadening and deepening the Acehnese rebellion, especially during the particularly repressive decade of the 1990s.

The large-scale mobilization in favor of Acehnese independence after May 1998, therefore, was a result of the paths taken at each institutional juncture after 1945. By this juncture, members of the civilian elite as well as the GAM seized the opportunity to demand, respectively, a referendum on independence or outright independence through armed rebellion. Few members of the elite trusted that, under the Indonesian Republic, any renewed institutional compromise could effectively provide Aceh with sufficient redress for past injustices and the political power to protect the Acehnese against future excesses from the center. The offer of wide-ranging autonomy only became later acceptable to part of the elite with the realization that continued struggle for independence would only be met with greater military repression.

More than anywhere else in Indonesia, the case of Aceh shows the dangers of securing the boundaries of the state through violent means as a precondition for negotiating ethnonationalist representation. Because the Indonesian armed forces had abused their power during the New Order regime and deepened the mistrust of the Acehnese toward the Indonesian state, the use of military force would have severe repercussions during the phase of democratization. Claiming democratic renewal while maintaining a hard line on secessionism, Suharto's successors to the presidency all approved large-scale military operations to eliminate secessionist rebellions and civilian movements associated with the option of independence. By doing so, they fed the mistrust already established during the New Order and, therefore, undermined their attempts to provide concessions in the form of institutional renewal. Jack Snyder contends that nationalist conflict can best be averted by first using coercion, or other means, to contain it and subsequently by weaving networks of civic institutions.[1] Yet, it may depend on the sequence of prior attempts to define and secure a nationalist vision. In the case of Aceh, the use of force against the secessionist movement narrowed the ability to convince the Acehnese population of the benefits of new institutional arrangements. Prior violence had created a perception of the Indonesian nation as alien, exploitative, and destructive for the Acehnese. The Indonesian government created almost insurmountable obstacles to regaining the "hearts and minds" of the people of Aceh.

The Indonesian revolution and Aceh's first rebellion

The integration of Aceh into the Indonesian Republic shows both a remarkable degree of adherence to the concept of the Indonesian nation and a strong regionalist identity. The Acehnese joined the Republic from a different starting point than many of the other regions. They had formed a unique sense of community through their past glory as a regional power, their resistance to the Dutch, and their strong Islamic identity. Yet, the elite group that gained most power and popular support in the dying days of Dutch colonialism and Japanese occupation were profoundly committed to the Republic. When the Republican government was forced to retreat because of the advances of the returning Dutch, the Acehnese formed a strong regional government and represented one of the Republic's strongholds.

The regionalist identity as Acehnese was not predetermined historically nor were there any "primordial" reasons why Aceh would become one of the most rebellious regions of Indonesia. The integration of the Republic was a defining moment that could have sealed a strong attachment to Indonesia. A regionalist identity re-emerged, however, when it became increasingly apparent to the Islamic elite in power that the nationalist leaders of the Republic did not share their goals. As nationalists and Islamists became increasingly divided on a national scale, the Acehnese felt betrayed that their strong commitment to the revolution was not rewarded with their participation in shaping the principles underlying the Indonesian nation. When nationalist leaders of the Republic regained ascendancy against the Dutch and established a unitary state in 1950, they also rejected Islam as a basis for the state. Furthermore, as the Acehnese expressed their disappointments with increasingly regionalist affirmation of their power, the unitary government abolished the province of Aceh, thereby weakening the established power base of the Islamic elite that had been the Republic's greatest ally. These decisions proved to be very costly, as they began the process of recreating a strong regionalist identity. While the rebellion that erupted in 1953 was neither a regionalist nor a separatist movement based on claims specific to Aceh, its resolution certainly had the effect of refocusing Aceh's elite on specifically regionalist objectives.

The Acehnese had a common sense of a distinct and glorious past. Despite a very diverse population, Aceh had a history as a distinct community from the regional strength of its sultanate in the sixteenth and seventeenth centuries. It had developed an expanded trade network in the sixteenth century and its influence was strong in parts of the Malay peninsula and along the coast of Sumatra. Its identity was already closely linked to the Islamic faith as it developed a vibrant culture with rich scholarly debates on Islam.[2]

The Dutch waged a costly war to gain control of Aceh. Although they succeeded in 1903, it was their most prolonged and costly colonial war, and it had a profound effect on the Acehnese. It reaffirmed the sense of collective experience and identity, as almost every Acehnese suffered from the destruction and deaths related to the conquest.[3]

The Dutch used indirect rule to govern Aceh. Before their arrival, the sultan had much symbolic power but real power resided with notables, the *uleebalang*. The *uleebalang* drew their power less from land than from control over trade and their own business ventures. When the Dutch took over, the *uleebalang* were transformed into a class of traditional *adat* chiefs and formed as "native" administrators. Their source of power shifted as they lost control over trade but gained greater possession of rice land and administrative powers, especially the administration of justice.[4]

Islamic scholars, the *ulama*, were always very influential and respected. Their power grew stronger under the Islamic revivalism of the 1920s and 1930s when new religious schools sprang up and modernist ideas spread rapidly. Among the rising modernist *ulama*, Daud Beureueh attracted a particularly strong following. Many *ulama* organized armed resistance to the Dutch during the colonial war, and some continued their resistance beyond 1904. As the *uleebalang* became close collaborators with the Dutch, the *ulama* increasingly turned their criticism toward them as well. Islam became a source of unification of the Acehnese in their resistance to the Dutch.[5]

The reformist *ulama* formed a distinctly Acehnese organization in 1939, the All-Aceh Ulama Association (PUSA). Originally created to coordinate educational activities, it became the main banner for resistance to the Dutch. Under the leadership of Daud Beureueh, PUSA and reformist *ulama* coordinated a mass uprising against the Dutch in March 1942, as Japanese forces were spreading rapidly across the Indies. In only four days, the revolt brought down the Dutch regime and, as the

Japanese arrived in Aceh on 12 March, they were greeted by enthusiastic crowds still enthralled by their victory.[6]

Under Japanese occupation, the *ulama*'s leadership role was further confirmed. In order to gain the support of the widely popular *ulama*, the Japanese created new courts and separated them from the influence of the *uleebalang*, who saw one of their strongest sources of power eliminated. They also created religious courts composed of prominent *ulama* and allowed them to rule on matters of religious importance. This partial recognition of Islamic law on certain issues contributed to the strengthening of the *ulama*'s formal authority.[7]

When the Japanese surrendered, the PUSA *ulama* joined the Indonesian revolution and shared the objectives of creating a single nation across the former Dutch East Indies. As Eric Morris argued, the revolution allowed the Acehnese to develop a consciousness as Acehnese, Islamic, and Indonesian without any contradictions in these identities. PUSA allied itself with an urban youth movement to struggle for the Republic. Islam provided the broad ideological support for this alliance as both groups shared the goals of an Islamic state. Yet, these goals were developed within a revolutionary consciousness that superseded Aceh and linked the movement to the broader revolution spreading across the archipelago.[8]

The revolution in Aceh was more profound than elsewhere. Known as the "social revolution," it led to the overthrow of the political power of the *uleebalang*. Elsewhere in the Indies, the revolution preserved the class of civil servants and traditional *adat* leaders that had supported the Dutch regime. In Aceh, however, there was a complete transformation of the power structure, as the old elite was replaced by the *ulama*. Forced to recognize this change, the central government of the Republic named Daud Beureueh military governor of the province of Aceh in July 1947. The alliance between the Acehnese *ulama* and the Indonesian Republic was sealed.[9]

The Acehnese subsequently played a key role in consolidating the Republic. When the Dutch returned and fought against the newly established Republic in 1947–48, Aceh became one of its strongholds. The Dutch regained control of the main cities in Java but stayed away from Aceh. The PUSA administration consolidated itself and refused Dutch offers to establish itself as a state in its proposed federal system. Furthermore, exports of rubber, tea, pepper, and coffee to Malaysia and Singapore kept Aceh in relatively good financial condition. Most of the revenues accrued to the region but a donation of gold was made to the Republic for the purchase of an airplane.[10]

From the revolutionary impetus against the Dutch and the consolidation of the Republic, therefore, the Acehnese elite and population were firmly behind the new Republic. The Acehnese adhered to the Indonesian nation in their common struggle against the Dutch and, furthermore, through a complete liberation by their social revolution. They shared the ideals and values that mobilized the masses behind the Indonesian nationalist movement.

By 1953, however, the Acehnese *ulama* rebelled against the Republican government. The rebellion began as Republican leaders' vision of the Indonesian nation diverged from that of the Acehnese. After briefly agreeing in 1949 to a federation between the Republic and states that remained under the control of the Dutch, the Republican leaders dissolved the federation in 1950 and adopted a unitary state. In addition, they rejected Islam as the basis of the state.

The Acehnese were disgruntled by the Republic's withdrawal of their status as a province. During negotiations with the Dutch over the transfer of sovereignty, the emergency government of the Republic of Indonesia had given Aceh provincial status. The Acehnese *ulama* had established an administrative structure under Daud Beureueh's leadership. Once the unitary state was adopted in 1950, however, Aceh was included in a larger province of North Sumatra. The Acehnese were disappointed that the Republican leaders had not consulted them nor recognized their strong loyalty throughout the revolution. From the Republic's perspective, the dissolution of the federal state and its replacement by a unitary state with ten provinces limited its capacity to extend provincial status to Aceh.[11]

The Acehnese *ulama* also resented the rejection of the Islamic state. They had fought in the spirit of an Islamic revolution. It was the unity of the *umma*, the Islamic community, that drove their common struggle with Muslims across the archipelago. Their nationalism was strongly enmeshed with the ideals of an Islamic state.[12] When President Sukarno and other leaders of the Republic chose to reaffirm the nationalist, secular orientation of the state over an Islamic vision, the *ulama* felt betrayed.

The Republican government finally tipped PUSA's leaders against it by taking firm steps to consolidate itself. It attempted to de-ethnicize the military and government by transferring Acehnese civil servants to the North Sumatran capital, Medan, and by reassigning Acehnese military officers to posts outside of the region. In turn, non-Acehnese were sent to Aceh. Furthermore, the Ministry of Religion refused to recognize the Islamic courts that had been established in Aceh.[13] The decision on the courts reaffirmed the sense among the Acehnese that the Islamic vision had been defeated.

The Acehnese population strongly supported the rebellion that began in 1953. PUSA leaders, and high-level civil servants and military officers, constituted the core members of the rebellion but tens of thousands of villagers joined. Even if the supply of arms limited their ability to fully participate, they supported the rebellion by monitoring Indonesian troop movements or providing material support. The *ulama* could mobilize the population in large part, as Nazaruddin Sjamsuddin argued, because of the respect they enjoyed among the Acehnese and because of their Islamic values and goals.[14]

The settlement of the rebellion narrowed the field of possibilities for future resistance in Aceh. Three aspects were most important. First, the violence associated with the Indonesian military created a precedent of military abuses that widened the gap between the Acehnese and the Indonesian government. As the rebellion was in full steam, in February 1955 the Republican forces shot more than one hundred people – most of the male population – in the villages of Cot Jeumpa and Pulot Leupung. Events that were perceived as using indiscriminate violence against the Acehnese population would become part of the repertoire of memories shaping the grievances against the state.[15]

Second, the compromise with the Republic allowed the Acehnese elite to redefine its objectives in regionalist terms, while abandoning its broader struggle. In order to appease the Acehnese, in late 1956 the Indonesian government had reinstated Aceh's provincial status, returned many PUSA members to their previous administrative positions, and reassigned Acehnese soldiers to serve in the region. It also gave back its own military regional command. The new regional commander, Sjammaun Gahuru, a former PUSA supporter, played an important role in convincing many rebel leaders to compromise and accept a settlement on Aceh.[16] When a cease-fire was reached in mid-1957, most rebels abandoned Daud Beureueh and joined Hasan Saleh's group which negotiated the compromise with the government. They asked for wide-ranging autonomy and the implementation of Islamic law. The government agreed only to extending wide-ranging autonomy in religion, education, and customary law, under a new status as "special region" (*daerah istimewa*).[17] It remained vague on the extent to which Islamic law could be applied in Aceh.

Third, the agreement with the government further divided the Acehnese political elite. Most of the civil servants and administrators of the area had joined the Darul Islam rebellion in 1953. They were not *ulama* but had strongly supported the PUSA leadership during the revolution. They joined Hasan Saleh and accepted the settlement with the government because a return of special status for Aceh would also mean a return to power. But the settlement was unacceptable to Daud Beureueh and other reformist *ulama*, for whom the struggle was essentially a moral one for the establishment of an Islamic Indonesia. They continued the resistance until mid-1962 and only abandoned it when Jasin, the new military commander for Aceh, declared that the special status did validate Islamic law for Aceh. He settled for an Islamic Aceh, far short of the broader goal of an Islamic state for Indonesia.[18]

By the end of the Darul Islam rebellion, peace was reached but Aceh had very different terms of inclusion in the Indonesian nation. It had failed, along with the Masyumi and other Islamists, to achieve an Islamic state in Indonesia. By 1960, the Islamists had been marginalized and the secular, nationalist vision reaffirmed in Sukarno's Guided Democracy. The resistance had solidified the Acehnese identity and experience as distinct from the rest of Indonesia. The population had suffered numerous casualties from the violence inflicted during the conflict. Furthermore, the settlement had institutionalized the Acehnese distinct identity by extending provincial status, the designation of "special region," and an informal recognition of Islamic law in Aceh. While institutionally it appeared that Aceh could pursue its unique way of life, at the same time it was bounded by the government's ultimate conception of the requisites of national unity.

The New Order and the emergence of the Free Aceh Movement

Authoritarian rule under Guided Democracy and the New Order tightened the institutional constraints on Aceh and promoted greater integration into the Indonesian national model. Aceh's special status faded rapidly with the centralization of political, economic, and military power. The regime legitimized its centralizing tendencies by appealing to the requisites of national unity, including institutional homogenization, military force to quell opposition (especially of a regionalist or separatist nature), and economic development.

This model created its own untenable tensions. The response in Aceh led to escalating violence. Because the Acehnese had been defeated in the Darul Islam rebellion, had a strong sense of communal identity, and had been given a special status, they reacted more negatively than elsewhere to the economic exploitation of their region and the use of military force to quell opposition. With every crisis in Aceh, the military increased its repressive approach, which had the direct effect of increasing support for Acehnese distinctiveness and, eventually, secession from the Republic. The crisis and violent response cycle further solidified the Acehnese common experience of violence and disillusion with a predatory central state.

The Guided Democracy and New Order institutional structures erased the special status that Aceh had gained. Under Guided Democracy, a return to the 1945 Constitution and to Pancasila ended the debate on the ideological basis of the state. The New Order regime continued this trend. Mobilization in favor of an Islamic state, whether in Aceh or elsewhere, was no longer tolerated. Furthermore, the president and the military consolidated their power relative to the legislature and political parties, which became very restricted. Patrimonial networks were the only means left of accessing resources and power. As a result, the regime could manipulate and divide the Acehnese elite.

After the promise that special status would allow for Islamic law to be implemented in Aceh, the New Order government reneged on the commitment. A regional regulation (no. 6) was passed in 1968 by the Acehnese regional assembly to implement elements of Islamic law. Despite its limited application, for example to minor issues such as the enforcement of certain dress codes, the regulation was never approved by the central government. In the realm of education, the *ulama* proposed modifications that would have reconciled the *madrasah* Islamic schools and the public elementary schools, so that every Acehnese would be exposed to both. The proposal never received an answer from the Ministry of Education and Culture, and was therefore never implemented.[19] The *ulama*, as a result, could no longer pursue their Islamic struggle: "Under the New Order, we weren't free. We were controlled by the central government. We requested autonomy for the Islamic religion, but were refused".[20] The *ulama* could no longer promote Islam in the political realm and were restricted even in the Islamic education system.

After the rebellion, there were few vehicles left to promote Islamic values. Masyumi had been banned and the freedom of other political parties was curtailed. The regime manipulated elections, and used incentives and intimidation to garner support for the government party, Golkar. Some *ulama* sought to use the new channels for access to the regime and its patronage network. They joined Golkar and the government-sponsored Indonesian Council of Ulama (MUI).[21]

With the gradual side-lining of the *ulama*, the central government fostered the development of a technocratic elite. Having received a modern education in Jakarta and abroad, yet strongly committed to Islamic values, this elite was sympathetic to the government's developmental goals. It gained ascendancy in administrative positions, the military, the provincial government, and the university, especially the local Syiah Kuala University. The technocratic vision began to supersede the Islamic vision of the *ulama*.[22]

The New Order regime allowed the Acehnese technocratic elite to penetrate its patronage network. Acehnese were able to rise to top positions in the military while others, such as Ibrahim Hasan, rose from university positions to become governors and subsequently cabinet ministers.

As head of the food procurement agency (Bulog), prominent Acehnese such as Ibrahim Hasan and Bustanil Arifin gained access to resources that served both to build their own wealth and to channel some resources back to Aceh.[23]

This penetration of the Jakarta elite by some prominent Acehnese differentiated Aceh from regions such as East Timor and Irian Jaya. In the latter areas, the elite remained marginalized and unable to tap into lucrative positions in Jakarta, thereby contributing to its active role and strong unity in the rebellion against the Indonesian state. In Aceh, however, such access to the center divided the Acehnese elite and created a constituency with a strong interest in preserving the New Order institutional order. This division contributed to the relatively weaker support that the rebellion in the 1970s and late 1980s received.[24]

Economic development was the main pillar of the New Order regime's legitimation and, in Aceh, was closely linked to the development of industrial enclaves. In 1971, large reserves of liquefied natural gas (LNG) were discovered in North Aceh. By 1977, an industrial zone had been created near Lhokseumawe where most of the LNG reserves were located. By the 1980s, Aceh was supplying 30% of the country's oil and gas exports, which were the government's main source of revenue. Other energy-dependent industries were also established, such as the ASEAN Aceh fertilizer plant and cement factories.[25]

The economic exploitation of these resources was managed by the central government following a centralized fiscal system. The logic of the system followed that of a unitary state with national development goals that superseded any regional or provincial considerations. As a result, almost all of the revenues from these investments accrued directly to foreign investors, their Indonesian partners in Jakarta, and the central government. The provincial government, in turn, received its annual budget through a system of allocation at the central government level and retained few rights to taxation. None of these gave any rights to tax the revenues from oil, gas, or other industrial activities. As a result, the provincial budget amounted to only a very small fraction of the total revenues generated in the province.[26]

For the Acehnese population, few benefits were derived from this economic activity. More than 70% of Acehnese remained employed in the agricultural sector and there were virtually no trickle-down effects from the industrial zone. Many of the skilled workers originated from outside Aceh and lived in gated compounds. A large proportion of Acehnese consequently saw little progress in their living standards, while LNG production and other industrial ventures boomed.[27]

Military repression constituted another pillar of the government's approach to Aceh. Under the New Order regime, the military had come to play a central role. The armed forces saw themselves as the ultimate guardians of national unity. As a result, they tolerated little opposition to the regime after the elimination of the Communist Party in 1965–66, especially if such opposition took the form of an ethnonationalist movement. Islamic groups were already curtailed because they were seen as a threat to the state, and Aceh had been a main region where the issue of an Islamic state had been strong. While a negotiated solution, brokered by Acehnese military officers and politicians, allowed Islamic rebels to reintegrate Acehnese society peacefully, the armed forces were not as tolerant of separatist rebels in the 1970s and late 1980s. By then, it was common for the armed forces to use military repression as a primary tool to maintain national unity, as it had already demonstrated in East Timor and Irian Jaya.

The rise of the Free Aceh Movement and the government's repressive response are a result of these three pillars of Indonesia's national model under the New Order – institutional homogenization, military force to quell opposition, and economic development. Disgruntled elites resented the central government's control over LNG and industrial production. When they formed a rebel movement and proclaimed Aceh's independence, they were firmly crushed by the Indonesian armed forces. A decade later, the movement rose again, this time with somewhat larger popular support, but the armed forces reacted with even greater repressive might. The extent of the military's use of violence, its arbitrariness, and its abuse turned the Acehnese against the military and the Indonesian state. A broad-based ethnonationalist movement emerged from the cycle of protest and repressive response.

The first emergence of the Free Aceh Movement (GAM) was marginal and had little support. Hasan di Tiro, who at the time was a local businessman and had previously been the representative of the Darul Islam at the United Nations, founded it in October 1976. He denounced the "Javanese" colonial empire and especially the exploitation of Aceh's natural resources and the use of military force to maintain control. With only a few hundred supporters, the movement declared the independence of Aceh-Sumatra in 1977, occasionally circulated propaganda, and raised the GAM flag in various locations, but undertook few military acts. The group was formed mainly of intellectuals, technocrats, and businessmen.[28] Eric Morris and Tim Kell agree in their respective analyses of the movement that it failed to capture wide support, in part because it barely mentioned Islam.[29] Certainly, the absence of an Islamic agenda kept the *ulama* from supporting the movement and some even denounced it. Among the broader population, it was too early in the development of the province's large gas resources for strong resentment at the few socio-economic benefits of industrial production to have arisen.

The ethnic appeals to an Acehnese independent state did not seem to capture a wide audience.

The re-emergence of the GAM in the late 1980s was different. The armed forces had arrested many supporters and virtually eliminated the threat by 1982, with no apparent sign that the movement was reorganizing. In 1989, however, GAM reappeared. It was better armed and waged a stronger insurgency but remained relatively small, with a core of a few hundred active fighters. This time, the movement seemed to enjoy much broader support among the local population, even prompting the regional military commander to complain that supporters might be everywhere, in every village. As in its first phase, the Acehnese were not necessarily supportive of the idea of an independent Aceh but they saw an opportunity to share in common grievances against the Indonesian government.[30] By the late 1980s, the continuing presence of the armed forces to protect industrial plants and the increasing gap created between the wealth surrounding LNG production relative to the poverty of the population were significant factors in the support for GAM.

In the second phase of GAM mobilization, therefore, the Acehnese had begun to shift the nature of their grievances. From the Darul Islam rebellion, they retained their sense of identity, which was distinct from that of the rest of the archipelago. They had fought for an Islamic Indonesia, had lost, and had retreated in a regionalist defense of Islam and local culture. As they became more marginalized, the autonomy for Islam was never implemented and only a small portion of the elite seemed to reap benefits from the New Order regime. From disgruntled elite members to a broader section of the population, the exploitation of LNG, other industrial production, and increased military presence showed that the Acehnese had little means to participate in, protest at, or reap benefits from development in their own territory.

The Indonesian armed forces' response to the rebellion was out of proportion to the estimate of GAM forces. In July 1990, 6,000 troops were sent to supplement the 6,000 already in the province, while GAM forces were numbered at only a few hundred. In what became a "shock therapy" approach, the armed forces went much beyond counter-insurgency tactics. Since they estimated that thousands of villagers supported GAM, soldiers used torture, arbitrary killings, arrests, detentions, and other means of weeding out supporters. They used fence-of-legs tactics, in which civilians formed a shield ahead of soldiers, in "sweeping" campaigns to track and corner GAM fighters in the forest.[31] From time to time, the armed forces lined up along roadsides the bodies of suspects they had killed.[32] It was estimated that 2,000 people were killed between mid-1989 and mid-1991.[33]

By 1993, the rebellion was crushed but the armed forces continued their operations. Having maintained the designation of parts of Aceh as a Military Operations Region (DOM), the armed forces kept an overwhelming presence in the province. Intelligence units continued to pursue suspected GAM supporters throughout the 1990s. A human rights group, Forum Peduli HAM, which was formed after the end of the New Order, estimated that hundreds of people had been killed even after the most intense period of violence from 1989 to 1992. Hundreds also disappeared during the decade from 1989 to 1998, and more than 2,300 people were tortured.[34] Well after the immediate insurgency was eliminated, the armed forces maintained a climate of fear and intimidation.

With the use of widespread violence, the New Order regime shifted Acehnese identity further away from an Indonesian national identity. The terms of inclusion in the nation became defined as the silent acceptance of exploitation of natural resources for national interests, with few local benefits and violent military repression of suspected opposition. Many Acehnese abandoned their loyalty to the Indonesian nation. The objectives of creating an Islamic state had long given way to disillusion and, now, disgust with the treatment of the Acehnese at the hands of the Republic's armed forces. A much broader section of the population was affected by their reign of terror and, therefore, many more Acehnese shifted their support to the opposition.[35] From a marginal movement, GAM came to symbolize resistance not only to the New Order but also to the Indonesian state and nation.

The New Order created a deeper pool of grievances that sealed the Acehnese sense of distinctiveness and laid the basis for a strong ethnonationalist movement to arise. Achmad Tirtosudiro, a former top general in the Indonesian armed forces, summed up the New Order's record in Aceh: "During the New Order, Aceh was ill-treated. Its wealth was taken away and violence was the response to its dissatisfaction".[36] Few Acehnese did not share the experience of violence at the hands of the armed forces and socio-economic discontent had spread considerably. The GAM had been crushed but it retained tremendous symbolic force as an organization through which all Acehnese grievances could be channeled.

Democratization and mobilization in favor of independence

The democratization of the regime allowed cumulated grievances to express themselves openly. Before the transition, the Acehnese had woven a hidden transcript of shared suffering, alienation from the Indonesian state, and anger at their treatment by the armed forces. Institutional change offered, first, the opportunity to express grievances and then, the possibility of effecting institutional change. At the moment of democratic opening, the Acehnese elite sought a unique institutional solution rather than a reform of Indonesia's institutions because they had developed a unique, shared experience that solidified their identity. An ethnonationalist movement arose because many Acehnese distrusted any solution within the institutional boundaries of the Indonesian state. The Acehnese had developed a distrust of the Indonesian state and a fear that any institutional concession could be subsequently withdrawn by the logic of a strong central state.

The sudden end of the New Order regime had an immediate effect in Aceh. The fall of Suharto and the hasty rise to power of B. J. Habibie revealed the tensions embedded in the New Order's institutions. While in most of Indonesia clamors for democracy accompanied the mantra of *reformasi* (reform), the Acehnese immediately focused on justice. Demonstrators demanded a withdrawal of soldiers from the region and investigations into human rights abuses committed by the armed forces over the past decade. Shortly after, a civilian movement began to demand a referendum on the future status of Aceh, with increasing evidence that a large proportion of the population supported independence. The GAM simultaneously resumed its armed guerilla struggle with much better organization than previously. A new cycle of violence began when the armed forces matched GAM's escalation. The civilian movement was caught in the middle of the armed struggle and faced repressive measures, as the Indonesian government suspected it had close ties to GAM.

The sequence of events following the first few months after Suharto's fall was crucial. The response of the Indonesian government to political mobilization was in large part responsible for widening the support for independence. Initially, pressures mounted to put an end to the DOM regime. As many Acehnese began to speak openly of the atrocities committed by the armed forces during the DOM years, students and intellectuals created human rights organizations and organized demonstrations to demand a lifting of the DOM and inquiries into these abuses. The Acehnese branch of MUI joined the students' voices and even Governor Syamsuddin Mahmud wrote a letter to President Habibie to request the lifting of the DOM.[37] In early August 1998, the armed forces commander, Wiranto, announced the end of Aceh's DOM status and the withdrawal of "non-organic" troops,[38] and he apologized for past abuses.

Nevertheless, the Indonesian government failed to respond to clamors for justice despite mounting evidence of human rights abuses. A parliamentary fact-finding team visited Aceh in July and accumulated numerous testimonies of killings, torture, and disappearances committed by the armed forces. A few weeks later, the National Human Rights Commission (Komnas HAM) investigated in more depth claims of abuses and uncovered several mass graves that proved many of the allegations.[39] Beyond apologies, Habibie and his government showed no signs of being ready to open formal investigations or to prosecute the perpetrators of the abuses.

These failings contributed to a rise in ethnonationalist demands. In the first few months of the Habibie presidency, the civilian movement might have supported *reformasi* and participated in an Indonesia-wide movement for deepening democratic reforms, if the central government had responded to claims for justice and shown a desire to break with its past. Instead, the announcement of the end of the DOM status and withdrawal of non-organic troops was accompanied by a renewed use of violent measures against the Acehnese.

The response to a few incidents triggered a return to violence. During the process of troop withdrawal, armed forces units left towns under the scorn and celebrations of local populations eager to witness their departure. In one incident, these demonstrations led to large-scale violence. In early September 1998, thousands of people gathered in Lhokseumawe to witness the departure of Special Forces units (Kopassus). A riot broke out and spread to other towns in the area, leading to extensive destruction of property, especially banks, government offices, and other property owned by the Indonesian government or investors from outside of Aceh. In response, Wiranto sent new units of non-organic troops from Medan to secure the town and, especially, the oil, gas, and fertilizer plants in the area. This response was strongly criticized by Acehnese intellectuals and NGOs, which favored a stronger role for the police instead of resorting to the armed forces.[40]

The armed forces increased their visibility when it became apparent that GAM might be resuming its guerilla activities. In November and December, hundreds of youths, many armed with weapons, established checkpoints in a few locations in North Aceh and stopped public buses, searching for ABRI (armed forces) members. In Lhoknibong, East Aceh, seven soldiers were taken away and killed. Some local NGOs blamed provocateurs and even suspected ABRI of engineering these incidents to justify its continuing presence in the area.[41] ABRI, instead, blamed GAM and responded accordingly. It began to undertake sweeping operations in which ABRI units raided villages in search of GAM members under a new operation named Operasi Wibawa 99 (Operation Authority 99). In early January 1999, eleven people were killed when troops opened fire on a crowd that was protesting the continued presence of

ABRI. A few days later, 1,000 soldiers stormed the village of Kandang (North Aceh) in search of a GAM leader.[42]

With the escalation of violence, a group of forty-two representatives from Aceh, comprising the governor, *ulama*, leaders of the local legislature (DPRD), leaders recognized by customary law (*adat*), and NGO, youth, and student leaders, met with Habibie in early January. It presented demands that included, most importantly, the prosecution of human rights abuses during the DOM years; the release and rehabilitation of political prisoners; special autonomy, with 80% of total provincial revenues accruing to the provincial government; specific clarifications about Aceh's status as a special region; and a statement that Aceh remained part of the Republic of Indonesia. Yet, Habibie ignored the claims, referring them instead to the parliament and to Wiranto. As the incidents of violence from ABRI and Acehnese armed groups continued, and as the civilian toll rose, Habibie visited Aceh at the end of March 1999 with specific promises. He apologized for abuses committed during the DOM years and promised to rehabilitate families affected by the DOM, to provide support for the proper burial of victims, and to free some political prisoners. He also undertook to establish a free port in Sabang and to provide funding to build eighty-five *madrasah* and for a new train and the extension of the airport.[43]

These promises came too late, as students had already mobilized in favor of a referendum. During a large congress on 4–6 February 1999, students from all over Aceh created the Centre for Information on an Aceh Referendum (SIRA). From mobilization against the DOM, the students sought a referendum to prevent further escalation of violence and to respond with a peaceful solution to what they perceived as the Acehnese people's aspirations. In their view, the population was increasingly disappointed with the failure of the central government to quickly respond to human rights abuses and cease military activities. They saw a growing support for independence that could be channeled through a peaceful approach. While some student groups were inclined to support independence, most sought to let people decide whether they wanted independence, autonomy, or federalism.[44] After Habibie had agreed that the East Timorese could have a referendum, SIRA sought the same opportunity for Aceh.

Habibie showed no indication of responding positively to demands for a referendum or to demands for an inquiry into human rights abuses. There appeared to be no space for negotiation or compromise to be reached between the civilian movement and the central government. Habibie depended for his political survival on the support of the armed forces and its commander, Wiranto, and therefore showed no desire to take any punitive action against them. He even disregarded the advice of his Presidential Advisory Team for Aceh that agreed with student and NGO groups on the main issue in Aceh: human rights abuses during the DOM years. Without prosecuting some perpetrators in the armed forces, it would be difficult to appease the Acehnese. But Wiranto held firm, Habibie took no action, and no charges were laid. The armed forces could not face the possibility that, once legal proceedings were taken against some of its members, subsequent inquiries and prosecution could reach its highest echelons and even cabinet ministers.[45]

The credibility of Habibie and the central government declined further as casualties continued to rise, despite promises of a cessation of violence. On 3 February, fifteen people were killed in Idi Cut (East Aceh) when soldiers opened fire on a crowd, demonstrating in favor of independence, after stones were thrown at an army post after a GAM meeting.[46] Occasional clashes between soldiers and GAM members occurred in the following months, but the most important event occurred in May. During a large meeting of GAM in Cot Murong (North Aceh), one soldier was caught in the crowd and taken away. The local military unit surrounded the village in search of him. During the confrontation in Krueng Geukeueh, the soldiers opened fire on a crowd that included women and children. Forty people were killed.[47]

The Krueng Geukeueh incident marked a turning point. Thereafter, the violence began to escalate. GAM began to issue public statements and a well-organized movement emerged, although it was unclear whether there were several groups using the GAM banner. In May, it undertook a campaign for the Acehnese to boycott the elections. Whether people were intimidated or threatened by GAM members, or whether they followed the directives as a protest against the government, registration was so low it had to be extended for several weeks. The actual election had to be delayed in North Aceh, Pidie, and East Aceh because too few people showed up at the polls.[48]

The following months began to involve more open clashes between GAM and the armed forces. Police/military units undertook sweeping operations in various locations and attacked villages suspected of harboring GAM soldiers. Meanwhile, GAM mounted attacks against military and police targets. ABRI increased its troops to close to 6,000, which reversed the policy of withdrawing non-organic troops from the area. Even if they were officially part of Operational Troops for Mass Revolt (PPRM), which included special units of the police (Brimob), they were no different in practise from troops posted during the DOM years.[49]

In many respects, the failure of the police to handle the increasing violence damaged any effort to convince the Acehnese that the policy toward Aceh had changed and the armed forces would be withdrawn. With the increased presence of troops and escalating violence, trust in the central government completely evaporated and the opportunity for reconciliation and compromise was lost.[50]

Until the end of his term, Habibie responded weakly to the state of war settling in Aceh. The armed forces caused the tensions to rise even more dramatically when a group of soldiers shot a respected *ulama*, Tengku Bantaqiah, and more than fifty of his followers during a raid in July 1999.[51] In August, NGOs successfully organized a mass strike on 3 and 4 August to protest against the presence of the PRRM troops. They were officially removed a few weeks later but would be replaced by more troops shortly thereafter.

Proposals for a peaceful solution began to arise. Governor Syamsuddin Mahmud suggested special autonomy for Aceh but received little support. A proposal for a law on Aceh's special status gained more immediate support from Habibie. The law on the implementation of the special status was passed on 23 September 1999. It specified what constituted Aceh's special status, which had been obtained several decades earlier but remained an empty title. It stipulated that elements of Islamic law would apply on religious and economic affairs, that Acehnese culture would inform the structure of local government, and that Islamic education would be integrated into the general education curriculum.[52] This law was inadequate compensation for the many demands for justice and a referendum over the previous months. As a result, it made little impact on the rising hostilities.

Abdurrahman Wahid's presidency was no less controversial on the issue of Aceh. Originally seen as a potentially strong broker to reach a compromise, he soon disappointed by his subsequent actions. As a committed democrat, Wahid had initially expressed no objections to a referendum but reversed his stance after he became president. Furthermore, he became embroiled in a power struggle with the armed forces and proved unable to reduce the escalating use of force in Aceh. He pursued negotiations with GAM but none of the agreements led to any reduction of violence in the territory. In the end, he sided with the armed forces' vision of military action aimed at preserving the unity of the state, while making little progress on extending more peaceful solutions. The main concession, special autonomy, arose from a proposal that originated with Governor Syamsuddin Mahmud and was passed by the national parliament.

Upon acceding to the presidency, Wahid closed the option of a referendum. On 13–14 September, he had attended in Banda Aceh a large meeting of *ulama* from boarding schools across Aceh. The *ulama* had adopted a resolution demanding a referendum on independence, and thereby strengthening support for it. Only a few days after Wahid's inauguration, SIRA organized a remarkable show of strength and support.

Hundreds of thousands of people demonstrated in the streets of Banda Aceh on 8 November in favor of a referendum. This was unprecedented evidence of the people's wishes, yet Wahid responded that he would not allow a referendum.[53]

The civilian movement reached its peak in November 1999 and was subsequently undermined by the rapid escalation of the war between GAM and the armed forces. A new level of violence was attained in December 1999 and January 2000. GAM leaders showed their control over their organization by promising and obtaining a peaceful celebration of the 23rd anniversary of the declaration of independence of Aceh on 4 December. Free Aceh flags were tolerated in response to Wahid's policy of allowing political expression and no violence was reported. No sooner were the celebrations over, however, than attacks were launched in full strength. Armed forces units accelerated their sweeping operations and GAM increased its attacks on military and police targets. By the end of January, the Commission for Missing Persons and Victims of Violence (Kontras) estimated that at least 105 people had died in December 1999 and January 2000 alone.[54]

Wahid's main approach to the conflict was focused on negotiations with GAM. Against criticism from parliamentarians and armed forces generals who were reluctant to negotiate with organizations seeking secession, Wahid approached GAM and reached an agreement on a "humanitarian pause." Under the mediation of the Henry Dunant Centre in Switzerland, the agreement was signed on 12 May 2000, in a meeting attended by Hasan Tiro, leader in exile of GAM. The "humanitarian pause" was initially seen as a major victory for Wahid as it occurred only three months after he became president.[55]

Yet, the policy failed to produce results. Only a few weeks later, the Joint Monitoring Committee (KBMK) responsible for implementing its modalities disagreed on the interpretation of the agreement. The government continued its raids with the argument that they constituted normal police operations, whereas GAM wanted a withdrawal of Indonesian troops. For the central government, such a demand contradicted what it deemed to be its sovereign right. Clashes continued regularly while the agreement was renegotiated in Geneva.[56]

Two subsequent agreements also failed to produce even a limited cessation of violence. In September 2000, the humanitarian pause was renewed until 2 December. Yet, during the first and second phases of the pause, casualties continued to rise steadily. In July 2000, Kontras had counted at least 8 incidents of armed conflict, 7 attacks on civilians, 8 attacks on security personnel, and 3 sweeping operations, in which 60 people died and 18 were injured.[57] TNI (Indonesian National Army, formerly ABRI) spokesman Rear Marshall Graito Usodo confirmed these

results by announcing that the first phase up to 2 September had seen
40 civilians dead and 122 injured, while 21 police/military officials had
been killed.[58] In October, clashes between TNI and GAM forces caused
at least 11 civilian deaths, as Brimob launched an attack against four
villages.[59] In November, a political dialogue (GAM–Indonesian government) was cancelled because of bloodshed during a massive rally organized by SIRA. The rally had been arranged to commemorate the mass
demonstration of November 1999. Although more than 400,000 people
were able to demonstrate on 10–11 November in favor of a referendum
on independence, many more were prevented from reaching the capital
by police and military units. In these confrontations, at least 39 people
were killed. Forum Peduli HAM recorded 960 people killed in 2000 as a
result of fighting between rebels and government troops, which was more
than double the number of deaths in 1999.[60]

Wahid appeared to apply a contradictory policy. He continually pressed
the need for political dialogue and pursued negotiations with GAM. Yet,
the violence not only continued but also actually increased throughout
2000, and the armed forces showed little restraint. GAM seemed to be
gaining greater strength and to be better organized. In fact, its targets
became increasingly daring. On 10 December, it launched a grenade
attack against the governor's house during the visit of Forestry Minister
Nurmahmudi Ismail. It also attacked the warehouses of Exxon Mobil, the
largest foreign gas producer in Aceh. After repeated attacks against its in-
stallations, Exxon suspended its production on 9 March 2001, causing gas
dependent companies such as the fertilizer producers PT Pupuk Iskandar
Muda and PT Asean Aceh Fertilizer to also cease production.[61] A last
attempt was made to agree to a cessation of hostilities within a restricted
zone in North Aceh and Bireun, and for only two weeks (from 22 March to
3 April). The armed forces also sent 2,000 additional troops to protect the
industrial zone and allow operations at Exxon to resume. Nevertheless,
even this limited agreement was broken. Only a few days later, a helicopter
carrying Minister of Energy and Mines Purnomo Yusgiantoro was fired
upon and further clashes between GAM and the police occurred in the
secure zone.[62]

Wahid was confronted with armed forces that did not share his "soft"
approach. Although he was not as dependent on the military as Habibie
had been, Wahid also failed to firmly establish civilian supremacy over it.
He successfully side-lined Wiranto in the first few months of his presidency but met with growing hostility when he attempted to place known
reformists in key positions.[63] The continuing war in Aceh showed the
difficulties of pursuing a policy of negotiation with GAM, when the
military advocated a repressive approach. Parliamentarians were also

critical of Wahid's policy toward Aceh. They blamed him for negotiating with GAM and for failing to find a way of reducing the violence in the province. They were particularly critical of contradictory statements and actions in Wahid's policy, such as the promise to allow a referendum in Aceh and the subsequent withdrawal of this offer. Many parliamentarians who were strong advocates of the unitary state and a firm approach to national unity still blamed Habibie for "losing" East Timor. The People's Consultative Assembly, primarily composed of the members of the national parliament (DPR), even went so far as to formally rebuke the president over his Aceh policy and noted his failure to prevent "separatist movements" from threatening the unitary state of Indonesia. They disapproved of negotiations with GAM and preferred, instead, to implement special autonomy while using force to eliminate the movement.[64]

As his personal power weakened, Wahid increasingly adopted a tough stance. As pressure mounted from the MPR, the DPR, and the TNI, Wahid himself announced a less compromising approach toward GAM during his accountability speech at the MPR session in August 2000. He stated that the government would "no longer tolerate any separatist movements and would take stern action against separatists".[65] He also announced that some form of special autonomy would be implemented before the end of the year. As the second humanitarian pause and more limited attempts to cease violent hostilities failed to produce a more peaceful environment, Wahid adopted the more repressive approach favored by the armed forces. In mid-March 2001, Minister of Defense Mahfud announced that a "limited military operation" would assist the ongoing police operations in Aceh. GAM was formally dubbed "separatist," a change of rhetoric that indicated an end to compromise. This stronger repressive approach was confirmed by Presidential Decree no. 4, 2001, issued on 11 April. The new policy focused on six points, including political dialogue and special autonomy, but the main emphasis was the provision of a political and legal umbrella for a new military operation.[66]

With the democratic transition already in its third year, another presidency ended with increased violence in Aceh. In May and June alone, 367 people were killed, according to the Aceh Legal Aid Institute (LBH).[67] Wahid had espoused a more peaceful solution based on democratic principles, negotiation, and dialogue. Yet, he ended his presidency by choosing a military option. Special autonomy was adopted in principle but the government had presented no proposal of its own. The civilian movement had faded under the intense violence escalating between GAM and the armed forces, while security forces became less tolerant of political demonstrations or demands for a referendum.

Coercion, wide-ranging autonomy, and democracy

Under the presidency of Megawati Sukarnoputri, the nationalist model and the unitary state were reinforced. Megawati was well known for favoring the Indonesian nation envisioned by her father, Sukarno. She therefore reiterated the policy adopted in the later months of the Wahid presidency that gave no room for compromise on secession. More comfortable with a freer role for the armed forces, she reaffirmed the military approach to eliminate GAM in Presidential Decree no. 7, 2001, and in her speech to the MPR on 1 November 2001. More troops were sent and the armed conflict intensified. To increase the military's logistical capability, Megawati approved the re-establishment of the Iskandar Muda military command for Aceh.[68]

Special autonomy and the implementation of Islamic law were concessions that steered away from the unitary state model. To supplement the military approach, special autonomy had been decreed by the MPR but never followed up with a concrete proposal by the government. Instead, Acehnese Governor Syamsuddin Mahmud had drafted a proposal that was adopted by the Acehnese regional parliament and forwarded to the national DPR. After months of stalling because of the political wrangling with President Wahid, the DPR had finally seized the proposal and adopted it with a few amendments. The province of Aceh would thenceforward be known as Nanggroe Aceh Darussalam and a large number of concessions were made. Several institutions were adopted to reflect Aceh's particular distinctiveness, including a flag and other cultural symbols, and Aceh would retain 80% of revenues from oil and gas exploration. Also, the new law provided for the implementation of Islamic law and superseded the law specifying the implementation of Aceh's special status. The law on Nanggroe Aceh Darussalam and Syariah law took effect on 1 January 2002.[69]

The Megawati government also reached a new agreement with GAM. A cessation of hostilities agreement was signed on 9 December 2002. The Indonesian government agreed to instruct its police units to resume normal policing activities, while GAM agreed to cease its violent actions and disarm. The agreement provided for a new all-inclusive dialogue with the Acehnese people on the basis of the special autonomy law on Nanggroe Aceh Darussalam. This dialogue was meant for both parties to discuss changes to the autonomy law and lead to democratic elections in Aceh.[70]

The cessation of hostilities did not, in itself, constitute a new critical juncture in Aceh's relations with the Indonesian nation. While it produced a new environment for constructive dialogue, it remained a weak basis for regaining Acehnese trust in the Indonesian nation. New terms of inclusion would have to be devised by democratic means before a majority of Acehnese would forget the abuses of the past. Special autonomy and democratic elections could provide such a basis but full acceptance of the Indonesian nation would take a long time.

10   Autonomy as a solution to ethnic conflict

The configuration of political institutions mediates ethnic tensions and can be a source of harmonious relations or conflict. At the most general level, democratic or authoritarian structures present very different means of negotiating resources, representation, and power between ethnic groups, or exerting partial or complete repression of one group by another. Similarly, different configurations in the distribution of power between levels of government, ethnic groups, or special territorial units can alter the probability of conflict.

Federalism, centralized unitary states, or various forms of autonomy constitute different institutional choices to extend or deny representation to ethnic groups. In federal systems, powers are divided between federal units and the central level of government. This division of power is usually specified in the constitution, and federal units and the central government negotiate changes through a formal process. In centralized unitary states, power is concentrated in the central government with minimal devolution to local governments. Various forms of autonomy usually imply a devolution of power from the center. Even though such devolution can lead to large transfers of powers to regional or local governments, the ultimate authority over the allocation of power remains with the central government. Unless protected by constitutional guarantees, various forms of autonomy can be reversed by the central government. In all cases, autonomy or federalism can be used to devolve power to minority ethnic groups (or share power), or to redraw territorial units in order to undermine ethnic group representation.[1]

At the time of Indonesia's independence, the leaders of the new republic chose a unitary state over a federal one. Despite a large, multi-ethnic, and multi-religious population scattered across hundreds of islands, they favored a unitary state as a means of institutionalizing and preserving a unified, Indonesian nation. During a brief negotiated settlement with the Dutch, republican leaders had agreed to a federal state with territorial entities still under Dutch control. The Dutch attempted to use a federal structure to secure the loyalty of ethnic groups residing outside the boundaries of the Republic. Nationalist leaders viewed these federal

184

arrangements as obstacles to the creation of a strong, single Indonesian nation. The unitary state, in their view, was the best means of preserving such unity.

Yet, when ethnic violence erupted in the late 1990s, political leaders questioned the unitary state. Under the New Order, the state had reached a high degree of centralization, with provincial, district, and sub-district governments constituting the implementing arms of the central government. Revenue flowed to the center before being redistributed to the provincial and regional levels via the central government's various programs. After the fall of Suharto, the loss of East Timor, the intensification of conflict in Aceh and Irian Jaya, as well rising clamors from many regions for decentralization, prompted the central government to provide greater autonomy in political and fiscal matters. Initially thought to be a pre-emptive attempt to stem conflict, two laws on autonomy and decentralization were insufficient in areas with ethnonationalist conflict. They were followed by special autonomy packages to respond to rising demands for secession.

Autonomy could redistribute political power, representation, and control over the state's resources to provincial or district levels. As such, it gave political elites in these territorial units more power to direct resources to their specific needs and to adopt regulations or laws that could enhance the specific cultural or religious identities of the ethnic groups represented in the area. Autonomy, therefore, could provide more flexibility and resources to meet group demands, provided that the elites in power were actually representative.

Autonomy could not, however, address the problems of national integration faced by East Timor, Aceh, and Irian Jaya. The Timorese overwhelmingly rejected a special autonomy package that would have resulted in a very significant devolution of power. Similarly, the autonomy packages for Aceh and Irian Jaya had little impact on the conflicts. They were rejected by ethnonationalist movements in both areas and were viewed suspiciously by supporters of these movements. The packages responded to many of the demands made by the ethnonationalists. They constituted in many ways a good basis for the formation of new terms of integration into the Indonesian nation. Yet, they failed to provide a strong, renewed sense of redress for past injustices and to fully restore confidence in the central government. For many Acehnese and Papuans, autonomy could be reversed at a later date. Furthermore, because they had suffered human rights abuses at the hands of the armed forces, many groups of Acehnese and Papuans wanted members of the armed forces to be prosecuted.

Ultimately, autonomy would reduce ethnonationalist demands only if combined with other measures that would reinvent the Indonesian national model with sufficiently new elements to fully include the Acehnese and the Papuans. From one period of institutional change to another, successive policies, laws, and regulations further pushed large numbers of Acehnese and Papuans to shed their identity as Indonesians and consolidate a loyalty to their respective Acehnese and Papuan nations.

Autonomy and its effects on ethnic conflict

Various forms of autonomy are often proposed to prevent ethnic conflict or respond to ethnonationalist demands. Skeptics argue that autonomy can sometimes exacerbate, rather than deflate, such conflicts but many scholars and policy-makers claim that it generally reduces them. A cursory review of the main arguments shows that the benefits are tenuous at best. While some form of autonomy can be a useful tool of ethnic conflict management, it is too often considered a panacea for all forms of ethnic and nationalist grievances.

The line between a federal or a unitary state is often blurred, and distinctions between federations and other forms of autonomy are more often concerned with the degree of constitutional formalization of the divisions of power between the center and its units than actual differences in the degree of devolution. Federal arrangements can sometimes be better than more informal means of devolution and regional autonomy if constitutional provisions help to clarify the divisions of power between the center and the units, as well as the areas of exclusive jurisdiction. Blurred divisions of power or clear jurisdictions nevertheless appear both in political systems with constitutionally guaranteed divisions of power and in those with other means of devolution to regional units.

In general, scholars argue that autonomy or federalism can reduce ethnic conflict, alleviate nationalist demands, and prevent secession. Where ethnic groups or nations are territorially concentrated, federations or autonomous regions can reduce conflict by removing it from the center and opening up new cleavages at the sub-national level. It gives a particular ethnic or national group the means to obtain cultural recognition, certain guarantees, laws, or advantages for itself. Institutionalized power through devolution or federation can allow groups, for example, to manage and develop their own education systems, religious institutions, or language laws.[2] It can also introduce flexibility and diversity in policies, programs, and resource allocations that centralized government cannot accomplish.

Some conditions are required, however, for autonomy to have positive effects on ethnic group relations. First, autonomy or federal units work best when their territorial boundaries coincide with a relatively homogenous group. Although it can be argued that the same benefits would apply to devolution toward more heterogeneous units, there are also some risks. Minorities can welcome their new status as majorities in a new autonomous territory, but newly created minorities might themselves seek a redivision into even smaller parcels of territorial autonomy.[3] Federalism is likely to involve an amalgamation of units, with some more homogenous than others.

Second, a democratic political environment is more conducive to successful devolution of political power.[4] Well-established democracies can better guarantee that negotiations over institutional changes are fully implemented and that a judicial process can be accessed for resolving disputes. Even at the time of reaching a compromise over a new form of autonomy, democratic participation might be crucial. An imposed solution or one that does not result from a broad consultation may fail to produce sufficient support to be adequately implemented. Members of groups benefitting from autonomy, for example, may contest new institutional forms on the basis that, later, autonomy might be reversed.

Third, there are better chances of reducing ethnic tensions when divisions of power, or devolution, between the center and various units are clear. Cooperative federalism, the right of the central government to veto or give directives to autonomous units, can reduce the effectiveness of such strategies, particularly in relation to powers relating to the protection of ethnic group identity.[5]

Fourth, some scholars argue that fiscal decentralization may be as important as political devolution. Political power without control over fiscal resources might be meaningless.[6]

In some instances, federalism might be a better option than autonomy. Federation can provide some constitutional guarantees that are more difficult to change or ignore than legislated autonomy or devolution. It works best when there are fewer ambiguities in the divisions of power between the center and the federated units. Autonomy can be particularly problematic if it is applied asymmetrically. Special status to a particular region, for example, can create grievances from those regions that do not benefit from similar devolution of power. The participation of ethnic groups in the institutions of the central government can be curtailed because they have their own region where they can obtain positions, resources, and representation.[7]

Skeptics of autonomy have two kinds of objections. While recognizing that it might be beneficial to ethnic relations, they observe that too much autonomy might lead nationalist groups to secession. In order to avoid being seen as conceding to separatists, central governments sometimes grant autonomy to all regions. In this instance, the central government can be perceived as weak, and therefore more susceptible to secessionist actions. In order to prevent such a vicious circle, Donald Horowitz cautions, it may be better for central governments to retain some ultimate power over regional governments.[8] A second kind of objection focuses on the institutional and material resources available to secessionist groups. When government functions and resources are transferred to autonomous units, they can be used as sources of patronage and mobilization. It can also increase a group's sense of distinct identity associated with a state.[9] Such objections are also raised in the context of federal states.

The relationship of autonomy to the concept of nation may be one additional factor of success. The form of autonomy that is offered, the degree of devolution, and its acceptability as an alternative to secession may be limited by the concept and model of the nation that has been developed by the central government. As in the case of Indonesia, where the nation became equated with a unique identity as Indonesian and the construction of a unitary state, any notion of federalism or diverse ethnic population had to be reconciled with the unity of the nation. While autonomy could potentially allow for a flexible set of institutions to decentralize power toward very diverse regions and maintain a degree of unified nationhood around common values and language at the national level, the ethnonationalist movements in Aceh, East Timor, and Irian Jaya found a more difficult space to articulate their unique identity within the confines of an Indonesian nation that was perceived to be antagonistic to their ethnic and regional identities. Autonomy, especially imposed from above and without broad consultation of local populations, would be more difficult to implement.

Unitary state, autonomy, and federalism

The crucial historical moment in the creation of the Indonesian state was 1950. After the withdrawal of the Dutch, many regions that had initially supported a federal system joined the Republic. Political leaders developed a strong consensus that a unitary state would be preferable to a federal structure, except in Maluku where a resistance movement formed shortly after the declaration of the unitary state. Subsequently, the debate shifted to the secondary issues involving the proper institutional relationship between regional units and the central government.

During the war against the Dutch between 1945 and 1949, a quasi-federal system was established. As the Dutch regained territorial control, they began to create constituent states within a form of federal system under Dutch control, whereas the Republic followed a unitary state model. Under agreements reached in 1948 and 1949, both parties created the Republic of the United States of Indonesia that became fully independent in December 1949. It comprised the states created by the Dutch and the Republic of Indonesia as its most important constituent state.[10]

The federal state lasted only seven months and was replaced by a unitary state. Shortly after the transfer of sovereignty, the federation began to collapse. As George Kahin has noted, "by most Indonesians it had been seen as an instrument of Dutch control and an obstacle to the attainment of their independence." To keep the federal system would have been to accept a legacy of the colonial past. Popular movements arose in the fifteen Dutch-created states for abolition of the federal state and a merger with the old Republic. In some areas, such as in Maluku and West Java (state of Pasundan), some former members of the Dutch colonial army resisted the movement for a unitary state. While this led to a direct confrontation in Maluku, where an independent Republic of South Maluku was declared, in other regions the conflicts were very brief. In August 1950, the unitary state of the Republic of Indonesia was created.[11]

The unitary state was elevated to a high symbolic level, as it became the embodiment of the Indonesian nation. Unitarianism was the product of a nationalist aim for unity, as it had been clearly expressed in the Constitution of 1945. For nationalist leaders, such as Sukarno and Hatta, the agreement on a federal system was only temporary. The ultimate aim had been the unitary state for achieving the objectives of a united Indonesian nation.[12]

The agreement on the unitary state was accompanied by strong demands for autonomy. Federal states agreed to disband but they also sought an institutional recognition of the vast diversity of conditions across the archipelago. "Autonomy" of regions became the main concern of these former federal states as well as regions included in the old Republic. During the first decade, the institutionalization of autonomy, its degree, and its form were subjects of intense debate, negotiation, and even conflict.

The new Republic retained the old structures that had been in place under Dutch colonial rule. In the western part of Indonesia, six levels of government were organized hierarchically and three were identified as self-governing regions (province, district, and village), with autonomy over "household affairs" and some other delegated powers. Provincial and district heads were named by the central government on the basis of a list selected by the newly created local parliaments (DPRD). In East Indonesia, former administrative structures were also maintained. These were less hierarchical, with fewer levels of government, and traditional rulers had a greater role at village and supra-village levels. In parallel to this structure, the government also maintained the vast network of civil servants, the *pamong praja*, who had administered the colonial system. They were posted at all levels of government as representatives of the center. Under Indonesia's new laws, the heads of each administrative level also combined the functions of *pamong praja* and were therefore accountable to the central government as much as to their constituencies. The two functions were deliberately blurred as a means of political control.[13]

The central government also showed its centralizing bias by ignoring established procedures. In 1950, aside from the village level, there was virtually no autonomy at the sub-national level after the federal states had been dissolved.[14] Because the government argued that administrative capabilities were inadequate, the local DPRD were constituted as temporary councils and members were nominated according to the estimated strength of particular political parties in each region (at the provincial and district levels). Furthermore, the heads of the administrative levels were directly appointed by the central government instead of following the DPRD lists. Even when elections were organized at the national level in 1955, members of the DPRD were allocated according to the votes obtained by region in the national elections, instead of separate local ballots being held.[15]

Fiscal power was also primarily in the hands of the central government. Sub-national units generated revenues from only small sources, such as taxes on dogs, bicycles, and vehicles, or returns from providing basic services such as water. Otherwise, they received some remittances from taxes collected on behalf of the central government. For instance, provinces retained 5% of the tax on households, and districts 15%. For the most part, they were dependent on grants-in-aid from the central government.[16]

In reaction to these established institutions, regions attempted to reassert their authority relative to the center but failed. Gains were made through the national parliament when Law no. 1, 1957, was adopted. It provided for a gradual elimination of the *pamong praja* and increased power for elected legislatures at the provincial and district levels. In a reversal of past practise, the law granted residual powers to these levels of government while specifying that only foreign affairs, defense, monetary policy, and a few other powers would remain with the central government. The law was never implemented.[17]

The centralization of government also provoked rebellion in several regions. During 1956–57, a number of regional military commanders, especially in Sumatra and Sulawesi, allied themselves with civilian leaders to resist the increasing centralization of power by Jakarta and Java. Various groups had begun to make demands for federalism and others had begun to organize along ethnic lines, with increasing anti-Javanese feelings. Regional military commanders were resisting actions by the armed forces commander, General Nasution, to transfer them to other positions and to centralize the military command structure. Military-led councils were formed in late 1956 and 1957, as divisions increased between the regionalists and Jakarta. A number of prominent national politicians, especially from the Muslim party Masyumi, joined the regionalist rebellion. By February 1958, they had declared an alternative Revolutionary Government of the Republic of Indonesia (PRRI). The effectiveness of the rebellion was short-lived as it was defeated militarily by the central government and most of its leaders were arrested.[18]

These events provided the opportunity for the central government to impose new, centralized institutional control. Many factors motivated Sukarno's decision to join with the armed forces and end the era of liberal democracy. Political stalemate within the Constituent Assembly, fierce competition between political parties over matters of state ideology, military dissent from regional commanders, as well as regionalist attempts to seize power, were among the most important ones. Certainly, the regional rebellions and their culmination in the declaration of an alternative government gave the opportunity for Sukarno to impose martial law and to accelerate the establishment of new political institutions.[19] The national legislature and the Constituent Assembly were suspended, many political parties were banned, a new regime of Guided Democracy was declared, and the armed forces asserted a primary position. The government suspended Law no. 1, 1957, and, instead, imposed more centralized control than had previously existed, as the regions were governed through military councils. The reinstatement in 1959 of the Constitution of 1945 laid the foundations of this system with a strong center and strong presidential power.

Centralization and authoritarian control under the New Order

Under the New Order regime, centralization was increased while regional resentment appeared to decline. After General Suharto and the armed forces seized power in 1965, they established even stronger authoritarian controls than the previous Guided Democracy. They espoused the argument that a strong nation required centralization,

military control, elimination of political opposition, and pressure to conform to the principles of the 1945 Constitution and the state ideology of
Pancasila. Sub-national institutions were reformed to homogenize administrative and political control across the country, while top-down
chains of command were strengthened. Tighter controls were accompanied by financial and political incentives to keep regional elites content
and opposition groups intimidated. The resulting system eliminated rebellious activities from most regions of Indonesia. Armed resistance
appeared only in Aceh, Irian Jaya, and East Timor. All of these represented, it could be argued, special cases that did not resemble the regional
resentment and demands for autonomy that had characterized the relationship between the center and regions in the 1950s.

Four aspects characterized the New Order's approach to administering the regions. First, it wanted to prevent a potential re-enactment
of the military-led regional rebellions of the 1950s, so it consolidated
the central control of the military command structure. Second, it maintained tight administrative control through its implementation of a new
law on regional administration. This law reaffirmed the principle of regional autonomy but, in its implementation, strengthened central control.
Third, the New Order increased its hold on fiscal resources and used
them to gain loyalty among regional elites. Fourth, it used Pancasila,
the Constitution of 1945, and development to legitimize its emphasis on
securing national unity through these military, political, and economic
levers.

The reorganization of the military command structure eliminated the
potential for regional rebellions. Suharto expanded territorial units that
had been revived under Guided Democracy for the purposes of internal security. The country was divided into four levels of military command: regional military commands (Kodam), military resort (garrison)
commands (Korem), district military commands (Kodim), and sub-
district military commands (Koramil).[20] He also created the Operations
Command for the Restoration of Security and Order (Kopkamtib), initially to eliminate PKI supporters, but it became the main instrument of
political control by using the territorial units as its intelligence network.
At the provincial level, the military maintained control over the civilian
administration through newly created Regional Leadership Consultative
Councils (Muspida) that were headed by the governor but included the
regional military commander. At the apex, Suharto held firm control over
Kopkamtib and the formal structure of operational command, placed
under the authority of the Ministry of Defense and Security.[21] These
structures maintained control and order over the regions and remained
essentially the same throughout the three decades of the New Order,
despite some changes in names and slight modifications.[22]

Staffing of the military and civilian administration further enhanced Suharto's grip on power. In order to prevent regional military commanders concentrating power, he shuffled them regularly, placed loyal generals in these positions, and never appointed locals of particular regions outside of Java. By 1977, the governors of 21 out of 27 provinces were active or retired military officers. While this proportion diminished in subsequent decades, it was still close to half in 1992. Also, in many cases where the governor was a civilian and from the region, the second most important provincial positions, the district heads (*bupati*) and mayors, were also mostly from the military. By 1969, 147 out of 271 districts and cities were headed by military officers (retired or active), while the proportion reached about two-thirds by 1971. It was still close to 50% in the 1990s.[23] These appointments prevented effective political resistance at the regional level.

The institutional structure of the civilian administration also reinforced central control. Law no. 5, 1974, established the structure of regional government under the New Order regime. It homogenized the bureaucratic structure across the archipelago and created two parallel institutional structures at three levels of sub-national government. Two autonomous levels were created (tgk I and tgk II). At each level, local legislatures (DPRD-I and DPRD-II) were composed of elected and appointed members. These levels were created alongside the administrative structures of the provinces (*propinsi*) and the districts (*kabupaten*), which were the implementing arms of the central government as well as the autonomous governments. A lower administrative level, the sub-district (*kecamatan*), had no autonomous status equivalent to the two upper levels (see Figure 2). At the bottom, the villages were organized as administrative structures responsible to higher levels, while village heads also played a role as representative of village interests. The villages were administered through separate legislation.[24]

The law was ambiguous in defining the extent of autonomy conferred to the regions and their degree of administrative responsibility for implementing central government programs and policies. It specified three principles of regional government, including decentralization of responsibilities to "autonomous" provincial and district governments, "deconcentration" of activities to regional offices of central ministries, and co-administration in which the provincial, district, and sub-district governments carried out activities on behalf of the central government. In practise, these divisions between autonomous activities and other administrative ones were blurred, as well as the dual functions of the governors and *bupati*. As a result, except for a few, very limited areas of authority that were specified in detail, the role of governments at the regional level was primarily to implement and monitor programs and

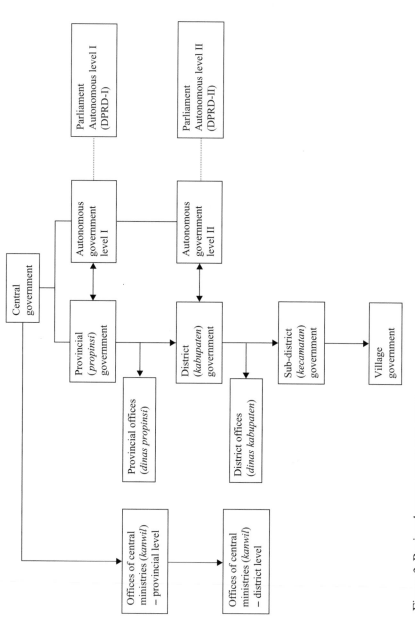

Figure 2 Regional government structures

policies decided by the central government. The regional offices of central ministries (*kanwil*) obtained the greater proportion of funds for development projects and were the most important offices. The provincial and district departments (*dinas*) had fewer resources and their roles were often indistinguishable from those of the *kanwil*.[25]

The very limited scope of autonomy at the institutional level was even more evident in fiscal matters. A comparative analysis of provincial and district budgets showed that, in 1979/80, 69.1% of the provincial budget came from central government subsidies for salaries and regular expenditures (57%) and from grants allocated under the various Presidential Instruction (Inpres) development funds (12.1%). This dependence rose to 72.8%, including 58.2% in subsidies and 14.6% in Inpres funds. Revenues from provincial sources represented less than 25% of the budget, with the largest item being a tax on motor vehicles.[26] District governments were even more dependent on the central government, with 75.02% of their budget in 1977/78 originating from subsidies (30.5%) and Inpres funds (44.5%). In 1980/81, this dependence had risen to 79.7%, with 30% from subsidies and 49.7% from Inpres funds. In their case, only around 20% of revenues came from district taxes and other local revenues, with the largest item being the district share of a property tax. This dependence contrasted with a stronger "autonomy" for districts relative to provinces in the early 1970s, when the central government's share of revenues was 60% rather than 80%. Districts saw the most rapid increase in dependence during the late 1970s and early 1980s.[27]

Central government funds were allocated with specific criteria on expenditures. A good proportion of the Inpres funds were specified for special sectors of development such as roads, schools, and health clinics. General Inpres funds allocated to provincial, district, and village governments provided some degree of control over expenditures. Part of the grant had to be spent on infrastructure or irrigation. The other portion could be spent on general development but was often accompanied by "guidance" on its use.[28]

The proportion of the national budget allocated to the provinces and districts is an alternative indicator of centralization. As a percentage of the national budget, total allocations to the province, district, and village levels of government in 1984/85 represented only 16.8% of the national budget (including subsidies (SDO) and Inpres grants). Most of these expenditures were tied to criteria determined by the central government, including all of the subsidies that went mostly to salaries and routine expenses (9.8%) and a good proportion of the Inpres funds (7%). These numbers were not significantly different from the proportion allocated to sub-national governments in previous years. In 1969/70, the total proportion was only slightly less at 14.6%. The SDO, however, was 13.1%

Table 3 Allocation of expenditures, National Budget of Indonesia, 1969/70, 1974/75, 1979/80, 1982/83, 1983/84, 1984/85 (%)

	1969/70	1974/75	1979/80	1982/83	1983/84	1984/85
Routine (excl. SDO)	51.6	41.7	42.4	39.9	37.8	39.3
SDO (incl. Irian)	13.1	10.4	8.4	9.2	8.5	9.8
Sectoral development	23.9	11.4	18.5	22.9	17.7	18.1
Inpres	1.5	6.5	5.7	6.8	7.1	7.0
PMP/Inpres pasar	2.4	4.7	3.3	2.4	3.3	1.9
Donor funded projects	7.5	10.1	16.4	13.5	21.3	17.7
Total SDO and Inpres	**14.6**	**16.8**	**14.1**	**16.1**	**15.7**	**16.8**

Note: Inpres = general grants; Inpres pasar = market loans; PMP = capital funds for state enterprises; SDO = autonomous region subsidies.
Source: Adapted from Devas, "Local government finance in Indonesia," p. 14.

relative to only 1.5% for Inpres funds. The proportion of SDO to Inpres grants diminished by 1974/75 and remained roughly similar throughout the following decade (see Table 3). Furthermore, sectoral development expenditures represented a higher proportion than total expenditures for all levels of sub-national government, at 18.1% of the national budget in 1984/85. These expenditures were usually spent in the regions and administered by offices representing the various ministries, under the direct control of the central government. As a result, provincial, district, and village governments controlled probably less than 5% of the national budget, and all three levels of sub-national government generated only 6% of total domestic revenue in 1983/84,[29] a fairly typical proportion that was representative of the situation throughout the 1970s and 1980s.

Despite the high dependence on the central government, sub-national levels of government received increasing funds throughout the 1970s and up to the mid-1980s. Even with little change in the proportions, these disbursements grew in real terms at a very rapid rate along with the increase in the national budget. Fueled by oil revenues in the 1970s, the real growth rate per capita of the national budget was around 14% per year from 1969/70 to 1980/81.[30] As a result, it was relatively easier for the central government to pursue its centralist policy while ensuring that the regions were somewhat satisfied.

By using its control over these growing fiscal resources, the New Order government established a vast network of patronage that bought loyalty to the regime. Formerly rebellious regions, such as West Sumatra and South Sulawesi, were devoid of significant political opposition during the decades of New Order rule. The restrictive political environment and the militarization of the bureaucracy partially explained this absence of opposition but Suharto's government also built in strong incentives. It increased its transfers to the regions, while also promoting business interests that involved local bureaucrats. West Sumatra, for example, received domestic investments and contracts to businesses owned by local Minangkabau firms, as well as projects from foreign aid agencies. In South Sulawesi, in a significant departure from other regions, Suharto allowed members of the region to hold most of the key positions. With the rise of M. Jusuf as commander of the Hasanuddin regional military command (which included South Sulawesi) and his eventual rise to the top of the armed forces, active and retired military figures from South Sulawesi played a strong role in the region as well as in Jakarta. As a result, patronage funds also flowed abundantly to the area.[31]

The ideological discourse of the New Order regime offered a legitimation formula for this system of governance. The regime called on developmental requirements to justify the need for centralization. The Constitution of 1945 was sufficiently vague on the role of the regions to allow for centralization of presidential power and its use in allocating development funds. Pancasila ideology was used profusely to sustain a strong, central government as were evocations of the requirements of national unity. The armed forces used a "dual function" (*dwi fungsi*) doctrine to justify its strong presence in civilian positions, as well as various appeals to national integrity, the "archipelagic principle" (*Wawasan Nusantara*), "Unity in Diversity" (*Bhinneka Tunggal Ika*, Indonesia's national motto), "national resilience," and other similar concepts to develop a framework that reinforced the goals of the single Indonesian nation, and its unity and indivisibility.[32]

During the 1990s, this centralized system began to weaken. Two sources of strain were embedded in the institutional structure. First, the centralization of fiscal resources and their method of management relied heavily on large oil revenues. It was only in times of surplus that the central government could keep increasing funds to fuel its patronage and provide resources to provinces and districts. Second, because formal positions in the administrative hierarchy were weak, regional politicians were mostly concerned with the informal networks of access to Suharto and his close aides. As a result, regional and ethnic representation in the highest positions of the military, the civil service, and the cabinet were often the best means of preserving patronage funds and favors from the regime. A decline in representation was often perceived as a loss for a particular ethnic group, province, or region.

Problems associated with fiscal centralization began to emerge. With rapidly declining state revenues from the drop in oil prices in the mid-1980s, the central government was increasingly incapable of providing funds to meet a rise in provincial and district infrastructural needs. The

economic growth of the previous two decades had led to rapid urbaniza-
tion and industrialization that increased the need for state-led projects
to ensure proper infrastructure and services. Administrative problems
were also frequent, including delays in financing caused by overburdened
central government departments, a reduction in the quality of development projects, poor accountability at sub-national levels of government, poor service provision, poor coordination in the implementation
of programs and services, and redundant administrative planning and
structures.[33]

At the political level, there were virtually no open signs of dissent
against the regime but some indications of discontent. In many regions,
the political elite complained of the lack of autonomy at the regional
level. There was growing discontent throughout the 1990s at the absence
of real political power and homogenous policies across the archipelago
that did not reflect the needs of particular regions.[34] In regions such as
Maluku or other areas of Eastern Indonesia, a low capacity for generat-
ing local revenue restricted their ability to adapt projects and development initiatives to local conditions. Furthermore, while revenues might
have been increasing under a new emphasis on Eastern Indonesia, these
funds remained vastly insufficient to tackle poverty and other regional
problems.[35]

Faced with these pressures, the New Order regime introduced mild
reforms that were designed to address some technical issues while avoiding political decentralization. Starting with the establishment of a new
tax on land and buildings (PBB) in 1985, the central government assisted districts in increasing local revenue to compensate for the decline
in the central government's capacity as a result of lessening oil revenues. In 1995, on the initiative of Minister of Home Affairs Rudini,
the government created "pilot areas" for a new decentralization initiative. Twenty-six districts were selected, one in each province, to test new
measures designed to increase the autonomy of the districts. As in Law
no. 5, 1974, the districts were designated as the desired level for more
autonomy.[36]

The reforms were merely administrative in nature and focused on technical aspects that did not significantly increase district autonomy. The
institutional structure remained in place, except for some administrative consolidation at the district level. In fiscal terms, the dependence
of districts and provinces remained prominent. Total Inpres funds remained close to 6.5% of the national budget, while sectoral development
funds were more than double. At its peak in 1994/95, the combined general Inpres funds for provinces, villages, and districts constituted only
5.8% of total expenditures reported in the national budget. Given that
a good proportion of these funds was already earmarked for specific

Table 4 Actual government expenditures, 1991–98 (%)

	1991/92	1992/93	1993/94	1994/95	1995/96	1996/97	1997/98
Total SDO	8.4	8.9	10.1	9.7	10.4	9.5	8.6
Sectoral development funds	14.4	16.6	15.9	15.0	13.9	12.3	9.4
Total Inpres funds	6.2	6.7	6.1	7.6	6.9	6.6	5.9
– villages	0.5	0.5	0.6	0.6	0.5	0.5	0.4
– districts	1.1	1.3	1.3	3.4	3.1	3.0	2.7
– provinces	1.1	1.2	1.1	1.8	1.6	1.4	1.3
Donor funded projects	16.5	17.5	15.6	13.2	11.4	12.1	11.2

Note: Inpres = general grants; SDO = autonomous region subsidies.
Source: National, provincial, and district financial data, Biro Pusat Statistik (various years).

infrastructural projects, fiscal control at the sub-national level was still relatively small compared to that of the central government. There was a significant increase in Inpres funds to districts during the 1990s, from 1.1% of total expenditures in 1991/92 to 3% or more from 1994/95 to 1996/97 (Table 4). This reflected the policy of increasing autonomy at the district level relative to other sub-national governments, but it was a very small change in relation to the fiscal power of the central government.

An analysis of provincial and district government budgets shows some growth in autonomous funding, but it was small in comparison to funding from the central government. At the provincial level, local revenues rose from 26.2% to 34.4% of total revenues between 1993/94 and 1996/97, a significant increase in taxes and charges under autonomous provincial authority (Table 5). While the direction of change suggests increased autonomy, the dependence on the central government nevertheless remained quite strong, at 47.2% in 1996/97. At the district level, the main increase in revenue came from the PBB reflected in the provincial share of tax and non-tax revenue. Yet, even combined with the local taxes and charges, the proportion remained much below that of the total contribution from the central government, at 65.6% in 1996/97. Given that the districts were supposed to be the focus of the decentralization policy, it was surprising that the share of central government contribution (subsidies and Inpres) funds in district budgets was still higher than that of the provinces (Table 6).

During its three decades, the New Order regime maintained strong fiscal and political control over the provinces and districts. Political control was maintained through a constant presence of the military at all levels of government, a persistent although diminishing presence of military personnel in top positions at both levels, a structure of administration

Table 5 Sources of provincial government revenue (tgk I), 1993–97 (%)

	1993/94	1994/95	1995/96	1996/97
Local government receipts	26.2	31.0	30.8	34.4
Provincial share of tax and non-tax revenue	7.7	7.8	9.2	9.5
Total central government contribution to provinces	60.9	54.7	51.0	47.2
– SDO	46.8	41.4	38.5	35.5
– Inpres funds	14.1	13.3	12.5	11.7
Other development funds	0.5	0.5	0.5	0.5

Note: Inpres = general grants; SDO = autonomous region subsidies; tgk I = level I.
Source: National, provincial, and district financial data, Biro Pusat Statistik (various years).

Table 6 Sources of district government revenue (tgk II), 1994–97 (%)

	1994/95	1995/96	1996/97
Local government receipts	13.0	13.7	13.9
District share of tax and non-tax revenue	15.3	15.3	16.3
Total central government contribution to districts	68.3	66.8	65.6
– SDO	33.4	35.1	35.2
– Inpres funds	35.0	31.6	30.4
Other development funds	0.9	1.1	1.2

Note: Inpres = general grants; SDO = autonomous region subsidies; tgk II = level II.
Source: National, provincial, and district financial data, Biro Pusat Statistik (various years).

that was subsumed under the authority of the central government and accountable only to it, and a network of patronage that provided incentives to remain loyal to this system of governance. A decline in oil revenues and growing evidence of the inefficiencies of overcentralization triggered some measure of decentralization, yet these changes had little overall impact on the low level of real autonomy.

Democratization, autonomy, and fiscal decentralization: A new direction

The fall of President Suharto in May 1998 marked the beginning of a new relationship between the central and sub-national governments. Already weakened by the Asian financial crisis of 1997, the central government was even more fragile after the weeks of political instability that accompanied Suharto's resignation. President Habibie initiated reforms that allowed an expansion of political participation and an increase in civilian control over the military. With political protest on the rise, demands for greater and more radical reforms of the political system, and a renewed mobilization of nationalist movements in East Timor, Aceh, and Irian Jaya, Habibie introduced two new autonomy laws on political devolution and fiscal decentralization. These laws represented a departure from the centralization of the previous three decades.

The protests in favor of reform and democratization expanded to the regions before and after Suharto's downfall. Calls for an end to corruption and nepotism at the national level were replicated at the provincial, district, and even village levels. Many regions also demanded fiscal independence from Jakarta and more political importance. Governors and district heads who had been appointed under the New Order regime came under intense scrutiny and more frequent calls were made for their resignation.[37]

With violence and protests on the rise, the Habibie government started to reform relations between the center and the regions. Within the confines of the New Order's procedures, it allowed local legislatures in provinces and districts to elect governors and *bupati* who were popular in the region. The home affairs minister began to ratify choices made by local legislatures rather than influence the selection process to favor Jakarta's candidates.[38] With protests increasing in East Timor, demands for a referendum and renewed mobilization of the Free Aceh Movement in Aceh, as well as similar demands on the rise in Irian Jaya, the Habibie government introduced new legislation to reform the political, administrative, and fiscal status of districts and provinces in relation to the central government.

Law no. 22, 1999, on regional government established a new framework of political and administrative institutions at the provincial and district levels.[39] It placed emphasis on wide-ranging autonomy at the district level. The new autonomous regions (districts) were given authority over all functions except national defense, international relations, justice, monetary and fiscal policy, religion, national management of natural resources, national development planning, fiscal equalization, and national standards. The law also specified a few functions that districts were obligated to perform, including health, education, environmental, and infrastructural services. Local legislatures (DPRD) gained much expanded powers, including the election of district heads (mayors and *bupati*), the right to propose and review legislation and regulations, and even the right to dismiss district heads.

Provinces remained primarily administrative regions with the responsibility of representing the central government and coordinating the implementation of its policies and programs. They were also given the ambiguous role of undertaking the tasks of the autonomous district governments that lacked administrative capacity. They were given autonomous power over unspecified areas, necessitating coordination among several districts. A DPRD was also created at the provincial level but with powers limited by the minimal autonomous jurisdiction of provinces. They had the same powers to dismiss governors but were more restricted in their powers to elect them. Candidates were to be selected by the legislature but the president had to be consulted on these candidates.

The devolution of power to districts had some limitations and ambiguities. The president could dismiss governors and *bupati*/mayors without consulting the DPRD under extraordinary conditions specified in the law. The central government was also given the right to annul regulations from provinces and districts that contradicted higher level legislation and executive decisions, or the general interest. The law in effect retained supervisory powers for the central government.

Law no. 25, 1999, provided for fiscal decentralization. The old subsidies (SDO) and development grants (Inpres) were eliminated and replaced with a general allocation fund (DAU) that represented at least 25% of central government revenues. Provinces received about 10% of these funds while districts received 90%. The law also specified new divisions of revenues from the exploitation of natural resources that kept a much greater proportion in the regions. The central government retained only 20% of revenues from mining and forestry, while the rest was distributed to provinces (16%) and to districts (64%), with a greater emphasis on districts where the revenue originated. Oil and natural gas revenues remained mainly in the hands of the central government (85% of oil revenues and 70% of gas revenues), but the 15% and 30%, respectively, that were allocated to provinces and districts represented a vast increase in revenues relative to the previous system of fiscal allocation. Other shared revenues, such as the land and property tax, were changed to favor the districts.[40]

Fiscal decentralization did not substantially change the central government's role in collecting and administering the allocation of revenues. More than 90% of the revenues at the provincial and district levels came from the DAU allocation, shared taxes, and natural resource revenues. Local government taxes and charges still represented only 7% of revenues. A new law (no. 34) was introduced in 2000 that greatly expanded the scope of the taxation powers of local governments.[41] Nevertheless, the role of the central government and ultimate control over fiscal resources remained high.

The autonomy laws relieved some of the tensions that were building up. As soon as the laws were passed, some districts and provinces began to use the new framework for electing governors and *bupati* even though the regulations for the operationalization of the laws were still being drafted. The protests and demonstrations that had accompanied the selection of regional heads diminished as districts and provinces gained greater empowerment. As a result, the potential for conflict between certain ethnic or regional groups against central control of the state was reduced.

The autonomy laws had the effect, overall, of appeasing some of the demands from the regions and prevented the mobilization of resentment against the center. They undercut some of the potential for a region to mobilize along ethnic lines in opposition to the center, although there were few signs of any new ethnonationalist movement aside from the well-established ones in East Timor, Aceh, and Irian Jaya. The debates and tensions surrounding the laws were more concerned with aspects of their implementation and technical issues than any fundamental rejection of the basis of the laws.

Problems that arose were mainly of a technical nature. The number of districts was expanded from 300 to 348 in 2002 and new provinces were created, despite continuing difficulties with staffing and capacity. There were also doubts about the effectiveness of autonomy distributed to almost 350 relatively small units. Most problems were due to the slow adoption of regulations to operationalize the implementation of the law, especially during the unstable presidency of President Wahid. Fiscal problems related to the difficulties in adopting clear criteria for determining transfers to districts and provinces for shared taxes, charges, and, especially, revenue from natural resources.[42]

Some evidence suggests that the autonomy laws might have contributed to conflict. The creation of a new province in North Maluku in 1999 may have sparked competition between the sultans of Tidore and Ternate for control of the position of governor. A similar argument was applied to violence against the Madurese in Central Kalimantan in 2001. An unsuccessful candidate in the gubernatorial election of 2000 allegedly fueled the violence against the local Madurese in a bid to mobilize political support among the Dayaks.[43]

Yet, these arguments are weak. It would be difficult to make the case that elite mobilization, prompted by the extension of autonomy and democratization, was a strong cause of these conflicts. The conflict in North Maluku was related to that in Ambon, where it was strongly influenced by the context of national uncertainty over the role of Islam in the polity. Where competition did exist, it involved positions in the civil service that much preceded the autonomy laws. The violence in Central Kalimantan was influenced by the conflict against the Madurese in West Kalimantan and was related to questions of marginalization and insecurity of the Dayaks that, again, predated the announcement of new autonomy laws.[44] Furthermore, the positions of governor, which were allegedly at the center of conflicts in North Maluku and Central Kalimantan, were the ones least affected by the new autonomy laws that were mainly focused on districts. Few resources were devolved to the provinces, and governors remained subject to the central government.

The major problem with the autonomy laws was their failure to have the intended effect on secessionist movements in Aceh and Irian Jaya. The People's Consultative Assembly had called for more autonomy for the regions in its special meeting of November 1998. The Habibie government had responded with its two autonomy laws. Nevertheless, demands for a referendum in Aceh and renewed mobilization of GAM activists grew. In Irian Jaya, similar demands for independence and a referendum began to be heard. In each case, the autonomy laws were viewed with suspicion and were immediately rejected, especially since they were focused on the districts and gave no power to the provincial level of government that was considered the locus of the regional identity for Aceh and Irian Jaya.

Events in East Timor strongly contributed to the government's change of policy toward Aceh and Irian Jaya. At the same time as the central government was preparing laws no. 22 and no. 25, it was abandoning their relevance for East Timor. Under pressure from renewed demonstrations in the territory and in donor countries, Habibie offered a new special autonomy for East Timor in its negotiations with Portugal. Under this agreement, a Special Autonomous Region of East Timor (Saret) was to be created.

The offer extended wide-ranging autonomy to the Saret, which gained authority in all matters except foreign relations, defense, and some areas of economic and fiscal policies (including monetary policy, central government assistance for development, national taxation under Indonesian law, and the control of "strategic or vital" natural resources). The Saret was given the authority to determine the rules regarding immigration to East Timor and the acquisition of East Timorese identity. A legislature was established with full powers in all areas under Saret jurisdiction, including the election of a governor. The governor was solely responsible to the Saret legislature, whereas the central government appointed a senior official for the implementation of its programs and policies in the region. The Saret obtained a system of independent courts in all civil, criminal, and administrative matters under its competence, although the Supreme Court of Indonesia was the final court of appeal.[45]

Some Acehnese and Papuan groups seized upon the offer of special autonomy for East Timor to demand the same kind of arrangement. The East Timorese rejected the offer in a referendum in August 1999 and supported independence. Acehnese and Papuan student and nationalist movements also demanded referendums to determine the future of their regions. The GAM and the Papuan Congress wanted full independence but other groups appeared open to the adoption of special autonomy status. In Aceh, the initiative came from the central government but its final proposal was preceded by a wide-ranging autonomy proposal from the governor of Aceh and other members of the region's political elite. This proposal became the basis of the special autonomy law for Aceh (Law no. 18, 2001) that was adopted by the DPR in July 2001 and became effective in January 2002. In Papua, the special autonomy law was developed after pressures from the central government to emulate the Acehnese proposal. In the wake of two Papuan Congresses that adopted strong resolutions in favor of independence, the central government and the governor of the province of Irian Jaya were under pressure to propose an alternative solution. The law on special autonomy for Papua was adopted by the DPR in October 2001 and became effective in January 2002.[46]

The Wahid and Megawati governments supported these special laws as it became evident that the autonomy laws of 1999 had had no effect on the conflicts. Instead, both violent conflict and civilian demands for independence grew steadily in both regions after the adoption of the 1999 laws. Their implementation in both regions was unnoticed and had been rejected even by the local governments in place. It was not completely surprising that the governors of Aceh and Irian Jaya played active roles in developing proposals for special autonomy, since provinces had been the main losers from the laws of 1999 that conferred autonomy on the districts.

The special autonomy law for Aceh gave wide-ranging autonomy to the province.[47] At the symbolic level, Aceh was recognized as a special area and, accordingly, changed its name to Nanggroe Aceh Darussalam (NAD, with "nanggroe" meaning "country or state", depending on the interpretation). It was also given the right to adopt symbols specific to the area, as long as they were not considered to be expressions of sovereignty. The government of NAD obtained the authority in all areas relating to its special autonomy. The law, however, did not specify which areas of jurisdiction were excluded or included and therefore remained a broad statement on autonomy rather than an actual specification of devolution of powers.

The institutions of government included organizations specific to Aceh, while preserving the basic structure of provincial governments in the rest of Indonesia. Legislative power was vested in the Regional People's Representative Assembly (DPRD-NAD), with wide powers that included the right to investigate the government and to demand accountability. The governor and *bupati* were to be elected directly by the people. This was a significant departure from standard practise in the rest of Indonesia. However, the governor also retained a role as representative of the central government, with the obligation to coordinate its programs and policies. Candidates for elections to the position had to be approved by the DPRD in consultation with the president. The governor was accountable to the DPRD-NAD as well as to the president. The law innovated by creating a "Wali Nanggroe" and a "Tuha Nanggroe," two unique institutions involved in the implementation and preservation of local customs. Their power was limited and small relative to that of the DPRD.

The law specified in detail the monetary and fiscal allocations to the government of NAD. In addition to the usual sources of local taxation and finance, the NAD government retained most of the portion of shared taxes and charges (90% of the tax on buildings and property), as well as 80% of revenue from fisheries and mining, 15% from oil, and 30% from gas. These proportions were the same as those specified in laws no. 22 and no. 25 on autonomy, but the amounts were distributed to the provincial government rather than mostly to the districts. The government of NAD retained the power to determine subsequently the proportion that would be distributed to the districts. In addition to these resources, the law on NAD specified additional revenues from the largest oil and gas industry that is prominent in Aceh. After taxes, the government of NAD would retain 55% of revenues from oil exploitation and 40% from gas during the following eight years. After this period, the proportion of revenues accruing to the NAD government would be reduced to 35% for oil and 20% for gas. These amounts constituted a vast increase in revenues for Aceh.

The law confirmed the application of Syariah law in NAD. Previous legislation had restricted Syariah to certain realms relating to religious affairs, but the law on NAD mentioned no such restrictions. Syariah courts obtained the right to oversee Syariah law and ensure its implementation. It was limited, however, by continued application of the secular laws of the Republic. Disputes between the Syariah and secular courts were to be resolved by the Supreme Court of Indonesia.

The special autonomy law for Papua shared many aspects of the law on Aceh, while including many more details on the role of the provincial government.[48] As a symbolic gesture, the province was officially renamed Papua (from Irian Jaya), and the government of Papua was given the right to adopt a flag, songs, and other symbols unique to Papua, while recognizing its integration into the Republic of Indonesia. The Papua government obtained authority over all matters except foreign policy, defense, monetary and fiscal policy, religion, justice, and specific areas to be determined by regulation. The government structure was supplemented with institutions specific to Papua. As in the case of Aceh, the principal legislative role was given to a provincial parliament, the Papuan People's Representative Assembly (DPRP), with similar powers. The governor was elected by the DPRP and *bupati* by district assemblies, as in the rest of Indonesia but differently from Aceh, where direct elections were to be held. However, the governor of Papua was also the central government's representative and therefore had responsibilities to coordinate the implementation of central government policies in Papua. As in Aceh and in the rest of Indonesia, the governor had a dual accountability to the provincial legislature and to the president. A Papuan People's Assembly (Majelis Rakyat Papua) was created, alongside the DPRP. Its members comprised indigenous Papuans from local customary (*adat*), religious, and women's groups. It was given responsibility for promoting and protecting the rights and customs of the Papuan people. It was given powers of consultation and assent over the candidates for the position of governor, representatives to the national People's Consultative Assembly in Jakarta, and decisions and regulations that infringed upon basic Papuan rights. Other powers or mandates were unclear but the language of the law gave more authority and involvement in the selection of the province's leaders than the customary institutions in Aceh that had no such powers.

On financial matters, specified revenues were similar to those in Aceh. In addition to local taxes and charges, the province received the same proportion of shared taxes and charges (90% of the PBB, for example). Revenues from natural resources accrued mainly to Papua, with 80% from forestry, 80% from mining, 80% from fisheries, 70% from oil and 70% from gas. The most significant revenue in Papua was from mining, given the important role of Freeport in the extraction of gold and copper. These allocations were to remain the same for the following twenty-five years.

The law on special autonomy also addressed the issue of Papua's integration into Indonesia. It specified the creation of a Truth and Reconciliation Commission to investigate the historical process by which West New Guinea had been integrated. The law indicated that the intent of this investigation would be to foster the continued unity of the Indonesian Republic.

A number of other areas of jurisdiction were specified. Most importantly, the law required the promotion of employment for indigenous Papuans, opening up the possibility of affirmative action programs.

Otherwise, it specified a large number of responsibilities for the provincial government in the realm of economic management, health, education, and other matters. In many articles, specific mention was made of the need to protect the rights of indigenous Papuans and their environment.

The special autonomy laws for Aceh and Papua devolved much power and resources to the provinces. Not only did they give broad powers in principle, they also specified areas of jurisdiction, especially in the case of Papua. In the case of Aceh, the principle of special autonomy was strongly stated, while it remained unclear which jurisdictions fell within the broad area of special autonomy. The jurisdictions and responsibilities of the Papuan government were spelled out, as well as the specific areas of exclusion that were to be retained at central government level. In fiscal and monetary terms, the two regions received much greater income than the already large allocations that had been specified in laws no. 22 and no. 25, 1999. The large proportion of revenues from oil and gas in Aceh and from mining in Papua represented very large sums, as they were some of the most important sources of domestic revenue from natural resources. In both regions, the provincial governments obtained the primary role for representing the people and identity of Acehnese and Papuans, with specific symbols and unique institutions to preserve and promote local customs and culture, including Islamic law in the case of Aceh.

Nevertheless, there were some weaknesses in both laws. Most important, there were large areas of jurisdiction that were left for future regulations of the national DPR. In the case of Aceh, the powers specific to special autonomy remained relatively unclear, since there were few specific responsibilities that were mentioned for the government of NAD and there were no specific areas of exclusion. Furthermore, for the most part, the language of the laws was quite broad and could be interpreted in different ways, with a potentially larger role for the central government. For example, the president's powers of consultation or ratification in the election of governors could be construed as a veto power. There were many areas of uncertain jurisdiction for Syariah courts in Aceh, the Wali Nanggroe and Tuha Nanggroe, as well as the Majelis Rakyat Papua. The effects of the governor's dual accountability to the provincial legislature and to the president were not clear. The role as representative of the central government could significantly constrain the autonomy of the provincial executive.

Despite these limitations, the laws on special autonomy provided real power over revenues. The governments of NAD and Papua received large sums and managed their distribution to the districts, as specified by provincial legislatures. By doing so, these laws effectively annulled the central government's attempts in previous legislation to weaken provincial governments and strengthen districts. Although the 1999 laws were implemented in both Aceh and Irian Jaya, the new governments of NAD and Papua now had the authority to specify the revenue allocations to districts. At least in terms of resource allocations, the laws were specific.

The laws on special autonomy were intended to undermine the secessionist movements in Aceh and Irian Jaya by providing wide-ranging autonomy. After the 1999 autonomy laws failed to have any effects, the 2001 laws were seen as concessions of much more autonomy. As they were adopted and implemented, President Megawati also closed the door to referendums on the future status of the regions. She also began new military campaigns against guerilla fighters in both areas, while increasing pressure to negotiate on the basis of autonomy.

Despite these concessions, the laws still failed, at least initially, to stem the support for independence. During the months that followed their implementation on 1 January 2002, GAM continued its struggle. At the end of 2002, it had agreed to a cease-fire and appeared to accept the principle of autonomy but had not formally rejected independence. In Papua, mistrust of the central government continued to rise, especially after the murder in November 2001 of the leader of the Papuan nationalist movement, Theys Eluay. Furthermore, repression of nationalist supporters continued in the province while autonomy was being implemented.

In Papua in particular, the process of implementation of the special autonomy law lacked legitimacy. When the governor had formed a team to draft the law, the consultation process had been hampered by protests and demonstrations against special autonomy. The governor's team, in the end, had drafted a proposed special law that took into account the grievances and demands made by nationalist leaders at two Papuan Congresses. The text had been written as a draft law on special autonomy and submitted to the DPR after it had been circulated in Papua as a consensus document. The team had also mentioned to the DPR that the text could not be changed without opposition from Papuans.[49] Yet, a comparison of the draft text and the actual law shows much dilution and compromise. The DPR reduced the importance of the MRP, eliminated some of the demands for oversight of Indonesian military activities in Papua, reduced the role of the provincial government to manage revenues from natural resources and other sources, and re-established controls by the central government over revenues and the responsibilities of the governor. It also eliminated demands for a Papuan Human Rights Commission as well as a clause on compensation to victims of mistreatment by the military since 1963. Perhaps most importantly, it eliminated a proposed clause that gave the right to the provincial government to hold a referendum on independence after five years if it found that the implementation of special autonomy had not been satisfactory.[50]

Autonomy and the prevention of ethnic violence in Indonesia

Special autonomy failed to stem ethnic violence in Aceh and Papua because of the path dependent context in which it was implemented. Since 1945, Indonesia's political leaders had always seen the political future of the nation as increasingly integrated within a unitary state. While ethnic and religious differences were recognized, they were accepted in as much as they were expressed in cultural events or local traditions, but not within the political realm. The ethnonationalist movements that arose in Aceh and Papua, as elsewhere in the 1950s, were seen as direct threats to this concept of the Indonesian nation and, consequently, as a fundamental breach of the principles of the unitary state. More often than not, expressions of ethnonationalism were crushed by military might with few concessions in return. In the cases of Aceh and Papua, special autonomy was conceded begrudgingly at a time when the state was weak.

If autonomy is sometimes seen as a concession to secessionist movements, certainly the case of East Timor reinforced this idea in the minds of Indonesia's political elite. The offer of wide-ranging autonomy was extended under considerable pressure when the central government, under the weak President Habibie, was facing unprecedented instability, a long financial crisis, and international pressure to resolve the long-standing conflict. While such autonomy was criticized for its concession to secessionists, it was the offer of a referendum that was most controversial, particularly since it led to a rejection of special autonomy in favor of independence. As a result, the possibility of holding referendums in any other area of Indonesia was effectively closed off.

The central government had tremendous difficulty in making regional autonomy a credible political arrangement. Federalism had been rejected because of its association with the divide-and-rule tactics of the Dutch and because it was thought to lack the necessary strength at the center to maintain the unity of the diverse peoples scattered across the archipelago. Young nationalists of all ethnic origins enthusiastically adopted the unitary state at the time of independence, with a common belief that the shared experience of colonialism under the Dutch, and commitments to modernity and shared political values, would allow for the development and prosperity of the nation.

Secessionist movements in the first decade after Indonesia's independence were not based on broad popular support. In South Maluku, South Sulawesi, and West Sumatra, rebellions emerged more from disgruntled military commanders who resisted centralization than from real, popular ethnonationalist movements against the idea of Indonesia. Once they were crushed, they faded away without difficulty as the broader populations had not developed an identity that was separate from Indonesia and elite loyalty was achieved through patronage and reward from the center. Other rebellions in the first decade, including Aceh's participation in the Darul Islam and the formation of a Revolutionary Government of the Republic of Indonesia, challenged the central government but not the unitary state or the Indonesian nation.

While there was always a problem with central–regional relations, these relations were not a threat to Indonesian unity. When various regions accepted the unitary state, they did so on the condition that broad autonomy be implemented to reflect the diversity of Indonesia. Such principles were embedded in every constitutional document of the early period following independence and every piece of legislation that was adopted in subsequent years to manage the relationship between the center and its regions.

The concept of autonomy lost much of its meaning during the New Order regime. An authoritarian context was not conducive to the implementation of devolution of power. While New Order leaders adopted the rhetoric of autonomy and diversity within a unitary state, they were more concerned about the means of securing political and economic control than of giving power to provinces and districts. The system that was implemented by the 1970s and maintained until the end of the New Order regime was highly centralized and allowed little regional autonomy.

This centralization of power was resisted in many areas but was not the cause of the rise of ethnonationalist movements. Many provinces grumbled at the centralization of authority, the control over fiscal resources, and Jakarta's control over revenues from natural resources. While all areas of Indonesia shared these grievances, only East Timor, Aceh, and Irian Jaya developed ethnonationalist movements. As other chapters have shown, the movements in Irian Jaya and East Timor resulted from the absence of shared experience with other regions of Indonesia and a process of integration through military force. In the case of Aceh, the transformation of rebellion from an effort to establish an Islamic state in Indonesia to an ethnonationalist movement was more complex. While the centralization of fiscal and political power contributed to the rise of the GAM, there were several other factors that led to an expansion of the movement. Most importantly, military repression in Aceh eliminated an already weak adherence to the idea of a common Indonesian nation and developed an Acehnese identity that was in opposition to an Indonesian one. In other resource-rich provinces with deep grievances against the center, such as in Riau and East Kalimantan, there was no development of ethnonationalist movements despite resentment of the central control over revenues from natural resources.

The extension of autonomy to all regions was therefore an adequate policy to address the grievances against the center but had little effect on secessionist movements. There was always a possibility that such movements might arise in provinces other than Aceh, Irian Jaya, and East Timor, but the evidence suggests that this was unlikely. Out of its fear of producing such movements, Jakarta offered autonomy to the districts rather than provinces. Many of the subsequent battles were to be fought over proper fiscal allocations, the role of provinces in such a system, and whether the fear of extending autonomy to provinces was justified. Many of these issues were more concerned about fine-tuning the institutions of governance than preventing ethnic violence.

Only in the cases of Aceh and Irian Jaya could autonomy be seen as a mechanism for such prevention, after the East Timorese had supported independence. Autonomy to the districts was flatly rejected and special autonomy was controversial. The problems came from the lack of credibility of the center. While it implemented special autonomy, it also continued to use repressive means against the populations of both regions, even when military repression was part of the experience that fueled separate ethnic identities and desire for a separate state. Democratization certainly increased the potential for special autonomy to be a successful tool to prevent secessionism, since it increased the possibility that the new legislation would be implemented and respected. The lack of clarity in the division of powers diminished these effects, as ambiguities and loopholes could be seen as opportunities for the central government to maintain its control over the two special regions. Furthermore, when Megawati's government showed signs of wanting to reimpose a more centralized government with a stronger role for the military, the credibility of special autonomy was even more undermined.

Autonomy was a successful policy to manage relations between the center and regions but insufficient to eliminate ethnonationalist movements in Aceh and Papua. While more decentralized political and fiscal power would meet many of the demands in several regions, it could prevent the future development of ethnic identification against the center. In the cases that already existed, however, other measures had to be taken to reduce the ethnonationalist threat. Special autonomy only addressed grievances based on the centralization of political and fiscal power, but was not sufficient to restore confidence in the center. It offered few guarantees that the center would not impose more centralization after it had overcome its weaknesses, it did not address demands for less repression, and it did not provide justice for human rights abuses committed in the two regions as a result of the New Order's rule.

11   Unity in diversity

Large, multi-ethnic societies are a challenge for states. Ethnic groups sometimes reach political compromises that ensure stable polities and relatively open politics. They regularly renegotiate, contest, or reaffirm their representation in the state, their access to resources and positions, their status, and their relations with other groups. Political institutions can be modified to accommodate these demands and reach new compromises. In many instances, however, negotiations and compromise break down and violence replaces civil politics. At times, ethnonationalist rebellions or conflicts between ethnic groups are endemic.

Multi-ethnicity in itself is not a source of conflict. Many ethnic groups live side-by-side without fighting each other. Even in societies, such as Indonesia, where ethnic violence has involved many different groups, a majority has maintained peaceful relations. A complex mix of factors such as institutional incentives and threats, elite interests, and state policies shape the politicization and mobilization of ethnic identities. Although groups identify themselves in ethnic terms and differentiate themselves from other groups along a variety of ethnic identifiers, such as language, religion, or race, these differences are not sources of conflict. Rather, grievances arising from different statuses for groups, discrimination, exclusion, or differentiated access to political representation or economic resources are much more plausible factors in violent outcomes.

Different views regarding the correspondence of states to nations have been at the core of many conflicts. In the Westphalian system, states have been the legitimate territorial unit deemed to represent nations. States and nations do not often coincide, but nations have aspired to obtain their own states while state leaders have sought to unify their constituents under the banner of a single nation. How nations are "imagined" out of common historical experiences, or how state leaders and political elites craft them, has a repercussion on relations between ethnic groups. Identities can be denied, modified, or incorporated as criteria for inclusion in a nation. While ethnic identities can sometimes flourish within a broadly defined national identity, at other times these

214

identities can be denied in order to promote a particular definition of the nation. Ethnonationalist response might ensue, or the criteria defining the nation might be renegotiated. In some instances, the compromise might include some recognition of several nations within one state, bound together by political principles.

The result of conflicts, negotiations, and compromises leads to the adoption of "national models." The most obvious national model defines the principles of a single nation within the state. Under this banner, ethnic groups are either recognized as sharing a unique as well as a common identity, or their identities are denied. Some groups may be included while others excluded. More complex models involve recognitions of several nations within the state, or various forms of recognition of ethnic identities. National models are the fundamental principles that define the inclusion/exclusion of groups and the terms of their inclusion. Are they equal to other groups? Must they shed their ethnic identities to be accepted as members of the nation? Are there political or cultural criteria of inclusion?

These national models become the explicit or implicit principles underlying state institutions. Choices about unitary or federal states, official recognition of particular languages, adoption of religions of state, power-sharing arrangements, and special provisions for particular groups represent the adoption of a particular national model. Often these principles become enshrined in preambles or the first few articles of constitutions. Other times they are subtler and can be subjected to various interpretations by state leaders and political elites. The accommodation of various demands by ethnic groups may entail modifications and adjustments to institutions, various forms of recognition, integration, or representation. These institutional changes tend to be relatively easy when they do not transgress the national model.

National models constrain the range of choices for institutional change. Not all negotiations over new or modified institutions raise as much controversy, fear, or sense of threat among various groups. Institutional changes that most directly affect an existing national model are likely to create most controversy. Changes from a unitary to a federal state, for example, would most likely be accompanied by a new way of thinking about the relation between nations, ethnic groups, and their respective territorial bases within the state. Changes from a secular to a religious state would also entail a renegotiation of the principles defining the national model and the role of religious criteria of inclusion. In other words, not all institutional changes are controversial or likely to raise high emotions.

Major institutional changes and renegotiations of national models occur at critical junctures. National models and basic institutions of the state that enshrine them rarely change. For the most part, political institutions change gradually and entail modifications that do not alter fundamental principles. Over time, however, national models become obsolete or their institutionalization creates unacceptable constraints on particular ethnic groups. These problems lead to tensions and grievances that eventually become bases for renegotiation. At those times, the principles of the national model come under attack, as well as the basic institutions of the state. Ethnic violence is more likely to rise when insecurities are high, and groups fear exclusion or unfavorable terms of inclusion.

Ethnic violence erupted in Indonesia at such a critical juncture in the 1990s. The institutional legacy of the New Order regime had intensified tensions between certain ethnic groups. Because Suharto interpreted Indonesia's national model and gave it an institutional expression that excluded certain groups, threatened others' identities, or repressed ethnic demands, some groups felt increasingly insecure. Specifically, his defense of the nation and the unitary state used primarily coercive means, with some measure of co-optation, without ever allowing a full debate on issues of ethnicity or religion.[1] His regime had "settled" the questions that led to ethnic violence in the past by fiat and full use of state instruments to prevent the mobilization of ethnic groups. When his regime began to show signs of decline, especially given his age, the uncertainty surrounding the future only exacerbated the fears and insecurities of groups that felt threatened. When the regime fell suddenly in May 1998, these fears and insecurities reached very high levels, as the basic institutions of the state and fundamental principles of the national model were open for renegotiation. Some groups also saw possibilities of breaking away from unfavorable terms of inclusion. The critical juncture that had begun to develop in the previous years suddenly reached a high peak.

Three sets of tensions became particularly salient toward the end of the New Order regime. First, groups that were previously marginalized or excluded saw opportunities for redress or feared that their status could worsen. Internal migration, combined with a national model that emphasized the modernity of Indonesian identity, threatened the identities and livelihoods of groups that were considered "backward." The Dayaks became violent, as they felt increasingly marginalized by a regime that considered them insufficiently modern to be considered on equal terms with other groups. The Madurese represented most visibly the migration that was encouraged by the New Order regime in its attempts to modernize "backward" groups, populate "isolated" areas, and reduce the importance of local identities. In the case of another excluded group, the Chinese, the outcome was different. The involvement of large Chinese conglomerates in the corrupt practises of the Suharto regime had intensified frustrations among non-Chinese Indonesians at the socio-economic gap between the two groups. With the sudden fall of Suharto, the Chinese became the first targets of violence, as in previous critical junctures, followed by rapid renegotiation of their status. The evidence of provocation by the armed forces and the elite's horror at the rapes of a large number of Chinese women triggered a swift response to begin reincluding the Chinese within Indonesia's national model.

Second, tensions between religious groups heightened. Christians feared that they might be excluded or marginalized in a post–New Order regime, while some Muslim groups seized opportunities to redress their past exclusion. The role of Islam remained ambiguous in the national model. Pancasila had become the sole ideology of the state and Islamists had been side-lined, but only through repression, manipulation, and co-optation of the Islamist political elite. Toward the end of the New Order, Islamic politics began to rise again, and tensions heightened with secularists and non-Muslims and then worsened with the fall of Suharto. Several riots degenerated into conflict between Christians and Muslims. In Maluku, they fueled already high tensions between Christian Ambonese and primarily Muslim migrants. Once the violence began, the conflict became large-scale and spread to pit all local and migrant Muslims against local Christians.

Third, the end of the regime opened up opportunities for renegotiating new terms of inclusion, or secession, for ethnonationalist groups. Aceh, East Timor, and Irian Jaya were three regions where the New Order had used military means to quell demands by local groups. Acehnese, Timorese, and Papuan grievances and demands were interpreted by the regime as threats to Indonesia's national model, because of the presence of secessionist groups. As a result, Suharto had used much more military force and coercion in these regions than elsewhere. In East Timor and Irian Jaya, problems of inclusion had been present since their integration into Indonesia through non-democratic means. A coercive approach was used from the very beginning to include Timorese and Papuans in the nation. As a result, both groups felt threatened by the national model and rejected Indonesian identity as it became interpreted as a loss of their own one. The Acehnese had been rebuked in their prior attempt to support an Indonesian national model based on Islam. In subsequent decades and particularly under the New Order regime, tensions rose to high levels and feelings of threats to their identity developed strongly in response to the repression of small separatist groups. The end of the Suharto regime provided the opportunity to renegotiate their inclusion and reduce the threat to their local identities. In all regions, civilian movements re-emerged to demand autonomy or secession. In Aceh, armed rebellion also resumed. Violence erupted as the post–New Order governments saw, once again, a strong threat from these regions to the national model based on a unitary state and an Indonesian nation.

The large number of conflicts, and their intensity after 1996, were not coincidental. Each event differed in terms of the nature of the conflict, its scale, and its causes. The motives for engaging in violent acts were often local, and many of the grievances also had local dimensions. Yet, the eruption or worsening of many conflicts in one limited time period could not be explained without reference to common factors. Among these, the institutional changes that accompanied the end of Suharto's regime and its aftermath were most significant. They had the effect of stimulating violent conflict where tensions already existed. These tensions were intensified dramatically by an expectation of potentially large changes in the fundamental principles of the Indonesian national model.

The configuration of the national model in the 1990s and the perceived threats to its basic principles were highly contingent on choices made by political leaders during previous critical junctures. At the end of such junctures in 1950 and 1968, certain institutional choices had been excluded and subsequently constrained future leaders from taking alternative paths. The initial decision to reject federalism and favor a unitary state as well as a single Indonesian nation would be difficult, if not impossible, to change in future generations. These pillars were the basis of an original compromise around which various regions had joined the Republic. Although the terms of inclusion could vary, such as wide-ranging regional autonomy, the return to a federalist model or the recognition of more than one, single nation within the Indonesian state was almost impossible. The strong Indonesian nationalism that had led to the creation of the initial institutions continued to feed support for this basic model.

Yet, other fundamental aspects remained open to negotiation. The role of Islam in defining the national model, for example, was left to subsequent debate. The degree of recognition of diversity or regional autonomy within a unitary state and a single nation also remained to be interpreted and negotiated as to their institutional expression. The implications of recognizing Indonesia's large diversity while promoting the development of a modern, Indonesian people were left to be implemented in various ways. In particular, it became difficult later to reconcile a largely inclusive membership criterion for the nation while simultaneously perceiving a section of the population as being "traditional," "backward," or "not conscious" enough to participate meaningfully as full citizens. Furthermore, even the boundaries of membership were left open to negotiation, as the status of the Chinese remained undefined.

Repressive means were used to resolve most of these issues while imposing criteria that excluded, marginalized, or silenced particular groups.

Open debates about Chinese citizenship, the role of Islam, the relative
power of regions, and the representation of ethnic groups characterized
the turbulent 1950s under liberal democratic institutions. When tensions
were high enough, they created pressures for institutional change in the
late 1950s. Guided Democracy and the New Order regime were the
responses of state leaders to these pressures.

The choice to use a repressive approach and to adopt authoritarian institutions had important consequences for future conflicts. Pancasila was
imposed, while Islamists were side-lined. Most Chinese were eventually
included as citizens but under terms that perpetuated their differentiation. Discussions of ethnic or religious issues became curtailed, while the
expression of diversity was limited to non-political forms and controlled
by the central government. Regional autonomy continued to be recognized in principle but was very limited in practise to give preponderance to
national policies. Groups that were deemed "backward" were subjected
to migratory pressure and policies to modernize and "Indonesianize"
them.

Indonesia's national model was modified to conform to the New
Order's interpretation of its requirements. Suharto's government not only
reaffirmed the principles of the unitary state and the Indonesian nation
but added several characteristics that it deemed necessary to ensure unity.
These included strict conformance to Pancasila, policies to homogenize
institutions and national cultural symbols across diverse regions, and political institutions to strengthen central control. The militarization of the
political system was legitimized in terms of the armed forces' unique
role in preserving national unity, as well as other features that restricted
political expression.

This particular definition of Indonesia's national model had especially
costly effects on groups that rejected it. Where there was ethnonationalist rebellion, the power of the military and the central state was used
forcefully. When East Timor and West New Guinea were integrated into
the nation, the choice of such an approach made much more difficult
the subsequent attempts by the central government to make them accept
their membership in the Indonesian nation. A similar divide was created
with the Acehnese, as Sukarno and Suharto rejected the Islamic variant
for Indonesia's national model and, later, used force and coercion against
rebellious groups.

The political crisis of the late 1990s showed that past choices had laid
the basis for ethnic conflict in several areas. Fears that Indonesia might
break up were overblown. The core principles of the national model continued to enjoy wide support. The bonds that were created out of colonial
experience, a revolution, and a new state remained strong among most
groups. In fact, despite the extent and intensity of ethnic violence in the

late 1990s, most groups continued to live peacefully with one another and considered themselves part of the nation, with no secessionist orientations. They contested their terms of inclusion but did not reject the Indonesian nation. East Timor seceded because the Timorese never considered themselves Indonesian, despite two decades of attempts to assimilate them. Coercion, military force, bureaucratic control, and political repression were used extensively in Papua and Aceh, as in East Timor. In these areas as well, the evidence showed that Papuan and Acehnese identity became increasingly divorced from inclusion in the Indonesian nation. While Papuans shared historical grievances that were similar to those in East Timor, the Acehnese did not, but an ethnonationalist movement grew stronger in response to the terms and means of inclusion imposed by the Indonesian government. Although the prospects for reconciliation in these two areas remained bleak, there were no other significant secessionist threats in the rest of Indonesia.

As the critical juncture unfolded after 1998, new terms of inclusion were being renegotiated. The administrations of Habibie, Wahid, and Megawati supported constitutional and institutional reforms that responded to the previous violence and the opportunity for groups to raise grievances openly. For the first time since the 1950s, various ethnic groups could debate and openly negotiate various aspects of the institutionalization of the Indonesian nation and unitary state. Changes were made to eliminate some institutionalized discrimination against the Chinese and accept them as full members of the nation, after the violence of May 1998.

A lively debate re-emerged concerning the role of Islam as a defining characteristic of the Indonesian nation. As violence in Maluku continued, the Laskar Jihad pursued their goals, and new groups pressed for an Islamist agenda, the debate was introduced in the country's highest legislative body, the MPR. The resurrection of the Jakarta Charter, which was widely seen as laying the basis for an Islamic state, was debated during discussions in 2002 over constitutional amendments. Its rejection by a majority of MPR members strongly reaffirmed the secular nature of the Indonesian nation and state but, this time, through a democratic process. Although the question of Islam in politics did not subsequently disappear, a new path had been set.

The unitary state was reconsidered to include greater autonomy for regions. Laws no. 22 and 25 of 1999 extended more autonomy to all regions and returned to the original conception of the unitary state that was developed in the late 1940s. Federalism was briefly discussed as an alternative but was rejected by most of the political elite. This shows the effects of the initial adoption of a unitary state in opposition to the Dutch supported federal state. Furthermore, special autonomy laws were passed to decentralize even more power than in other regions and to recognize specific cultural differences in Aceh and Papua.

The effects of special autonomy on the unitary state and nation were ambiguous. They constituted the boldest attempt to decentralize political and fiscal authority to particular regions since Indonesia was created. By doing so, the central government hoped to offer new terms of inclusion and to diminish ethnonationalist sentiments. Yet, at the same time, they significantly diluted some of the interpretations of the requirements of Indonesian unity, by allowing the adoption of institutions and symbols that were specific to local Acehnese and Papuan cultures. In some sense, it represented recognition that diversity posed strong limits on attempts to define an elaborate national model based on a single, Indonesian nation. At the same time, the autonomy laws did not go so far as to reconceptualize Indonesia in terms of more than one nation.

The Indonesian nation and the unitary state were not, in themselves, sources of ethnic violence. It was their interpretation and their institutionalization in different forms that created tensions. Attempts to define more criteria and a more precise common culture around the national model were mostly responsible for excluding groups, marginalizing them, or creating unfavorable terms of inclusion.

The recognition of diversity and its greater inclusion in political institutions promised more stable ethnic relations. While maintaining an Indonesian nation and a unitary state, these modifications began to accommodate demands for greater diversity of institutions at the local and regional level. A more diluted conception of the nation could allow the reconciling of a common identity, while permitting a fuller expression of cultural diversity, a flourishing of local languages, and even institutions and symbols representing local distinctiveness, such as in Aceh and Papua. The national model might be maintained at its core while moving toward a multiculturalist model. The Indonesian government seemed set to abandon the previously strong emphasis on unity in its national motto, "Unity in Diversity," and to recognize instead the benefits of strengthening its diversity.

Indonesia's experience is not unique and suggests that an analysis of ethnic conflict should address three issues. First, such conflict is partly a product of the institutions that, over time, shape, define, and redefine ethnic identities in relation to other groups, the state, and the nation. Second, even the most inclusive forms of nationalism often produce marginalization, or even exclusion, of groups. More often than not, they create unequal terms of inclusion between different groups. Third, diverse and multicultural societies pose a real challenge for political leaders seeking to create unified political communities. The emphasis on unity at the expense of diversity can be a source of ethnic conflict.

Past choices affect current outcomes. Explanations for ethnic violence can benefit from an analysis of the critical junctures when institutions were created or modified with profound impacts on ethnic relations. During those periods, state leaders and political elites see opportunities to shape the configurations of relative group status and power within a state. They are also moments when ethnic identities are either recognized in constitutional or institutional structures, or ignored for the purposes of building a united political community. Original conceptions of the nation, relative representation of groups, or recognition of particular groups at the time of state creation greatly constrain future possibilities. Moving away from past choices is costly and rarely entails the creation of completely new institutional structures. Past negotiations, compromises, and conflicts that set a particular pattern of ethnic relations are developed explicitly or implicitly into national models. Tensions and grievances arise from these institutions and eventually give rise to new critical junctures. The legacies of the past, however, always remain. For instance, opportunities to choose federal structures, once rejected in the past, may never be feasible in the future. Autonomy may lead to more secessionism, depending on the levels of tension and grievance created by highly centralized states.

The implementation of new institutional structures is highly contingent, therefore, on past institutional choices. The adoption of federal structures or even of autonomy can have very different consequences, depending on past choices in favor of unitary states, negative experiences with federalism, or national models that deny recognition of ethnic groups with regional concentration. While institutional incentives or constraints to ethnic cooperation can be derived theoretically, their effects in particular societies depend on past choices. Only rarely, such as in South Africa in the 1990s, can new constitutions and radically new institutional structures be adopted. Most often, changes are unlikely to depart radically from entrenched institutional paths.

One of the greatest constraints to institutional choices lies in the conception of nation and national models underlying political institutions. When a national model has been built around the idea of a single nation, political institutions reflect the unity of the nation over the representation of various groups. Conversely, when a national model is based on ideas of the primacy of one ethnic group over others, or of shared power between several groups or nations, the constitution and state institutions are structured around these basic characteristics. In either case, it is very difficult for subsequent generations to move away from the initial model. Institutional change will tend to remain within the constraints posed by the basic principles of the initial national model.

The constraints can have varying effects on ethnic relations, depending on the degree of inclusiveness. While ethnic forms of nationalism are often most restrictive, they are not exclusively so. Even some broadly inclusive forms, such as Indonesian nationalism, often exclude or marginalize certain groups. National models are rarely, if at all, based on purely political, civic principles. Where citizenship is broad and inclusive, there are still attempts by political leaders to create national cultures around values that distinguish them from other nations. At a minimum, political communities develop over time a common culture around official languages or values that can become criteria for exclusion or unequal terms of inclusion.

Multicultural or multi-ethnic societies, therefore, pose a challenge for building unified political communities. National models based on single nations or cultural criteria that exclude or marginalize groups may produce much violence. Political leaders sometimes choose to consolidate states first, before crafting nations or national models. In these circumstances, state repressive instruments are often used to quell secessionist rebellions or groups whose perspectives may differ from that of state leaders. In the end, however, nationalist dreams cannot escape the realities of multi-ethnic or multicultural diversity.

Notes

1 Introduction

1 In this book, "ethnic" identities refer to groups defined by ascriptive character-istics that include cultural, linguistic, religious, or racial criteria. "Ethnic con-flict" refers to conflict between groups that identify themselves as distinct from others according to one or more of these criteria. The literature has more often emphasized ethnic "conflict" than ethnic "violence." Conflict includes violent and non-violent forms. The factors that explain violence can be different from the causes of the broader conflict. See Brubaker and Laitin, "Ethnic and na-tionalist violence." However, the explanatory factors that shape the boundaries and conditions of conflict generally tend to be the same whether the conflict takes a violent or non-violent form.

2 See, for example, a special report entitled "Bangsa (Nation)," *Tiras* 3, no. 6, 6 March 1997.

3 Figures are compiled from the following sources: on Maluku, see International Crisis Group, *Indonesia*; on Aceh, see International Crisis Group, *Aceh*, for 2001 figures. For 1999–2000, see figures from Care Human Rights Forum, reported in *Agence France-Presse*, 6 January 2001. On West Kalimantan, see Human Rights Watch, *Indonesia: Communal Violence in West Kalimantan*; on Central Kalimantan, see International Crisis Group, *Communal Violence in Indonesia*, p. 5; on East Timor, see US State Department, "1999 Indonesia country report on human rights practices," and "Unfinished business: Justice for East Timor," press release, Human Rights Watch, New York, 30 August 2000.

4 "Police arrest main suspect in Bali blasts," *Reuters*, 21 November 2002.

5 See, for example, Hefner, *Civil Islam*, pp. 167–213. For a general account of the role of criminal gangs in inciting violence, see Barker, "State of fear"; and Ryter, "Pemuda Pancasila."

6 On the lack of evidence in Poso, Central Sulawesi, and Maluku, see Aragon, "Communal violence in Poso, Central Sulawesi"; Bertrand, "Legacies of the authoritarian past"; and van Klinken, "Indonesia's new ethnic elites."

7 See Aragon, "Communal violence in Poso," on Poso (Central Sulawesi); van Klinken, "The Maluku wars," on Maluku; and van Klinken, "Indonesia's new ethnic elites," on Kalimantan.

8 On Papua, see Mote and Rutherford, "From Irian Jaya to Papua."

9 See Peluso and Harwell, "Territory, custom and the cultural politics of ethnic war in West Kalimantan, Indonesia."

10 Robinson, "*Rawan* is as *rawan* does," and particularly the revised version in Anderson, *Violence and the State in Suharto's Indonesia.*

2 Critical junctures, nationalism, and ethnic violence

1 There are many definitions of "ethnic" identities. In this study, I use an inclusive definition that refers to attributes such as skin color, religion, language, or others associated with common origin.

2 The view that ethnic identities are malleable and change over time has been identified with the constructivist and situationalist approaches. See Barth, *Ethnic Groups and Boundaries*, for a good example of a situationalist conception. The "constructivist" approach accepts the malleability of ethnic identity but emphasizes that ethnic boundaries are also "enduring social constructions."

3 The debate on institutions is extensive, but more often limited to issues of conflict management. For an argument favoring a "consociational" model, a form of power-sharing between major ethnic groups, see Lijphart, *Democracy in Plural Societies*. For a perspective that favors incentives for cross-ethnic alliances, see Horowitz, *Ethnic Groups in Conflict*; Horowitz, "Democracy in divided societies."

4 Young, *The Politics of Cultural Pluralism*; Tambiah, *Leveling Crowds*; Brass, *Theft of an Idol*; Anderson, *Imagined Communities.*

5 See Brass, *Ethnic Groups and the State*. On ethnonationalist mobilization, also with an emphasis on elites, see Snyder, *From Voting to Violence.*

6 See Geertz, *The Interpretation of Cultures*. For a view based on a socio-biological perspective, see Van den Berghe, *The Ethnic Phenomenon.*

7 Young, *The Politics of Cultural Pluralism.*

8 Horowitz, *Ethnic Groups in Conflict*, p. 187.

9 Other explanations place less emphasis on group anxieties and psychological factors. Some focus more on structural factors. Hechter (*Internal Colonialism*), for example, emphasized internal colonialism. This approach stresses the economic disparities created by unequal control over state power and resources. Other types of economic explanations focus on the class interests of ethnic groups, conflicts between "middlemen" traders and other groups, or economic marginalization. See Bates, "Modernization, ethnic competition, and the rationality of politics in contemporary Africa." Ted Gurr emphasizes a large number of factors that explain why ethnocultural groups choose political action, but he particularly stresses economic, political, and cultural discrimination. See Gurr, *Peoples Versus States*; Gurr et al., *Minorities at Risk.*

10 See Scott, *Domination and the Arts of Resistance.*

11 Horowitz, *The Deadly Ethnic Riot*, pp. 268–9. For a rational choice perspective on why ethnic relations most often remain tense but not violent, see Fearon and Laitin, "Explaining interethnic cooperation."

12 See Brass, *Theft of an Idol*, for an argument that state actors and the police, among other elites, often construct "riots" or other forms of violence in terms of ethnic violence and, as a result, intensify precipitant events.

13 On this hypothesis, see Gurr, *Why Men Rebel*; Gurr et al., *Minorities at Risk*, pp. 43–6. Esman, *Conflict and Peacemaking in Multiethnic*

Societies, argues that economic growth has little effect on alleviating ethnic conflict.

14 Gurr, *Peoples Versus States*, pp. 115–19.

15 On rational choice analyses, see Posen, "The security dilemma and ethnic conflict"; Hechter, "Explaining nationalist violence"; Carment et al., "Third party intervention and ethnic conflict"; Fearon and Laitin, 'Explaining interethnic cooperation'. For an excellent discussion of the role of passion, emotion, and rationality of fear in ethnic riots, see Horowitz, *The Deadly Ethnic Riot*, pp. 522–65.

16 Horowitz, *The Deadly Ethnic Riot*, offers a compelling explanation of the causes of riots, their various forms, and their effects on group relations. Brass, *Theft of an Idol*, emphasizes the role of discourse in explaining the perpetuation and intensification of collective violence.

17 Horowitz, *Ethnic Groups in Conflict*, uses "ethnic conflict" as a general category that is inclusive of various forms of ethnic violence. Gurr, who analyzes a large number of groups, uses the category "ethnopolitical" action, expressed as protest (violent/non-violent) and rebellion (which includes ethnonationalist rebellion), to explain the sources of violence (see Gurr et al., *Minorities at Risk*, pp. 93–137).

18 See, for instance, Kedourie's argument (in *Nationalism*) of nationalism as an ideology (or doctrine) which, he contends, leads to violence: "Ideological politics is thus necessarily and inevitably caught up in a perpetual disastrous and self-destructive tension between ends and means" (p. xiv); "The attempts to refashion so much of the world on national lines has not led to greater peace and stability. On the contrary, it has created new conflicts, exacerbated tensions, brought catastrophe to numberless people innocent of all politics" (pp. 133–4).

19 Most scholars on nationalism share this view, although they have very different analyses on its origins and its characteristics. See Gellner, *Nations and Nationalism*, for a modernist account; Anderson, *Imagined Communities*, for a constructivist approach; and Smith, *The Ethnic Origins of Nations*, for a primordialist approach.

20 Kymlicka, *Multicultural Citizenship*, p. 13.

21 See Anderson, *Imagined Communities*.

22 For an interesting discussion of state nationalism in developing countries, see Anderson's concepts of "Russification" and "official nationalism," in Anderson, *Imagined Communities*, pp. 83–140.

23 See Greenfeld, *Nationalism*. For an earlier and similar classification of nationalism, as Western and Eastern, see Kohn, *The Idea of Nationalism*.

24 Xenos, "Civic nationalism," offers an interesting critique of the attempt to classify the United States as a purely civic model.

25 Kymlicka, *Multicultural Citizenship*, p. 24. See fn. 15, p. 200 for an interesting critique of the distinction between civic and ethnic nationalism and its basis, he contends, on a misreading of American history.

26 See Yack, "The myth of the civic nation," p. 208.

27 See Yashar, "Democracy, indigenous movements, and the postliberal challenge in Latin America."

28 Taylor, *Multiculturalism and "The Politics of Recognition."*

29 Ibid., p. 64. Emphasis in original text.

30 On group worth and conflict, see Horowitz, *Ethnic Groups in Conflict*, pp. 141–228.

31 See Lijphart, *Democracy in Plural Societies*.

32 Identities and the substance of negotiation at critical junctures are also shaped by "rhetorical frames" that limit the field of possibilities in terms of particular groups' views of themselves and the world. See Cruz, "Identity and persuasion."

33 See Lijphart, *Democracy in Plural Societies*; Lijphart, "The puzzle of Indian democracy."

34 Horowitz, *Ethnic Groups in Conflict*, pp. 598–9, 601–52.

35 See Collier and Collier, *Shaping the Political Arena* (pp. 29–39), for an elaboration of the critical juncture framework and analysis.

36 This is not unusual in the analysis of critical junctures. Collier and Collier analyze critical junctures that relate specifically to relations between the state and the labor movement in Latin America, particularly periods of incorporation.

37 Pierson, "Increasing returns, path dependence, and the study of politics," p. 263.

38 On the third wave of democratization, see Huntington, *The Third Wave*.

39 Horowitz, "Democracy in divided societies."

40 Linz and Stepan, "Political identities and electoral sequences," p. 124.

41 Linz and Stepan, *Problems of Democratic Transition and Consolidation*, p. 36.

42 Marx, "Apartheid's end," pp. 489–92.

43 Linz and Stepan, "Political identities and electoral sequences," p. 125.

44 This argument implicitly rejects Snyder's account of ethnonationalist violence during periods of democratization (see *From Voting to Violence*). While Snyder places more emphasis on the role of elites who are likely to lose power as a result of regime change, I argue that elites could not mobilize groups without existing tensions and grievances that are prior to regime change. These tensions and grievances are more important in explaining the violence. They can also be traced back to previous junctures when institutions were formed or changed in such a way that they contributed to deteriorating relations between groups and the development of opposing identities.

3 The national model and its institutional history

1 On the role of Muslim groups in the nationalist movement, see Benda, *The Crescent and the Rising Sun*.

2 On the Communist International and Moscow's position on the orientation of the Indonesian Communist Party, see Kahin, *Nationalism and Revolution in Indonesia*, pp. 78–9. Stalin was specifically supportive of an alliance between Indonesian communists and the non-communist nationalist organizations.

3 Many scholars argue that the Budi Utomo, formed in 1908, was the first nationalist organization. Yet, it was mainly a Javanese organization that was not able to supersede ethnic boundaries in the same way as Sarekat Islam did. On Budi Utomo, see Nagazumi, *The Dawn of Indonesian Nationalism*; and Anderson, "A time of darkness and a time of light."

4 Kahin, *Nationalism and Revolution*, pp. 64–78.

5 Ibid., pp. 90–1.
6 Ibid., pp. 101–33.
7 Ibid., pp. 123–6.
8 Hefner, *Civil Islam*, p. 42. For an elaborate discussion of the Jakarta Charter and the events surrounding its rejection, see Boland, *The Struggle of Islam in Modern Indonesia*, pp. 27–35.
9 Kahin, *Nationalism and Revolution*, pp. 351–90.
10 For a detailed analysis of the movement to establish an independent Republic of South Maluku, see Chauvel, "Ambon"; Chauvel, *Nationalists, Soldiers, and Separatists*. For a detailed account of the regions' participation and role in the revolution, as well as their support for the unitarian state, see Kahin, *Regional Dynamics of the Indonesian Revolution*.
11 On the Darul Islam, see van Dijk, *Rebellion under the Banner of Islam*; Boland, *The Struggle of Islam*.
12 Kahin, *Nationalism and Revolution*, pp. 256–303, 326–31. For a detailed analysis of the communist rebellion, see Swift, *The Road to Madiun*.
13 Legge, *Central Authority and Regional Autonomy in Indonesia*, p. 9.
14 Feith, *The Decline of Constitutional Democracy in Indonesia*, pp. 212–14.
15 For a detailed analysis of the rebellion in Sulawesi, see Harvey, *Permesta*.
16 Feith, *The Decline of Constitutional Democracy*, pp. 487–500, 521–38.
17 Ibid., pp. 584–9.
18 Ibid., pp. 590–7.
19 See Crouch, *The Army and Politics in Indonesia*, 1st edn, p. 155; Robinson, *The Dark Side of Paradise*, pp. 235–302. See Anderson and McVey, *A Preliminary Analysis of the October 1, 1965 Coup in Indonesia*, for an argument that the coup attempt was a result of divisions within the armed forces rather than instigated by the Communist Party. The numbers of people killed in 1965–66 reached the hundreds of thousands but there are differences in the actual estimates, ranging from 100,000 to 700,000–800,000. For the best discussion of this issue, see Cribb, *The Indonesian Killings, 1965–66*.
20 See Crouch, *The Army and Politics*, pp. 221–44, 333–45.

4 Exclusion, marginality, and the nation

1 The following account of events is taken mainly from the 1997 Human Rights Watch (HRW) report, *Indonesia: Communal Violence in West Kalimantan*. The paucity of reporting on these events makes an exact account difficult. The HRW report has the most balanced description of events.
2 Ibid., p. 1.
3 See, for instance, HRW, *Indonesia: Communal Violence*, which considers the cultural explanation as important as other explanations. See also reports in *D&R*, no. 28, 1 March 1997. Interviews with Syarif Ibrahim Alqadrie, Professor of Sociology (University Tanjungpura, Pontianak), offer contradictory accounts. In one interview, he elaborates on a cultural explanation (*Berita Buana*, 6 February 1997), while in others he rejects it and favors instead socio-economic explanations (see *D&R*, 18 January 1997). The foreign media often placed much emphasis on the circulation of a "red bowl" as a cultural appeal to war among the Dayaks. Such reports also focused on instances of heads severed and livers eaten by Dayaks, some of whom were reported to be "in

trance," thereby suggesting a "primitive" cultural explanation to the violence. See, for example, "Murder and mayhem," *Far Eastern Economic Review* 160, no. 8, 20 February 1997.

4 The ICG report on the 2001 violence gives some important weight to such an explanation (see International Crisis Group, *Communal Violence in Indonesia*).

5 See, for example, the report in *Tiras* 3, no. 6, 6 March 1997; and discussion in HRW, *Indonesia: Communal Violence*.

6 HRW, *Indonesia: Communal Violence*, discusses such an explanation while pointing to the absence of evidence to substantiate it. On the East Java *ulama* and subsequent withdrawal of allegations made by the armed forces, see *D&R*, no. 28, 1 March 1997; *Media Indonesia*, 21 February 1997; *Forum Keadilan* 5, no. 24, 10 March 1997.

7 See, for example, the ICG report's rejection of such explanation for the 2001 violence (ICG, *Communal Violence in Indonesia*, p. 20).

8 Sudagung, *Mengurai Pertikaian Etnis*, pp. 80–5; HRW, *Indonesia: Communal Violence*.

9 Sudagung, *Mengurai Pertikaian Etnis*, p. 64.

10 See Dove, "Dayak anger ignored," *Inside Indonesia*, no. 51, July–September 1997, for an argument that the ethnic tensions in Kalimantan resulted from economic inequities between a national entrepreneurial class and local communities, especially in relation to plantation projects in the area.

11 Peluso and Harwell, "Territory, custom and the cultural politics of ethnic war in West Kalimantan, Indonesia."

12 See King, *The Peoples of Borneo*, pp. 29–31. The term "Malay" was also a label to denote the Muslim populations of the coastal areas, as opposed to the non-Muslims of the interior (Dayaks). For this reason, when some Dayaks began to convert to Islam, they often adopted the label "Malay" and talked of "entering Malay" (*masuk Melayu*).

13 Miles, *Cutlass & Crescent Moon*, pp. 103–9.

14 Ibid., p. 104.

15 Ibid., p. 114; Schiller, *The Formation of Federal Indonesia, 1945–1949*, pp. 100–3.

16 Schiller, *The Formation of Federal Indonesia*, pp. 100–3.

17 Miles, *Cutlass & Crescent Moon*, p. 114; see also endnote 33, p. 154, and endnotes 53 and 54, p. 155.

18 See Feith, *The Indonesian Elections of 1955*, pp. 69–70. The only other significant parties that were somewhat based on ethnic groups, although less avowedly so, were Baperki representing the Chinese Indonesians; PRD (Villlage People's Party) and PRIM (Party of the People of Free Indonesia) which were based in West Java, among the Sundanese; and AKUI, based in Madura. Of these parties, Baperki was probably most significant because of the amount of support relative to the Chinese population, while PRD, PRIM, and AKUI obtained a relatively small percentage of support in the regions where they ran candidates.

19 Miles, *Cutlass & Crescent Moon*, pp. 119–23.

20 See Peluso and Watts, *Violent Environments*, p. 99.

21 Interview with Juwono Sudarsono, vice-governor, National Defense Institute, Jakarta, 22 April 1997.

22 Peluso and Watts, *Violent Environments*, p. 100. A more general argument
about "backward" and "primitive" groups under the New Order can be found
in Li, "Marginality, power and production"; Kahn, "Culturalising the Indonesian uplands"; and Persoon, "Isolated groups or indigenous peoples."
23 The Village Law of 1979 (no. 5) implemented a new form of village government with homogenous features across the archipelago and modeled after the
Javanese village. For its effects on Dayak villages, see ICG, *Communal Violence
in Indonesia*, p. 19.
24 Peluso, "Whose woods are these," pp. 392–4; Peluso and Watts, *Violent
Environments*, pp. 93–6; McCarthy, "The changing regime," pp. 93–6.
25 McCarthy, "The changing regime," p. 99, fn. 17.
26 HRW, *Indonesia: Communal Violence*.
27 Sudagung, *Mengurai Pertikaian Etnis*, pp. 61–2.
28 Sudagung, *Mengurai Pertikaian Etnis*, pp. 61–2, 64, 86–7, 105.
29 Horowitz, *The Deadly Ethnic Riot*, pp. 135–47.
30 Specifically, there were nine incidents before 1996. Only one, in 1979, involved more than a couple of people and led to riots in which more than twenty
people were killed. See HRW, *Indonesia: Communal Violence*; and Petebang,
Dayak Sakti, pp. 102–4.
31 For an account of the conflict in 1999, as well as interviews with Indonesian scholars about the conflict, see Petebang and Sutrisno, *Konflik Etnik
Di Sambas*. See also *Tempo* 28, no. 3, 23–29 March 1999; *Tempo* 28, no. 4,
30 March – 5 April 1999; *Forum Keadilan* 7, no. 25, 22 March 1999; *Forum
Keadilan* 7, Special edition, 29 March – 4 April 1999; *Gatra* 5, no. 19, 27
March 1999.
32 Petebang and Sutrisno, *Konflik Etnik*, p. 16.
33 Ibid., pp. 124–6.
34 For an account of the violence, see *Tempo* 30, no. 2, 12–18 March 2001;
Tempo 30, no. 7, 16–22 April 2001; ICG, *Communal Violence in Indonesia*,
pp. 2–6.
35 ICG, *Communal Violence in Indonesia*, p. 5.
36 Ibid., p. 16. The ICG report emphasizes the economic and political marginalization of the Dayaks, as well as the effects of migration (pp. 2–6). It places
too much stress, however, on cultural stereotypes as a cause of conflict, rather
than a symptom of the tensions between both groups.
37 Ibid., pp. 13–15.
38 See Peluso and Watts, *Violent Environments*, for factors specific to West Kalimantan; van Klinken, "Indonesia's new ethnic elites," for factors specific to
Central Kalimantan.
39 *Asli* (original, indigenous) and *pribumi* (native, indigenous) have essentially
the same meaning and have been used at different periods to distinguish "sons
of the soil" from the non-indigenous. These categories were essentially used
to differentiate the Chinese from all other Indonesians.
40 John Sidel, for example, strongly emphasizes the anti-Chinese riots of the
late 1990s as being attacks on capital. See Sidel, "Riots, church burnings,
conspiracies." See also Harymurti, "Challenges of change in Indonesia,"
p. 77; and Thee Kian Wie, "Masalah 'Cina' Dan Nasionalisme Ekonomi
Indonesia [the 'Chinese problem' and Indonesia's economic nationalism]."
41 Coppel, *Indonesian Chinese in Crisis*, pp. 28–9.

42 "Native" was a colonial category that divided people in the Dutch East Indies along racial lines.
43 Kahin, *Nationalism and Revolution in Indonesia*, pp. 8–10. For a detailed analysis of the economic system under Dutch colonial rule and its effects on the structure of society, including the differentiation of the Chinese from the "Natives," see Furnivall, *Netherlands India*.
44 Suryadinata, *Peranakan Chinese Politics in Java, 1917–1942*, pp. 1–3.
45 Siauw, *Siauw Giok Tjhan*, pp. 18–20; Suryadinata, *Peranakan Chinese Politics*, p. 22. For a detailed study on the rise of Chinese nationalism, see Williams, *Overseas Chinese Nationalism*.
46 Kahin, *Nationalism and Revolution*, p. 67. On the formation of the Sarekat Islam and its link to fear and hostility against the Chinese, see Shiraishi, *An Age in Motion*, pp. 41–69.
47 See Shiraishi, "Anti-Sinicism in Java's New Order."
48 For a detailed account of the different waves of Chinese migration and the formation of *peranakan* and *totok* Chinese communities, see Skinner, "The Chinese minority," pp. 104–10; Williams, *Overseas Chinese Nationalism*, pp. 10–11.
49 Suryadinata, *Peranakan Chinese Politics*, pp. 22, 39–82.
50 Ibid., pp. 136–7, 158–70; Siauw, *Siauw Giok Tjhan*, p. 48; Coppel, *Indonesian Chinese*, p. 16.
51 Kahin, *Nationalism and Revolution*, pp. 158, 171 (fn. 42); Siauw, *Siauw Giok Tjhan*, pp. 99, 104.
52 Siauw, *Siauw Giok Tjhan*, pp. 102–3.
53 Ibid., p. 169.
54 Ibid., pp. 184–9.
55 Coppel, *Indonesian Chinese*, pp. 43–4.
56 Somers, "*Peranakan* Chinese Politics in Indonesia", p. 147.
57 Coppel, *Indonesian Chinese*, pp. 38–40.
58 Ibid., pp. 36–7.
59 Ibid., p. 44.
60 Ibid., pp. 58–60.
61 Ibid., pp. 70, 112–13. On the Dayak attacks against the Chinese, see Coppel, *Indonesian Chinese*, pp. 145–9. For a detailed account, see Davidson and Kammen, "Indonesia's unknown war and the lineages of violence in West Kalimantan."
62 Mackie, "Anti-Chinese outbreaks in Indonesia, 1959–1968," pp. 111, 129–38.
63 Coppel, *Indonesian Chinese*, pp. 110–12, 135; Heidhues, "Who wants to be non-pribumi?," p. 51.
64 Coppel, *Indonesian Chinese*, pp. 110–12, 153.
65 Coppel, *Indonesian Chinese*, pp. 110–12, 144. On Suharto's policies and regulations in the late 1960s, see also Tan, "The social and cultural dimensions of the role of ethnic Chinese in Indonesian society."
66 Coppel, *Indonesian Chinese*, pp. 156–7, 162–4.
67 Interview with Frans Winarta, Jakarta, 21 April 1997. See also Kwik, "Masalah pri dan non-pri dewasa ini," pp. 19–20; Suryadinata, "Patterns of Chinese political participation in four ASEAN states," pp. 296–7; and *Jakarta Post*, 17 September 1998.

68 Coppel, *Indonesian Chinese*, pp. 156–7.
69 Interview with Frans Winarta.
70 For a good analysis of the formation of these conglomerates and their growth, see Robison, *Indonesia*. See also Mackie, "Towkays and tycoons," on the rise of Liem Sioe Liong, the most powerful Chinese businessman in the New Order; and Crouch, *The Army and Politics in Indonesia*.
71 This figure was contested by Thee Kian Wie, an economist at Indonesia's Institute of Sciences (LIPI), who nevertheless argued that public perception was more important than the actual facts. Interview with Thee Kian Wie, Jakarta, 18 May 1999.
72 Schwarz, *A Nation in Waiting: Indonesia's Search for Stability*, pp. 158–9.
73 See "Us and them," *Far Eastern Economic Review*, 12 February 1998, pp. 16–17; "Ready, set . . .," *Far Eastern Economic Review*, 19 February 1998, pp. 46–50; "Playing with ire," *Far Eastern Economic Review*, 5 March 1998, pp. 18–19.
74 A report published by Tim Relawan Kemanusiaan estimated the number of deaths at 1200 and rapes at 44 (*Tempo Interaktif*, 20 June 1998). In the final report, the numbers were revised upwards to 168 cases. These rapes were subject to much controversy in the Indonesian media, with accusations that the numbers were fabricated. See Human Rights Watch, *Indonesia: The Damaging Debate on Rapes of Ethnic Chinese Women*. A government-named independent fact-gathering team on the May events reported evidence of armed forces involvement in the riots and killings, with the main suspect being Lt. Gen. Prabowo Subianto (*Tempo* 27, no. 5, 3–10 November 1998). The number of rapes was estimated to be closer to 90.
75 See *Laporan Akhir Tim Gabungan Pencari Fakta Peristiwa Tanggal 13–15 Mei 1998* (Final Report of the Joint Fact-Finding Team on the May 13–15 1998 Riots).
76 Interview with Harry Tjan Silalahi, vice-chair of the board, Centre for Strategic and International Studies, Jakarta, 10 May 1999. See also statements by Amien Rais in *Jakarta Post*, 4 August 1998.
77 See Suryadinata, "Chinese politics in post-Suharto Indonesia," pp. 509–15; and *Jakarta Post*, 7 November 1998.
78 Suryadinata, "Chinese politics," pp. 517–19.
79 *Jakarta Post*, 15 October 1998; *Jakarta Post*, 19 January 2000; *Tempo* 30, no. 52, 25 February – 3 March 2002.

5 Islam and nation

1 Feith, *The Decline of Constitutional Democracy in Indonesia*, pp. 487–507, 521–38, 578–89.
2 Smith-Kipp and Rodgers, "Introduction: Indonesian religions in society," p. 19.
3 Boland cites Christian reports showing figures of several hundred thousand Indonesians converting to Christianity. See Boland, *The Struggle of Islam in Modern Indonesia*, p. 231. Others support the finding of massive conversions to Christianity without precise figures. See Webb, *Palms and the Cross*; Hefner, "Of faith and commitment," p. 113.

4 Hefner, "Of faith and commitment"; Boland, *The Struggle of Islam*, p. 231; Webb, *Palms and the Cross*, p. 203; Spyer, "Serial conversion/conversion to seriality."

5 Webb, *Palms and the Cross*, p. 153; Coppel, *Indonesian Chinese in Crisis*, pp. 109–10.

6 The term *"abangan"* refers to the distinction between Javanese following a syncretic form of Islam, as opposed to the *santri* who were more strict adherents to the precepts of Islam. See Geertz, *The Religion of Java*.

7 Boland, *The Struggle of Islam*, pp. 231–2; Webb, *Palms and the Cross*, p. 153. McVey notes that many also converted to *kebatinan*, a Javanese mysticism that became the first non-universal religion to be recognized by the state. Many New Order officials, especially military personnel, were adherents of *kebatinan*. See McVey, "Faith as the outsider," p. 203. On the role of Muslims in the massacre, see Brackman, *The Communist Collapse in Indonesia*, pp. 114–18.

8 On the role of NU supporters, see McVey, "Faith as the outsider."

9 An Islamic ruling on religious duty.

10 Boland, *The Struggle of Islam*, pp. 147, 151.

11 For a very sophisticated account of the differences in policies toward secular nationalists, Muslim traditionalists, and Muslim modernists, see Hefner, *Civil Islam*, chs 4 and 5.

12 Crouch, *The Army and Politics in Indonesia*, 2nd edn, pp. 260–2.

13 Schwarz, *A Nation in Waiting*, p. 32.

14 McVey, "Faith as the outsider," pp. 205–6.

15 Ibid., pp. 215–16.

16 Ibid.

17 Atkinson, "Religions in dialogue," p. 177.

18 Schwarz, *A Nation in Waiting*, p. 172; Steenbrink, "Muslim–Christian relations in the Pancasila state of Indonesia," p. 328.

19 Bresnan, *Managing Indonesia*, pp. 218–26; Ramage, *Politics in Indonesia*, pp. 37–8.

20 McVey, "Faith as the outsider," p. 199.

21 Boland, *The Struggle of Islam*, p. 230; Steenbrink, "Muslim–Christian relations," pp. 329–30.

22 Boland, *The Struggle of Islam*, p. 233; Webb, *Palms and the Cross*, pp. 243–4.

23 Boland, *The Struggle of Islam*, p. 231.

24 Ibid., pp. 234–5; Steenbrink, "Muslim–Christian relations," p. 330.

25 Steenbrink, "Muslim–Christian relations," p. 330.

26 Ibid., p. 331; see also Boland, *The Struggle of Islam*, p. 230.

27 Webb, *Palms and the Cross*, p. 158.

28 Steenbrink, *Dutch Colonialism and Indonesian Islam*, pp. 145–6, 331–2.

29 Jenkins, *Suharto and His Generals*, p. 29.

30 Crouch, *The Army and Politics*, pp. 242–3, 271–2; Jenkins, *Suharto and His Generals*, p. 21.

31 The Kopkamtib became one of the most important instruments of government political control under the New Order. See Crouch, *The Army and Politics*, p. 223.

32 Jenkins, *Suharto and His Generals*, pp. 56–7.

33 Green is the colour of Islam. The Indonesian media portrayed these changes as a "greening" (*penghijauan*) of the New Order's policies and institutions.

34 Vatikiotis, *Indonesian Politics under Suharto*, p. 133.
35 Liddle, "The Islamic turn in Indonesia".
36 Hefner, "Of faith and commitment," pp. 1–37. See also Hefner, *Civil Islam*, pp. 128–45.
37 Hefner, "Islam and nation in the post-Suharto era," pp. 40–7; Hefner, "Islamization and democratization in Indonesia," pp. 90–1; Aminudin, *Kekuatan Islam Dan Pergulatan Kekuasaan Di Indonesia*, pp. 212–13.
38 Hefner, "Islamization and democratization," pp. 80–1; Hefner, *Civil Islam*, pp. 113–15.
39 Hefner, *Civil Islam*, pp. 113–15; Aminudin, *Kekuatan Islam*, pp. 142–53.
40 Aminudin, *Kekuatan Islam*, pp. 153–6, 168–70.
41 Ibid., pp. 176–9.
42 Hefner, "Islamization and democratization," pp. 86–8; Hefner, *Civil Islam*, pp. 113–21.
43 Aminudin, *Kekuatan Islam*, p. 230.
44 Schwarz, *A Nation in Waiting*, pp. 175, 333–4.
45 Aminudin, *Kekuatan Islam*, pp. 182–92.
46 Ibid., p. 330.
47 Hefner, "Islamization and democratization," pp. 76–9; Hefner, "Islam and nation," pp. 48–52.
48 Hefner, "Islam and nation," p. 48.

6 The escalation of religious conflict

1 The Indonesian term "Maluku" is used instead of the European "Moluccas."
2 Tirtosudarmo, "The political-demography of national integration and its policy implications for a sustainable development in Indonesia," p. 373. See also Hoshour, "Resettlement and the politicization of ethnicity in Indonesia," p. 558; Guinness, "Transmigrants in South Kalimantan and South Sulawesi"; and Elmhirst, "Space, identity politics and resource control in Indonesia's transmigration programme," pp. 814–15.
3 Aditjondro, "Transmigration in Irian Jaya," pp. 71–2.
4 One exception is the early policy of settling transmigrants in border areas where guerilla organizations operated. This policy was used in East Kalimantan during the Confrontation with Malaysia, and later in Irian Jaya to constrain the activities of the OPM (Free Papua Movement). See Aditjondro, "Transmigration in Irian Jaya," p. 68.
5 Spontaneous migrants receive partial subsidies from the government, whereas voluntary migrants are self-funded.
6 Tirtosudarmo, "The political-demography," p. 378.
7 On Irian Jaya, see Defert, *L'Indonésie et la Nouvelle-Guinée-Occidentale*, p. 339; on Maluku, see Biro Pusat Statistik, *Beberapa Ciri Pemeluk Agama di Indonesia 1990*, p. 59.
8 Aditjondro, "Transmigration in Irian Jaya," p. 78.
9 Tirtosudarmo, "The political-demography," p. 381.
10 Human Rights Watch/Asia, *Deteriorating Human Rights in East Timor*.
11 Associated Press, 24 July 1995.
12 CNRM press release, Apakabar Internet List, 18 September 1995; *Republika*, 9 and 11 September and 13 October 1995.

13 It is of course possible that the statistics on migration to East Timor were not reliable and may have underestimated the total number of migrants. The absence of statistics for the period 1975–85 may be particularly significant.
14 Sherlock, "Political economy of the East Timor conflict," p. 839. Original quote from Soetrisno et al., *East Timor, the Impact of Integration*, pp. 55–6.
15 "We want to be free: Interview with Bishop Carlos Ximenes Belo," Matra (Jakarta), reprinted in *Inside Indonesia*, 32, September 1992, p. 11.
16 Sherlock, "Political economy," p. 839.
17 "Refleksi Dan Rekomendasi Para Pimpinan Gereja Dan Tokoh Umat Katolik, Nusa Tenggara Tentang Masalah Penodaan Dan Penyelesaiannya," p. 7. The exact number of cases of host desecrations varies. Steenbrink has recorded 32 between 1990 and 1995 (see "Muslim-Christian relations in the Pancasila state of Indonesia," p. 336).
18 On the Maumere riot, see *Gatra* 1, no. 26, 13 May 1995; on the Larantuka riots, see *Pos Kupang*, 13 June 1995, and "Refleksi Dan Rekomendasi," p. 9. I am indebted to Gwen Evans for clarification on a number of details regarding the riots in Maumere and Larantuka.
19 Interviews with Longginus da Cunha, Vice-Archbishop of Ende (appointed archbishop, February 1996), and with Father Huberto Thomas Hasilie, SVD, Ledalero, Flores, February 1996.
20 Interview with Donatus Djagom, SVD, Archbishop of Ende, February 1996. I am also indebted to Daniel Dhakidae on this point (discussion, Jakarta, March 1996).
21 Interview with Father John Prior, SVD, Ledalero, Flores, February 1996.
22 Interview with Donatus Djagom, February 1996. Gwen Evans also communicated this point to me.
23 Interview with Gabriel Lado, Golkar representative, DPRD-II, Kabupaten Sikka, Maumere, February 1996.
24 Interviews with Longginus da Cunha, February 1996.
25 "Refleksi Dan Rekomendasi," pp. 10, 11 and 15.
26 Interviews with John Prior and with Longginus da Cunha, February 1996.
27 Interview with former head of Department of Agriculture, Kabupaten Sikka. This point was also made by Daniel Dhakidae.
28 Interview with Romo P. D. da Lopez, LPPS, Maumere, February 1996. Romo da Lopez is known as an excellent source for local history and runs LPPS, a church-related NGO focusing on socio-economic development.
29 Interview with Donatus Djagom.
30 Interview with Laurens da Costa, Father Rector of the Seminari Tinggi St-Paulus, Ledalero, Flores, February 1996, and with Professor Cornelis Lay, political scientist and specialist on Nusa Tenggara Timur, Universitas Gadjah Mada, Yogyakarta, January 1996.
31 Interviews with Laurens da Costa, Donatus Djagom, and Daniel Dhakidae.
32 Interview with Donatus Djagom.
33 Interviews with Laurens da Costa and Donatus Djagom.
34 Confidential interviews with religious leaders, Flores, February 1996.
35 *D&R*, 19 October 1996; *Gatra* 2, no. 50, 26 October 1996; "Kerusuhan Situbondo: Situbondo, Kamis, 10 Oktober 1996: Draft Buku Putih [The Situbondo Riot: Situbondo, Thursday 10 October 1996]," unpublished document, Situbondo, 1996, p. 1.

36 Yayasan LBH Nusantara dan Forum Pemuda Pelajar dan Mahasiswa Garut, *Kerusuhan Tasikmalaya Dan Ngabang*, pp. 3–6; *Kompas*, 18 February 1997; *Suara Karya*, 20 February 1997.
37 Yayasan LBH Nusantara dan Forum Pemuda Pelajar dan Mahasiswa Garut, *Kerusuhan Tasikmalaya Dan Ngabang*, pp. 3–6; *Republika*, 8 January 1997; *Kompas*, 2 January 1997.
38 *Media Indonesia*, 31 January 1997; *Republika*, 31 January 1997; *Suara Pembaruan*, 31 January 1997.
39 See Bertrand, "False starts, succession crises, and regime transition"; Hefner, *Civil Islam*, pp. 131–8.
40 *Tempo* 27, no. 5, 3–10 November 1998.
41 *Tempo* 27, no. 5, 3–10 November 1998, and no. 7, 17–23 November 1998.
42 *Tempo* 27, no. 8, 24–30 November, and no. 10, 8–14 December 1998; *Suara Pembaruan*, 30 November 1998.
43 *Kompas*, 1 and 5 December 1998; *Republika*, 1 December 1998; *Media Indonesia*, 3 December 1998; *Jakarta Post*, 5 December 1998; *Tempo* 27, no. 10, 8–14 December 1998.
44 *Suara Pembaruan*, 30 December 1998; *Kompas*, 31 December 1998; *Bisnis Indonesia*, 31 December 1998.
45 For an explanation that focuses on the congruence of broader national problems with local particularities, with an emphasis on religious identities and patronage politics, see Aragon, "Communal violence in Poso, Central Sulawesi."
46 *Jakarta Post*, 9 June 1998.
47 *Gatra* 4, no. 42, 5 September 1998.
48 *Gatra* 5, no. 9, 9 January 1999.
49 *Gatra* 4, no. 52, 14 November 1998; *Tempo* 27, no. 4, 27 October – 3 November 1998.
50 *Gatra* 5, no. 36, 24 July 1999; *Forum Keadilan*, no. 27, 10 October 1999.
51 *Forum Keadilan*, no. 27, 10 October 1999, and no. 28, 17 October 1999.
52 *Gatra* 5, no. 50, 30 October 1999;*Forum Keadilan*, no. 30, 31 October 1999.
53 Interview with Radius Prawiro, Jakarta, 21 April 1997.
54 Interview with Cardinal Julius Darmaatmadja, Jakarta, 11 May 1999.
55 Yayasan LBH Nusantara dan Forum Pemuda Pelajar dan Mahasiswa Garut, *Kerusuhan Tasikmalaya Dan Ngabang*, pp. 24–5.
56 Interview with Munawir Sjadzali, chair of Komnas HAM and former minister of religion, and with Miriam Budiarjo, first vice-chair of Komnas HAM.
57 *Media Indonesia*, 9 January 1997.
58 *Kompas*, 2 January 1997.
59 Interview with Mulya Lubis, Jakarta, 21 April 1997.
60 *Kerusuhan Situbondo*, pp. 40–5; *Suara Pembaruan*, 14 January 1997. Hefner's analysis of the riots supports Wahid's view and even quotes Wahid as pointing to a "dirty tricks" bureau within ICMI as being responsible for instigating the riots. Hefner does not sufficiently examine, however, the other causes of riots nor does he show evidence to support this claim, beyond Wahid's assertions. See Hefner, "Islam and nation in post-Suharto," pp. 57–8.
61 *Media Indonesia*, 18 June 1997.
62 *Republika*, 17 June 1997; *Suara Karya*, 17 June 1997.

63 *Adil*, 14 January 1997.
64 Interview with Munawir Sjadzali and Miriam Budiardjo.
65 Interviews with Laksamana Sukardi, PDI-P executive committee, and Megawati Sukarnoputri, PDI-P leader, Jakarta, 22 April 1997.
66 *Jakarta Post*, 12 December 1997.
67 *Suara Pembaruan*, 2 February 1997.
68 *Suara Pembaruan*, 12 February 1997.
69 Interview with Juwono Sudarsono, 22 April 1997.

7 Conflict in Maluku

1 The province of Maluku encompasses the Moluccas islands, often known as the Spice islands, once at the heart of the Dutch East Indies spice trade. The Indonesian "Maluku" is used here, with "Moluccan" to describe its inhabitants or as an adjective.
2 For an analysis of these patrimonial networks and their effects on the conflict, see van Klinken, "The Maluku wars."
3 See Chauvel, *Nationalists, Soldiers, and Separatists*, especially chs 2 and 3, and see also pp. 168–9.
4 Ibid.
5 Interview with Job Syauta, economist, advisor to the Agency for Regional Development (Bappeda), Maluku, and head of the Unpatti research institute, Ambon, May 1996. South Sulawesi was also a concern for the Suharto regime, because of its participation in a rebellion in the 1950s against the central government. See Harvey, *Permesta*.
6 Interviews with Jan Nanere, rector of Unpatti, P. J. Siwabessy, vice-rector of Unpatti, and Jopi Papilaja, head of PDI, Maluku, and professor of economics, Unpatti, Ambon, May 1996.
7 Interview with the Rev. Sammy Titaley, head of GPM, May 1996.
8 On the *pela-gandong*, see Bartels, "Guarding the Invisible Mountain."
9 Interview with Nicolas Radjawane, former head of GPM and former rector of UKIM.
10 Interview with Nicolas Radjawane.
11 Interviews with Sammy Titaley, P. J. Siwabessy, Abraham Soplantila, former head of GPM, and Mgr Andreas Sol, former Catholic Bishop of Maluku.
12 Interview with Jopi Papilaja.
13 Interview with Sammy Titaley, Jopi Papilaja.
14 Intervews with Sammy Titaley, Jopi Papilaja, and Jan Nanere.
15 Interview with Mgr Andreas Sol.
16 Interview with Mgr Andreas Sol.
17 Interview with Sammy Titaley.
18 Interview with Abdullah Soulissa, head of Ambon's Al-Fatah mosque foundation, Ambon, May 1996.
19 Interview with Sammy Titaley.
20 Interview with Mgr Andreas Sol.
21 Confidential interview, Ambon, May 1996.
22 Interview with Abdullah Soulissa.

23 These trends were confirmed by interviews with Sammy Titaley, Nick Radjawane, and Jopi Papilaja.

24 Interview with Jopi Papilaja.

25 Based on fieldwork observation and personal communications, Ambon, February–May 1993.

26 For an interesting argument along these lines, see Anderson, *Violence and the State in Suharto's Indonesia.*

27 For a different explanation, which also draws on the context of political change and its effects on competition for resources and jobs, see Sidel, "Riots, church burnings, conspiracies."

28 The two leading newsmagazines, *Tempo* and *Gatra*, presented different accounts of the incident. See *Tempo* 27, no. 17, 26 January – 1 February 1999; *Gatra* 5, no. 11, 30 January 1999.

29 Human Rights Watch, *Indonesia: The Violence in Ambon*; *Suara Pembaruan*, 4 February 1999.

30 *Tempo* 27, no. 17, 26 January – 1 February 1999.

31 Personal communication, Ambon, May 1996.

32 *Kompas*, 15 December 1998; *Suara Karya*, 15 December 1998.

33 HRW, *Indonesia: The Violence*, pp. 22–5; *Gatra* 5, no. 15, 27 February 1999; *Republika*, 15 February 1999.

34 *Republika*, 16 February 1999; HRW, *Indonesia: The Violence*, p. 26.

35 *Indonesia: The Violence*, pp. 27–8; *Tempo* 27, no. 23, 9–15 March 1999.

36 *Tempo* 27, no. 18, 1–8 February 1999, and no. 23, 9–15 March 1999.

37 HRW, *Indonesia: The Violence*, p. 29; *Kompas*, 4 March 1999.

38 *Republika*, 6 March 1999; *Kompas*, 4 and 6 March 1999; *Forum Keadilan*, no. 25, 22 March 1999.

39 *Tempo* 28, no. 6, 13–19 April 1999.

40 *Forum Keadilan*, no. 1, 11 April 1999.

41 Ibid.; *Tempo* 28, no. 11, 17–24 May 1999.

42 *Gatra* 5, no. 37, 31 July, and no. 38, 7 August 1999; *Tempo* 28, no. 22, 2–8 August, and no. 24, 16–22 August 1999.

43 *Gatra* 5, no. 42, 4 September 1999.

44 *Gatra*, 31 August 1999; *Forum Keadilan*, no. 20, 22 August, no. 22, 5 September, and no. 25, 26 September 1999; *Gatra* 5, no. 48, 16 October 1999.

45 *Gatra* 5, no. 53, 20 November 1999; *Gatra* 6, no. 10, 22 January, and no. 12, 5 February 2000.

46 Tomagola, "The bleeding Halmahera of North Moluccas," pp. 8–10.

47 Ibid, pp. 5–6.

48 *Tempo* 28, no. 44, 3–9 January 2000.

49 *Tempo* 28, no. 41, 13–20 December, and no. 42, 20–26 December 1999; *Gatra* 6, no. 10, 22 January 2000.

50 *Gatra* 6, no. 10, 22 January, and no. 11, 29 January 2000.

51 *Jakarta Post*, 14 April 2000; *Tempo* 29, no. 7, 17–23 April, and no. 12, 22–28 May 2000.

52 International Crisis Group, *Indonesia*, pp. 7–10.

53 *Gatra* 6, no. 11, 29 January 2000.

54 *Tempo* 28, no. 8, 24–30 April 2000; *Tempo* 29, no. 15, 12–18 June 2000.

55 International Crisis Group, *Indonesia*, pp. 17–18.

56 *Kompas*, 16 October 2002.

8 Late integration into the nation

1 Defert, *Timor-Est, Le Génocide Oublié*, pp. 45–6; Taylor, *Indonesia's Forgotten War*, p. 16.
2 Defert, *Timor-Est*, pp. 57–9; Jolliffe, *East Timor*, pp. 61–5, 68, 79.
3 Jolliffe, *East Timor*, p. 68; Defert, *Timor-Est*, pp. 69, 71.
4 Defert, *Timor-Est*, p. 71. The word "Maubere" originates from the Mambai tribe and means "friend." It was elevated to the level of an ideology of "Mauberism" with an emphasis on a struggle for the common people. See also Taylor, *Indonesia's Forgotten War*, p. 42; Jolliffe, *East Timor*, p. 94.
5 Jolliffe, *East Timor*, pp. 112–16, 131–44, 150–5; Defert, *Timor-Est*, pp. 75–80; Taylor, *Indonesia's Forgotten War*, pp. 36–8.
6 Dunn, *The Timor Affair*, p. 7, quoted in Jolliffe, *East Timor*, p. 161.
7 Jolliffe, *East Timor*, pp. 277–8.
8 Taylor, *Indonesia's Forgotten War*, pp. 80, 85–7; Defert, *Timor-Est*, pp. 109, 116.
9 Taylor, *Indonesia's Forgotten War*, pp. 86–7, 117–18. There are numerous sources that describe details of Indonesia's military invasion and occupation of East Timor, as well as human rights abuses. Jolliffe, *East Timor*, Taylor, *Indonesia's Forgotten War*, and Defert, *Timor-Est*, provide excellent descriptive accounts that cover the various periods from the 1970s to the early 1990s. Regular reports by Tapol (Indonesian Human Rights Campaign) and Human Rights Watch (HRW) are also excellent sources.
10 Taylor, *Indonesia's Forgotten War*, pp. 110–11; Defert, *Timor-Est*, pp. 157–9, 163–6, 169–79, 188–92.
11 Taylor, *Indonesia's Forgotten War*, pp. 123–6; Defert, *Timor-Est*, pp. 188–92; Soetrisno et al., *East Timor*, pp. 47–50.
12 Defert, *Timor-Est*, pp. 180–1; Taylor, *Indonesia's Forgotten War*, p. 128.
13 Defert, *Timor-Est*, pp. 182–3.
14 Ibid., pp. 184–5.
15 Mubyarto, *East Timor*, p. 65.
16 Defert, *Timor-Est*, pp. 202–3.
17 Jolliffe, *East Timor*, pp. 93–4.
18 Taylor, *Indonesia's Forgotten War*, p. 154.
19 Schwarz, *A Nation in Waiting*, pp. 208–11.
20 The government named a National Commission of Inquiry to investigate the shooting. While the commission and the government were critical of the armed forces, they blamed the protesters for instigating the violence leading up to the shooting. The NCI report gave a figure of 50 people dead, while an Amnesty International report estimated about 100 people had been killed. See National Commission of Inquiry into the 12 November 1991 Incident in Dili, *Advance Report*; Amnesty International, *East Timor*; Amnesty International, *Indonesia/East Timor – Santa Cruz*.
21 On these demonstrations, see "East Timor rises again," *Economist*, 20 June 1998, p. 46. Student demonstrations were held in Dili as well, demanding a referendum on independence. See "Demo Mengusung mayat," *Gatra* 4, no. 32, 27 June 1998.
22 The armed forces began reducing troops in the territory in August 1998, shortly after Habibie's offer of special autonomy and indication of his

willingness to find a solution to the conflict. See "Timor Timur: Mereka
Meninggalkan Dili," *Gatra* 4, no. 39, 15 August 1998.

23 Between July and December 1998, protests and violence escalated. Even UN
Special Envoy for East Timor Jamsheed Marker had to flee Dili after being
attacked by a mob of 50,000 people demanding a referendum. See *Tempo* 27,
no. 13, 29 December 1998 – 4 January 1999. On the offer of independence,
see *Tempo* 27, no. 18, 1–8 February 1999.

24 Early reports raised suspicions that armed pro-integration militias were being supplied with weapons by supporters in the Indonesian armed forces.
For example, see statements by Clemento Dos Reis Amaral, general secretary of Komnas HAM, in "Tembakan Peringatan dari Dili," *Gatra* 5, no. 12,
6 February 1999, and *Tempo* 27, no. 19, 9–15 February 1999. Reports of
escalating violence and the suspected links of the militias to the armed forces
were made quite forcefully by East Timorese representatives at a roundtable in Ottawa in February 1999 (attended by the author. See Canadian
Centre for Foreign Policy Development, *East Timor Roundtable Report*). On
Operasi Sapu Jagad, see "Indonesia's dirty war in East Timor," *Tapol Bulletin*,
7 June 1999. On armed forces' involvement in the violence, see Interna-
tional Commission of Inquiry on East Timor, *United Nations Report of the
International Commission of Inquiry on East Timor to the Secretary-General*;
Commission to Investigate Human Rights Violations in East Timor (KPP-
HAM), *Executive Summary Report on the Investigation of Human Rights
Violations in East Timor*.

25 "East Timorese choose independence," Associated Press, 3 September 1999.

26 The Indonesian Human Rights Commission named high-level officers suspected of involvement in the post-referendum violence. See Commission to
Investigate Human Rights Violations, *Executive Summary Report*.

27 *Tempo* 28, no. 35, 1–7 November 1999; *Gatra* 6, no. 4, 11 December, and
no. 6, 25 December 1999; *Tempo* 28, no. 43, 27 December 1999 – 2 January
2000.

28 Prior to 1969, the territory was most often known as West New Guinea.
The Indonesians called it West Irian (Irian Barat) before President Suharto
changed its name to Irian Jaya at the opening of the Freeport mine in 1973.
The province was again informally renamed, Papua, under the Wahid admin-
istration. In 2001, the name was formally changed to Papua. The term "West
Papua" is used by Papuan nationalists.

29 Defert, *L'Indonésie Et La Nouvelle-Guinée-Occidentale*, pp. 56–62, 75–6,
81; Bone, *The Dynamics of the Western New Guinea (Irian Barat) Problem*,
pp. 15–19, 22, and fn. 43, p. 140.

30 Lijphart, *The Trauma of Decolonization*, pp. 12–15.

31 The most important study of Dutch interests in West New Guinea and the
dispute with Indonesia is Lijphart, *The Trauma of Decolonization*. On the question of the Eurasion migration project, see pp. 96–106.

32 Bone, *The Dynamics of the Western New Guinea*, pp. 85–6.

33 Ibid., pp. 27, 32.

34 Lijphart, *The Trauma of Decolonization*, p. 33.

35 Interview with Frans A. Wospakrik, rector of Uncen, Abepura, 20 August
2001. He was among the first generation of the Dutch-educated elite to
benefit.

36 Lijphart, *The Trauma of Decolonization*, pp. 18–20; Defert, *L'Indonésie Et La Nouvelle-Guinée-Occidentale*, p. 171.
37 Defert, *L'Indonésie Et La Nouvelle-Guinée-Occidentale*, pp. 149–50.
38 Interview with Frans Wospakrik.
39 Defert, *L'Indonésie Et La Nouvelle-Guinée-Occidentale*, pp. 171–3.
40 Anderson, *Imagined Communities* (2nd edn, 1991), especially pp. 113–40; see Kahin, *Nationalism and Revolution in Indonesia*, on the evolution of Indonesian nationalism.
41 Bone, *The Dynamics of the Western New Guinea*, p. 128; Ministry of Information, "The autonomous province of West Irian."
42 Defert, *L'Indonésie Et La Nouvelle-Guinée-Occidentale*, pp. 171–3.
43 The *konoor* were believed to be descendants of Manggundi whose return is awaited.
44 Defert, *L'Indonésie Et La Nouvelle-Guinée-Occidentale*, pp. 91–104.
45 Osborne, *Indonesia's Secret War*, pp. 34, 41–8; Defert, *L'Indonésie Et La Nouvelle-Guinée-Occidentale*, pp. 243–4.
46 Confidential interview with a high-level civil servant, Jayapura, August 2001.
47 Confidential interviews, Jayapura, August 2001.
48 Osborne, *Indonesia's Secret War*, pp. 36–9, 45.
49 These incidents were witnessed by an Australian team hired by the government to map the area. See Osborne, *Indonesia's Secret War*, pp. 66–72.
50 See Defert, *L'Indonésie Et La Nouvelle-Guinée-Occidentale*, note 74, p. 379.
51 Amnesty International, *Indonesia: Continuing Human Rights Violations in Irian Jaya*, p. 5.
52 See Münninghoff, *Report of Human Rights Violations toward Local People in the Area of Timika, District of Fak Fak, Irian Jaya, 1994–1995*.
53 Amnesty International, *Indonesia – Irian Jaya*, pp. 2–3.
54 Gereja Kemah Injil Indonesia, Paroki Tiga Raja and Gereja Kristen Injili di Irian Jaya, *Laporan Pelanggaran Hak Asasi Manusia Dan Bencana Di Bela, Alama, Jila Dan Mapnduma, Irian Jaya*.
55 Osborne, *Indonesia's Secret War*, pp. 78–9, 112–13.
56 "Trik-ular nasib sandera di Wamena," *Forum Keadilan* 4, no. 24, 11 March 1996.
57 Osborne, *Indonesia's Secret War*, pp. 117–19.
58 *Gatra* 2, no. 20, 30 March 1996.
59 Defert, *L'Indonésie Et La Nouvelle-Guinée-Occidentale*, pp. 316–17. Interview with Michael Rumbiak, lecturer and head of Population Research Centre, Uncen, Abepura, 25 August 2001.
60 Interviews with anthropologist Yos Mansoben, Uncen, Abepura, 24 August 2001, and Yohanis G. Bonay, director, Elsham–Papua, Abepura, 20 August 2001.
61 Interview with Michael Rumbiak.
62 Defert, *L'Indonésie Et La Nouvelle-Guinée-Occidentale*, pp. 347–8.
63 Although originally a word from Biak used to identify the mainland, many Papuans believed that it was an acronym meaning "Ikut Republic Indonesia Anti-Nederland" (Follow the Indonesian Republic against the Dutch), which would have been used by the Indonesians during the 1950s.
64 Defert, *L'Indonésie Et La Nouvelle-Guinée-Occidentale*, p. 271.
65 Osborne, *Indonesia's Secret War*, p. 137.

66 Defert, *L'Indonésie Et La Nouvelle-Guinée-Occidentale*, pp. 369–70.
67 On the Arnold Ap case, see Osborne, *Indonesia's Secret War*, pp. 148–54. On the 1984 flag incident and defections, see Defert, *L'Indonésie Et La Nouvelle-Guinée-Occidentale*, pp. 369–70; Osborne, *Indonesia's Secret War*, pp. 99–100. On the Wanggai case, see Amnesty International, *Indonesia: Continuing Human Rights*, pp. 8–10; Amnesty International, *Indonesia – Irian Jaya*, pp. 2–3.
68 *Media Indonesia*, 7 July 1998; *Forum Keadilan* 7, no. 8, 27 July 1998; *Gatra* 4, no. 35, 18 July 1998.
69 *Media Indonesia*, 8 July 1998.
70 *Kompas*, 7 July 1998; *Forum Keadilan* 7, no. 8, 27 July 1998; *Gatra* 4, no. 34, 11 July 1998. For a detailed account of the events of July and October 1998, as well as a detailed assessment of casualties and arrests, see HRW, *Indonesia: Human Rights and Pro-Independence Actions in Irian Jaya*.
71 *Republika*, 29 July 1998; *Forum Keadilan* 7, no. 10, 24 August 1998. The special meeting of the MPR in November 1998 subsequently instructed the government to implement laws to fulfill regional autonomy.
72 *Adat* means "custom, tradition" and was broadly used in Indonesia to identify the cultural traditions and laws of the vast number of different tribes and ethnic groups across the archipelago. The government often sponsored the formation of organizations representing traditional *adat* groups. For a detailed discussion of Foreri, see HRW, *Indonesia: Human Rights and Pro-Independence Actions in Papua, 1999–2000*.
73 Interview (Jayapura, 22 August 2001) with Benny Giay, lecturer at STT-Walter Post, Jayapura, and head of team preparing terms of reference for Team 100 meeting.
74 *Gatra* 5, no. 16, 6 March 1999; *Forum Keadilan* 7, no. 25, 22 March 1999; *Tempo* 28, no. 22, 2–8 March 1999. See also HRW, *Indonesia: Human Rights and Pro-Independence Actions in Papua, 1999–2000*, pp. 11–13.
75 Interview with the Rev. Phil Erari, director of Center for Research and Development, Indonesian Council of Churches, Jakarta, 12 May 1999; Erari was closely involved in Team 100 and associated meetings. See also HRW, *Indonesia: Human Rights and Pro-Independence Actions in Papua, 1999–2000*, p. 16.
76 *Gatra* 5, no. 25, 8 May, and no. 47, 9 October 1999; *Tempo* 28, no. 9, 4–10 May 1999. On the division of the province, see *Tempo* 28, no. 35, 1–7 November 1999; *Forum Keadilan* 7, no. 29, 24 October, and no. 30, 31 October 1999; on its cancellation, see *Gatra* 6, no. 3, 4 December 1999.
77 *Tempo* 28, no. 39, 30 November – 5 December 1999; *Gatra* 6, no. 2, 27 November 1999.
78 The latest figure is from Elsham–Irian Jaya. See HRW, *Indonesia: Human Rights and Pro-Independence Actions in Papua, 1999–2000*, pp. 27–30.
79 "*Kitorang* nanti 1 Desember 1999 kasih naik bendera dan selesai; *kitorang* merdeka sudah!" Van den Broek et al., *Memoria Passionis Di Papua*, pp. 70–1.
80 *Jakarta Post*, 2 January 2000. The name change was never officially implemented under Wahid's presidency.
81 Interview (Abepura, 23 August 2001) with Agus Alua, vice secretary general of PDP, secretary of Mubes organizing committee, and head of Congress organizing committee.

82 Interview with Benny Giay. He was named one of three moderators of PDP at People's Congress.
83 Interview with Agus Alua. For details on the Mubes and Congress, see also Van den Broek and Szalay, "Raising the Morning Star."
84 See *Komunike Politik Papua*, signed by Theys Eluay and Tom Beanal as great leaders of the Papuan people, Sentani-Port Numbay (Jayapura), 26 February 2000.
85 See *Resolutions as agreed by the members of the Papuan Congress, 29 May – 4 June, 2000*, Port Numbay (Jayapura), 4 June 2000. Signed by members of the Congress steering committee.
86 Interview with Agus Alua.
87 Interview with Benny Giay. See also Van den Broek et al., *Memoria Passionis*, pp. 72–3.
88 Interview with Theys Eluay, PDP chair, Sentani, 21 August 2001.
89 Interview with Agus Alua.
90 *Tempo* 29, no. 33, 15–22 October 2000.
91 On the Nabire incident, see Van den Broek and Szalay, "Raising the Morning Star," pp. 87–9.
92 See Institute for Human Rights Study and Advocacy – Irian Jaya, *Laporan "Kasus Abepura 07 Desember 2000"*; Human Rights Watch, *Indonesia: Violence and Political Impasse in Papua*; *Tempo* 29, no. 40, 4–10 December 2000.
93 Kepolisian Negara Republik Indonesia Daerah Irian Jaya, *Rencana Operasi "Tuntas Matoa 2000" Polda Irja (Confidential)*, p. 9.
94 See Majelis Permusyawaratan Rakyat Republik Indonesia, *Ketetapan MPR-RI Nomor IV/MPR/1999 Tentang Garis-Garis Besar Haluan Negara Tahun 1999–2004*, section IV-G (2); for the instructions to the president in response to the president's report to the MPR, see Majelis Permusyawaratan Rakyat Republik Indonesia, *Ketetapan MPR Nomor VIII/MPR/2000 Tentang Laporan Tahunan Lembaga-Lembaga Tinggi Negara Pada Sidang Tahunan MPR 2000*, Appendix 1.1.
95 See Chapter 10 for a full discussion of special autonomy.
96 Interview with Yos Mansoben, Uncen faculty member and head of organizing committee of governor's team on special autonomy, Jayapura, 24 August 2001; interview with Frans Wospakrik, rector of Uncen and member of team steering committee, Jayapura, 20 August 2001.
97 *Tempo* 30, no. 10, 7–13 May 2001; "Masih ada diskriminasi," *Cendrawasih Pos*, 28 August 2001; "Gubernur Papua tolak bertemu demonstran," *Kompas*, 18 December 2001.

9 Aceh's ethnonationalist conflict

1 Snyder, *From Voting to Violence*, p. 321.
2 Morris, "Islam and Politics in Aceh," pp. 19–24. For a more detailed account of this period, see Reid, "Trade and the problem of royal power in Aceh"; Lombard, *Le Sultanat D'Atjeh Au Temps D'Iskandar Muda, 1607–1636*.
3 Reid, *The Blood of the People*, pp. 8–11.
4 Ibid., pp. 12–13; Morris, "Islam and Politics," pp. 61–72.

5 Morris, "Islam and Politics," pp. 25–53, 57–9; Reid, *The Blood of the People*, pp. 8–11.
6 Morris, "Islam and Politics," pp. 75–94; Reid, *The Blood of the People*, pp. 87–9.
7 Reid, *The Blood of the People*, pp. 94–5, 128; Morris, "Islam and Politics," pp. 94–114, 130–2.
8 Morris, "Islam and Politics," pp. 116–25.
9 Ibid., pp. 145–50; Reid, *The Blood of the People*, pp. 200–5.
10 Reid, *The Indonesian National Revolution, 1945–1950*, p. 147, see fn 4; Morris, "Islam and Politics," pp. 152–4.
11 Morris, "Islam and Politics," pp. 180–1; Sjamsuddin, *The Republican Revolt*, pp. 34–41.
12 Morris, "Islam and Politics," p. 148.
13 Ibid., pp. 190–1.
14 Sjamsuddin, *The Republican Revolt*, p. 177, rejects a socio-economic explanation for support of the rebellion. Van Dijk, *Rebellion under the Banner of Islam*, pp. 386–9, cautions as well against a socio-economic interpretation, noting that land redistribution had already occurred as a result of the social revolution that eliminated the power of the *uleebalang*. Yet, he provides an explanation based on the agrarian structure.
15 Sjamsuddin, *The Republican Revolt*, pp. 140–4; van Dijk, *Rebellion under the Banner*, pp. 326–7.
16 Morris, "Islam and Politics," pp. 216–24. The events leading to this compromise are complex. The central government was faced with a rebellion of army commanders in several regions, including North Sumatra, of which Aceh was part. Gahuru distanced himself from his superior, Col. Simbolon, who joined the rebellion, which became known as the Permesta. By the end of 1957, the army commanders had allied themselves with leaders of Masyumi and proclaimed the PRRI. These events put much pressure on the government to reach a settlement with Darul Islam rebels in Aceh.
17 Morris, "Islam and Politics," pp. 226–34; Sjamsuddin, *The Republican Revolt*, pp. 293–4.
18 Sjamsuddin, *The Republican Revolt*, pp. 300–10. In his book, Sjamsuddin makes the interesting distinction between the *ulama* and the *zuama*, the non-*ulama* members of PUSA, most of whom became the civil servants and administrators during PUSA's leadership of the Aceh military region.
19 Morris, "Islam and Politics," pp. 273–7, 281.
20 Interview (Banda Aceh, 4 May 1999) with Teungku Soufyan Hamzah, head imam, Aceh's Great Mosque (Mesjid Raya), and one of the heads of MUI, Aceh.
21 Kell, *The Roots of the Acehnese Rebellion, 1989–1992*, pp. 50–2.
22 Morris, "Islam and Politics," pp. 255–6, 260–5.
23 On the centralization of power, the selection of governors and regional heads (*bupati*), as well as the role of connections to prominent Acehnese in Jakarta, see Kell, *The Roots of Acehnese Rebellion*, pp. 28–40.
24 I am indebted to Abdul Hakim Garuda Nusantara, head of Elsham, for a particularly insightful analysis of this issue. (Interview, Jakarta, March 1996.)
25 Kell, *The Roots of Acehnese Rebellion*, pp. 14–16.

26 Beyond the logic of this fiscal system, a significant proportion of revenues at the national level was siphoned off by corruption. Redistributions at the provincial level were also subject to graft.

27 Kell, *The Roots of Acehnese Rebellion*, pp. 22–3.

28 Ibid., pp. 61–6.

29 Morris, "Islam and Politics," pp. 300–1; Kell, *The Roots of Acehnese Rebellion*, p. 65.

30 Kell, *The Roots of Acehnese Rebellion*, pp. 66–74.

31 Ibid., pp. 74–7.

32 Discussions with Jafar Siddiq Hamzah, Acehnese human rights lawyer, Medan and Lhokseumawe, May 1996. For a more detailed account of the strategies and abuses of the armed forces, see Robinson, "*Rawan* is as *rawan* does," pp. 139–45.

33 Kell, *The Roots of Acehnese Rebellion*, p. 75.

34 Interview with Saifuddin Bantasyam, executive director, Forum Peduli HAM, Banda Aceh, 1 May 1999. The figure for tortures is from Bantasyam, "A note on torture of civilians during the military operation in Aceh," p. 1. On disappearances, one compilation of cases reported by a variety of NGOs and governmental sources estimates a total of 1,834 people between 1989 and 1998. See Al-Chaidar et al., *Aceh Bersimbah Darah*, p. 257. Al-Chaidar and others also report the preliminary findings of a team from Komnas HAM. During this period, 871 died in prison as a result of violent acts, 387 disappeared and were found dead, 550 disappeared and were not found, 360 were tortured, and 102 were raped (this data was mainly for Pidie, Aceh Besar, and Aceh Timur).

35 Robinson, "*Rawan* is as *rawan* does," p. 140.

36 Interview with Tirtosudiro, chair of Supreme Advisory Council, Jakarta, 19 May 1999.

37 *Gatra* 4, no. 33, 4 July, and no. 38, 8 August 1998.

38 This term was used by the Indonesian military to make a distinction between regular military units assigned to the territory for purposes of national defense and troops assigned under special operations.

39 *Gatra* 4, no. 38, 8 August, and no. 41, 29 August 1998.

40 *Gatra* 4, no. 43, 12 September 1998.

41 *Gatra* 4, no. 52, 14 November 1998; *Gatra* 5, no. 8, 9 January 1999; *Forum Keadilan* 7, no. 21, 25 January 1999.

42 *Tempo* 27, no. 15, 12–18 January 1999.

43 Ibid.; *Gatra* 5, no. 20, 3 April 1999.

44 Interview with Aguswandi, secretary general of SMUR, Banda Aceh, 5 May 1999; interview with executive members of Karma, Banda Aceh, 1 May 1999.

45 Interview with Usman Hasan, head of Presidential Advisory Team for Aceh, Jakarta, 29 April 1999.

46 *Gatra* 5, no. 13, 13 February 1999; *Forum Keadilan* 7, no. 24, 8 March 1999.

47 *Tempo* 28, no. 10, 1999; *Gatra* 5, no. 26, 15 May 1999; interview with Ahmad Humam Hamid, chief coordinator of Forum Peduli HAM, Banda Aceh, 3 May 1999.

48 Interview with Basir Achmad from the presidium of Forum LSM Aceh, and Afrizal Tjoetra, executive secretary of Forum LSM Aceh, Banda Aceh, 3 May

1999. Forum LSM was involved in voter education for the election and claimed there were no reports that people were intimidated into boycotting the election; *Gatra* 5, no. 31, 19 June 1999.

49 *Forum Keadilan* 8, no. 16, 25 July 1999.

50 Even as early as the Krueng Geukeueh incident, little faith was left in the government's approach to Aceh. A meeting between the Presidential Advisory Team for Aceh, local NGOs, and students showed the complete disillusionment with the government's policy and approach to the violence, even among members of the team, who expressed their outrage at the shootings and the failure of Habibie to take decisive action against abuse by the armed forces. Meeting attended by the author, Banda Aceh, 4 May 1999.

51 *Tempo* 28, no. 22, 2–8 August 1999.

52 *Forum Keadilan* 8, no. 31, 17 October 1999.

53 *Gatra* 6, no. 1, 20 November 1999; *Forum Keadilan*, no. 33, 21 November 1999; "Alarms in Aceh," *Far Eastern Economic Review*, 18 November 1999.

54 On 4 December celebrations, see *Tempo* 27, no. 40, 6–12 December 1999; on Kontras statistics, see *Jakarta Post*, 29 January 2000.

55 *Tempo* 29, no. 11, 15–22 May 2000.

56 *Tempo* 29, no. 17, 26 June – 2 July 2000.

57 *Kompas*, 18 July 2000.

58 *Jakarta Post*, 22 September 2000.

59 *Tempo* 29, no. 35, 30 October – 5 November 2000.

60 *Tempo* 29, no. 37, 13–19 November 2000; *Agence France-Presse*, 11 and 14 November 2000, and 6 January 2001.

61 *Agence France-Presse*, 10 December 2000; *Tempo* 30, no. 3, 19–25 March 2001.

62 *Agence France-Presse*, 17 and 25 March 2001.

63 See Liddle, "Indonesia in 2000," pp. 211–12.

64 See appendix to Majelis Permusyawaratan Rakyat Republik Indonesia, *Ketetapan MPR-RI Nomor VIII/MPR/2000 Tentang Laporan Tahunan Lembaga-Lembaga Tinggi Negara Pada Sidang Tahunan MPR 2000*.

65 *Jakarta Post*, 7 August 2000.

66 *Tempo* 30, no. 7, 16–22 April 2001

67 *Tempo* 30, no. 18, 2–8 July 2001.

68 See Megawati's speech to the MPR, 1 November 2001. On reinstatement of Iskandar Muda military command, see *Jakarta Post*, 11 January 2002.

69 *Tempo* 29, no. 5, 3–9 April 2000; *Jakarta Post*, 27 November 2000, 18 May 2001, and 2 January 2002.

70 *Tempo* 31, no. 41, 8–15 December 2002. For full text, see "Cessation Of Hostilities Framework Agreement Between Government Of The Republic Of Indonesia And The Free Acheh Movement" http://www.hdcentre.org/Programmes/aceh/aceh%20COH.htm (accessed 15 January 2003).

10 Autonomy as a solution

1 For discussions on definitions, see Ghai, *Autonomy and Ethnicity*, pp. 9–11; Horowitz, *Ethnic Groups in Conflict*, p. 602, fn 2.

2 Horowitz, *Ethnic Groups in Conflict*, pp. 614–17; Hechter, *Containing Nationalism*, p. 144.

3 Horowitz, *Ethnic Groups in Conflict*, pp. 617–19.
4 Ghai, *Autonomy and Ethnicity*, pp. 20–2.
5 Ibid.
6 Ghai, "Decentralization and the accommodation of ethnic diversity."
7 Horowitz, *Ethnic Groups in Conflict*, p. 622.
8 Ibid., pp. 623–4.
9 See Hechter, *Containing Nationalism*, p. 144, for a good presentation of these arguments and a critique. See also Nordlinger, *Conflict Regulation in Divided Societies*, pp. 31–2.
10 See Kahin, *Nationalism and Revolution in Indonesia*, pp. 224–9, 446–69. For a detailed account of Indonesia's brief experience with federalism, see Schiller, *The Formation of Federal Indonesia, 1945–1949*.
11 See Kahin, *Nationalism and Revolution*, pp. 446–69.
12 Finkelstein, "The Indonesian federal problem," p. 286.
13 Legge, *Problems of Regional Autonomy in Contemporary Indonesia*, pp. 5–6, 10–12; Kahin, "Regionalism and decentralization," p. 204.
14 Finkelstein, "The Indonesian federal problem," p. 288. L. G. M. Jacquet responded to Finkelstein by mentioning the much higher degree of autonomy in self-governing territories under "native" states, present mainly in areas outside Java and Eastern Indonesia. See Jaquet, "The Indonesian federal problem reconsidered," p. 172.
15 Legge, *Problems of Regional Autonomy*, pp. 16–18, 26–7; Finkelstein, "The Indonesian federal problem," p. 290.
16 Legge, *Problems of Regional Autonomy*, p. 41.
17 Kahin, "Regionalism and decentralization," pp. 206–7.
18 Feith, *The Decline of Constitutional Democracy in Indonesia*, pp. 487–507, 521–38, 578–89. For a detailed account of these complex events, see Harvey, *Permesta*; Lev, *The Transition to Guided Democracy*. On West Sumatra and South Sulawesi, see Amal, *Regional and Central Government in Indonesia*.
19 Kahin, "Regionalism and decentralization," pp. 207–8.
20 Crouch, *The Army and Politics in Indonesia*, 1st edn, pp. 222–3.
21 Malley, "Resource Distribution, State Coherence, and Political Centralization in Indonesia, 1950–1997," pp. 146–7.
22 For example, in a mid-1980s reform of the armed forces, Kopkamtib was eventually replaced by Bakorstanas, which played essentially the same role.
23 Crouch, *The Army and Politics*, p. 244; Malley, "Resource Distribution," p. 149.
24 Malley, "Resource Distribution," pp. 150–5. Village structures were homogenized under Village Law no. 5, 1979. The new structures provided for village councils and village officers in a structure that was modeled after the Javanese village. See Bertrand, "Compliance, Resistance, and Trust."
25 Devas, "Indonesia," p. 354; Amal, "The dilemmas of decentralisation and democratisation," pp. 218–19; Morfit, "Pancasila orthodoxy," pp. 58–62; Malley, "Resource Distribution," pp. 150–5. These tendencies were confirmed in discussions with regional specialists on Maluku (Idrus Tatuhey, Department of Social and Political Affairs, Pattimura University, Ambon, May 1996), and Nusa Tenggara Timur (Cornelis Lay, Department of Social and Political Affairs, Gadjah Mada University, March 1996).

26 Kristiadi, "Masalah sekitar peningkatan pendapatan daerah," pp. 37–9. See also Ranis and Frances, "Decentralisation in Indonesia," p. 46, for a similar account of dependence on central government funds. For a detailed analysis, see Devas, *Financing Local Government in Indonesia*.

27 Kristiadi, "Masalah sekitar peningkatan," p. 40; Booth, "Central government funding of local government development expenditures," pp. 203–4. A Gadjah Mada University study found a lower percentage of dependence on central government funds (70%) in its analysis of twenty-five districts, but this amount refers to the average for the period 1973/74 to 1980/81. See Thoha, "Masalah sekitar peningkatan pendapatan daerah," p. 27, for a summary of findings. The discrepancy can be largely explained by the rise in dependence toward the late 1970s as a result of the increase in the Inpres program.

28 See Davey, "Central–local financial relations," pp. 173–6; Booth, "Central government funding," pp. 196–7; Devas, "Local government finance in Indonesia," p. 23; Ranis and Stewart, "Decentralisation," p. 51.

29 Devas, "Local government finance," p. 21.

30 Ibid., p. 19.

31 Amal, *Regional and Central Government*, pp. 155–60, 162–83.

32 On Pancasila, see Morfit, "Pancasila orthodoxy"; on *Wawasan Nusantara* and its relationship to national unity, see Lubis, *Ketatanegaraan Republik Indonesia*.

33 Smoke and Lewis, "Fiscal decentralization in Indonesia," p. 1284.

34 Interview with Asmara Nababan, executive secretary of INFID and member of Human Rights Commission, Jakarta; interview with Abdul Hakim Garuda Nusantara; interviews in Medan, Flores, Ujung Pandang, Maluku, Aceh, and Irian Jaya.

35 Interviews with Daniel Dhakidae, Jopi Papilaya, John Mailoa.

36 Devas, "Indonesia," p. 359.

37 See Malley, "Regional protest and reform in post-Suharto Indonesia," pp. 5–8.

38 Ibid., pp. 9–10.

39 See Law no. 22, 1999, on regional government.

40 Hofman and Kaiser, "The making of the big bang and its aftermath," pp. 12–14; Law no. 25, 1999, on fiscal decentralization.

41 Hofman and Kaiser, "The making of the big bang and its aftermath," pp. 12, 15.

42 For a good assessment of many of these technical issues in the implementation of the laws, see Hofman, "The making of the big bang and its aftermath."

43 Van Klinken, "The Maluku wars"; van Klinken, "Indonesia's new ethnic elites."

44 See chapters on the conflict in Maluku and the conflict in Kalimantan.

45 "A Constitutional Framework for a Special Autonomy for East Timor."

46 For an account of the process surrounding the special autonomy proposals, see chapters on Aceh and on East Timor and Irian Jaya.

47 The following is based on an analysis of Law no. 18, 2001, on Special Autonomy for the Province of Special Region of Aceh as the Province of Nanggroe Aceh Darussalam (Undang-undang no. 18, 2001 tentang otonomi khusus bagi provinsi Daerah Istimewa Aceh sebagai provinsi Nanggroe Aceh Darussalam), Jakarta, 2001.

48 The following is based on an analysis of Law no. 21, 2001, on Special Autonomy for the Province of Papua (Undang-undang no. 21, 2001 tentang otonomi khusus bagi provinsi Papua).

49 Interview with Frans A. Wospakrik, rector of Uncen, Abepura, 20 August 2001. He was a member of the team that drafted Papua's special autonomy bill.

50 See draft of law on special autonomy for the province of Papua, submitted to the DPR in April 2001.

11 Unity in diversity

1 Liddle, "Coercion, co-optation, and the management of ethnic relations in Indonesia."

Glossary

Abangan	Javanese syncretic form of Islamic practise. *See also* Santri
ABRI	Angkatan Bersenjata Republik Indonesia (Armed Forces of the Republic of Indonesia): the amalgamated military and police forces during the Suharto years
Adat	Customary law: a term broadly used to identify the cultural traditions and laws of the vast number of different tribes and ethnic groups across the archipelago
AKUI	Small Muslim party of the 1950s, based in Madura
Aliran kepercayaan	Spiritual beliefs stream (some spiritual beliefs became officially recognized by the New Order state, in addition to the major world religions)
Apodeti	Associação Popular Democrática Timorense (Popular Democratic Association of Timorese)
ASDT	Associação Social Democrática Timor (Social Democratic Association of Timor)
ASEAN	Association of Southeast Asian Nations
Asli	*see* Pribumi
Bakin	Badan Koordinasi Intelijens Negara (State Intelligence Coordinating Body)
Bakorstanas	Badan Koordinasi Bantuan Pemantapan Stabilitas Nasional (Coordinating Agency for National Stability)
Baperki	Badan Permusjawaratan Kewarganegaraan Indonesia (Consultative Body for Indonesian Citizenship): organization representing Chinese Indonesians in the 1950s
Bappenas	Badan Perencanaan Pembangunan Nasional (National Development Agency)
Barisan Nasional	National Front
Bhinneka Tunggal Ika	Unity in Diversity: the national motto
BPPT	Badan Pengkajian dan Penerapan Teknologi (Agency for the Assessment and Application of Technology)

250

Brimob	Brigade Mobil (mobile brigades): special units of the police
Bulog	Badan Urusan Logistik (National Logistics Board)
Bupati	District heads
Camat	Sub-district heads
CHH	Chung Hwa Hui: Chinese peranakan political organization in the 1930s
CIDES	Centre for Information and Development Studies
CNRM	National Council for the Maubere Resistance
CSIS	Centre for Strategic and International Studies
Daerah istimewa	Special region
DAU	Dana Alokasi Umum: general allocation fund
Dayak	Common term for the indigenous people of Kalimantan, used originally by Europeans to mean people of the "interior" and to distinguish them from the Muslim Malays
Dayak Besar	Great Dayak: a semi-autonomous administrative unit
DDII	Dewan Dakwah Islamiyah Indonesia (Indonesian Islamic Preaching Council)
Desa	Village
Dewan Papua	Papuan Assembly
Dinas	Provincial and district departments
DOM	Daerah Operasi Militer (Military Operations Region)
DPR	Dewan Perwakilan Rakyat (People's Representative Assembly): Indonesian legislature
DPRD	Dewan Perwakilan Rakyat Daerah (Regional People's Representative Assembly): district and provincial legislatures
DPRD-NAD	Dewan Perwakilan Rakyat Daerah – Nanggroe Aceh Darussalam (Regional People's Representative Council of the State of Aceh)
DPRP	Dewan Perwakilan Rakyat Papua (Papuan People's Representative Assembly)
Dwi fungsi	Dual function: doctrine of the armed forces to justify its dual role of defending the homeland and participating in the civilian institutions of the state
Elsham	Institute for Human Rights Study and Advocacy
Falintil	Military wing of Fretilin
Fatwa	An Islamic ruling on religious duty
FKIP	Fakultas Keguruan dan Ilmu Pendidikan (Faculty of Education)
Foreri	Forum Rekonsiliasi Masyarakat/Rakyat Irian Jaya (Forum for the Reconciliation of Irian Jaya Society)
Forkap-Malut	Forum Komunikasi Masyarakat Provinsi Maluku Utara (People's Communication Forum for the Province of North Maluku)
Forkot	Forum Kota (City Forum)

Forum LSM Aceh	Forum Lembaga Swadaya Masyarakat Aceh (Aceh People's Self-Help Organizations Forum): Aceh NGO forum
Forum Peduli HAM	Care Human Rights Forum: an Acehnese human rights organization
FPI	Front Pembela Islam (Front for the Defense of Islam)
Fretilin	Frente Revolucionária de Timor Leste Independente (Revolutionary Front of Independent East Timor), formerly the ASDT
Furkon	Forum Umat Islam Penegak Keadilan dan Konstitusi (Islamic Forum for the Upholding of Justice and the Constitution)
GAM	Gerakan Aceh Merdeka (Free Aceh Movement)
Gandi	Gerakan Perjuangan Anti Diskriminasi Indonesia (Indonesian Anti-Discrimination Movement)
Golkar	Golongan Karya (functional groups): an organization representing functional groups and effectively operating as a large government party under the New Order regime
GPM	Gereja Protestan Maluku (Protestant Church of Maluku)
HAM	Hak Asasi Manusia: human rights
Harga diri	Self-respect
HKBP	Huria Kristen Batak Protestan (Batak Protestant Church)
HMI	Himpunan Mahasiswa Islam (Association of Muslim Students)
IAIN	Institut Agama Islam Negeri (State Institutes for Islam)
ICMI	Ikatan Cendekiawan Muslim se-Indonesia (Indonesian Association of Muslim Intellectuals)
INFID	International NGO Forum on International Development
Inpres	Instruksi Presiden (Presidential Instruction): general grants directly under presidential directives, allocated to sub-national levels of government
Inpres pasar	Market inpres: specific loans for the construction of markets
IPKI	Ikatan Pendukung Kemerdekaan Indonesia (League of Upholders of Indonesian Freedom)
IPTN	Industri Pesawat Terbang Nusantara: state aircraft manufacturer and industry
Jihad	Holy war
Jilbab	Islamic head-dress
Ka'bah	Symbol of the Muslim shrine in Mecca
Kabupaten	District
Kammi	Komite Mahasiswa Muslim Indonesia (Indonesian Committee of Muslim Students)

Kanwil	Kantor Wilayah (regional offices of central ministries)
Karma	Kesatuan Aksi Reformasi Mahasiswa Aceh (Aceh Student Union for Reform)
KBMK	Komite Bersama Modalitas Keamanan (Joint Monitoring Committee)
Kebatinan	A Javanese mystical practise
Kecamatan	Sub-district
Kepala desa	Village heads
Kisdi	Komite Indonesia untuk Solidaritas Dunia Islam (Indonesian Committee for World Islamic Solidarity)
KNIP	Komite Nasional Indonesia Pusat (Central Indonesian National Committee): temporary legislative body in the early days after independence
Kodam	Komando Daerah Militer (regional military command)
Kodim	Komando Distrik Militer (district military command)
Komnas HAM	Komisi Nasional Hak Asasi Manusia (National Human Rights Commission)
Kongress Papua	Papuan People's Congress
Konoor	Millenarian leaders of the Koreri movement in West New Guinea
Kontras	Komisi untuk Orang Hilang dan Korban Tindak Kekerasan (Commission for Missing Persons and Victims of Violence)
Kopassandha	Komando Pasukan Sandi Yudha (Special Forces)
Kopassus	Komando Pasukan Khusus (special elite forces), formerly Kopassandha
Kopkamtib	Komando Operasi Pemulihan Keamanan dan Ketertiban (Operations Command for the Restoration of Security and Order)
Koramil	Komando Rayon Militer (sub-district military command)
Korem	Komando Resort Militer (military resort (garrison) command)
Kostrad	Komando Cadangan Strategis Angkatan Darat (Army Strategic Reserve Command)
Koteka	Penis-sheaths worn by some local populations of the Papuan highlands
LBH	Lembaga Bantuan Hukum (Legal Aid Institute)
Lembaga Ketahanan Nasional	National Defense Institute
LIPI	Lembaga Ilmu Pengetahuan Indonesia (Indonesian Institute of Sciences)
Liurai	Traditional village heads in East Timor
LMMDD-KT	Lembaga Musyawarah Masyarakat Dayak dan daerah Kalimantan Tengah (Dayak and Central Kalimantan Representative Association)

LPKB	Lembaga Pembina Kesatuan Bangsa (Institute for the Promoters of National Unity)
Madrasah	Islamic school
Majelis Rakyat Papua	Papuan People's Assembly
Majelis Ulama Indonesia	Indonesian Council of Ulama
Masuk melayu	"Entering Malay"
Masyumi	Modernist Islamic party in the 1950s
Maubere	Term designating the people of East Timor. Originating from the Mambai "friend," it was elevated to the level of an ideology of "Mauberism" with an emphasis on a struggle for the common people.
MPR	Majelis Permusyawaratan Rakyat (People's Consultative Assembly)
Mubes	Musyawarah Besar: the first congress of the Papuan people
Muhammadiyah	One of the largest Muslim organizations in Indonesia
MUI	Majelis Ulama Indonesia (Indonesian Council of Ulama)
Musholla	Muslim prayer house
Muspida	Musyawarah Pimpinan Daerah (Regional Leadership Consultative Council)
NAD	Nanggroe Aceh Darussalam: designating the special state of Aceh ("Nanggroe" means "country or state")
NGO	Non-governmental organization
NTT	Nusa Tenggara Timur: Indonesian province of East Nusa Tenggara
NU	Nahdlatul Ulama (Association of Muslim Scholars)
Operasi Sapu Jagad	Operation Global Clean-Sweep
Operasi Wibawa 99	Operation Authority 99
OPM	Organisasi Papua Merdeka (Free Papua Movement)
Opsus	Operasi Khusus (Special Operations)
Paksaan	Pressure
Pamong praja	Civil servants, during colonial rule
PAN	Partai Amanat Nasional (National Mandate Party)
Parmusi	Partai Muslimin Indonesia (Muslim Party of Indonesia)
Parpindo	Partai Pembauran Indonesia (Indonesian Assimilation Party)
Partai Warga Bangsa Indonesia	Indonesian Citizen-Nation Party
Parti	Partai Reformasi Tionghoa Indonesia (Chinese Indonesian Reform Party)
PBB	Pajak Bumi dan Bangunan (tax on land and buildings)
PBB	Partai Bulan Bintang (Crescent Star Party)
PBI	Partai Bhinneka Tunggal Ika (Unity in Diversity Party)

PDI	Partai Demokrasi Indonesia (Democratic Party of Indonesia)
PDI-P	Partai Demokrasi Indonesia-Perjuangan (Democratic Party of Indonesia for the Struggle)
PDP	Presidium Dewan Papua (Presidium of the Papuan Assembly)
Pela or pela-gandong	Moluccan traditional institution designed to maintain peaceful relations between different religious groups
Pemikiran baru	New thinking
Pemuda Sosialis Indonesia	Indonesia-wide Socialist Youth of Indonesia
Penghijauan	Greening: refers to the "greening" of the New Order under Suharto, since green is the color of Islam
Peranakan	Mixed descendants of early Chinese migrants, born in the Indies
Pesantren	Islamic boarding school
PKB	Partai Kebangkitan Bangsa (National Awakening Party)
PKI	Partai Komunis Indonesia (Communist Party of Indonesia)
PMP	Penyertaan Modal Pemerintah: capital fund for state enterprises
PNI	Partai Nasionalis Indonesia (Nationalist Party of Indonesia)
POSKO	Communication posts
PPD	Partai Persatuan Dayak (United Dayak Party)
PPP	Partai Persatuan Pembangunan (Development Unity Party)
PPRM	Pasukan Penindak Rusuh Massa (Operational Troops for Mass Revolt)
PPTI	Persatuan Pengamal Tarekat Islam (Association for the Practise of Islamic Mysticism)
PRC	People's Republic of China
PRD	Partai Rakyat Desa (Village People's Party)
Pribumi	Indigenous or native people. Pribumi and asli (original, indigenous) have essentially the same meaning and have been used at different times to distinguish native "sons of the soil" from non-natives.
PRIM	Partai Republik Indonesia Merdeka (Party of the People of Free Indonesia)
Propinsi	Province
PRRI	Pemerintah Revolusioner Republic Indonesia (Revolutionary Government of the Republic of Indonesia)
PPRM	Pasukan Penindak Rusuh Massa (Operational Troops for Mass Revolt)

PTI	Partai Tionghoa Indonesia (Indonesian Chinese Party)
PUSA	Persatuan Ulama Seluruh Aceh (All-Aceh Ulama Association)
Putera	Advisory council set up by the Japanese during their occupation
Reformasi	Reform
RMS	Republik Maluku Selatan (South Moluccan Republic)
Rp	Rupiah
Santri	Student of a traditional Muslim school. Also refers to Javanese who practice a stricter observance of Islamic precepts. *See also* Abangan.
SARA	Suku, Agama, Ras, Antar golongan: an acronym referring to ethnic, religious, racial, and tribal issues that should not be publicly discussed
Saret	Special Autonomous Region of East Timor
Sawah	Wetland rice field
SDO	Subsidi Daerah Otonom (autonomous region subsidy)
Sekwilda	Sekretaris Wilayah Daerah (Regional Secretary)
SI	Sarekat Islam (Islamic League): first major Indonesian nationalist organization (1910s and 1920s)
SI–MPR	Sidang Istimewa – Majelis Permusyawaratan Rakyat (Special Session of the People's Consultative Assembly)
SIRA	Sentra Informasi Referendum Aceh (Centre for Information on an Aceh Referendum)
SMUR	Solidaritas Mahasiswa untuk Rakyat (Student Solidarity for the People)
Solidaritas Nusa Bangsa	National Solidarity Organization
Sukuism	Tribalism
Tapol	Indonesian Human Rights Campaign
Tgk	Tingkat (Level)
THHK	Tiong Hoa Hwee Kwan (Chinese Association)
TNI	Tentara Nasional Indonesia (Indonesian National Army)
Totok (or singkeh)	Chinese migrants born in China
Tuha Nanggroe	A unique institution involved in the implementation and preservation of local customs in Aceh
UDT	União Democrática Timorense (Democratic Union of Timorese)
UKIM	Universitas Kristen Indonesia Maluku (Christian University of Indonesia, Maluku)
Ulama	Islamic scholars
Uleebalang	Acehnese notables
Umma	The Islamic community
Uncen	Universitas Cendrawasih (Cendrawasih University)

Unpatti	Universitas Pattimura (Pattimura University)
UNTAET	United Nations Transitional Administration in East Timor
UNTEA	United Nations Temporary Executive Authority
Wali Nanggroe	Head of the state of Aceh
Wawasan Nusantara	Archipelagic principle, used as an armed forces concept
Zuama	Non-ulama members of PUSA, in Aceh

Bibliography

Aditjondro, George, "Transmigration in Irian Jaya: Issues, targets and alternative approaches," *Prisma* 41 (1986), 67–82.

Al-Chaidar, Sayed Mudhahar Ahmad, and Yarmen Dinamika, *Aceh Bersimbah Darah: Mengungkap Penerapan Status Daerah Operasi Militer (DOM) Di Aceh, 1989–1998* [Aceh Drenched in Blood: Revealing the Application of the Status of Military Operation Area in Aceh, 1989–1998], Jakarta: Pustaka Al-Kautsar, 1999.

Amal, Ichlasul, *Regional and Central Government in Indonesia: West Sumatra and South Sulawesi 1949–1979*, Yogyakarta: Gadjah Mada University Press, 1992.

—— "The dilemmas of decentralisation and democratisation." In David Bourchier, and J. D. Legge (eds), *Democracy in Indonesia 1950s and 1990s*, Melbourne: Centre of Southeast Asian Studies, Monash University, 1994, 214–22.

Aminudin, *Kekuatan Islam Dan Pergulatan Kekuasaan Di Indonesia: Sebelum Dan Sesudah Runtuhnya Rezim Suharto* [Islamic Forces and the Struggle for Power in Indonesia before and after the Fall of Suharto's Regime], Yogyakarta: Pustaka Pelajar, 1999.

Amnesty International, *Indonesia: Continuing Human Rights Violations in Irian Jaya*, ASA 21/06/91, New York: Amnesty International [April 1991].

—— *East Timor: After the Massacre*, AI Index: ASA 21/24/91, London: Amnesty International [21 November 1991].

—— *Indonesia/East Timor – Santa Cruz: The Government Response*, AI Index: ASA 21/03/92, Washington: Amnesty International [February 1992].

—— *Indonesia – Irian Jaya: Recent Arrests*, ASA 21/21/96, London: Amnesty International [May 1996].

Anderson, Benedict R. O'G., *Imagined Communities: Reflections on the Origin and Spread of Nationalism*, London: Verso, 1983 (2nd edn, 1991).

—— "A time of darkness and a time of light." In Benedict R. O'G. Anderson (ed.), *Language and Power: Exploring Political Cultures in Indonesia*, Ithaca, NY: Cornell University Press, 1990, 241–70.

Anderson, Benedict R. O'G. (ed.), *Violence and the State in Suharto's Indonesia*, Ithaca, NY: Southeast Asia Program, Cornell University, 2001.

Anderson, Benedict R. O'G., and Ruth McVey, *A Preliminary Analysis of the October 1, 1965 Coup in Indonesia*, Ithaca, NY: Interim Reports Series, Modern Indonesia Project, Southeast Asia Program, Cornell University, [1971].

Aragon, Lorraine V., "Communal violence in Poso, Central Sulawesi: Where the people eat fish and fish eat people," *Indonesia*, no. 72 (October 2001), 45–79.

Atkinson, Jane Monnig, "Religions in dialogue: The construction of an Indonesian minority religion." In Susan Rodgers, and Rita Smith-Kipp (eds), *Indonesian Religions in Transition*, Tucson: University of Arizona Press, 1987, 171–86.

Bantasyam, Saifuddin, "A note on torture of civilians during the military operation in Aceh: Its development and program rehabilitation," paper for workshop on Rehabilitation Program for Torture Victims, a collaboration between Syiah Kuala University and International Rehabilitation Council for Torture Victims, Denmark, 26 April 1999.

Barker, Joshua, "State of fear: Containing the criminal contagion in Suharto's New Order." In Anderson, *Violence and the State in Suharto's Indonesia*, 20–53.

Bartels, Dieter, "Guarding the Invisible Mountain: Intervillage Alliances, Religious Syncretism, and Ethnic Identity among Ambonese Christians and Muslims in the Moluccas," PhD thesis, Cornell University, 1997.

Barth, Fredrik (ed.), *Ethnic Groups and Boundaries: The Social Organization of Culture Difference*, Boston: Little, Brown, 1969.

Bates, Robert, "Modernization, ethnic competition, and the rationality of politics in contemporary Africa." In Donald Rothchild, and Victor A. Olorunsola (eds), *State versus Ethnic Claims: African Policy Dilemmas*, Boulder, CO: Westview Press, 1983, 152–71.

Benda, Harry J., *The Crescent and the Rising Sun: Indonesian Islam under the Japanese Occupation, 1942–1945*, The Hague and Bandung: W. van Hoeve Ltd., 1958.

Bertrand, Jacques, "Compliance, Resistance, and Trust: Peasants and the State in Indonesia," PhD dissertation, Princeton University, 1995.

—— "False starts, succession crises, and regime transition: Flirting with openness in Indonesia," *Pacific Affairs* 69, no. 3 (Fall 1996), 319–40.

—— "Legacies of the authoritarian past: Religious violence in Indonesia's Moluccan Islands," *Pacific Affairs* 75, no. 1 (Spring 2002), 57–86.

Biro Pusat Statistik, *Beberapa Ciri Pemeluk Agama Di Indonesia 1990*, Jakarta: Biro Pusat Statistik, 1990.

Boland, B. J., *The Struggle of Islam in Modern Indonesia*, The Hague: Martinus Nijhoff, 1982.

Bone, Robert C., *The Dynamics of the Western New Guinea (Irian Barat) Problem*, Ithaca, NY: Modern Indonesia Project, Southeast Asia Program, Dept. of Far Eastern Studies, Cornell University, 1958.

Booth, Anne, "Central government funding of local government development expenditures." In Devas, *Financing Local Government in Indonesia*, 191–211.

Brackman, Arnold, *The Communist Collapse in Indonesia*, New York: Norton, 1969.

Brass, Paul R. (ed.), *Ethnic Groups and the State*, London: Croom Helm, 1985.

—— *Theft of an Idol: Text and Context in the Representation of Collective Violence*, Princeton, NJ: Princeton Studies in Culture/Power/History, Princeton University Press, 1997.

Bresnan, John, *Managing Indonesia: The Modern Political Economy*, New York: Columbia University Press, 1993.

Brubaker, Rogers, and David D. Laitin, "Ethnic and nationalist violence," *Annual Review of Sociology* 24 (1998), 423–52.

Canadian Centre for Foreign Policy Development, *East Timor Roundtable Report*, Ottawa: Canadian Centre for Foreign Policy Development [22 February 1999].

Carment, David, Dane Rowlands, and Patrick James, "Third party intervention and ethnic conflict: Riskiness, rationality and commitment." In Gerald Schneider, and Patricia A. Weitsman (eds), *Enforcing Cooperation: Risky States and Intergovernmental Management of Conflict*, New York: Macmillan St. Martin's Press, 1997, 104–32.

Chauvel, Richard, "Ambon: Not a revolution but a counter-revolution." In Kahin, *Regional Dynamics of the Indonesian Revolution*, 237–64.

——— *Nationalists, Soldiers, and Separatists*, Leiden: KITLV Press, 1990.

Collier, Ruth B., and David Collier, *Shaping the Political Arena: Critical Junctures, the Labor Movement and Regime Dynamics in Latin America*, Princeton, NJ: Princeton University Press, 1991.

Commission To Investigate Human Rights Violations in East Timor (KPP-HAM), *Executive Summary Report on the Investigation of Human Rights Violations in East Timor*, Jakarta: Indonesian Human Rights Commission, [31 January 2000].

"A Constitutional Framework for a Special Autonomy for East Timor: Annex to the Agreements Signed by Portugal and Indonesia at the United Nations 5 May 1999" [cited 2 July 2002]. Available from http://www.etan.org/etun/annex.htm.

Coppel, Charles A., *Indonesian Chinese in Crisis*, New York: Oxford University Press, 1983.

Cribb, Robert, *The Indonesian Killings, 1965–66: Studies from Java and Bali*, Melbourne: Centre of Southeast Asian Studies, Monash University, 1990.

Crouch, Harold, *The Army and Politics in Indonesia*, Ithaca, NY: Cornell University Press, 1978 (2nd edn, 1988).

Cruz, Consuelo, "Identity and persuasion: How nations remember their pasts and make their futures," *World Politics* 52, no. 3 (April 2000), 275–312.

Davey, Kenneth, "Central–local financial relations." In Devas, *Financing Local Government in Indonesia*, 169–88.

Davidson, Jamie S., and Douglas Kammen, "Indonesia's unknown war and the lineages of violence in West Kalimantan," *Indonesia* 73 (April 2002), 53–87.

Defert, Gabriel, *Timor-Est, Le Génocide Oublié: Droit D'un Peuple Et Raisons D'Etats* [East Timor, the Forgotten Genocide: A People's Right and State Motives], Paris: Recherches Asiatiques, L'Harmattan, 1992.

——— *L'Indonésie Et La Nouvelle Guinée Occidentale: Maintien Des Frontières Coloniales, Ou, Respect Des Identités Communautaires* [Indonesia and West New Guinea: Maintenance of Colonial Boundaries, or, Respect of Communal Identities], Paris: Harmattan, 1996.

Devas, Nick, "Local government finance in Indonesia: An overview." In Devas, *Financing Local Government in Indonesia*, 1–51.

——— "Indonesia: What do we mean by decentralization?," *Public Administration and Development* 17, no. 3 (August 1997), 351–67.

Devas, Nick (ed.), *Financing Local Government in Indonesia*, Athens, OH: Monographs in International Studies, Ohio University Center for International Studies, 1989.

Dove, Michael, "Dayak anger ignored," *Inside Indonesia*, no. 51 (July–September 1997).

Dunn, James S., *The Timor Affair: From Civil War to Invasion by Indonesia*, Canberra: Parliamentary Library Legislative Research Service, 1976.

Elmhirst, Rebecca, "Space, identity politics and resource control in Indonesia's transmigration programme," *Political Geography* 18, no. 7 (1999), 813–35.

Esman, Milton, "Economic performance and ethnic conflict." In Joseph Montville (ed.), *Conflict and Peacemaking in Multiethnic Societies*, Lexington, Mass.: Lexington Books, 1990, 477–90.

Fearon, James, and David Laitin, "Explaining interethnic cooperation," *American Political Science Review* 90, no. 4 (1996), 715–35.

Feith, Herbert, *The Indonesian Elections of 1955*, Ithaca, NY: Interim Reports Series, Modern Indonesia Project, Southeast Asia Program, Dept. of Far Eastern Studies, Cornell University, 1957.

—— *The Decline of Constitutional Democracy in Indonesia*, Ithaca, NY: Cornell University Press, 1962.

Finkelstein, Lawrence, "The Indonesian federal problem," *Pacific Affairs* 24, no. 3 (1951), 284–95.

Furnivall, J. S., *Netherlands India: A Study of Plural Economy*, Cambridge: Cambridge University Press, 1939 (reprint 1944).

Geertz, Clifford, *The Religion of Java*, Chicago: University of Chicago Press, 1960.

—— *The Interpretation of Cultures*, New York: Basic Books, 1973.

Gellner, Ernest, *Nations and Nationalism*, Oxford: Basil Blackwell, 1983.

Gereja Kemah Injil Indonesia, Paroki Tiga Raja, and Gereja Kristen Injili di Irian Jaya [churches], *Laporan Pelanggaran Hak Asasi Manusia Dan Bencana Di Bela, Alama, Jila Dan Mapnduma, Irian Jaya* [Report on the Violation of Human Rights and Calamity in Bela, Alama, Jila, and Mapnduma, Irian Jaya], Timika, Irian Jaya, 1998.

Ghai, Yash P., "Decentralization and the accommodation of ethnic diversity." In Crawford Young (ed.), *Ethnic Diversity and Public Policy: A Comparative Inquiry*, New York: St. Martin's Press, 1998, 31–71.

—— *Autonomy and Ethnicity: Negotiating Competing Claims in Multi-Ethnic States*, Cambridge: Cambridge Studies in Law and Society, Cambridge University Press, 2000.

Greenfeld, Liah, *Nationalism: Five Roads to Modernity*, Cambridge, Mass.: Harvard University Press, 1992.

Guinness, Patrick, "Transmigrants in South Kalimantan and South Sulawesi." In G. W. and H. V. Richter Jones (eds), *Population Resettlement Programs in Southeast Asia*, Canberra: Australian National University Press, 1982, 63–72.

Gurr, Ted R., *Why Men Rebel*, Princeton, NJ: Princeton University Press (for Center of International Studies, Princeton University), 1970.

—— *Peoples Versus States: Minorities at Risk in the New Century*, Washington, DC: United States Institute of Peace Press, 2000.

Gurr, Ted R., Barbara Harff, Monty Marshall, and James R. Scarritt, *Minorities at Risk: A Global View of Ethnopolitical Conflict*, Washington, DC: US Institute of Peace Press, 1993.

Harvey, Barbara S., *Permesta: Half a Rebellion*, Ithaca, NY: Modern Indonesia Project, Southeast Asia Program, Cornell University, 1977.

Harymurti, Bambang, "Challenges of change in Indonesia," *Journal of Democracy* 10, no. 4 (1999), 69–83.

Hechter, Michael, *Internal Colonialism: The Celtic Fringe in British National Development, 1536–1966*, Berkeley: University of California Press, 1975.

—— "Explaining nationalist violence," *Nations and Nationalism* 1, no. 1 (1995), 53–68.

—— *Containing Nationalism*, New York: Oxford University Press, 2000.

Hefner, Robert W., "Of faith and commitment: Christian conversion in Muslim Java." In Robert W. Hefner (ed.), *Conversion to Christianity: Historical and Anthropological Perspectives on a Great Transformation*, Berkeley: University of California Press, 1993, 99–125.

—— "Islamization and democratization in Indonesia." In Robert W. Hefner, and Patricia Horvatich (eds), *Islam in an Era of Nation-States: Politics and Religious Revival in Muslim Southeast Asia*, Honolulu: University of Hawaii Press, 1997, 75–127.

—— "Islam and nation in the post-Suharto era." In Adam Schwarz, and Jonathan Paris (eds), *The Politics of Post-Suharto Indonesia*, New York: Council on Foreign Relations Press (distributed by Brookings Institution Press), 1999, 40–72.

—— *Civil Islam: Muslims and Democratization in Indonesia*, Princeton, NJ: Princeton University Press, 2000.

Heidhues, Mary Somers, "Who wants to be non-pribumi? The use of parentheses." In Hans Dieter Kubitscheck, Thomas Engelbert, and Andreas Schneider (eds), *Ethnic Minorities and Nationalism in Southeast Asia: Festschrift, dedicated to Hans Dieter Kubitscheck*, New York: Peter Lang, 2000, 49–60.

Hofman, Bert, and Kai Kaiser, "The making of the big bang and its aftermath: A political economy perspective," paper presented at Can Decentralization Help Rebuild Indonesia? conference, Georgia State University, 1–3 May 2002.

Horowitz, Donald L., *Ethnic Groups in Conflict*, Berkeley: University of California Press, 1985.

—— "Democracy in divided societies." In Larry J. Diamond, and Marc F. Plattner (eds), *Nationalism, Ethnic Conflict, and Democracy*, Baltimore: Johns Hopkins University Press, 1994, 35–55.

—— *The Deadly Ethnic Riot*, Berkeley: University of California Press, 2001.

Hoshour, Cathy A., "Resettlement and the politicization of ethnicity in Indonesia," *Bijdragen Tot De Taal, Lande- En Volkenkunde* 153, no. 4 (1997), 557–76.

Human Rights Watch, *Indonesia: Communal Violence in West Kalimantan*, A Human Rights Watch Report, New York/London: Human Rights Watch, 1997.

—— *Indonesia: Human Rights and Pro-Independence Actions in Irian Jaya*, New York/London: Human Rights Watch, 1998.

—— *Indonesia: The Damaging Debate on Rapes of Ethnic Chinese Women*, New York/London: Human Rights Watch, 1998.

—— *Indonesia: The Violence in Ambon*, New York/London: Human Rights Watch, 1999.

—— *Indonesia: Human Rights and Pro-Independence Actions in Papua, 1999–2000*, New York/London: Human Rights Watch, 2000.

—— *Indonesia: Violence and Political Impasse in Papua*, New York: Human Rights Watch, 2001.

Human Rights Watch/Asia, *Deteriorating Human Rights in East Timor*, A Human Rights Watch Report, New York/London: Human Rights Watch, 1995.

Huntington, Samuel P. *The Third Wave: Democratization in the Late Twentieth Century*, The Julian J. Rothbaum Distinguished Lecture Series, Norman: University of Oklahoma Press, 1991.

Institute for Human Rights Study and Advocacy – Irian Jaya (Elsham–Irian Jaya), *Laporan "Kasus Abepura" 07 Desember 2000* [Report of the "Abepura Case" of 7 December 2000], Jayapura: Elsham–Irian Jaya [December 2000].

International Commission of Inquiry on East Timor, *United Nations Report of the International Commission of Inquiry on East Timor to the Secretary-General*, New York: United Nations [January 2000].

International Crisis Group, *Communal Violence in Indonesia: Lessons From Kalimantan*, ICG Asia Report no. 18, Jakarta/Brussels: ICG, 2001.

—— *Aceh: A Slim Chance for Peace*, ICG Asia Briefing Paper, Jakarta/Brussels: ICG [30 January 2002].

—— *Indonesia: The Search for Peace in Maluku*. ICG Asia Report no. 31, Jakarta/Brussels: ICG [8 February 2002].

Jaquet, L. G. M., "The Indonesian federal problem reconsidered," *Pacific Affairs* 25, no. 2 (1952), 170–5.

Jenkins, David, *Suharto and His Generals: Indonesian Military Politics, 1975–1983*, Ithaca, NY: Modern Indonesia Project, Cornell University Press, 1984.

Jolliffe, Jill, *East Timor: Nationalism and Colonialism*, Brisbane: University of Queensland Press, 1978.

Kahin, Audrey R., "Regionalism and decentralization." In David Bourchier, and J. D. Legge (eds), *Democracy in Indonesia 1950s and 1990s*, Melbourne: Centre of Southeast Asian Studies, Monash University, 1994, 204–13.

Kahin, Audrey R. (ed.), *Regional Dynamics of the Indonesian Revolution: Unity from Diversity*, Honolulu: University of Hawaii Press, 1985.

Kahin, George McT., *Nationalism and Revolution in Indonesia*, Ithaca, NY: Cornell University Press, 1952.

Kahn, Joel S., "Culturalising the Indonesian uplands." In Tania Murray Li (ed.), *Transforming the Indonesian Uplands: Marginality, Power and Production*, Amsterdam: Harwood Academic Publishers Institute of Southeast Asian Studies, 1999, 79–101.

Kedourie, Elie, *Nationalism*, Oxford, UK/Cambridge, Mass.: Blackwell, 1993 (4th edn).

Kell, Tim, *The Roots of the Acehnese Rebellion, 1989–1992*, Ithaca, NY: Modern Indonesia Project, Cornell University, 1995.

Kepolisian Negara Republik Indonesia Daerah Irian Jaya [Republic of Indonesia Police in Irian Jaya], *Rencana Operasi "Tuntas Matoa 2000" Polda Irja* [Plan for Operation "Tuntas Matoa 2000" of the Regional Police of Irian Jaya] (Confidential), No. Pol.: R/Renops/640/XI/2000, Jayapura, [November 2000].

King, Victor T., *The Peoples of Borneo*, Peoples of South-East Asia and the Pacific, Oxford, UK/Cambridge, Mass.: Blackwell, 1993.

Kohn, Hans, *The Idea of Nationalism: A Study in Its Origins and Background*, New York: Macmillan, 1946 (3rd printing, with additions – ed.).

Kristiadi, J. B., "Masalah sekitar peningkatan pendapatan daerah [Problems relating to the increase of regional revenues]," *Prisma* 12 (1985), 35–43.

Kwik Kian Gie, "Masalah pri dan non-pri dewasa ini [The 'pri'/'non-pri' problem in this era]." In *Masalah Pri Dan Nonpri Dewasa Ini*, Jakarta: Pustaka Sinar Harapan Bekerja Sama Dengan Yayasan Dharma Wulan, 1998, 13–60.

Kymlicka, Will, *Multicultural Citizenship: A Liberal Theory of Minority Rights*, Oxford Political Theory, Oxford/New York: Clarendon Press, 1995.

Laporan Akhir Tim Gabungan Pencari Fakta Peristiwa Tanggal 13–15 Mei 1998: Ringkasan Eksekutik [Final Report of the Joint Fact-Finding Team on the 13–15 May 1998 Riots: Executive Summary], Jakarta: Joint Fact-Finding Team, [23 October 1998].

Legge, John David, *Problems of Regional Autonomy in Contemporary Indonesia*, Ithaca, NY: Modern Indonesia Project, Southeast Asia Program, Dept. of Far Eastern Studies, Cornell University, 1957.

——*Central Authority and Regional Autonomy in Indonesia*, Ithaca, NY: Cornell University Press, 1961.

Lev, Daniel S., *The Transition to Guided Democracy: Indonesian Politics, 1957–1959*, Ithaca, NY: Modern Indonesia Project, Southeast Asia Program, Dept. of Asian Studies, Cornell University, 1966.

Li, Tania Murray, "Marginality, power and production: Analysing upland transformation." In Tania Murray Li (ed.), *Transforming the Indonesian Uplands: Marginality, Power and Production*, Amsterdam: Harwood Academic Publishers Institute of Southeast Asian Studies, 1999, 1–44.

Liddle, R. William, *Leadership and Culture in Indonesian Politics*, Sydney: Asian Studies Association of Australia in association with Allen & Unwin, 1996.

——"The Islamic turn in Indonesia: A political explanation," *Journal of Asian Studies* 55, no. 3 (August 1996), 613–34.

——"Coercion, co-optation, and the management of ethnic relations in Indonesia." In Michael E. Brown, and Sumit Ganguly (eds), *Government Policies and Ethnic Relations in Asia and the Pacific*, Cambridge, Mass.: MIT Press, 1997, 273–319.

——"Indonesia in 2000: A shaky start for democracy," *Asian Survey* 41, no. 1 (2001), 208–20.

Lijphart, Arend, *The Trauma of Decolonization: The Dutch and West New Guinea*, New Haven: Yale Studies in Political Science, Yale University Press, 1966.

——*Democracy in Plural Societies*, New Haven: Yale University Press, 1977.

——"The puzzle of Indian democracy: A consociational interpretation," *American Political Science Review* 90, no. 2 (1996), 258–68.

Linz, Juan J., and Alfred Stepan, "Political identities and electoral sequences – Spain, the Soviet Union, and Yugoslavia," *Daedalus* 12, no. 2 (Spring 1992), 123–39.

—— *Problems of Democratic Transition and Consolidation: Southern Europe, South America, and Post-Communist Europe*, Baltimore/London: Johns Hopkins University Press, 1996.

Lombard, Denys, *Le Sultanat D'Atjeh Au Temps D'Iskandar Muda, 1607–1636* [The Acehnese Sultanate at the Time of Iskandar Muda, 1607–1636], Paris: École Française d'Extrême-Orient, 1967.

Lubis, Solly M., *Ketatanegaraan Republik Indonesia* [State Structures of the Republic of Indonesia], Bandung: Penerbit Mandar Maju, 1993.

McCarthy, J. F., "The changing regime: Forest property and Reformasi in Indonesia," *Development and Change* 31, no. 1 (2000), 91–129.

Mackie, J. A. C., "Anti-Chinese outbreaks in Indonesia, 1959–1968." In J. A. C. Mackie (ed.), *The Chinese in Indonesia: Five Essays*, Honolulu: University Press of Hawaii in association with Australian Institute of International Affairs, 1976, 77–138.

—— "Towkays and tycoons: The Chinese in Indonesian economic life in the 1920s and 1980s," *Indonesia* Special Issue on "The Role of the Indonesian Chinese in Shaping Modern Indonesian Life" (1991), 83–96.

McVey, Ruth, "Faith as the outsider: Islam in Indonesian politics." In James Piscatori (ed.), *Islam in the Political Process*, Cambridge: Cambridge University Press, 1983, 199–225.

Majelis Permusyawaratan Rakyat Republik Indonesia, *Ketetapan MPR-RI Nomor IV/MPR/1999 Tentang Garis-Garis Besar Haluan Negara Tahun 1999–2004* [Decree of the MPR-RI no. IV/MPR/1999 on the Broad Outlines of State Policy 1999–2004], 1999.

Majelis Permusyawaratan Rakyat Republik Indonesia, *Ketetapan MPR-RI Nomor VIII/MPR/2000 Tentang Laporan Tahunan Lembaga-Lembaga Tinggi Negara Pada Sidang Tahunan MPR 2000* [Decree of the MPR-RI no. VIII/MPR/2000 on State Institutions Progress Reports to the 2000 MPR Annual Session], Jakarta, 2000.

Malley, Michael, "Regional protest and reform in post-Suharto Indonesia," conference paper to annual meeting of Association of Asian Studies, Boston, 11–14 March 1999.

—— "Resource Distribution, State Coherence, and Political Centralization in Indonesia, 1950–1997," PhD dissertation, University of Wisconsin-Madison, 1999.

Marx, Anthony W., "Apartheid's end: South Africa's transition from racial domination," *Ethnic and Racial Studies* 20, no. 3 (July 1997), 474–96.

Miles, Douglas, *Cutlass & Crescent Moon: A Case Study of Social and Political Change in Outer Indonesia*, Sydney: Centre for Asian Studies, University of Sydney, 1976.

Ministry of Information, "The autonomous province of West Irian," Jakarta: Ministry of Information, Republic of Indonesia, 1958.

Morfit, M., "Pancasila orthodoxy." In C. MacAndrews (ed.), *Central Government and Local Development in Indonesia*, Singapore: Oxford University Press, 1986, 42–55.

Morris, Eric E., "Islam and Politics in Aceh: A Study of Center–Periphery Relations in Indonesia," PhD dissertation, Cornell University, 1983.

Mote, Octovianus, and Danilyn Rutherford, "From Irian Jaya to Papua: The limits of primordialism in Indonesia's troubled east," *Indonesia*, no. 72 (October 2001), 115–40.

Mubyarto, Loekman Soetrisno, Hudiyanto, Edhie Djatmiko, Ita Setiawati, and Agnes Mawarni, *East Timor, the Impact of Integration: An Indonesian Socio-Anthropological Study*, Northcote, Australia: Indonesia Resources and Information Program, 1991.

Münninghoff, H. F. M., *Laporan Pelanggaran Hak Asasi Terhadap Penduduk Lokal Di Wilayah Sekitar Timika, Kabupaten Fak-Fak, Irian Jaya, Tahun 1994/1995* [Report of Human Rights Violations toward Local People in the Area of Timika, District of Fak Fak, Irian Jaya, 1994/1995], Bishop's Office, Jayapura, 1 August 1995.

Nagazumi, Akira, *The Dawn of Indonesian Nationalism: The Early Years of the Budi Utomo, 1908–1918*, Tokyo: Institute of Developing Economies, 1972.

National Commission of Inquiry into the 12 November 1991 Incident in Dili, *Advance Report*, Jakarta: Government of the Republic of Indonesia [1991].

Nordlinger, Eric A., *Conflict Regulation in Divided Societes*, [Cambridge, Mass.]: Center for International Affairs, Harvard University, 1972.

Osborne, Robin, *Indonesia's Secret War: The Guerilla Struggle in Irian Jaya*, Sydney/Boston: Allen & Unwin, 1985.

Peluso, Nancy Lee, "Whose woods are these: Counter-mapping forest territories in Kalimantan, Indonesia," *Antipode* 27, no. 4 (1995), 383–406.

Peluso, Nancy Lee, and Emily Harwell, "Territory, custom and the cultural politics of ethnic war in West Kalimantan, Indonesia." In Peluso, and Watts, *Violent Environments*, 83–116.

Peluso, Nancy Lee, and Michael Watts (eds), *Violent Environments*, Ithaca, NY: Cornell University Press, 2001.

Persoon, Gerard, "Isolated groups or indigenous peoples: Indonesia and the international discourse," *Bijdragen Tot De Taal-, Land- En Volkenkunde* 154, no. 2 (1998), 281–304.

Petebang, Edi, *Dayak Sakti: Pengayauan, Tariu, Mangkok Merah: Konflik Etnis Di Kalbar, 1996/1997* [Superstitious Dayak: Headhunting, Trance, Red Bowl: Ethnic Conflict in West Kalimantan], Cet. 2. ed. [Pontianak]: Institut Dayakologi, 1999.

Petebang, Edi, and Eri Sutrisno, *Konflik Etnik Di Sambas* [Ethnic Conflict in Sambas], Cet. 1. ed. [Jakarta]: Institut Studi Arus Informasi, 2000.

Pierson, Paul, "Increasing returns, path dependence, and the study of politics," *American Political Science Review* 94, no. 2 (June 2000), 251–67.

Posen, Barry, "The security dilemma and ethnic conflict," *Survival* 35, no. 1 (1993), 27–47.

Ramage, Douglas E., *Politics in Indonesia: Democracy, Islam, and the Ideology of Tolerance*, New York: Routledge, 1995.

Ranis, Gustav, and Frances Stewart, "Decentralisation in Indonesia," *Bulletin of Indonesian Economic Studies* 30 (1994), 41–72.

"Refleksi Dan Rekomendasi Para Pimpinan Gereja Dan Tokoh Umat Katolik, Nusa Tenggara Tentang Masalah Penodaan Dan Penyelesaiannya [Reflection and Recommendations by Catholic Church and Community in East Nusa Tenggara about Host Desecrations and How to End the Problem]," 19–20 June 1995.

Reid, Anthony, *The Indonesian National Revolution, 1945–1950*, Melbourne: Longman, 1974.

—— "Trade and the problem of royal power in Aceh. Three stages: c. 1550–1700." In Anthony Reid, and Lance Castles (eds), *Pre-Colonial State Systems in Southeast Asia: The Malay Peninsula, Sumatra, Bali-Lombok, South Celebes*, [Singapore]: Council of the Malaysian Branch of the Royal Asiatic Society, 1975, 45–55.

—— *The Blood of the People: Revolution and the End of Traditional Rule in Northern Sumatra*, Kuala Lumpur: Oxford University Press, 1979.

Robinson, Geoffrey, *The Dark Side of Paradise: Political Violence in Bali*, Ithaca, NY: Cornell University Press, 1995.

—— "*Rawan* is as *Rawan* does: The origins of disorder in New Order Aceh," *Indonesia* 66 (October 1998), 127–58.

Robison, Richard, *Indonesia: The Rise of Capital*, Sydney: Allen & Unwin, 1986.

Ryter, Loren, "Pemuda Pancasila: The last loyalist free men of Suharto's order?," *Indonesia*, no. 66 (October 1998), 45–73.

Schiller, A. Arthur, *The Formation of Federal Indonesia, 1945–1949*, The Hague: W. van Hoeve, 1955.

Schwarz, Adam, *A Nation in Waiting: Indonesia's Search for Stability*, Boulder/San Francisco: Westview Press, 2000.

Scott, James C., *Domination and the Arts of Resistance*, New Haven: Yale University Press, 1990.

Sherlock, Stephen, "Political economy of the East Timor conflict," *Asian Survey* 36, no. 9 (1996), 835–51.

Shiraishi, Takashi, *An Age in Motion: Popular Radicalism in Java, 1912–1926*, Ithaca, NY: Cornell University Press, 1990.

—— "Anti-sinicism in Java's New Order." In Daniel Chirot, and Anthony Reid (eds), *Essential Outsiders? Chinese and Jews in the Modern Transformation of Southeast Asia and Central Europe*, Seattle: University of Washington Press, 1997, 187–207.

Siauw Tiong-djin, *Siauw Giok Tjhan: Riwayat Perjuangan Seorang Patriot Membangun Nasion Indonesia Dan Masyarakat Bhineka Tunggal Ika* [Siauw Giok Tjhan: Story of the Struggle of a Patriot To Build the Indonesian Nation and a People Characterized by Unity in Diversity], Jakarta: Hasta Mitra, 1999.

Sidel, John T., "Riots, church burnings, conspiracies: The moral economy of the Indonesian crowd in the late twentieth century." In Ingrid Wessel, and Georgia Wimhoefer (eds), *Violence in Indonesia*, Hamburg: Abera, 2001, 47–61.

Sjamsuddin, Nazaruddin, *The Republican Revolt: A Study of the Acehnese Rebellion*, Singapore: Institute of Southeast Asian Studies, 1985.

Skinner, G. William, "The Chinese minority." In Ruth T. McVey (ed.), *Indonesia*, New Haven: Southeast Asian Studies, Yale University, 1963, 97–117.

Smith, Anthony D., *The Ethnic Origins of Nations*, Oxford, UK/New York: B. Blackwell, 1986.

Smith Kipp, Rita, and Susan Rodgers, "Introduction: Indonesian religions in society." In Rita Smith-Kipp, and Susan Rodgers (eds), *Indonesian Religions in Transition*, Tucson: University of Arizona Press, 1987, 1–29.

Smoke, Paul, and Blane D. Lewis, "Fiscal decentralization in Indonesia: A new approach to an old idea," *World Development* 24, no. 8 (1996), 1281–99.

Snyder, Jack L., *From Voting to Violence: Democratization and Nationalist Conflict*, New York: Norton, 2000.

Somers, Mary F., *"Peranakan* Chinese Politics in Indonesia," PhD dissertation, Cornell University, 1965.

Spyer, Patricia, "Serial conversion/conversion to seriality: Religion, state, and number in Aru, Eastern Indonesia." In Peter Van Der Veer (ed.), *Conversion to Modernities: The Globalization of Christianity*, New York: Routledge, 1996, 171–98.

Steenbrink, Karel A., *Dutch Colonialism and Indonesian Islam: Contacts and Conflicts, 1596–1950*, Amsterdam/Atlanta, GA: Rodopi, 1993.

—— "Muslim–Christian relations in the Pancasila state of Indonesia," *The Muslim World* 88, no. 3/4 (1998), 320–52.

Sudagung, Hendro Suroyo, *Mengurai Pertikaian Etnis: Migrasi Swakarsa Etnis Madura Ke Kalimantan Barat* [Explaining Ethnic Differences: The Voluntary Migration of Ethnic Madurese to West Kalimantan], Cet. 1. ed. [Yogyakarta?]: Institut Studi Arus Informasi bekerja sama dengan Yayasan Adikarya IKAPI dan the Ford Foundation, 2001.

Suryadinata, Leo, *Peranakan Chinese Politics in Java, 1917–1942*, Singapore: Singapore University Press, 1981.

—— "Patterns of Chinese political participation in four ASEAN states," *Contemporary Southeast Asia* 15, no. 3 (December 1993), 292–308.

—— "Chinese politics in post-Suharto Indonesia – Beyond the ethnic approach?," *Asian Survey* 41, no. 3 (2001), 502–24.

Swift, Ann, *The Road to Madiun: The Indonesian Communist Uprising of 1948*, Ithaca, NY: Modern Indonesia Project, Southeast Asia Program, Cornell University, 1989.

Tambiah, Stanley Jeyaraja, *Leveling Crowds: Ethnonationalist Conflicts and Collective Violence in South Asia*, Berkeley: Comparative Studies in Religion and Society, University of California Press, 1996.

Tan, Mely G., "The social and cultural dimensions of the role of ethnic Chinese in Indonesian society," *Indonesia* Special Issue on "The Role of the Indonesian Chinese in Shaping Modern Indonesian Life" (1991), 83–96.

Taylor, Charles, *Multiculturalism and "The Politics of Recognition": An Essay*, with commentary by Amy Gutmann (ed.), Princeton, NJ: Princeton University Press, 1992.

Taylor, John G., *Indonesia's Forgotten War: The Hidden History of East Timor*, London Atlantic Highlands, NJ: Zed Books/Sydney: Pluto Press, 1991.

Thee Kian Wie, "Masalah 'Cina' Dan Nasionalisme Ekonomi Indonesia [The 'Chinese problem' and Indonesia's economic nationalism]," paper presented at Mencari Format Baru Pembauran Bangsa [Searching for a new form of national assimilation] conference, 2 November 1998.

Thoha, Mifta, "Masalah sekitar peningkatan pendapatan daerah [Problems relating to the increase of regional revenues]," *Prisma* 12 (1985), 25–34.

Tirtosudarmo, Riwanto, "The political-demography of national integration and its policy implications for a sustainable development in Indonesia," *Indonesian Quarterly* 23, no. 4 (1995).

Tomagola, Thamrin Amal, "The bleeding Halmahera of North Moluccas." In *Proceedings of the Political Violence in Asia*, Centre for Development and Environment, University of Oslo, June 2000.

US State Department, "1999 Indonesia country report on human rights practices," Bureau of Democracy, Human Rights, and Labor, US Department of State, 25 February 2000.

Van den Berghe, Pierre L., *The Ethnic Phenomenon*, New York: Elsevier, 1981.

Van den Broek, T., and A. Szalay, "Raising the Morning Star – Six months in the developing independence movement in West Papua," *Journal of Pacific History* 36, no. 1 (2001), 77–92.

Van den Broek, Theo, J. Budi Hernawan, and Candra Gautama, *Memoria Passionis Di Papua: Kondisi Hak Asasi Manusia Dan Gerakan Aspirasi Merdeka: Gambaran 1999* [Memoria Passionis in Papua: Human Rights Conditions and the Separatist Movement in 1999], Seri Memoria Passionis Di Papua. Cet. 1. ed. [Jayapura]: Diterbitkan atas kerjasama Sekretariat Keadilan dan Perdamaian, Keuskupan Jayapura [dan] Lembaga Studi Pers dan Pembangunan, Jakarta, 2001.

Van Dijk, Cornelis, *Rebellion under the Banner of Islam: The Darul Islam in Indonesia*, The Hague: Martinus Nijhoff, 1981.

Van Klinken, Gerry, "The Maluku wars: Bringing society back in," *Indonesia* 71 (April 2001), 1–26.

—— "Indonesia's new ethnic elites." In Henk Schulte Nordholt, and Irwan Abdullah (eds), *Indonesia: In Search of Transition*, Yogyakarta: Pustaka Pelajar, 2002, 67–105.

Vatikiotis, Michael R. J., *Indonesian Politics under Suharto: Order, Development and Pressure for Change*, London/New York: Routledge, 1993.

Webb, Paul, *Palms and the Cross: Socio-Economic Development in Nusatenggara*, Townsville: Centre for South East Asian Studies, James Cook University of North Queensland, 1986.

Williams, Lea E., *Overseas Chinese Nationalism: The Genesis of the Pan-Chinese Movement in Indonesia, 1900–1916*, Glencoe, IL: Free Press, 1960.

Xenos, Nicholas, "Civic nationalism: Oxymoron?," *Critical Review* 10, no. 2 (1996), 213–31.

Yack, Bernard, "The myth of the civic nation," *Critical Review* 10, no. 2 (1996), 193–211.

Yashar, Deborah J., "Democracy, indigenous movements, and the postliberal challenge in Latin America," *World Politics* 52, no. 1 (October 1999), 76–104.

Yayasan LBH Nusantara dan Forum Pemuda Pelajar dan Mahasiswa Garut, *Kerusuhan Tasikmalaya Dan Ngabang: Kumpulan Investigasi* [The Tasikmalaya and Ngabang Riots: Results of the Investigation], Bandung: Lingkar Studi Reformasi, 1997.

Young, Crawford, *The Politics of Cultural Pluralism*, Madison: University of Wisconsin Press, 1976.

Index

ethnic tensions under, 39, 41–2, 135, 168
instability in the 1990s, 2–3, 7, 40, 42, 56,
    111, 113
institutionalization of, 39, 43
massacres of 1965–66, 2, 63, 74, 75, 112
patronage under the, 41, 59, 66, 67, 69, 112,
    114, 115, 116, 169, 172, 196, 197
policy legacies and conflict, 8, 50, 54–5, 57,
    64–6, 68, 69, 73, 114, 169, 173, 216
political stability of, 2, 83
September 1965 coup attempt, 37, 63, 75
shift to Islam, 73, 83–9, 90, 114, 118, 121

Pakat Dayak, 50, 51, 52, 53
pamong praja, 36, 39, 190
Pamungkas, Sri Bintang, 87
Pancasila. *See* nationalism, Indonesian; Sukarno
Panggabean, Maraden, 82
Papuans, 8, 41, 135. (*See also* Irian Jaya)
Peluso, Nancy, 49
People's Consultative Assembly (MPR), 38, 48,
    70, 86, 88, 89, 109, 143, 144, 157, 181,
    182, 207
  election of President and Vice-President, 42,
    90, 107
  instructions on special autonomy for Irian Jaya
    and Aceh, 158
  special session of, 103, 104, 204
People's Republic of China, 62, 63, 65
People's Representative Assembly (DPR), 38, 88,
    154, 155, 158, 182, 205, 208, 209
Pierson, Paul, 24
Portugal, 136, 142, 204
Poso. *See* Muslim–Christian conflict
Prawiro, Radius, 82, 109
pribumi, 29, 46, 66, 67, 70, 102
  non-pribumi, 45, 46, 59, 67, 68
Protestant Party of Indonesia, 77, 116

Radjawane, Nicolas, 118
Rahardjo, Dawam, 85
Rais, Amien, 87
  as leader of Muhammadiyah, 85, 103
  as PAN leader, 70, 105, 106, 108, 109, 131
Ramos Horta, José, 141, 142
Rangel, Sebastio (Gomes), 142
Raweyai, Yorrys, 126, 157
regionalist rebellions, 35–6, 41, 53, 72, 190, 196,
    211. (*See also* Aceh; Revolutionary
    Government of the Republic of Indonesia
    (PRRI); Sulawesi; Sumatra)
Renan, Ernest, 17
Revolutionary Government of the Republic of
    Indonesia (PRRI), 36, 37, 72, 191, 211
Riau, 92, 212
riots. (*See also* ethnic conflict, in Indonesia;
    Muslim–Christian conflict)

anti-Chinese, 1, 40, 42, 43, 45, 60, 63, 64, 67,
    101, 102
  May 1998, 3, 42, 45, 67, 68
  Muslim–Christian, 78
    in East Timor, 94–6, 98
    in Flores, 96–100
    in Java, 1, 48, 67, 100–2
    in post-Suharto era, 104, 132
  origins of, 14
Riwut, Tjilik, 51, 53
Rukmana, Siti Hardiyanti, 43

Saefuddin, Ahmad Muflih, 108
Saleh, Hasan, 167
Sarekat Islam, 30, 31, 50, 60
Sasono, Adi, 87
Seda, Frans, 81, 100
Siahaan, Hotman, 112
Singapore, 165
Sjadzali, Munawir, 110, 111
Sjahrir, Sutan, 31, 61
Sjamsuddin, Nazaruddin, 167
Sjarifuddin, Amir, 61
Snyder, Jack, 162
Soedirman, Basofi, 111
Soetrisno, Lukman, 112
Sol, Andreas, 121
Solossa, J. P., 158
Soulissa, Abdullah, 120, 126
South Africa, 26, 222
Soviet Union, 2, 26, 111
Spain, 26
Stalin, 30
states. (*See also* ethnic conflict; nation;
    nationalism)
  and "politics of recognition", 19
  links to nations, 15, 16
  multination, 15, 16
  unitary states and ethnic group representation,
    184, 186
Subianto, Prabowo, 68, 88
Sudarsono, Juwono, 112
Sudiono, Yohanes, 119
Sudomo, 81
Sugama, Yoga, 81
Suharto, 76, 99, 137, 157
  alliance with Muslims, 39, 83, 84, 87, 90
  and distrust of Islamic groups, 81, 82
  and political control, 38, 41, 91, 192, 193
  and question of Islamic state, 38
  and September 1965 coup attempt, 37
  close advisors, 81
  corruption, 3, 42, 66, 69, 70, 84, 90, 112, 201
  end of rule, 3, 5, 28, 40, 42–3, 45, 46, 58, 102,
    103, 200
  erosion of legitimacy, 98
  influence over Golkar, 88

CAMBRIDGE ASIA–PACIFIC STUDIES

Other titles in the series: